Seeing Complexity in Public Education

Seeing Complexity in Public Education

Problems, Possibilities, and

Success for All

Donald J. Peurach

OXFORD
UNIVERSITY PRESS

OXFORD
UNIVERSITY PRESS

Oxford University Press, Inc., publishes works that further
Oxford University's objective of excellence
in research, scholarship, and education.

Oxford   New York
Auckland   Cape Town   Dar es Salaam   Hong Kong   Karachi
Kuala Lumpur   Madrid   Melbourne   Mexico City   Nairobi
New Delhi   Shanghai   Taipei   Toronto

With offices in
Argentina   Austria   Brazil   Chile   Czech Republic   France   Greece
Guatemala   Hungary   Italy   Japan   Poland   Portugal   Singapore
South Korea   Switzerland   Thailand   Turkey   Ukraine   Vietnam

Published by Oxford University Press, Inc.
198 Madison Avenue, New York, New York 10016
www.oup.com

Oxford is a registered trademark of Oxford University Press, Inc.

Library of Congress Cataloging-in-Publication Data
Peurach, Donald J., 1962-
Seeing complexity in public education: problems, possibilities, and success for all/Donald J. Peurach.
    p. cm.
Includes bibliographical references and index.
  ISBN-13: 978-0-19-973653-9 (hardcover)
  1. Public schools—United States. 2. School improvement programs—United States. I. Title.
  LA217.2P49 2011
379.1—dc22 2011001671

987654321

Printed in the United States of America on acid-free paper

To Connie and Annie,

with love and thanks.

PREFACE AND ACKNOWLEDGEMENTS

In the United States, the great ambition of education reform is to ensure the academic success of each and every child who walks through the doors of a public school. The great puzzle of U.S. education reform is learning how to make that happen. Possibilities lie in widely publicized instances of remarkable transformations, often in long-struggling schools in challenging urban contexts. Such transformations are rarely the result of targeted interventions. Rather, they are often the product of systems of interdependent solutions to systems of interdependent problems that routinely undermine student achievement, implemented over time and adapted in response to changing needs, circumstances, and understandings. Problems, then, lie in the small number of such transformations when compared to the many schools that continue to struggle.

Two questions follow: What is the day-to-day, shoulder-to-the-grindstone work of devising, implementing, and adapting systemic school improvement strategies? What is it about the work that makes it so challenging?

The following study aims to shed light on these questions, though from an unusual-but-revealing perspective. The study examines the work of a nonprofit organization that, for over 20 years, has operated outside the formal system of U.S. educational governance to support a voluntary, state-sized system of elementary schools, each implementing a common program of systemic improvement. Over that period, this organization, the Success for All Foundation, has been viewed as the darling of U.S. education reform by some and as everything that is wrong with U.S. education reform by others.

The study spanned nearly 14 years, from 1996 to 2010. It was conducted within the Consortium for Policy Research in Education as part of the Study of Instructional Improvement at The University of Michigan. The work reported here was conducted in collaboration with three teams of researchers. One team studied the work of three nongovernmental organizations as they pursued a specific form of systemic improvement called comprehensive school reform: the Accelerated Schools Project, America's Choice, and the Success for All Foundation. A second team conducted case studies of program implementation in 12 schools. And a third team used surveys and instructional logs to study program implementation and effects in 115 schools.

To enlist the interest and intelligence of a wide array of people, the results of the study of the Success for All Foundation are reported in the form of a story. Impatient readers can read the introduction and the conclusion and get a complete picture. More patient readers, however, will benefit from the rest. For it is in the middle chapters that they will see the work of systemic school improvement up close and in detail—and, with that, much of what makes the work so challenging.

* * * * * *

One cannot conduct a study such as this without considerable support from many people and organizations over an extended period of time. I gratefully acknowledge funding received from the Atlantic Philanthropies USA, the William and Flora Hewlett Foundation, the U.S. Department of Education, and the National Science Foundation's Interagency Educational Research Initiative. I also gratefully acknowledge the support of the Consortium for Policy Research in Education and the Study of Instructional Improvement at The University of Michigan. Additional funding was provided by Eastern Michigan University and Michigan State University through resources provided to new faculty members. Please note that none of these organizations or their affiliates are responsible for views expressed in this book.

My thanks to Success for All staff members, teachers, and school leaders who, for many years, have been both open and patient as I sought to learn about their work and its challenges. A complete list of their names would literally fill this page. I owe special thanks to: Robert Slavin and (especially) Nancy Madden, who opened their enterprise to me; Jane Harbert, who befriended me early in my field work and helped me make my way into the enterprise; and a collection of good folks who provided endless ad hoc assistance—Liesel Rupprecht, Sharon Fox, Susan Davis, Lynda Hamilton, Tylvia Koromah, Julie Farver, and Tracey Taylor.

At that same time that I acknowledge its members, I wish to make clear that I am in no way affiliated with the Success for All Foundation, nor have I received compensation of any sort from the organization in conducting this research. The organization did extend three courtesies: complementary copies of several manuals; waivers for several conference fees; and four nights of hotel expenses (out of 138 total nights in the field), at a conference in which the organization had overbooked (and already paid for) rooms for its own trainers. Otherwise, all materials and training were purchased at the same costs incurred by schools.

I am indebted to my colleagues on the Study of Instructional Improvement (SII) at The University of Michigan. The principal investigators have worked with me as teachers, mentors, and colleagues for many years: Deborah Ball, Brian Rowan, and (especially) David K. Cohen. For over ten years, I have counted on our project team for weekly analysis, debate, and support: Simona Goldin, Karen Gates, Joshua Glazer, and David K. Cohen. I have called on other SII colleagues, past and present, over the entire period of my study: Carol Barnes, Eric Camburn, Ruben Carriedo, Richard Correnti, Joseph Hesse, Heather Hill, Kristi Holmstrom, Matthew Janger, Bonita Kothe, Jeanne Kuo, Angus Mairs,

Diane Massell, Katie Mikesell, Robert Miller, Geoffrey Phelps, Terri Ridenour, Seneca Rosenberg, Jennifer Smith, James Taylor, Charles Vanover, Chris Weiss, and many others.

Other family, friends, and colleagues have read drafts, found time to talk, and provided moral support. Kiera Book expressed trust and confidence at the earliest stages of this work that can never be repaid. Members of my dissertation committee encouraged me to develop my dissertation into this book: David K. Cohen (chair), Annemarie Palincsar, Jeffrey Mirel, and Michael D. Cohen. Anonymous reviewers put much time and thought into their very helpful comments. Colleagues at Eastern Michigan University and Michigan State University provided encouragement and support, especially Marilyn Amey, Tom Buffet, Melinda Mangin, Barbara Markle, Gary Marx, Susan Printy, BetsAnn Smith, and Jackie Tracey. Graduate students reviewed drafts and helped wrestle with some of the stickier issues, especially Jeff Bohl, Chris Elliott, Laura Kirklen, Tom Lietz, Celena Mills, and Ken Wright. Participants in the 2009 Van Leer Education Conference in Jerusalem engaged in very helpful conversations about my work. Finally, the editorial team at the Oxford University Press provided the opportunity, guidance, and encouragement needed to bring the project to fruition: Lori Handelman, Sarah Harrington, Abby Gross, Karen Kwak, Joanna Ng, and Anindita Sengupta.

While these people (and many others) provided endless support, please know that any errors or problems in this analysis are mine, alone.

Above all, I would like to thank my family. Connie and Annie, my wife and daughter, have been partners in this work. Connie and I set out together many years ago to serve children through public education. Through this entire study, Connie provided endless support, and she held fast to our commitment to service. As for Annie, she worked up an entire comedy routine called "Dad, Writing." She provided constant reminders that laughing helps. And our cats, Chip and Dip, kept me company in my many early morning writing sessions. Looking at our motley crew, you might think that we couldn't complete a coherent sentence, let alone a book. But, by the grace of God, we did.

CONTENTS

Seeing Complexity in Public Education

Introduction

This is a story of one organization, the Success for All Foundation, and its 20+ year effort to improve education for millions of at-risk students attending thousands of schools across the United States. The story begins with the organization's founders pursuing an elementary strategy: improving achievement by improving how students work together in classrooms. The story ends over 20 years later, this elementary strategy having drawn the organization into coordinated, continuing improvement efforts spanning the entire system of U.S. public education.

This is, at its roots, a story about complexity: about the many concerns to be taken into account in improving education for at-risk students; about their dense, tangled, interdependent relationships; and about the time needed to sort them all out. For that reason, it is an unusual story, simply because its focus on complexity is at odds with how we reformers often approach improving schools. Rather than taking on these dense, tangled, interdependent relationships, we try to slice through the complexity with that one innovation so incisive and fundamental that it quickly changes everything: that new instructional method, or curriculum, or leadership strategy, or funding stream, or state assessment. There is a world of difference between these two approaches: the difference between seeing education as a full world, its parts densely connected, tangled, and interdependent; and seeing education as an empty world in which we can sidestep these complexities, insert our quick fix, and still make substantive improvements.

This is not a story about learning to hone that one, incisive innovation that slices through the complexity and changes everything. This is a story about learning to see the world of education and the work of improving it fundamentally differently.

PROBLEMS

Millions of U.S. students are at risk of academic failure. According to 2001 U.S. Census Bureau estimates, 46% of all U.S. students—approximately 24 million children and adolescents—experienced at least one of seven conditions that put them at risk of academic failure: the inability to speak English; the presence of a personal disability; one or more instances of grade retention; the absence of either or both parents; at least one foreign-born parent of recent immigration; low family income; and/or the absence of any employed parent or guardian.[1] 18% of all U.S. students—over 9 million children and adolescents—experienced two or more compounding risk factors.[2] These students were of all races and ethnicities. They were distributed among central cities, suburbs, and rural areas. If their risk factors were contagious, then being at risk of academic failure would be pandemic.

In an ideal world, the educational system would be organized so that students at risk of academic failure would be channeled into schools with the most able teachers and leaders, dedicated professionals who would collaborate to bring the most advanced knowledge and expertise to bear on their very difficult educational challenges. In an ideal world, schools serving large numbers of at-risk students would be unusual in their capabilities, functioning as something akin to teaching hospitals: capable of diagnosing and treating the specific problems of individual students; capable of continuing professional development for new and experienced members; and capable of generating and evaluating new knowledge and treatments. These teaching hospitals, in turn, would be supported by an array of organizations, private and public, that conducted basic and applied research, devised and tested technologies and treatments, and trained specialists with unique expertise.

In today's real world, that's not the case. The educational system is organized so that students at risk of academic failure are channeled into the same schools as everybody else: their neighborhood schools. A consequence is that large numbers of at-risk students attend "Title I" schools: over 50,000 public schools that receive funding under Title I of the federal Elementary and Secondary Education Act. In over 31,000 Title I schools, 40% or more of students live in poverty.[3] Some of these schools surely resemble our teaching hospital: centers of diagnosis, treatment, systematic learning, and continuous improvement, surrounded by an array of supporting organizations. Many others, however, do not.

Many at-risk students attend chronically underperforming public schools in which being at risk of academic failure is a self-fulfilling prophecy, a consequence of interdependent problems that stretch from classrooms to environments. Deeply held beliefs about innate ability and motivation breed low expectations for at-risk students; so, too, do beliefs about the effects of their family and social environments. The bar is lowered to meet those expectations by asking that at-risk students learn facts and skills, though often without asking that they learn to think. Teachers face the challenges of at-risk students in structural and social isolation—in their own, private, autonomous classrooms. Though rife with supplemental student services, these services are uncoordinated with each other and with classroom instruction, and plagued by administrative burdens. Leadership is bureaucratic, administrative, and disconnected from the work of improving the performance of students and teachers. Districts, states, universities, and others provide funding, oversight, and even some assistance, though far removed from the day-to-day realities of practice and its improvement.

The preceding is something of an exaggeration: a worst case that begins to tease out the universe of potential, interdependent problems that undermine the academic achievement of at-risk students. To be sure, pockets of hope and strength exist in even the most challenged schools and in the environments supporting them. Even so, some subset of these problems likely exists in every school and the environments in which they function. The persistent and considerable achievement gap between at-risk students and their less challenged peers suggests that such problems manifest themselves in greater numbers, in more confounding ways, and toward more dire ends in schools and environments serving large numbers of at-risk students. Unless we are to blame these students, themselves, then we are left to assume that something is wrong with these schools and their environments—or, more likely, many, interdependent things.

These many, interdependent problems have proven stubborn and difficult to remedy. Not that we haven't tried. Educational reforms are like opinions, and opinions are like . . . well, noses. Everybody has one: politicians at all levels of government, leaders in education and business, teachers, pundits, academics, office workers, laborers, you, and me. Indeed, educational reform is among the great American pastimes, ubiquitous activity that plays out continuously in schools, in capitol buildings, in board rooms, in ivory towers, in polling places, and around water coolers—largely unregulated and open to all comers. Though motivations, targets, and intended outcomes vary, the tie binding educational reformers is the assumption that the problems of schools can be solved from the outside in, by people and organizations such as themselves, and their aspirations and ideas for improvement.

But educational reform is, itself, a problem. In the 50+ years since *Brown vs. Board of Education* and Sputnik ushered in the modern era of educational reform, educational reformers have struggled to transform the schools that exist into the schools that they desire. Though the problems to be solved are many and interdependent, educational reform, as a national enterprise, has lacked a coherent, organizing agenda for solving them. Individual reforms have tended to be piecemeal, uncoordinated, and faddish silver bullets: curriculum reforms, pedagogical innovations, smaller class sizes, professional learning communities, and many more. Moreover, these reforms have tended to be at least as responsive to ever-churning cycles of electoral politics and government funding as the specific problems of individuals schools—if not more. Compared to the sheer number of educational reforms, few have advanced beyond rhetoric to serious attempts at improvement. Of those that have, fewer still have effected deep change in either practice or achievement, reached large-scale operations, or remained viable over time. Indeed, enthusiasm for individual reforms more often derives from their novelty and their promise than from evidence of effectiveness.

An unintended consequence of 50+ years of uncoordinated, prolific, and relentless educational reform has been to make the challenge of fixing schools from the outside in more difficult. Like bacteria to antibiotics, schools have become resistant to external reform, able to stave off, incorporate-and-marginalize, and/or ingest-and-pass external efforts to improve them. Likewise, the broader system has become resistant to reformers in the same way that schools have become resistant to reform, with the "population ecology" of the school improvement industry such that successful reformers either die off (due to problems of funding, capitalization, and simple burnout) or are incorporated into larger, established organizations (and subsequently smothered by their conservative inclinations).

Narrowing our lens and looking at individual schools, the net effect is described as turning schools into veritable Christmas trees, decorated with the accumulated artifacts of piecemeal, faddish, and ineffective reforms. Zooming out to incorporate more schools, the effect is described as a pattern of tinkering and marginal adaptation, primarily in the structures and resources in schools, yet persistence in the day-to-day practices of teachers and school leaders. Teaching is said to be inherently conservative—for that matter, leadership, school organization, and public education, too. Zooming out even farther, to include environments, we see an unregulated, multi-billion dollar school improvement industry running alongside the formal system of education, open to all comers yet dominated by conservative, commercial interests.[4]

No matter the level at which we zoom, we struggle to see consistently the intended outcomes at the very foundation of the modern era of educational reform: equity and excellence.

SOLUTIONS

The 1980s saw the emergence of a new logic of reform: a new way of thinking and reasoning about improving schools, their environments, and, with that, the achievement of at-risk students. This new logic of "systemic reform" began with the intended ends: equity and excellence.[5] The essential goal of systemic reform was to enable all students to master the same, ambitious academic content at the same, high standards, including (and especially) students historically at risk of academic failure. The expectation was not only that all students would be able to read complex texts and respond to factual questions, or that all students would be able to perform complex computational algorithms. The expectation was that all students would interpret text and data, draw (and defend) inferences, make (and support) conjectures, and more.

The logic of systemic reform held that ambitious outcomes would not be realized with piecemeal, uncoordinated reforms. Rather, the problems to be solved were understood to be many and interdependent. Within the logic of systemic reform, *systems* of interdependent problems required *systems* of coordinated, interdependent solutions. It wasn't classroom instruction that needed to be improved, or curriculum, or supplemental services, or professional development, or school and district leadership, or environmental organizations. It was the entire lot, in interaction, at a very large scale: nationwide, in the tens of thousands of schools serving millions of at-risk students, and in the many organizations supporting them. Indeed, the ambition was for no less than fundamental, coordinated transformation of public education's most enduring institutions in order to achieve multiple ends, including reducing social inequality, maintaining economic prominence, and ensuring national defense.

The logic of systemic reform became intertwined with specific policy movements that aimed both to improve and to coordinate schools and their environments. "Comprehensive school reform" (also called "whole school" and "schoolwide" reform) took the entire school as the unit of treatment, the strategy centered on targeting schools with an integrated, coordinated suite of improvement initiatives responsive to the many, interdependent problems undermining achievement. "Standards-based reform" targeted systemic change in environments, the strategy centered on using a small set of state-level policy instruments to motivate and to coordinate improvement efforts, system-wide: common standards for academic content; common standards for student performance; and common student assessments with which to measure whether students were, in fact, mastering the intended content at the intended standards.

There was a rationality to systemic reform and these associated movements that ran counter to the usual faddism and incoherence of educational reform: the notion of establishing high, shared goals for student achievement and then, developing and coordinating new capabilities throughout the system of U.S. public education to achieve those goals. Indeed, with the logic of systemic reform came new attention to effectiveness: leveraging research-validated strategies as the basis for specific improvement programs; using formal research methods to validate the effectiveness of programs prior to large-scale dissemination; and supporting not only the adoption of new programs but, also, their effective use in schools. With new attention to effectiveness came new attention to accountability: sanctions for schools whose students failed to perform at standard; political and financial consequences for districts and states that failed to help those schools; and market failure for providers of ineffective programs.

From the logic of systemic reform followed the watchwords of the national educational reform agenda: "systemic improvement"; "scale"; "sustainability"; and "effectiveness." This was not a marginal set of ideas. Rather, the logic of systemic reform and its associated watchwords were central to a litany of loosely coordinated federal policy initiatives that spanned 20 years: the Hawkins-Stafford Amendments to the 1988 reauthorization of Elementary and Secondary Education Act; America 2000 in 1991; Goals 2000 in 1994; the Improving America's Schools Act of 1994; the Obey-Porter Comprehensive School Reform Demonstration Act of 1997; the Reading Excellence Act of 1998; and the No Child Left Behind Act of 2001. The rhetoric of these initiatives was matched with resources, as billions of federal dollars flooded into the system over this 20-year period in support.

This 20-year run of federal policy sustained a coherent agenda of systemic reform within an educational system prone, historically, to fragmentation and incoherence. Yet this new coherence was relative. For federal policy fueled reform activity throughout the system, and system-wide reform activity fueled the evolution of federal policy. Over this 20-year period, the work of developing, refining, and legitimizing content standards, performance standards, and assessments was in motion across the 50 states, though differently in each state, and with varying degrees of success. Across the country, program developers, publishers, researchers, and others worked to generate and evaluate essential programs and services. Philanthropists and investors contributed additional resources to support the work, including $130 million from the New American Schools initiative: a private enterprise that championed seven "break the mold" designs for comprehensive school reform.[6] Increasing numbers of schools worked to heed increasing resources and incentives for improvement. And increasing numbers of districts and states worked to develop the capabilities to provide those schools with substantive assistance.

Indeed, it wasn't as if some intelligent designer could devise a new, systemic, rational world of education and, then, cut over to it with the flick of a switch. Systemic reform was emerging as a solution amidst the very system of problems that it sought to solve. This swirl of loosely coordinated policy activity, proprietary activity, research, and school-level use proceeded amidst continuing dysfunction that risked overwhelming it: for example, weak capabilities and coordination throughout the system; institutionalized understandings and processes that continued to favor piecemeal, faddish reforms; professional and political opposition; and candidates for everything from local school board to U.S. president continuing to run on their own platforms for educational reform. This was not social problems *solved*. This was social problem *solving*.

Thus, in the reforming system of U.S. public education, coherence was a matter of perception, not reality, a sort of optical illusion akin to the beautiful woman and the old hag. Concentrating hard and squinting just right, the image of the beautiful woman leaps from the page, vivid and clear and unmistakable. Lose your concentration for a moment, and her image dissolves into that of the old hag. So, too, coherence and lingering dysfunction. Was the system coherent? Was the system dysfunctional? It was both, at the same time.

THE SUCCESS FOR ALL FOUNDATION

Over this 20-year span, an organization emerged and rose to national prominence for its success navigating the complex mix of coherence and dysfunction in the reforming system of U.S. public education: the Success for All Foundation (SFAF).[7] SFAF was no armchair reformer slinging silver bullets. Rather, SFAF was a 200+ person organization, the core mission of which sat at the intersection of the deepest convictions of its founders and the essential parameters of the federal policy agenda. SFAF was founded on the commitment to improve the academic achievement of as many at-risk students as possible by solving as many systemic, interdependent, undermining problems as necessary. SFAF was equally committed to the cause of rationality in education: to leveraging every available resource to inform, evaluate, and adapt all educational activity toward that goal, in every corner of the formal system.

For SFAF, systemic, rational reform was not a theoretical approach to improvement but, instead, a practical approach that drove the day-to-day work of the organization. The work of SFAF began with designing and supporting programs for improving schools. SFAF's cornerstone program was called, simply, Success for All. Among the nation's original and preeminent comprehensive school reform programs, Success for All was two things at once. It was a design for school restructuring: a blueprint for coordinated, simultaneous change in norms and culture, instructional organization, curriculum and instruction, supplemental services, and school-level leadership, all toward the goal of on-grade-level reading achievement in grades K–6. It was also a system of supports for replicating and sustaining that design at scale, across large numbers of chronically underperforming schools. As SFAF's cornerstone program, Success for All functioned as a springboard for developing coordinated designs and supports beyond K–6 reading and beyond chronically underperforming schools: K–6 writing and mathematics; pre-K and middle school reading and writing; district and state leadership; and more.

Efforts to devise designs and supports for schools were matched with efforts to scale-up operations. By the time of this writing, SFAF had achieved an astounding scale of operations, essentially operating its own system of education in interaction with the formal system. SFAF sat at the hub of this system, joined by two collaborating organizations that its executives helped to found and to manage: the Center for Data Driven Reform in Education and the Institute for Effective Education. Together with these collaborating organizations, SFAF was supporting 1,200 schools that were using its core, comprehensive school reform program—a network of elementary schools larger than that served by all but 14 states, though composed almost entirely of chronically underperforming Title I schools.[8] Beyond comprehensive school reform, SFAF was providing a combination of technical resources and/or assistance to an additional 2,500 schools, 380 districts, and 7 states.

While operating at scale, SFAF acted on its commitment to rationality by working to continuously improve the technical effectiveness of its programs. SFAF anchored its programs in strategies shown by research to be both effective and replicable, it adapted its programs as new knowledge and technologies emerged, and it worked tirelessly to leverage its organization, its networks, and its broader environments for ideas and knowledge to improve the program. At the same time, SFAF constantly subjected its programs to internal and external evaluations of program effectiveness, the product of which was a formidable body of evidence demonstrating positive effects on student achievement. This evidence included matched comparison studies, a randomized experiment, meta-analyses and other research syntheses, and re-analyses of state-level achievement data. SFAF's claim was *not* that this was unequivocal evidence of absolute success. Rather, SFAF's claim was that this was growing evidence of the *possibility* for systemic, rational, large-scale reform in schools, districts, and states.

All of this work depended on SFAF working aggressively to sustain the enterprise for the time required to bring it to fruition. Over this 20-year period, SFAF did so by doing two things at once. SFAF worked to align its organization and its programs with reforming environments. For example, specific requirements were attached to the use of the billions of federal dollars flooding the system to support systemic reform, and SFAF worked to ensure that its capabilities and programs aligned with those requirements. SFAF was particularly mindful of periodic reauthorizations of the federal Elementary and Secondary Education Act, which SFAF recognized as having implications for virtually all schools, districts, and states. By aligning with the Elementary and Secondary Education Act, SFAF sought to position itself at the nexus of system-wide reform activity. At the same time that it aligned with reforming environments, SFAF sought to influence those same environments to secure conditions that favored the organization and its programs. SFAF advocated for systemic reform and rationality in both policy and academic circles, and it held up the organization, its programs, and their effectiveness as evidence of the success that could be had by sustaining that agenda.

None of this was easy. Over these 20 years, SFAF faced tremendous challenges that greatly complicated its work. These challenges came from within SFAF's own system of schooling: from its clients—thousands of underperforming schools, districts, and states; from its systemic, complex, multicomponent programs; and from its own organization. These challenges came from the reforming and dysfunctional system of U.S. public education, including stiff criticism of SFAF's motivations, methods, and claims of effectiveness. And these challenges came from beyond education entirely: political turbulence, including six presidential elections, ten House elections, and three complete cycles of Senate elections; an economy that boomed and busted at least three times in SFAF's existence; two wars abroad; and unprecedented security threats at home.

All of it was fragile. SFAF was operating its own system of education in interaction with the broader, reforming, turbulent system of U.S. public education. It was doing so absent formal authority or institutionalized funding, in voluntary relationships with schools, districts, and states that remained card-carrying members of the broader system. Moreover, SFAF was doing so in competition with the many other program providers that populated the U.S. school improvement industry (included highly resourced, deeply institutionalized commercial publishers). Indeed, the boundaries between SFAF's system and the broader system were permeable (if not illusory), and fully buffering SFAF's system from the broader system was folly. Turbulence in the broader system meant turbulence in the SFAF system. And, ironically, that which effected some of the greatest shocks to SFAF and its system of education was that by which SFAF oriented most strongly: the federal Elementary and Secondary Education Act.

THE STORY

This is one account of SFAF, from its genesis in the early 1980s through the school year 2007/2008. The story might best be described as a blend of contemporary history and organizational ethnography: an attempt to understand the complexity of one of this period's most pervasive attempts at large-scale, sustainable educational reform (the shift to systemic, rational approaches to improvement) by exploring the work of one of this period's preeminent reformers (SFAF).

The research methods used to construct this story are detailed in an appendix that follows it. This appendix is a small story unto itself, and important context in considering the merits of the broader story. Because critics have long charged external researchers as complicit with SFAF and biased in their positive claims, and because SFAF has long charged critics as self-interested and biased in their negative claims, readers concerned about such issues should pause after the introduction to read the appendix before proceeding with the story of SFAF. Otherwise, such concerns are sure to complicate their reading.

By way of précis, this story is one product of the Study of Instructional Improvement (SII) at The University of Michigan: a longitudinal, mixed-methods study comparing the organization, design, implementation, and effects of Success for All and two other leading comprehensive school reform programs (America's Choice and the Accelerated Schools Project). SII featured three components: a survey component focused on implementation and effects in 115 schools; a case study component focused on program implementation in 12 schools; and a second case study component focused on understanding the three comprehensive school reform programs, their sponsoring organizations, and the evolution of the programs and organizations over time. This study of SFAF was conducted within the second case study component.

Within the Study of Instructional Improvement, the goal of the research reported here was to improve understanding of the work of launching and sustaining large-scale, externally developed improvement programs for underperforming schools in the turbulent environments of U.S. public education. Data collection ran from 1996 through 2010, a period that began amidst the New American Schools movement, Goals 2000, and the Improving America's Schools Act and that ended amidst such federal and national initiatives as Race to the Top, the Investing in Innovation program, and the Common Core Standards movement. Data collection centered on four domains: participant-observation in 34 training events for Success for All teachers, leaders, and trainers spanning 80 contact days; 77 interviews with SFAF executives, developers, trainers, researchers, and staff members; compilation of a vast library of program materials, reports, research, media accounts, and other documents; and thousands of informal conversations with Success for All teachers, leaders, and staff members. Analysis ran concurrent with data collection and in interaction with complementary analyses of the Accelerated Schools Project and America's Choice, with a focus on developing analytic frameworks capturing the work of these organizations and the challenges routinely experienced in that work.

Central to these strategies for data collection and analysis was developing close, long-term relationships with SFAF executives, developers, trainers, researchers, and staff members, with two key goals: observing and understanding their work; and cultivating trust as the basis for critically analyzing their work. As such, the structure of this story draws from the work of SFAF, such that each chapter focuses on a specific dimension of the work at a specific period in SFAF's evolution as an organization: designing externally sponsored school improvement programs; devising supports for implementation; scaling up the installed base of schools and the sponsoring organization; continuously improving while working at scale; and sustaining the enterprise in turbulent environments.

Such work is novel in the history of U.S. public education: working to effect large-scale improvement in the technical capabilities of schools, with the goal of all students mastering the same, ambitious academic content at the same, high standards. Such work is increasingly ubiquitous. This is work being done by reformers operating outside the formal system: organizations like SFAF, that seek to improve large numbers of existing schools; and organizations such as charter management organizations, that seek to build alternative systems of schools. Increasingly, this is the work being done by institutionalized organizations within the formal system, including state, regional, and local education agencies.

While the story runs thick with ironies, paradoxes, and other twists, chief among them is this: Despite rationality as the very goal, the work of systemic, rational reform as enacted by SFAF did not adhere to conventional models of rational problem solving. Conventional models portray such work as a straight-forward sequence of steps: study the problem; establish the goal; generate knowledge via basic and applied research; design and pilot; disseminate and use; and assess progress.[9] However, for SFAF, the functional work of systemic, rational reform was reciprocally interdependent, the essential tasks concurrent and con-founded.[10] Further, the knowledge needed to fuel the effort was not generated entirely (or even primarily) in advance of dissemination and use, with chronically underperforming schools the downstream recipients. Rather, essential knowledge was generated through the *experience* of dissemination and use, with chronically underperforming schools critical partners in the production of essential knowledge. Thus, while the story explores the functional work in a specific sequence (i.e., designing, supporting, scaling up, continuously improving, and sustaining), this sequence should not be read as "what came next. . . ." Rather, it should be read as "what was being done in addition to . . ." (including producing the very knowledge needed to support the enterprise).

Stories about organizations and their work are necessarily stories about people, and this story of SFAF is no different: It is a story about SFAF's executives, managers, developers, trainers, and many others. Yet an equally important (and very complex) character in this story is SFAF's cornerstone comprehensive school reform program, Success for All. From its inception through the time of this writing, Success for All was the heart and soul of the organization, its public identity, and the raw material from which most of its other programs and services were fashioned. Moreover, as a character in this story, Success for All plays against type. Throughout the educational reform community, Success for All has come to be viewed by many as the archetype of a top-down, bureaucratic, control-focused intervention. In this story, Success for All is portrayed quite differently: specifically, as a resource supporting the professional practice and professional learning of teachers and leaders in chronically underperforming schools.

Introductions to this cast of characters span the story. In Chapters 1 and 2, in the context of exploring the work of designing and supporting, we meet Success for All and its founders. In subsequent chapters, we meet other members of SFAF, and we learn about their capabilities, motivations, norms, values, and relationships. For example, in Chapter 3, in the context of exploring the work of scaling up, we learn about SFAF's training organization, its members, and their relationships with teachers and leaders in schools. In Chapter 4, in the context of exploring the work of continuous improvement, we learn about SFAF's development organization, its members, and their relationships with members of the training organization. And in Chapter 5, in the context of exploring the work of sustaining the enterprise, we learn about SFAF's executive team, its members, and their work with members of both the development and training organizations.

As we meet these characters and explore their work, one task as an analyst (whether writer or reader) is to maintain a balanced perspective. On the one hand, one needs to be empathetic toward SFAF and its members to appreciate and to understand their work as they chose to enact it. After all, at the time of this writing, SFAF and its members likely had more street-level experience working to improve more chronically underperforming schools than most people vested in improving U.S. public education. Whatever SFAF and its members elected to do to improve education for at-risk students, it is a safe assumption that there were very good reasons for it. On the other hand, one needs to be thoughtfully critical in order to learn from SFAF's successes and failures. After all, not every idea is a good idea, no matter how well reasoned. Maintaining a balanced perspective is made more important and more complicated by complex methods, motives, and tactics that, over its history, have polarized proponents and critics of SFAF: methods that included supporting both adaptive, locally responsive use of the program *and* consistent, conventional use within and between schools; motives that included both helping as many at-risk children as possible *and* securing the success of SFAF as an organization; and tactics that included both producing rigorous, objective research on program effectiveness *and* actively lobbying and marketing to secure advantage for the organization and its programs.

One means of maintaining a balanced perspective lies in keeping alive the voices of SFAF's critics. Over its history, SFAF and Success for All have been the subjects of widespread criticism, with its critics ranging from high-profile researchers and advocates to classroom teachers. Like SFAF, the methods, motives, and tactics of these critics were complex. Some of their critiques appeared to be motivated by genuine concern; others appeared to be motivated by competition. After all, critics, themselves, sometimes had their own irons in the fire. Some of their critiques were leveled thoughtfully; others were leveled harshly. Many of their critiques drew responses from SFAF: some genuine and thoughtful; others competitive and harsh.

Despite differences in opinions, viewpoints, and ideologies, a good many of these critics bore keen resemblance to SFAF: gravely concerned with problems undermining the academic success of at-risk students; hopeful about the possibilities of solving those problems; and committed to acting on their best knowledge in doing so. In keeping alive their voices, one intent is to keep alive an awareness that SFAF continuously operated amidst self-effected environmental turbulence, as the organization, its cornerstone program, and its interpretation of activity in schools ran up against others who saw matters quite differently. Another intent is to keep alive the equivocality of the Success for All enterprise: the simple fact that everything about it could be interpreted from multiple perspectives.

A second (and primary) means of maintaining a balanced perspective lies in recognizing that SFAF's greatest strengths were also its greatest weaknesses. This "strengths-as-weaknesses" dialectic begins with accepting SFAF on its own terms, and exploring how the organization gained unique leverage on key challenges of large-scale educational reform: designing programs; supporting implementation; scaling up; continuously improving; and sustaining its operations. This dialectic continues, then, with critical analysis of how the very methods that provided SFAF unique leverage also interacted to create new and steep problems for the organization (including intense criticism).

This "strengths-as-weaknesses" dialect is used to structure each chapter, with the beginning of each chapter detailing strengths of SFAF, and with the remainder of each chapter providing critical analysis of how those strengths interacted to yield new and steep problems. Both strengths and weaknesses emerge and accumulate across chapters. At the beginning of the story, we see the strengths of SFAF accumulating to create unique potential to address systemic problems that often undermine the achievement of at-risk students. At the same time, we see the weaknesses of SFAF accumulating to risk adverse interpretations and misuse of the program in chronically underperforming schools. By the end of the story, we see the strengths of SFAF accumulating to create unusual capabilities to support large-scale improvement—not only in chronically underperforming schools but, also, in higher-performing schools, districts, and states. At the same time, we see the weaknesses of SFAF accumulating to raise important questions about the effectiveness of SFAF's programs, the influence of SFAF in educational and political environments, and the continued viability of SFAF as an organization.

Another task as an analyst is to pursue multiple, complementary means of establishing the validity of such claims. After all, this is but one account of SFAF, constructed by a particular person, at a particular period in time. Circumstances of this account heighten the need: for example, interpretations of Success for All that run counter both to the charges of its critics and to the public image cultivated by its founders; existing camps of proponents and critics, both loaded for bear; and strategies for data collection and analysis that involved developing close, personal, extended relationships with the people under study.

Efforts to establish validity rest in several domains. One is the study design, itself, which included opportunities to observe Success for All for an extended period of time, triangulate among multiple sources of evidence, further investigate contrary and confusing evidence, and share and examine interpretations with Success for All staff, teachers, and leaders. Another is the Study of Instructional Improvement as a context for this research, which included simultaneous, complementary case studies of two other leading comprehensive school reform programs (the Accelerated Schools Project and America's Choice), with these case studies themselves conducted in interaction with quantitative and qualitative studies of program implementation and effects. Yet another is the effort taken to incorporate external perspective and criticism: for example, interviewing several of SFAF's most vocal critics; maintaining surveillance of reports on Success for All in academic journals and in the popular press; making extensive use of the academic literature; and presenting components of the analyses as papers at academic conferences, thus opening the analysis to criticism and feedback. Again, a complete account of the research methods is included as an appendix following the story of SFAF.

ANALYTIC FRAMEWORK

While the work of SFAF structures the primary narrative (i.e., designing, supporting, scaling up, continuously improving, and sustaining), a sub-narrative emerges and develops over the course of the story. This sub-narrative explores the strengths and weaknesses of SFAF as arising from the complex interactions among the four essential parts of SFAF's self-constructed system of education: the clients served (i.e., schools, districts, and states); the programs provided to them; the organization needed to develop programs and support clients (i.e., SFAF); and the environments in which all function (both educational environments and broader environments). Throughout SFAF's history, each of these parts has functioned as a source of critical problems, as a target of ambitious solutions, and as a source of new challenges that followed from enacting those solutions. In the case of SFAF, rather than tidy and tractable, the relationships between these parts were "networky" and "web-like," such that the different parts, problems, solutions, and challenges pushed against each other in complex and often hard-to-discern ways, and with federal policy functioning as a sort of "deep structure" that motivated and constrained their interactions.

This sub-narrative emerges immediately and explicitly in the very beginning of the story, in an initial analysis of the strengths and weaknesses that arose in the work of designing Success for All. It is developed and used throughout the remainder of the story as an analytic framework: that is, as a way of seeing the work of large-scale, sustainable, systemic educational reform as sitting at the nexus of complex interactions among clients, programs, the sponsoring organization, and their environments.

This analytic framework is used here to explore the work of SFAF: that is, designing improvement programs; devising supports for implementation; scaling up; continuously improving; and sustaining the enterprise. It is used elsewhere to guide the comparative analysis of SFAF and the two other leading comprehensive school reform providers that participated in the Study of Instructional Improvement: the National Commission on Education and the Economy (which developed America's Choice); and the Accelerated Schools Project (which developed the Accelerated Schools Project).[11] The conjecture that follows is that this analytic framework will be generally useful for exploring, understanding, and critically analyzing the increasingly ubiquitous work of large-scale, sustainable, systemic educational reform, as enacted by organizations operating both within and beyond the formal system of U.S. public education.

Thus, the story of SFAF is not intended to advance a theoretical framework: a series of propositions about the relationship between independent and dependent variables that can be subjected to empirical investigation. Nor is the story intended to advance SFAF and Success for All as exemplars to be replicated by those seeking to perform similar work. Rather, the story is intended to advance an analytic framework: a means of seeing complexity that would otherwise go unnoticed, both in the system of U.S. public education and in the work of improving it.

COMPLEXITY

That, then, is the essential condition that drove the work of SFAF: complexity, both in the system of U.S. public education and in the work of improving it. That complexity, in turn, was rooted in interdependence: in the many concerns to be taken into account in improving education for at-risk students; in their dense, tangled relationships; and in the time needed to sort them all out. Interdependence spanned the parts of SFAF's self-constructed system of education: its clients, its programs, its own organization, and their environments. Interdependence spanned the functional work of SFAF: designing, supporting, scaling up, continuously improving, and sustaining. SFAF's primary strength was recognizing (and seeking to manage) education as a complex system ripe with interdependence. SFAF's primary struggle was exactly the same.

Indeed, there is much in this story of SFAF—the parts, the work, the interdependencies—to challenge our usual ways of thinking about complex systems and the work of improving them. Herbert Simon, a Nobel Prize-winning economist and pioneering student of complex systems, described these usual ways of thinking as beginning with one, fundamental observation: that many complex systems have a hierarchic, nested, "boxes-within-boxes" structure, the elements of which are nearly independent in the short term and only weakly interdependent in the long term. Simon explained that the near-independence between levels and elements of such systems simplifies the work of designing improvements, because it enables designers to isolate parts of the system, understand them, and improve them, all while paying comparatively scant attention to the broader system. Simon generalizes this premise as the "empty world hypothesis": "most things are only weakly connected with most other things; for a tolerable description of reality only a tiny fraction of all possible interactions needs to be taken into account."[12]

These usual ways of thinking are well represented in our usual ways of thinking about education as a complex system—ways of thinking to which many vested in improving U.S. public education hold fast. For example, we think in terms of hierarchy, with students in classrooms, classrooms in schools, schools in districts, and districts in states. We think of "loose coupling" within and between educational organizations.[13] And we think in terms of incisive, targeted interventions that are designed, disseminated, and implemented using straightforward, rational methods of problem solving and management.

Our problem is that, when viewed from the perspective of SFAF, a leading reformer working at a unique moment in the history of U.S. educational reform, education does not appear to be *that* type of complex system, nor does the work of improving education appear so straightforward. Standing on the shoulders of SFAF and looking out, we don't see U.S. public education as an empty world but, instead, as a full world: a world full of at-risk students; a world full of complex parts, problems, solutions, and challenges, all in dense, interdependent, networked relationships; and a world full of individuals, organizations, and groups working in interaction to apprehend, confront, and reform these many parts and their dense, interdependent relationships. This complexity challenges the work of designing improvements, because it drives designers to consider multiple parts of the system, to understand them and their interactions, and to improve them in interaction, all while paying careful attention to the broader system.

The general formalization of this premise would be a "full world hypothesis": in considering education as a complex system, many things are strongly connected to many other things; for a tolerable description of reality, a large number of all possible interactions needs to be taken into account. Simon recognizes the possibility of full worlds: complex systems ripe with many parts in dense, interdependent, non-hierarchic relationships. He also cautions that such systems are so complex as to escape our capacity to observe and to understand them:

> The fact that many complex systems have a nearly decomposable, hierarchic structure is a major facilitating factor enabling us to understand, describe, and even "see" such systems and their parts. Or perhaps the proposition should be put the other way around. If there are important systems in the world that are complex without being hierarchic, they may to a considerable extent escape our observation and understanding. Analysis of their behavior would involve such detailed knowledge and calculation of the interactions of their elementary parts that it would be beyond our capacities of memory or computation.[14]

That, then, is the premise of this book: not that the system of U.S. public education is beyond improving, but that we reformers are just now beginning to see and understand the full complexity of improving it. And this, then, is the purpose of this book: to help more people learn to see complexity in U.S. public education, so that we reformers can begin thinking and talking more clearly about its problems, our solutions, and the possibility of academic success for all students. Nothing more. Nothing less.

Notes

1. Kominski, Jamieson, and Martinez (2001:6).
2. Kominski, Jamieson, and Martinez (2001:6).

3. For reports on the number of Title I schools as of 2007, see Stullich, Eisner, and McCrary (2007:xix). Stullich, Eisner, and McCrary report that, as of 2005, a total of 54,454 schools received Title I funding. Of these, 31,782 were pursuing schoolwide Title I programs, which requires that over 40% of students in those schools be in poverty.

4. For example, see: Sebring and Bryk (2000), on Christmas tree reform; Tyack and Cuban (1995), Cuban (1992; 1993), and Lortie (1975), on incremental change and inherent conservatism in public education; and Rowan (2002), on the population ecology of the school improvement industry.

5. For seminal research and analysis in the development of the logic of systemic reform, see: Purkey and Smith (1983; 1985); Smith and O'Day (1991): O'Day and Smith (1993). See, also, Puma, Raphael, Olsen, and Hannaway (2000), who detail a design for evaluating systemic reform that includes a comprehensive discussion of the underlying principles.

6. Berends, Bodilly, and Kirby (2002:157).

7. Throughout this analysis, I refer to the Success for All *Foundation* as "SFAF," and I refer to the Success for All *program* as "Success for All."

8. See Williams, Blank, Toye, and Petermann (2007): a report prepared by the Council of Chief State School Officers for the U.S. Department of Education that includes the total number of elementary schools per state as of school year 2002–2003.

9. See Rogers (1995:131–160) for a widely cited rendering of the conventional research-development-diffusion model of innovation. Rowan, Camburn, and Barnes (2004:3) describe this model as an "RDDU" strategy for educational change: research, development, dissemination, and utilization.

10. Findings of the functional work of effective, large-scale, sustainable educational reform as concurrent, confounded, and inconsistent with conventional models of research and development directly mirror findings in two related lines of research: research on the organizations and programs that participated in the New American Schools initiative (see Berends, Bodilly, and Kirby, 2002); and broader research on 13 leading large-scale educational reform initiatives over a 20 years period (see Glennan, Bodilly, Galegher, and Kerr, 2004).

11. See Cohen, Gates, Glazer, Goldin, and Peurach (in press).

12. Simon (1996: 209). See, also, Simon (1962).

13. For seminal research on loose coupling in educational organizations, see: Bidwell (1965); Weick (1976); Meyer and Rowan (1983); and Meyer, Scott, and Deal (1983).

14. See Simon (1996:207).

1

Designing

Not more than 15 years ago, Ronald Edmonds put forth three assertions: (a) We can, whenever and wherever we choose, successfully teach all children whose schooling is of interest to us; (b) We already know more than we need to do that; and (c) Whether or not we do it must finally depend on how we feel about the fact that we haven't so far. . . .

The greatest importance of research on Success for All and Roots and Wings is that it brings us close to making Edmond's vision a reality. Only when we have confidence that we can take a typical school serving disadvantaged children and ensure the success of virtually every child can we really force the essential political and policy question: Given that we know that we can greatly improve the educational performance of at risk children, **are we willing to do what it takes to do so?**

ROBERT SLAVIN, NANCY MADDEN, LAWRENCE DOLAN,
AND BARBARA WASIK, 1996[1]

uccess for All is a comprehensive school reform program initially developed in 1987/88. Put plainly by the program's developers, their ambition was "to make the idea that all children can learn a practical, daily organizing principle for schools, especially those serving many students placed at risk."[2]

From one perspective, Success for All quickly became an evangelical crusade, its mission anchored in unwavering belief in the academic potential of all students and the professional potential of all educators. From such beliefs came moral responsibility to work at a large scale, serving as many students, teachers, and leaders as possible. Salvation was possible for the nation's weakest schools—ironically, through science: specifically, through the use of rigorous research both as a basis for the program and to validate its effectiveness. From another perspective, Success for All quickly became a player in a new, niche market for school improvement services, one determined to push the essential political and policy question: Are we willing to do what it takes to enable academic success for all children?

Over its first ten years of operations, the Success for All movement gained considerable momentum. Enthusiasm gathered in some circles. Criticism gathered in others.

BEGINNINGS

Success for All was not the product of amateur reformers, nor was it created overnight from whole cloth. Rather, the heritage of Success for All was a rich one, steeped in knowledge and experience designing external improvement programs for schools, and in relationships with other reformers doing the same.[3] Its beginnings coincided with dramatic changes in U.S. educational environments that provided legitimacy, guidance, resources, and incentives supporting its core mission: comprehensive, large scale, sustainable reform in schools serving large numbers of at-risk students. Even so, its very ambitions for schools brought Success for All face-to-face with a host of interdependent and deeply institutionalized problems that often undermine student achievement.

Heritage: The Organization and the Program

Success for All was initially founded and developed by a research group led by the husband and wife team of Robert Slavin and Nancy Madden. The project team and the program were originally headquartered in one of the nation's oldest publicly funded educational research centers, in one of the nation's original and preeminent research universities: the Center for the Social Organization of Schools (CSOS) at Johns Hopkins University in Baltimore, MD. CSOS was cofounded by sociologist James Coleman in 1966, virtually concurrent with the publication of *Equality of Educational Opportunity*—the famous Coleman Report.[4]

Slavin and Madden had extensive experience working as designers of external improvement programs for schools. While undergraduates at Reed College in the early 1970s, Slavin and Madden received funding to design "WorldLab," which blended instruction in social studies and science with authentic problem solving and small-group investigations among diverse groups of students. Slavin and Madden fielded WorldLab in a Portland-area school district, with the experience serving as the basis for Slavin's senior thesis.[5] The program and its developers reflected that particular moment in U.S. history: a period of social upheaval and reconstitution led by coming-of-age baby boomers, marked with great concern for people of all stripes learning to live and to work in harmony.

In the mid-1970s, as researchers in CSOS, Slavin and Madden began working with colleagues to design and support additional improvement programs targeting classroom instruction. Rather than addressing elements of instruction in isolation, Slavin, Madden, and colleagues developed programs that simultaneously addressed the student role in instruction, the teacher role in instruction, and classroom-level curriculum materials. Initial efforts focused on a strategy for cooperative learning in classrooms, with the goal of developing "positive inter-dependence" among student teams that would improve their motivation, their social relations, and, with that, their potential to learn.[6]

Two subsequent efforts combined cooperative learning with individualized instruction and coordinated curriculum materials: Team Accelerated Instruction (TAI) in mathematics, designed and fielded in 1980; and Cooperative Integrated Reading and Composition (CIRC), designed and fielded in 1983. These efforts and their underlying instructional strategies were formally evaluated and the results published, with Slavin, Madden, and colleagues arguing that findings supported claims of generally positive effects on academic, affective, and social outcomes of instruction.[7]

Beginning in 1985, Slavin, Madden, and colleagues extended these earlier (and, in their view, promising) development efforts with a project called "the coopera-tive elementary school." Evolving beyond classroom-by-classroom improvement, the cooperative elementary school sought to improve the school as a whole by combining TAI and CIRC with organizational restructuring, the integration of special education services, and family support programs. As explained by Slavin and his colleague, Robert Stevens, the aim of the cooperative elementary school was to develop positive interdependence not only among students but, also, among teachers and school leaders:

> We attempted to use cooperation as a philosophy to change the school and classroom organization and the way members of the school community interacted. Peer coaching was used as a form of cooperation where teachers would help one another improve their teaching (Joyce, Hersh, & McKibbin, 1983). Similarly, teachers and the principal were encouraged to collaborate in planning instruction and to develop interdependence within the faculty so they would take collective responsibility for the learning of all students.[8]

At the same time that he was deeply engaged in program design, Slavin was also drawing recognition as a leading educational researcher. In 1986, Slavin was awarded the Raymond B. Cattell Early Career Award for Programmatic Research by the American Educational Research Association (AERA), primarily for his work on cooperative learning. In 1988, Slavin was awarded the Palmer O. Johnson award for the best article in an AERA journal, which introduced "best evidence synthesis" as a formal method for synthesizing findings on a given topic across studies.[9]

In 1986, with what members recalled as important encouragement and support from Kalman Hettleman, former Maryland Secretary of Human Resources, Slavin, Madden, and colleagues launched Success for All, a research and development program aimed at improving education for at-risk students.[10] Success for All was first fielded in 1987/1988. The program was novel by the standards of the day. Success for All was not a remedial program targeting struggling students or a professional development series promoting a specific instructional method (then-conventional approaches to externally supported improvement). Rather, Success for All was the next step in the evolution of the cooperative elementary school, the intent being to blanket schools with an even more comprehensive suite of coordinated solutions that stretched from the classroom level to the school level and into family, community, and political environments.

The novelty extended beyond the program itself, to the approach that its developers took to designing the program: that is, to deciding what needed to be done differently in schools to increase the achievement of at-risk students. For Success for All, designing was not to be a distributed task, with developers consulting with leaders and teachers school-by-school to devise customized, school-specific programs. Such a strategy was viewed by developers as unnecessary and inefficient. They saw enough in common among chronically underperforming schools to support the development of a more general program for use in many schools. Designing, thus, became a centralized task through which developers devised a conventional array of coordinated program components to be replicated across multiple, chronically underperforming elementary schools. Indeed, from the earliest days of Success for All, developers' approach to designing was linked tightly to their ambitions for large-scale operations.

With an eye on replicable effectiveness, developers took a principled approach to the work of designing. Developers sought to avoid the uncertainty and costs of pure invention, and they sought to sidestep the dogmatic debates that often plagued educational reform. Instead, developers stayed true to their organizational and professional roots by anchoring Success for All in methods and strategies shown by research both to be effective in improving student achievement and replicable across schools. They drew heavily from their own basic research and from their own research-validated programs, including Slavin's research on cooperative learning and Madden and Slavin's joint work on CIRC. Developers also drew heavily from formal meta-analyses and best-evidence syntheses of relevant research. Among these was *Effective Program for Students at Risk*, a federally supported volume edited by Slavin, Madden, and CSOS colleague Nancy Karweit that sought to compile "the best available information on what is known about effective programs for students at risk of school failure."[11] Beyond anchoring Success for All in research, developers also renewed their commitment to evaluating program effectiveness using rigorous research methods and to publishing their results.

Developers balanced their principled approach to design with a healthy dose of pragmatism. By 1987/1988, they had over fifteen years of experience designing and fielding educational improvement programs, and they drew heavily on that experience in designing Success for All. Moreover, they continued to refine, adapt, and evolve Success for All as they accumulated additional experience. Among developers, the work of designing was not detached from the work of program implementation. Rather, developers were committed to supporting implementation, such that their collaborative work with schools combined with ever-developing research and technologies to fuel continuous improvement of the program.

Just as the program evolved, so, too, did the project team. In 1994, the Success for All project team moved to the newly formed and federally funded Center for the Study of Students Placed at Risk (CRESPAR), which paired with CSOS to operate jointly within Johns Hopkins University. The move had several advantages, including shoring up the legitimacy and identity of the Success for All enterprise and providing the resources needed to grow and sustain it. CRESPAR was a major undertaking, involving collaboration on multiple programs by researchers spanning an array of formidable institutions: Johns Hopkins University, Howard University, the University of California at Santa Barbara, the University of California at Los Angeles, the University of Oklahoma, the University of Chicago, Manpower Research Demonstration Corporation, WestEd Regional Laboratory, the University of Memphis, and the University of Houston-Clear Lake. The mission of Success for All and the mission of CRESPAR were virtually indistinguishable, including the ambition of achieving large scale operations:

> The mission of the Center for Research on the Education of Students Placed at Risk (CRESPAR) is to conduct the research, development, evaluation, and dissemination needed to transform schooling for students placed at risk. The work of the Center is guided by three central themes—ensuring the success of all students at key development points, building on students' personal and cultural assets, and scaling up effective programs—and conducted through seven research and development programs and a program of institutional activities.[12]

Thus, from the inception of Success for All, designing shaped up as centralized, principled, and pragmatic activity. It also shaped up as activity inextricably bound with the work of supporting implementation, scaling up operations, continuously improving the program, and acquiring the legitimacy and resources needed to sustain the enterprise.

A New, Niche Market

Success for All and its project team emerged in interaction with supporting environmental conditions. Amidst growing enthusiasm for systemic, rational reform, a loosely coordinated stream of policies and initiatives gave rise to a new, niche market for precisely that which Success for All's founders and developers sought to provide: comprehensive school reform programs for chronically underperforming schools. Chief among these policies and initiatives was the federal Elementary and Secondary Education Act (ESEA). ESEA was a federal statute first signed into law in 1965 and, thereafter, amended and reauthorized roughly every five to seven years. In contrast to general aid to public schools, ESEA was the first federal policy to provide funding to schools, districts, and states to support specific categories of school improvement. Consequently, ESEA was an omnibus policy that, over its history, included funding for such initiatives as schools libraries, supplemental student services, professional development, parent involvement, bilingual education, and more.

From its inception, Title I was one of ESEA's cornerstones, providing funding to schools, districts, and states to improve the education of students at risk of academic failure.[13] Initially, schools were required to use Title I funding to provide supplemental services to individual students, either through "pull out" programs or through classroom-based assistance. However, recognizing the difficulty of providing effective supplemental assistance to large numbers of at-risk students, a series of reauthorizations of ESEA made it increasingly possible for schools to shift away from supplemental, targeted assistance and toward systemic, whole school improvement. The 1978 reauthorization allowed schools with 75% of students in poverty to use Title I funds to support schoolwide improvement, with the requirement that districts provide matching funds. Concurrent with the founding of Success for All, the 1988 reauthorization dropped the requirement for district matching funds. In 1994, concurrent with Success for All's movement to CRESPAR, the reauthorization of ESEA as the Improving America's Education Act (IASA) reduced the threshold for qualifying schools to those with 60% of students in poverty (in 1995/1996) and, then, to those with 50% of students in poverty (in 1996/1997).

One effect of these amendments to Title I was to provide increased legitimacy to comprehensive, schoolwide reform as a strategy for improvement. A second effect was to make billions of dollars available to schools to pursue comprehensive school reform, either by developing their own programs or by contracting with external developers. Indeed, by the time of Success for All's emergence in the late 1980s, Title I was pumping $4.6 billion annually into all 50 states, 93% of all public school districts, and 71% of all public elementary schools.[14] A third effect was to begin formalizing guidance for schools and external developers regarding programs that would qualify for federal funding. With the 1994 reauthorization, ESEA (now IASA) specified eight criteria for qualifying schoolwide programs (see Table 1.1), including requirements for the use of "effective" strategies for improving instruction and achievement.

Legitimacy, guidance, and resources for comprehensive school reform were matched with incentives, as interdependent federal and state policy activity led to the emergence of the "standards-based reform" movement: for example, the Charlottesville Education Summit of 1989, America 2000 in 1991, Goals 2000 in 1994, and IASA in 1994. Beyond holding schools fiscally accountable for the use of federal funding, the standards-based reform movement sought to hold schools accountable for their effectiveness as measured by what IASA described as "adequate yearly progress" improving student achievement.[15] Using a combination of newly created state-level content standards, performance standards, and accountability assessments, one intent was to increase expectations for achievement beyond basic facts and skills to ambitious academic content and cognitive strategies. A second intent was to coordinate system-wide improvement activity around common core standards and assessments. A third intent was to motivate chronically underperforming schools to use available resources to embark on self-designed or self-selected programs of improvement, the "basic bargain" of standards-based reform being accountability in exchange for autonomy.[16]

Table 1.1 IMPROVING AMERICA'S SCHOOLS ACT: CRITERIA FOR QUALIFYING
SCHOOLWIDE PROGRAMS*

Key components of schoolwide programs under IASA included:

1. A comprehensive needs assessment of the entire school that is based on information on the performance of children in relation to the State content standards and the State student performance standards.

2. Schoolwide reform strategies that provide opportunities for all children to meet the State's proficient and advanced levels of student performance, are based on effective means of improving achievement, and use effective instructional strategies.

3. Instruction by highly qualified professional staff.

4. Professional development for teachers and aides, and, where appropriate, pupil services, personnel, parents, principals, and other staff to enable all children in the school to meet the State's student performance standards.

5. Strategies to increase parental involvement, such as family literary services.

6. Plans for assisting preschool children in the transition from early childhood programs, such as Head Start, Even Start, or a state-run preschool program, to local elementary school programs.

7. Measures to include teachers in the decisions regarding the use of assessments described in section 1112(b)(1) in order to provide information on, and to improve, the performance of individual students and the overall instructional program.

8. Activities to ensure that students who experience difficulty mastering any of the standards required by section 1111(b) during the course of the school year shall be provided with effective, timely additional assistance.

*U.S. Department of Education (1994b).

Possible sanctions for failing to improve included reductions in funding, the replacement of administrators, or the complete reconstitution of the school.

Resources and incentives for schools were matched with resources and incentives for program developers. In 1991, as part of President George H. W. Bush's America 2000 Initiative, the New American Schools Development Corporation (later renamed New American Schools, or NAS) was founded as a private, nonprofit corporation to support seven design teams in developing, scaling up, and evaluating "break the mold" designs for comprehensive school reform, one of which was Roots and Wings (an expanded version of Success for All).[17] NAS was a high profile initiative: founded by members of the Business Round Table; led by David Kearns, Chairman Emeritus of Xerox Corporation and then Deputy Secretary of Education; and funded to the tune of $130 million.[18] Besides providing additional legitimacy, resources, and incentives for comprehensive school reform, NAS also sought to bring business acumen to bear on educational reform: for example, by using a conventional, sequential research-development-diffusion model to structure the work of the design teams over a six-year period; by creating a market for comprehensive school reform, and brokering relationships between design teams and schools; and by providing guidance for establishing the design teams and their programs as self-sustaining enterprises. This last point was particularly important, as a key goal of NAS was not only for design teams to achieve large-scale operations but, also, to sustain those operations over time.

Public and private support for both comprehensive school reform and standards-based reform were themselves enabled by supporting conditions in broader environments. The two reform movements first emerged concurrent with political and economic turbulence: the stock market crash of 1987, subsequent recession, and the first Gulf War. However, political conditions abroad soon stabilized, and the economy began to grow (fueled, in part, by rapid growth in the information technology sector). Benefits included new opportunity to focus the domestic policy agenda on educational reform, along with increased public and private financial contributions to educational reform.

Buoyed by support in broader environments, this combination of legitimacy, guidance, resources, and incentives led to a rapid expansion in the number of schools using Title I funding to pursue comprehensive, schoolwide improvement. Following the 1978 reauthorization of ESEA, requirements that districts match federal Title I funding had only small numbers of schools pursuing schoolwide improvement programs.[19] By 1991, with the 1988 reauthorization having relaxed the requirement for district matching funds, 10% of eligible schools (1,200 of approximately 12,000 schools) were using Title I funds to pursue schoolwide improvement programs. By 1996, almost 50% of eligible schools (8,000 of approximately 16,800 schools) were using Title I funds to pursue schoolwide improvement programs.[20] By 1998, the number of schools using Title I funds to pursue schoolwide programs had risen to 17,000 of 22,000 eligible schools, or approximately 77%: a formidable market for comprehensive school reform programs that simply had not existed ten years earlier.[21]

Thus, by historical standards, Success for All was something of an odd duck, its central tenets uncommon in U.S. educational reform: that is, this business of comprehensive and research-based solutions, rigorous evaluation, large-scale operations, continuous improvement, and long-term sustainability. Yet in the reforming environments in which it emerged, Success for All was one of seven privileged programs in a new, niche market for comprehensive school reform, its central tenets stitched into national education policy and reform. Between its founding in 1987/88 and the passage of IASA in 1994, Success for All had become a player.

Goals and Targets

In the late 1980s and early 1990s, as enthusiasm for systemic, rational reform was taking root in U.S. educational environments, developers of comprehensive school reform programs faced the novel challenge of devising means of achieving policy-specified goals for student achievement. With that, effectiveness emerged as a driving concern: effectiveness as a criterion for selecting strategies on which to base programs, effectiveness as demonstrated through evaluations of implementation, and effectiveness as demonstrated by measurable gains in student achievement.

From its inception in 1987/88, Success for All developers elected to pursue effectiveness along a strategically-selected dimension of schooling: K–6 reading. From the perspective of program developers, reading instruction was the primary work of U.S. elementary schools, with reading achievement the foundation for learning in all other content areas. Literature, science, and social studies all require reading as a prerequisite skill—and, with increasing emphasis on complex and authentic analyses, mathematics, too. With funding from NAS in 1992/93, program developers leveraged past development efforts and initiated new ones to create programs in writing, mathematics, and integrated science and social studies, which they bundled into an even more comprehensive model called Roots and Wings. Even so, the cornerstone program—the foundation on which all other programs were built—was the original K–6 Success for All reading program.

The overarching goal of Success for All was straightforward and measurable: for all students—especially at-risk students—to read at or above grade level by the end of each grade, in terms of decoding, fluency, and (especially) reading comprehension.[22] Among developers, the operative notion was that of "neverstreaming." Rather than assigning struggling students to special education and then mainstreaming them into regular classrooms, the goal was to achieve and sustain success at each critical stage of development, thus precluding their assignment to special education. Asked later to reflect on their initial motivations and aspirations, early developers reported that Success for All was neither intended nor designed as a "basic skills" program for struggling readers. Rather, they reported that it was intended and designed as a program for scaffolding the initially weakest readers to the same, high levels of reading performance as all other students and, then, sustaining that success over time.

The overarching goal of on-grade-level reading performance was not only straightforward and measurable. It was also ambitious. At-risk students often entered elementary school behind their age-mates in their readiness to begin formal reading instruction. At the extreme, they were kindergartners and first graders who spoke English as a second language (if at all), who did not know to hold a book with the spine to the left and the cover facing up, who didn't know that text flowed from top to bottom and left to right, and who didn't know the association between printed symbols and sounds. Closing the achievement gap required that these same students be the fastest learners in the schools if they were ever to read at the same levels as their less-challenged peers. Indeed, an adage among program developers was that Success for All was not a remediation program but, instead, an acceleration program, one intended and designed to close that gap.

There was a tension in focusing on elementary reading. On the one hand, developers saw the focus as strategic. Though K–6 reading was but one drop in a big bucket of schooling, Success for All sought to transform the entire bucket by changing that drop—and with it, the life chances of at-risk students. As cited by Success for All trainers, studies suggest that a student who doesn't read on grade level by the end of first grade has a 50/50 chance of ever reading on grade level.[23] Difficulties with early reading quickly lead to difficulties in other academic content areas, which then interact with other risk factors to drive a downward spiral of academic and life failure. As cited by Success for All trainers, studies suggest that (a) a male student in third grade, (b) who is a member of a racial or ethnic minority, (c) who has repeated a grade, (d) who is reading below grade level, (e) and who attends a school with more than 50% of students in poverty has a near-zero probability of graduating from high school.[24] By this analysis, much of the life-history of that student can be written by the time he is eight or nine years old.

On the other hand, the focus on K–6 reading was narrow and thus, risky. After all, reading represented but one-half of the usual language arts curriculum in schools, the other half being writing. Further, language arts was but one academic content area in elementary schools, the others being mathematics, science, and social studies—never mind music, art, physical education, computer lab, library, and other "specials" courses. In many ways, improving reading achievement depended on success in these other content areas: for example, in writing, so that students would develop the capability to construct meaningful written responses to provide evidence of reading comprehension; and in social studies, science, and math, so that students would acquire broader knowledge to support reading comprehension. Indeed, despite developers' identification of Success for All as a comprehensive school reform program, the narrow focus on K–6 reading ran the risk that lingering dysfunction in other content areas would overwhelm efforts to improve reading achievement.

Steep Challenges

With rationality taking root, enthusiasts could argue that Success for All had the textbook characteristics of a good plan. Its goals were specific and measurable. Its targets were both ambitious (so as to make a difference) and narrow (so as to be doable). On a more basic level, it sounded right. Why target improvements in any other content areas if students lacked the fundamental capability for academic success: the capability to read and to understand text?

At the same time, critics could argue just as easily that the very strengths of Success for All were also its most fundamental weaknesses. The weaknesses went well beyond risks arising from the strategic (but narrow) focus on K–6 reading. Specifically, setting high goals for student achievement and electing comprehensive school reform as the means of achieving those goals ran Success for All developers straight into a host of compounding and deeply institutionalized problems that often undermined student achievement, especially for at-risk students in chronically underperforming schools. Straightforwardly, there was little infrastructure within schools or their environments upon which the Success for All project team could build.

The problems began with expectations and responsibility for achievement. A fundamental problem in chronically underperforming schools was that few teachers or leaders expected at-risk students to learn—certainly not challenging content, certainly not at the same level as less-challenged students, and perhaps not at all.[25] In some cases, expectations followed from deeply rooted biases and prejudices. In other cases, expectations followed from careers' worth of experience witnessing the failure of at-risk students, despite what teachers and leaders saw as their best efforts. As much out of self-preservation as malpractice, they had long absolved themselves of responsibility for students' failure, locating it, instead, in the very characteristics that had students at risk of failing: for example, language difficulties, family circumstances, and community dysfunction. Low expectations, powerlessness, and non-responsibility exacerbated achievement problems, which exacerbated low expectations, powerlessness, and non-responsibility, which exacerbated achievement problems—again, a downward spiral that too often ended in students' academic and life failure.

Problems carried beyond norms and culture to conventional means of organizing instruction. Rather than standardizing and prioritizing time for reading instruction to support at-risk students, reading often competed with other academic content areas, announcements, assemblies, supplemental services, and "specials" classes for the time and attention of students and teachers.[26] The annual assignment of teachers and students to classes further complicated matters. Such conventional practices as social promotion, inclusion, and promoting diversity guaranteed that teachers would face tremendous variation in students. The result was a lose-lose situation. Whole class instruction required striking compromises between the learning needs of students at very different levels of performance. Managing student variation via ability-based reading groups meant partial attention from the teacher and extended time for independent work—risky practices for students already at risk of academic failure.[27]

Problems stretched further, into the core work of classroom instruction. As a general matter, instruction in U.S. public schools was notoriously weakly coordinated, rarely bound by the consistent use of coherent methods and materials between classes (let alone methods and materials tailored to the specific needs of at-risk students).[28] Rather, long-held norms of teacher autonomy meant that methods and materials often varied from teacher to teacher—maybe loosely constrained by a schoolwide textbook series and an associated "scope and sequence" of topics, but often cobbled teacher-by-teacher from personal and professional experience.[29] With instruction largely private and individually determined conducted in solitary classrooms and behind closed doors, teachers often had little basis or opportunity to coordinate their work, even if so inclined.

Reading instruction was particularly problematic. One problem was that, concurrent with the emergence of Success for All, reading instruction was plagued by dogmatic debates between proponents of phonics and whole language, with no socially agreed-upon standards for grade-level reading performance, and with no socially agreed-upon means of measuring grade-level reading performance.[30]

A second problem was that, in many schools, reading instruction was reduced to little more than straightforward usage of commercially published basal reading programs. A common result was reading instruction that favored low-level reading skills, with little attention either to developing or to assessing general strategies for comprehending more complex texts.[31]

Ironically, supplemental programs for struggling students often did more to exacerbate problems than to solve them.[32] Students often were not eligible for supplemental services until they performed significantly below students their same age. The consequence was to predicate opportunity for academic success on academic failure—a deep hole out of which to dig. Participating in supplemental programs often required that already-struggling students miss regular classroom instruction—if not in reading, then in other content areas. Supplemental programs were often weakly (if at all) coordinated with regular classroom instruction and with each other, and often required that students master "the basics" as a prerequisite to richer academic content and instruction. Some supplemental programs were staffed by highly specialized teachers expert in addressing the specific problems of struggling students. Many others, however, were staffed by well-intended paraprofessionals with little formal training as teachers.

With school leadership focused on improving both instruction and achievement, schools may have been able to overcome such problems. But such leadership was the exception, not the rule.[33] Conventionally, leadership roles were weakly developed in elementary schools: typically, a single principal, with norms of egalitarianism precluding formal leadership from rising within the teacher ranks, itself.[34] Leadership influence over instruction was widely recognized as weak, and for a set of complex and interacting reasons: centuries-old tensions between administrators and teachers; norms of autonomy and privacy among teachers; a weak knowledge base supporting instructional leadership; and an environment that, historically, had not held leaders accountable for achievement, thus providing no incentives to actively manage instruction.[35] Instead, the work of leadership typically focused on such matters as student discipline, resource acquisition and allocation, contract and personnel administration, building maintenance, and parent/district/community relations—but rarely on comprehensive, simultaneous efforts to improve norms, structures, and practices in order to improve student achievement.

A combined effect of conventional norms, structures, practices, and leadership was that schools bore close resemblance to holding companies: collections of autonomous operations under an umbrella management organization. One result was inefficiency, as teachers and students coped with the need to "unlearn" and "relearn" classroom norms, routines, and even academic content from year to year. Another result was more damning. Absent coordination by adults, students were tacitly delegated the task of coordinating their own instructional experiences over time—very risky business for students already at risk of academic failure.

Worse yet, it wasn't clear how schools could improve themselves from within. For many of the same features of schooling that undermined students' learning also undermined teachers' learning, such that it was difficult for a teacher to develop the knowledge and expertise to organize and conduct reading instruction any differently. Structural isolation in "egg crate" classrooms and norms of privacy meant that teachers lacked opportunity and incentives for on-going, collaborative learning. A cost of individual autonomy over instruction was that teachers lacked a social infrastructure to develop their technical capabilities: for example, shared language, experiences, and instructional artifacts that would support substantive interaction around specific problems in their daily work. Teachers might sample and share tools, materials, and techniques, and they might experiment and tinker at the margins of their own practice. However, teachers had few incentives or resources that would enable them to leverage colleagues to tackle deep problems in their daily practice. Conventional "in-service" education (often leader-determined or district-mandated) was no better, and reminiscent of the sort of supplemental services provided students: uncoordinated with the challenges of regular classroom instruction, partial in relation to the magnitude of the problems, and with little follow-up in practice. Leaders, themselves, struggled to improve from within: isolated in individual schools, both from colleagues in other schools and from their own teachers; drawing from a weak technical knowledge base; and targeted by blizzards of uncoordinated, partial, and often irrelevant guidance for their work.

If enthusiasts could draw hope from Success for All having become a player, then critics could quickly point out that Success for All had dealt itself into a very tough game. It was a game that required solving not one problem, but many. For any one problem put a dent in the possibility of at-risk students learning to read; the combination seemed expertly designed to defeat that possibility. By both the logic of the day and the experiences of Success for All's developers, these problems couldn't be solved independently or serially, for they formed a system of interdependent, compounding problems. If all students were to succeed in reading on grade level, these problems needed to be solved systemically.

THE ORGANIZATIONAL BLUEPRINT

In seeking to establish positive interdependence within and among schools and their environments, the motivations, experiences, and methods of Success for All developers brought them to the cusp of a system of interdependent problems that routinely undermine both student achievement and efforts to improve it. This was not news to developers. Rather, over Success for All's first decade of operations, developers worked to devise and refine a design for comprehensive school reform with multiple, interdependent components targeting these multiple, interdependent problems.

At the highest level, the design was an organizational blueprint for transforming chronically underperforming schools from holding companies into professional organizations resembling teaching hospitals: that is, into centers of professional practice and professional learning. With respect to professional practice, teachers and leaders would collaborate within an evidence-driven diagnosis-and-treatment model to identify and to address the academic and nonacademic problems of individual students. As intended by program developers, a Success for All school "does not merely provide services to children, it constantly assesses the results of the services it provides and keeps varying or adding services until every child is successful."[36] Routine problems were to be identified and addressed in regular classroom instruction; nonroutine problems were to be identified and addressed in supplemental venues.

With respect to professional learning, teachers and leaders would constantly collaborate to review cases, to observe and reflect on practice, and to share information and knowledge. Sustained, on-going professional development was described by cofounder Robert Slavin as "Job 1" for a Success for All school, to be pursued 180 days per year, as part and parcel with students' learning.[37] These schools would be linked into a coherent, professional network with the Success for All project team as the coordinating hub, partners in a widely distributed, knowledge-producing enterprise aimed at improving both the design and its use in schools.

Aspirations for professional practice and learning were not unique to Success for All. Rather, they were consistent with an agenda promoting "teacher professionalism" that emerged and developed virtually concurrent with the emergence and development Success for All.[38] The focus of the movement was on recognizing teachers' knowledge and expertise as the essential resource bearing on student achievement, and on improving schools to support diagnostic instruction and practice-based learning anchored in evidence of instructional processes and outcomes. In the language of the day, Success for All teachers would be engaged in joint work, co-enacting a version of pedagogical reasoning and action to develop, share, and refine wisdom of practice.[39]

Aspirations for linking schools thus transformed into a professional network were not unique to Success for All, either. Rather, as explained by Success for All founder Robert Slavin in an interview in March of 2003, they were common among other, early developers of comprehensive school-reform programs:

> Developers of comprehensive school-reform programs were basically saying, "We are going to give you, the school, an identification that will last, that will transcend your own superintendent. We will be here. We've been here many years. We're going to be here many more. Your superintendent won't. You need a professional identification with people who have high standards for you and can help you to accomplish what you need to accomplish. You need a professional identification that is not dependent on this year's superintendent and this year's funding level." That was our way of thinking. We and other program developers were thinking that we would have schools all over, and that they would have sort of a transnational, transdistrict identification for their professional development. Districts would be reduced to making sure that the buses and the meals get done and they hire the teachers and so on. But the real professional identification would be with the entire network of schools involved in a particular model.

Again, as viewed by Success for All developers, the transformation from holding company to professional organization could neither be accomplished with a single, incisive intervention nor by advancing a set of piecemeal and disconnected initiatives. Rather, as explained by Slavin, the transformation would require a "simultaneous heart and lung transplant": interdependent changes in culture, instructional organization, curriculum and instruction, supplemental services, and leadership.[40] With these changes, student achievement would no longer be the non-product of isolated, uncoordinated, and unmanaged activities and services. Instead, student achievement would be the product of coordinated, schoolwide activity among teachers and leaders.[41]

First Principles

Consistent with Success for All's heritage in CSOS, restructuring began with attention to the social organization of schools: their core beliefs, values, and norms. An adage among developers was that Success for All was "1% program and 99% belief system," with three beliefs most central: the belief that all students enter school eager, excited, and expecting to learn; the belief that it is possible for every student to learn rich academic content at high levels of mastery; and the belief that student achievement ultimately depends on whether the adults in schools are willing to do everything possible to ensure it.[42]

Developers elaborated these foundational beliefs as a set of "first principles" appropriate to all professional human service enterprises, from medicine to social work to education: prevention, early intervention, and relentlessness.[43] The aim was to prevent problems of achievement from occurring in the first place by enacting "best practices" validated by research and experience, to intervene aggressively and coherently at the first sign of problems, and to relentlessly pursue and coordinate alternative courses of treatment and action until a given problem was solved. These first principles then became the foundation for rational action within the school. As explained by program developers:

> . . . There is one feature we try to make consistent in all [Success for All schools]: a relentless focus on the success of every child. It would be entirely possible to have tutoring and curriculum change, and have family support, and other services, yet still not ensure the success of at-risk children. Success does not come from piling on additional services but from coordinating human resources around a well-defined goal, constantly assessing progress towards that goal, and never giving up until success is achieved.[44]

Working within these beliefs and by these first principles, each child would be treated as an individual and unique case, with teachers and leaders working collectively to bring knowledge and expertise to bear on diagnosing their unique problems, proposing a treatment regimen, monitoring outcomes, and making necessary adaptations. Teachers and school leaders would doggedly pursue academic success for each and every child, exhausting every possible resource to solve each child's academic and nonacademic problems. No child would fall between the cracks—the Hippocratic Oath for Success for All schools, and the core mission driving the Success for All development team, itself.

Program Components

Developers recognized that advancing only "first principles" would do little to help historically weak schools actually do anything differently, in part because schools lacked roles and structures to support the work and, in part, because schools lacked the knowledge to apprehend abstract and novel ideas and to translate them into action. As such, developers supported first principles with a comprehensive design for restructuring schools: a plan for coordinated change in instructional organization, curriculum and instruction, supplemental services, and school leadership (see Table 1.2, below).

Instructional organization: Success for All sought to prioritize, increase, and standardize time for reading instruction through the creation of a 90-minute reading block in grades 1 through 6. The reading block was a "non-negotiable"

Table 1.2 Success for All: Primary Program Components

Component	Description
Instructional Organization	
90 Minute Reading Block	Uninterrupted reading instruction, concurrently, schoolwide, using all instructional staff.
Quarterly Assessment/ Regrouping	Students are assessed quarterly and regrouped for instruction across classes and grade levels based on current reading performance level.
Curriculum and Instruction	
Early Learning	Theme-based kindergarten curriculum that combines conventional, nurturing elements of kindergarten with instruction in oral language, reading readiness, emergent writing, and early reading.
KinderRoots	Additional kindergarten curriculum focused on initial reading activities using controlled texts.
Reading Roots	Grade 1 level curriculum emphasizing systematic presentation of letter sounds (phonics), word attack skills, fluency, and beginning metacognitive comprehension strategies using controlled texts.
Reading Wings	Grades 2–6 level curriculum emphasizing cognitive skills and strategies for comprehending complex texts independently, though with continued attention to vocabulary development and word attack skills.

Table 1.2 Success for All: Primary Program Components (Cont'd)

Component	Description
Supplemental Services	
Tutoring	20 minutes daily of supplemental reading instruction for lowest-performing students, coordinated with classroom instruction.
Family Support	Unifies responsibility for attendance monitoring, social work, special education pre-referral activities, parental involvement activities, and community outreach activities. Includes school-based intervention process for addressing non-academic problems of individual students.
Leadership	Three member team (reading facilitator, family support coordinator, and principal) responsible for operational, analytical, and developmental support of reading instruction, including integrating Success for All with environmental expectations for schools.

around which all else was built. Reading would taught concurrently, schoolwide, at the same time every day, over a sustained block of time likely exceeding that spent on reading instruction in most U.S. schools at that time. Reading instruction was to become the primary activity of the school, scheduled first thing every morning, though with cushion to allow for late busses, tardy students, and other beginning-of-the-day distractions. This was to be sacred time, not to be interrupted by announcements, assemblies, or supplemental instructional activities.

With reading taught concurrently, schoolwide, all students were to be regrouped for reading instruction across classes and grade levels roughly every quarter (8–10 weeks). Transient students were to be placed upon entry to the school. Assignment of students to reading classes was to be based on a quarterly analysis of each student's current reading mastery level, which included a standardized reading assessment, curriculum-based tasks and assessments, and anecdotal reports from teachers. With no other instructional activities scheduled during the 90-minute reading block, all certified teachers (including "specials" teachers, Title I teachers, and other supplemental teachers) could be assigned to teach reading, reducing the average size of reading classes and increasing informal coordination between regular classroom instruction and supplemental services.

The quarterly, schoolwide regrouping of students into small, performance-based reading classes created opportunities to organize instruction and other services to address the specific needs of individual students on a regular basis: for example, by accelerating high-performing students; by identifying low-performing students in need of supplemental services; and by grouping teachers and students based on individual strengths and needs. Within classes, reduced variability in students' current reading performance created new opportunities for teachers to focus instruction on the specific needs of students. Whole-group instruction could be tailored to the needs of students performing at a particular level, rather than targeted at some middle ground above and below large numbers of students. The need for ability-based reading groups as a means of differentiating instruction would also be eliminated. Instead, small group instruction could have all students collaborating in the performance of the same, substantive tasks. Teachers would have both fewer students to monitor and a narrower band of likely reading needs and problems to address. As explained by program developers:

> Having all students at one reading level avoids any need for the use of reading groups within the class. The problem with reading groups is that when the teacher is working with one group, the other groups are at their desks doing seatwork or other independent tasks of no instructional value. To have a full 90 minutes of active, productive instruction, having only one reading group is essential. Research on cross-grade grouping, often called the Joplin Plan, has shown that this method increases student achievement (Slavin, 1987).[45]

Curriculum and Instruction: Complementing the design for instructional organization, Success for All included an extensive design for curriculum and instruction that pushed deeply into the day-to-day work of students and teachers. The aims included binding the school into a coherent K–6 instructional system, as well as raising the level and coordination of academic content and instruction for all students.

The design began with a reading curriculum that aimed to scaffold at-risk students into reading readiness, decoding, fluency, and comprehension, all while cultivating students' joy and love of reading. The reading curriculum was composed of three components spanning K–6: Early Learning, Reading Roots, and Reading Wings. Early Learning replaced the school's existing kindergarten curriculum. To ensure that all students entered first grade excited and prepared to learn, Early Learning (along with KinderRoots, a reading-specific subcomponent) was designed to combine the nurturing, supportive elements of conventional kindergarten with instruction in oral language, reading readiness, emergent writing, and early reading. In contrast to notions of first mastering "the basics" before proceeding to more advanced reading tasks, Early Learning (as well as Reading Roots and Reading Wings) used listening comprehension lessons and oral language development exercises to begin developing capability for reading comprehension concurrent with developing the capability for independent reading.

Reading Roots replaced the school's first-grade reading curriculum. The primary focus of Reading Roots was the systematic presentation of letter sounds (phonics), word attack skills, fluency, and beginning metacognitive comprehension strategies, all in the context of reading actual texts. As in Early Learning, listening comprehension lessons and oral language development exercises ran in parallel, with the goal of developing capabilities for reading comprehension and independent reading concurrently. Reading Roots was also available in a Spanish language edition ("Lee Conmigo"), as well as in editions tailored to special student populations: for example, students speaking English as a second language (ESL), or upper elementary students reading at the first grade level.

As such, Spanish-language, ESL, and other students would all receive instruction in precisely the same format as English language instruction, using a curriculum designed to scaffold their transition into English language instruction.

In Reading Wings (grades 2–6), the primary focus shifted to developing cognitive skills and strategies for comprehending complex texts independently, with continued attention to vocabulary development and word attack skills. The relevant academic content was *not* the particular text at hand but, instead, the skills and strategies used to make meaning of texts. Rather than replacing the existing curriculum (often an unrealistic expectation for schools, given sunk costs and district requirements), and to align Success for All with district-adopted or state-adopted reading curricula, Reading Wings restructured the use of the existing reading curriculum to support instruction in reading comprehension. "Treasure Hunts" guided students' exploration of texts, and supplemental "Reading Comprehension Lessons" structured instruction in specific comprehension skills and strategies. Reading Wings was designed for use with over 100 children's novels, as well as with many commercially- published basal series and literature anthologies (e.g., Houghton-Mifflin, Scott Foresman, Holt, HBJ, Macmillan, McGraw Hill, Silver Burdett-Ginn, and Open Court).[46] Reading Wings was also available in a Spanish language edition ("Alas Para Leer"), with novels as the core texts.

Consistent across Reading Roots and Reading Wings was the inclusion of specific unit and lesson plans. These plans were leveled by reading mastery level, tailored to students reading at that particular level, and ordered to support an intentional developmental sequence of reading skills and strategies. In combination with Success for All's assessment and regrouping process, students could thus be placed strategically within the curriculum on a quarterly basis, with instruction then tailored to their current performance level. All units and lessons were spiraled within and across reading levels, so that on-going review and remediation were incorporated routinely into regular classroom instruction.

The Success for All curriculum was matched with the use of a specific instructional model. In Success for All, the intent was to shift instruction out of a recitation model into more complex, dynamic form of instruction in which both students and teachers assumed much more active roles.

The bedrock for all instruction was a cooperative learning model devised by Success for All cofounder Robert Slavin. In this model, students were to work in diverse teams of 4 or 5 members. Students began by collaborating in shared tasks. Gradually, students assumed responsibility for independent performance with peer assistance. One goal was to provide multiple opportunities for students to practice the use of reading skills and strategies, to formulate and express interpretations, and to discuss and debate texts—all with assistance from their peers. A second goal was to provide students a lively and inherently motivating learning experience, along with the multiple opportunities for substantial interactions with a diverse group of peers. As explained in the Reading Wings *Teacher's Manual*:

Reading Wings is a product of more than 25 years of research and development on cooperative learning at the Johns Hopkins University Center for

Social Organization of Schools. Research has shown that using cooperative learning in the classroom has positive effects on academic achievement, interethnic relationships, developing English proficiency, acceptance of mainstreamed and academically handicapped students, self-esteem, liking of self and others, and attitude towards school and teachers. In cooperative learning, students work together to learn; work is not completed until *all* team members have learned the material being studied. This positive inter-dependence is an essential feature of cooperative learning.[47]

Cooperative learning was embedded in a "cycle of diagnostic instruction" used consistently throughout Success for All to scaffold students into independent use of reading skills and strategies.[48] The cycle began with direct instruction in which the teacher explained and modeled the use of reading skills and strategies in whole group format, with opportunities for partner practice, teacher monitoring, and immediate remediation. The cycle continued with team practice in which coop-erative learning teams worked collaboratively on the use of skills and strategies. Team practice was followed by individual assessment in which students produced a piece of work or completed an assessment that provided evidence of their under-standing and use of reading skills and strategies. The cycle concluded with recog-nition and celebration of cooperative work and academic success, with the aim of transforming the cultures of classrooms from failure to success.

Beyond the intentional scaffolding of skills and strategies, one central feature of the cycle of diagnostic instruction was the creation of multiple opportunities for the teacher to assess, diagnose, and model the use of reading skills and strategies—essential both to notions of prevention and early intervention and to notions of "professional practice" in education. The opportunities began with opportunities for partner practice during whole group instruction. They continued into team practice and individual assessment, tasks in which students routinely made evi-dent their thinking and their application of skills and strategies: for example by articulating ideas, supporting their ideas with reasoning, and demonstrating methods for understanding text.

Indeed, ambitions for students' cooperative learning were matched with ambi-tions for a dynamic, active instructional role for teachers. As described in the Reading Wings *Teacher's Manual*:

Role of Teacher[49]

Monitoring teams during practice is crucial to successful cooperative learning. Look for frequent opportunities to:

- give immediate feedback and reinforcement for learning;
- re-teach, clarify, or challenge students to higher levels of understanding;
- encourage oral elaboration and explanation;

- model appropriate partnering/teaming behaviors;
- assess student reading fluency and comprehension by observing individual students;
- record observations on the assessment summary form using the indicators as a guide;
- offer encouragement and praise;
- encourage teams to solve their own problems; and
- catch kids being good.

Working in leveled and carefully designed units, in cooperative learning teams, and within the cycle of diagnostic instruction, regular classroom instruction became a primary means both of preventing problems of achievement and of intervening at the first signs of problems. However, all would be for naught unless at-risk students could successfully co-enact their novel and ambitious roles in cooperative learning teams. Recognizing that, developers designed the reading curriculum to include means of developing students' capabilities to co-enact their new roles: for example, by having students first work in pairs (rather than teams) in Early Learning and Reading Roots; by developing oral language skills to support collaborative work; and by standardizing unit and lesson formats K–6 so that students would not have to relearn their instructional roles and responsibilities from year to year and teacher to teacher. Students were further supported by a separate social-problem-solving curriculum called Getting Along Together, which was designed to scaffold students into the Success for All cycle of diagnostic instruction, to provide common standards for cooperative learning and classroom discourse, and to establish schoolwide routines for classroom management and conflict resolution.

Supplemental Services: To complement regular classroom instruction, Success for All included two components that restructured supplemental services for students: tutoring and family support. The former addressed academic needs; the latter addressed nonacademic needs. The supplemental service components were intended as resources supporting both prevention and early intervention, and as loci for coordinating all instructional and noninstructional activities for students.

The tutoring component was designed to provide 20 additional minutes of one-on-one reading instruction daily for the lowest-performing students, bringing their total daily reading instruction to 110 minutes (close to one-third of the typical school day). The intent was for tutoring to directly support regular classroom instruction by featuring a combination of both basic and advanced reading skills and strategies. Tutoring responsibilities were to be shouldered by a team composed of certified teachers (preferably with training and experience in special education, primary reading, or compensatory education) and qualified paraprofessionals. Tutors were to collaborate with regular classroom teachers to analyze students' needs based on formal and informal assessments, to construct student-specific instructional plans, and to formally coordinate those plans with regular classroom instruction. Like classroom teachers, tutors were to take an active role in instruction. In one-on-one tutoring sessions, tutors would have the opportunity to closely observe students' use of specific reading skills and strategies, diagnose problems, and provide immediate remediation. As explained in the Success for All *Tutoring Manual*:

> **One-on-one tutoring is the most effective form of instruction, especially for students with reading problems.** The effectiveness of one-to-one tutoring results from the fact that tutors have the opportunity to give constant, immediate feedback to the student. If a student makes an error when reading, immediate corrective feedback can be provided, and the instruction needed to prevent further errors can be conducted. This immediate diagnostic assessment and feedback is not possible when working with an entire class.
>
> In addition, tutors can make individual plans that fit each student's needs and can spend as much time as needed to teach a particular sound blending or comprehension strategy.
>
> Because tutors have the opportunity to spend intensive instruction time with individual students, they learn about the student's strengths and weaknesses. They know which approaches work best with each student. Tutors can capitalize on this knowledge and use it in presenting the class material in the best way to help each student learn and remember the information.[50]

The family support component brought under one umbrella a suite of conventional programs and activities targeting students, their families, and the community: for example, attendance monitoring; social work; special education pre-referral activities; parental and community outreach; and more. The goal was to coordinate these activities and to focus them both on preventing nonacademic problems (e.g., attendance, health, nutrition, behavior) and on intervening as early as possible when those problems arose. These responsibilities were to be shouldered by a team composed of a newly appointed family support coordinator, a newly appointed reading facilitator, the school principal, the school social worker/guidance counselor, a parent/family liaison, and an attendance monitor. As with tutoring, individualized plans were to be devised in collaboration with teachers, and they were to be coordinated with teachers' own problem-solving efforts. As explained by program developers, the core goal spanning all activities was "to identify and to build on the strengths of parents, communities, and individual children."[51]

Leadership: Success for All included a design for leadership that sought to develop the roles and responsibilities of schools leaders, and to orient their work squarely towards improving the core work of teaching and learning. Consistent with then-emerging understandings of "distributed leadership," the Success for All leadership component began with the construction of a three-member leadership team that blurred the usual distinctions between teaching staff, "special services," and administrative staff, thus bringing diverse knowledge, experience, and interests to bear on the work of school leadership.

The reading facilitator was a newly created, full-time position responsible for the implementation and effectiveness of the Success for All program. Developers advised staffing the position with an experienced and respected teacher with expertise in reading instruction and/or education for at-risk students. The family support coordinator was responsible for the family support component. Developers advised that this either be a part-time or full-time position (depending on school size) staffed by a counselor or social worker. The school principal was responsible for assisting in the leadership of Success for All while continuing to perform the on-going executive and administrative functions of the school, including managing all other content areas and maintaining community and district relations. Especially important was that the principal set a high bar by demonstrating commitment to the program and by participating in its implementation, thereby signaling to teachers the expectation for *their* commitment and participation.

Of the three leadership roles, most central and most novel was the role of reading facilitator. The reading facilitator functioned as the "change agent" within the school, the primary liaison with the Success for All project team and the person responsible for ensuring the quality, effectiveness, and integration of all program elements.[52] Originally, Success for All developers performed the responsibilities of the reading facilitator. However, with the goal of scaling up operations, it became necessary for schools to hire a full-time reading facilitator who would then be mentored by program developers.[53] The role of reading facilitator was designed to be entirely formative and free of the usual personnel-related responsibilities that often drive tensions between teachers and schools leaders. As explained by program developers, facilitators "need to spend their time working as change agents, not facilitating the school's routine day-to-day operations."[54]

Collectively, the leadership team was responsible for a set of interacting organizational, developmental, and analytical responsibilities. In Success for All, the organizational responsibilities of leadership included a core set of tasks: scheduling the 90-minute reading block; quarterly assessment and regrouping; maintaining and distributing curriculum materials; scheduling and coordinating the work of the tutoring and family support teams; and maintaining and distributing information generated throughout the school. These were zero-order responsibilities in Success for All schools. Botch this work, and implementation of Success for All became difficult, if not impossible.

Development responsibilities focused on the on-going professional development of school staff, both in relation to implementing Success for All and in relation to environmental expectations for student achievement. In some cases, work with teachers was to be conducted one-on-one, either via classroom observation and peer coaching by the reading facilitator or via teacher-to-teacher relationships brokered by the reading facilitator. In other cases, the reading facilitator worked with groups of teachers in the context of regularly scheduled "component team meetings." These meetings functioned as an essential venue for bringing collective knowledge to bear on problems of practice in specific program components (e.g., Early Learning, Reading Roots, Reading Wings, tutoring, and family support). They also functioned as a venue for enlisting the experiences, knowledge, and expertise of teachers in the management of the program as a whole.

Analytical responsibilities involved working from multiple sources of information to monitor the overall implementation and effectiveness of Success for All, both in relation to the internal goal of on-grade-level reading achievement and the external goal of improved performance on state standardized assessments. The analytical work of leadership was intended to inform the organizational and developmental work: for example, the strategic grouping of students and teachers into classes, and the design of professional learning opportunities for teachers. School leaders were also to relay their analyses and findings to teachers for use in instruction, tutoring, and family support. As explained in *The Facilitators Manual*, the success of Success for All depended on the reading facilitator routinely enacting these analytical responsibilities:

> The most important responsibility of the SFA facilitator is ensuring that the program is guaranteeing student success, not just providing services. This means the facilitator is constantly checking on the operation of the program and its outcomes, including monitoring the teachers' proficiency of implementation, pacing, classroom management, tutoring, and family support activities. **The facilitator makes sure that no child is being forgotten or being allowed to fail, and that all staff are working together effectively.** . . . .
>
> As the person with the most training and expertise in Success for All and the best opportunities to see how teachers are faring in implementation, you are responsible for assuring that all staff members extend their knowledge and skill within the program.[55]

Thus, Success for All was not designed as a program that would support top-down, administrative leadership. Rather, it was designed as a program fundamentally dependent on collegial leadership under the direction of a lead teacher. Moreover, classroom teachers were to function as key partners in the work of leadership: for example, by providing timely, valid, and reliable information on student performance; by opening their doors to observation and formative feedback; and by participating in collegial learning opportunities. This was tough work, uncommon (if not unprecedented) at that time in U.S. public schools, and requiring unusual knowledge and expertise in a host of matters: the design of the Success for All program; reading instruction; environments and their expectations for schools; analysis of messy and noisy data; teachers' professional development; and much more.

A New Image

The product of a decade's worth of designing was a comprehensive school reform program that challenged the image of schools as holding companies with a new image: that of schools as centers of professional practice and learning, linked into professional networks that transcended the geographic constraints of districts. These schools would not be static, conservative, and closed, but dynamic, responsive, and open: centers of diagnosis, treatment, experimentation, and systematic reflection; joined by a common design for schooling; all leveraging and responding to environmental resources and expectations. Teachers and leaders would treat the achievement of each individual student as an authentic puzzle to be solved, and they would learn in order to solve those puzzles.

The intent was *not* for all of the preceding to be available only to exceptional schools with access to extraordinary resources. Rather, Success for All developers sought to make the design affordable for the modal, chronically underperforming school. To do so, developers locked onto Title I of ESEA and its associated funding criteria as comparatively stable features of otherwise-turbulent U.S. educational environments. Designed within these constraints, the program could be adopted and funded in schools at a rough, average cost of $100,000 per year.[56] With that, Success for All would not be a boutique program for exceptionally resourceful schools but a program available to thousands of chronically underperforming schools serving millions of at-risk students in all 50 states.

CHALLENGES, REDEFINED

Over its first decade, the goals and methods of the Success for All project team steered the work of design into a thicket of twisted, interdependent problems. By centralizing design activity, mining available research, and leveraging extensive experience, they devised what, in their analysis, was one way out of that thicket: not a decisive hack that cut through the complexity but, instead, a complex, multicomponent design for untangling the lot.

But there was a recurring irony to the work of designing, at least as enacted in Success for All: However strategic and sensible, the work of designing (and the resulting designs) did as much to redefine the problems to be solved as to solve them. Viewed from this perspective, the Success for All design was, in many ways, its own twisted thicket of solutions and begotten problems, with that thicket providing still more kindling for critics.

Indeed, implementing Success for All in any U.S. school would have been no little feat, never mind the many chronically underperforming schools to which designers aspired. On the matter of implementation, developers had put themselves at a decided disadvantage. Rather than working as consultants *within* schools to devise school-specific designs for improvement, they had elected to work *outside* of schools, using centralized design activities to devise a general set of solutions. And there they sat, absent any formal authority to act on the very problem at hand: carrying their comprehensive, complex design into schools and making it both operational and effective.

There was much in the interactions between external programs, chronically underperforming schools, and U.S. educational environments to challenge successful implementation. These challenges, too, came to rest with the Success for

All project team as an organization working from the outside in to improve chronically underperforming schools.

External Programs

Challenges began with the program itself, and they went well beyond those that arose from the strategic (yet narrow) focus on K–6 reading. However well reasoned, researched, and evaluated, every component of Success for All stood to be challenged by critics with different understandings, beliefs, and concerns about schools and their improvement. Instructional grouping by reading mastery level risked charges of academic tracking. Allocating 110 minutes per day to reading instruction risked charges of denying the most struggling students opportunities to learn other skills and content that would support their development as readers. That students could be assessed quarterly, grouped at some similar "level," and targeted with common forms of instruction risked charges of "batch processing" from critics who held more organic understandings of students, content, and learning. The focus on cooperative learning risked charges of giving too much control over instruction to at-risk students. Centralizing leadership responsibilities in a formal team (no matter its members) risked concerns of inhibiting the emergence of informal teacher leaders. The list goes on.

Beyond the specifics of the program, the simple reality of being an externally developed program had the entire enterprise starting out in a deep hole—in any U.S. school, never mind the chronically underperforming schools for which Success for All was intended. The "we-they"/"inside-outside" culture of U.S. public education was centuries old, as were schools' means of apprehending and responding to external guidance in ways that defeated designers' best intentions.

Indeed, education research dating to the 1960s identified steep challenges associated with implementing ambitious, externally sponsored reform initiatives in U.S. schools, the most famous being the Rand Change Agent Study.[57] Findings from this body of research identified formidable disconnects between programs-as-intended and programs-as-implemented, and argued for "mutual adaptation" and "backward mapping" as imperatives for on-the-ground success.[58] In the main, findings were so discouraging as to lead to an axiom shared among many education reformers that externally sponsored change was futile, and that effective school improvement could only be initiated and designed from within, school-by-school.

In implementing externally developed programs, the problems often began at the most fundamental level: with the way that schools apprehended and interpreted those programs.[59] One interpretation had external programs as "bureaucratic" and "top-down," thus in conflict with such deeply institutionalized norms as local control over schools and teacher autonomy in classrooms. Apprehended as bureaucratic, external programs often evoked a set of predictable responses far short of relentless, adaptive, empowered use. One response was active resistance and, sometimes, active subversion. Another was more subtle, but just as subversive: by-the-book compliance, doing no more and no less than directed, irrespective of any local circumstances, in ways that absolved implementers of responsibility and that indicted external designers in any consequent failure.

Another interpretation was more hopeful: external improvement programs as a sort of technocratic, prescribed cure, automatically successful if administered as directed (and ineffective and/or harmful if not). Apprehended as technocratic, the response was motivated by trust and enthusiasm, rather than distrust and resistance. Yet, ironically, the response was exactly the same: by-the-book compliance, doing no more and no less than directed, irrespective of any local circumstances, in deference to the knowledge and expertise of designers.

In the case of Success for All, the risk of evoking such interpretations was exacerbated by the very novelty of Success for All's strategy: a sort of "professionalism by design." The strategy rested on the alchemy of an external program of improvement as a mechanism for effecting professional practice and learning in schools.

Problematic was that, at that period in the history of education reform, notions of "professionalism" were coupled tightly with long-held norms of teacher autonomy and discretion, and long used as a first defense against anything perceived as external, bureaucratic, and top down. The standard defense was that it was teachers (not external designers) who had intimate knowledge of the problems of students and schools, and it was teachers (and not external designers) who would solve them. Indeed, for many, the notion of "professional practice" often did not speak to ways in which teachers interacted with students and academic content. Instead, the notion of "professional practice" was frequently a political claim to authority over the design and performance of work. Never mind that the ultimate goals of Success for All were consistent with an agenda of teacher professionalism: that is, establishing infrastructure that would empower teachers to lead improvement efforts in classrooms and schools. For those well practiced in this first defense (and there were many), the very notion of "professionalism by design" would have been an oxymoron that confounded two antithetical approaches to reform: teacher professionalism and externally developed programs.

Out of the gate, the combination of conventional understandings and a novel strategy had Success for All at risk of adverse interpretations and, thus, weak implementation: bureaucratic or technocratic, and not professional; and thus, rote and mechanistic, not relentless and adaptive.

Chronically Underperforming Schools

Compounding challenges of external programs were challenges in the targeted schools: chronically underperforming schools, especially Title I schools in which over 50% of students were in poverty. The challenges, again, stretched far beyond the lack of infrastructure on which to begin building. These were battled-hardened schools, subject to decades of external reform, highly resistant to deep change, fragmented with diffuse and uncoordinated programs, fraught with tensions (internally, between teachers and leaders, and externally, between schools and districts), and littered with the remnants of past change efforts. Under increasing environmental pressure to improve, conditions were ripe for these schools to interpret Success for All as either a bureaucratic, top-down imposition or as a technocratic, quick fix.

Yet even if schools actually understood the intentions of Success for All developers and sought to use the program as intended, enacting it would still pose formidable challenges. On a purely practical level, Success for All created much new work for teachers and leaders: for example, quarterly assessment and regrouping; continuous formative assessment in the context of instruction; coordination between regular classroom instruction and supplemental services; and more. The demands of the work increased with the size and complexity of the school. To be sure, quarterly assessment and regrouping in a school with 1,000 students and 40 teachers would require more work than in a school with 250 students and 10 teachers. Further, any new work required by Success for All was to be performed alongside the continuing work of teachers and leaders: for example, instruction in other content areas; quarterly report cards; and the other, usual work of operating an elementary school.

Even more challenging were the demands on capabilities and beliefs, in that Success for All required that teachers and leaders enact a novel design for which they likely had no formal education and no practical experience—while, at the same time, selectively abandoning conventional practices in which they had extensive education and extensive experience. Further, enacting the design as intended required resources likely beyond those found in the modal, chronically-underperforming school: standardized, quarterly assessments; information systems with which to manage, communicate, and analyze evidence; shared, technical knowledge and vocabulary to support practice-based collaboration; mechanisms and routines for formally coordinating work; productive, collegial relationships among teachers; and more. Finally, convincing teachers and leaders that improvement of the sort intended by Success for All was even possible was no small matter, considering careers' worth of experience to the contrary.

Indeed, Success for All's designers faced a fundamental paradox. On the one hand, developers targeted chronically underperforming schools with a comprehensive, complex design precisely because these schools lacked what organizational theorists describe as "absorptive capacity": the capability to identify, incorporate, and effectively use new knowledge and expertise to expand their capabilities and to solve their own problems.[60] On the other hand, absorptive capacity is argued to be a function of an organization's current capabilities, such that organizations learn by building on existing knowledge, expertise, and capabilities. The knowledge-rich get knowledge-richer, and the knowledge-poor don't. This, then, is the paradox: The very weaknesses that demanded a comprehensive, complex design limited schools' capabilities to incorporate and use exactly such a design.

Reforming and Dysfunctional Environments

The accumulating list of potential, interacting challenges grew longer with the addition of potential challenges in environments. Success for All and the schools that it targeted existed in weak family and community environments and in dynamic policy environments. These policy environments were ripe with emerging resources and incentives supporting comprehensive school reform: policies legitimizing comprehensive school reform as a strategy for improvement; funding to develop and to pursue comprehensive school reform programs; the carrots and sticks of standards-based reform; and more. Both Success for All developers and schools had incentives to heed these environments. Never mind the "internal" goal of on-grade-level reading performance. The legitimacy of Success for All and its schools depended increasingly on improving performance on state accountability assessments.

Yet heeding environments was no simple matter. The emergent nature of the resources and incentives supporting the new, niche market for comprehensive school reform meant that the targets to be hit by both developers and schools were moving. What qualified as a "legitimate" comprehensive school reform program was under constant revision, the specific criteria growing and changing with each iteration of federal policy. No more stable were the specific targets to be hit by schools. Within individual states, the policy instruments of standards-based reform were under near-constant development, with variation between content areas and grade levels and, at times, a lack of coordination between standards and assessments. Working at a national scale had Success for All developers encountering such problems times fifty.

Challenges within reforming environments were matched with challenges beyond. The rise of comprehensive school reform and standards-based reform did nothing to tame the usual blizzard of external guidance to schools: from districts, states, universities, labs and centers, commercial interests, and others. In the late 1980s and early 1990s, approaches to instruction in reading and language arts were hotly debated, captured best in dogmatic debates between proponents of phonics and whole language. Disciplinary knowledge of reading instruction was diffuse and fragmented, and in the throes of synthesis—and, even then, miles ahead of complementary work on educational leadership. While calls for accountability were creating incentives for leaders to manage instruction, historically rapid cycles of innovation in education favored a "wait and see/business as usual" attitude among leaders: exploit environments for whatever resources they provided, while buffering the school from any sort of deep change.

One option for Success for All developers was to manage uncertain environments by asserting influence in them. Indeed, stitched into the core goals of the organization was that of pushing the essential political and policy question: Are we willing to do what it takes to enable academic success for all children?

But this, too, was difficult. Developers attempted to assert influence at the federal and national levels: for example, by participating in CRESPAR and NAS, two high profile initiatives; by publishing research on the design, implementation, and effects of Success for All; and by advocating for the use of research both to construct and to evaluate programs. Despite these extensive efforts, developers lacked the resources to exert sufficient influence at the federal level and across all 50 states to stabilize and standardize expectations for schools, just as they lacked the resources and influence to tame the usual blizzard of external guidance directed at them. Indeed, in the US, no organization had such influence—no government organization, no nongovernment organization, and certainly no project team operating within a research center in a university. Environmental uncertainty was a fact of life, a challenge to be managed concurrent with challenges of external design and challenges of chronically underperforming schools.

A Complex and Novel Organization

Responsibility for managing these challenges circled back to the Success for All project team, itself: challenges with external design as a form of improvement; challenges with chronically underperforming schools as contexts for reform; and challenges with U.S. educational environments both supporting and hindering improvement. And, in circling back, these challenges interacted to complicate all else that Success for All developers were committed to doing to ensure the success of the program.

For example, developers were committed to supporting effective implementation in schools. However, doing so would require working proactively to stem possible interpretations of Success for All as bureaucratic or technocratic: for example, by clearly communicating ambitions for professional practice and learning, and by clearly communicating how those ambitions could be achieved through the implementation of an external design. Supporting effective implementation would also require being sensitive to the absorptive capacity of schools by structuring implementation developmentally, over time: for example, by minding the weak, initial capabilities of chronically underperforming schools; structuring early implementation to expand schools' capabilities; and leveraging those expanding capabilities to enable more ambitious use of the program.

Providing such support at a large scale would be no simple matter. It would require developing close, long-term relationships with large numbers of schools. In working with schools, team members would need to mind the evolving absorptive capacity of many individual schools: for example, by assessing and monitoring the progress of schools and, then, tailoring guidance and assistance to match their immediate needs. They would also need to collaborate with many schools to mind their proximal environments, working school-by-school to buffer environmental dysfunction and to align the program with local expectations for improvement. Finally, they would need to engage in close collaboration with schools without exacerbating the risk that schools would interpret their support as intrusive, bureaucratic, and top down.

Working over time to improve the design and its associated supports would be at least as complicated. Such work would require that developers take a systemic approach to their own work, identifying and targeting multiple areas of the program for improvement while still maintaining the overall integration and coordination of the program's many interdependent components. Developers would need to devise means of disseminating improvements to large numbers of schools while, at the same time, explaining to schools the difference between an evolving, external design for improvement and the usual environmental churn. And to ensure the program's continued viability, it would require looking beyond schools to evolving environments to identify relevant reform activity and, then, to adapt the enterprise in response.

Finally, sustaining the enterprise would require developing, adapting, and managing the project team as a complex and novel organization able to perform the work of design-based school improvement in the face of the many, steep challenges that came with it. This, too, would be no simple matter, for there were no conventional models to emulate in structuring the organization and in managing its operations. Few educational organizations had ever sought to advance and sustain such a complex design at a large scale with such a commitment to effectiveness. With only a few exceptions, such work had never been the province of state or local education agencies: administrative arms of government, not centers of research-and-development. At best, the project team could turn to other organizations participating in the New American Schools initiative, both partners and competitors in the new, niche market for comprehensive school reform. But they were no farther down this particular road than Success for All.

The Success for All project team could have lightened its own load: for example, through less comprehensive intervention, by placing geographic limits on their operations, by limiting the number of participating schools, or by relaxing their own standards for effectiveness. But doing so would have required compromising their very mission. For the project team, success for all was much more than a rallying cry. It was a practical, daily organizing principle—not only for schools, but for the project team, itself. The project team was committed to demonstrating the willingness to do whatever it took to take a typical school serving at-risk children and to ensure the success of virtually every child in it.

Their commitment ran deep. No matter how hard and stubborn, every problem had a solution, either anchored in research or drawn from experience. Solutions could be combined into an interdependent system with which to target systems of interdependent problems. Results could be evaluated against goals, and solutions refined and adapted. That stood to move the project team and schools toward their goals. It also stood to foster new problems and new criticisms. Such was the irony of designing in Success for All.

GATHERING ENTHUSIASM

Success for All appeared to be an aggressive, strong, and sensible player in the new, niche market of comprehensive school reform—a player with a keen knack for the work of designing. Developers set a high bar for the achievement of at-risk students, their scope of intervention into chronically underperforming schools, their scale of operations, and their standards of success. They targeted a strategic dimension of schooling (K–6 reading), centralized design activity, and played the odds by drawing on strategies and methods validated by research and experience. The resulting strengths appeared to be in the way that its founders leveraged policy activity in educational environments to devise a program and an organization coordinated closely with the needs of its primary client: chronically underperforming schools serving large numbers of at-risk students.

Despite its strengths, Success for All appeared to be a long shot. It was not as if targeting K–6 reading in chronically underperforming schools somehow enabled developers to draw a tight box around a small set of problems and then solve them. While every problem had a solution, every solution also appeared to bring with it a new challenges, and interdependent systems of solutions yielded interdependent systems of new challenges. And, interestingly, the resulting weaknesses in Success for All appeared to derive from the very same source as its strengths: interactions among the targeted schools, the program, external environments, and the project team as an organization.

Yet against long odds, Success for All experienced unlikely success. Between 1987/1988 and 1997/1998, in little more than a decade of operations, Success for All became the exemplar of comprehensive school reform. Its status derived, in part, from its scale of operations. Success for All was first implemented in 1987/1988 in a single Baltimore school, with five additional schools added in the second year of operations. Over the next eight years, annual growth averaged an incredible 74% per year. By 1997/1998, as it began its second decade of operations, Success for All was being implemented in 750 schools, roughly as many elementary schools as in the state of Oregon.[61] Though rivaling them in number, Success for All's schools were not nearly as diverse as the population of elementary schools in a given state, in that almost all were high poverty Title I schools. In effect, Success for All had constructed a state-sized education system composed of some of the nation's weakest and most impacted schools, among the first to feel the pressure of accountability.

Success for All's status also derived from evidence of effectiveness. True to its roots and its commitment, the project team immediately began evaluating program effectiveness and publishing the results.[62] Success for All also attracted the attention of external researchers, including those studying the New American Schools initiative. By 1996, the founders of Success for All made the bold claim that "with individually administered test data on thousands of children in many schools in many districts, Success for All is without any doubt the most extensively evaluated schoolwide restructuring program ever developed."[63]

To the project team, more important than the volume of research was their interpretation of the findings. In the analysis of the team, research on Success for All was showing positive effects on achievement, with some of the most impacted students, in some of the nation's most impacted schools. To make the case, the project team drew most heavily on a series of internal and external studies (the latter conducted by Success for All-funded research teams at the University of Memphis and the Southwest Regional Educational Laboratory).[64] The favored research design compared Success for All "treatment" schools to carefully matched "control" schools, such that the two sets of schools were as similar as possible along key dimensions prior to implementation (e.g., school size, socio-economic composition, and achievement).

By 1996, these studies provided longitudinal data on 23 Success for All schools and comparison schools in nine districts and eight states. These schools had implemented the program from three to seven years. The data set included students who had been in Success for All schools continuously since first grade and, thus, received the entire "treatment." Reading skills and strategies (e.g., word identification, word attack, and reading comprehension) were assessed using three tests: the Woodcock Reading Mastery Test; the Durrell Analysis of Reading Difficulty; and the Gray Oral Reading Test. Outcomes were typically reported as "effect sizes," a statistic used to estimate the magnitude of the effects of Success for All on specific outcomes in treatment schools as compared to control schools.

Indeed, in the new, niche market for comprehensive school reform programs, effect sizes were the coin of the realm: the widely agreed upon means of measuring and comparing the effectiveness of different programs. Even so, effect sizes could be reported in multiple forms: odds ratios, correlation coefficients, and standardized mean differences (also referred to as "Cohen's d," and the measure used by Success for All).[65] Further, there were no firm rules for interpreting effect sizes, with different sources both providing guidelines and urging caution in their use. Widely cited guidance suggested that effect sizes of 0.20 generally be interpreted as "small," 0.50 as "medium," and 0.80 and above as "large."[66] However, these guidelines came with the caveat that effect sizes in education-related fields were likely to be smaller, owing to challenges of generating valid outcome measures and to the complex nature of interventions. Heeding that caveat, the federally funded Comprehensive School Reform Quality Center (CSRQ) ultimately adopted the following as rough estimates of program impact: moderate (0.15 to 0.19), moderately strong (0.20 to 0.24), and very strong effects (0.25 and above).[67] Success for All cofounder Robert Slavin posed 0.25 as the standard for "educationally significant" effects, with an effect size of 1.00 equated either to a 100 point gain on the SAT test or a 15 point gain on an IQ test.[68]

In 1996, complete syntheses of internal research on Success for All were published in two sources: a trade book called *Every Child, Every School: Success for All*, which detailed the program design and summaries of research for a wide audience; and the first edition of the CRESPAR-published *Journal of Education for Students Placed at Risk*.[69] In 1998, reduced-form summaries of these syntheses were published in two other sources alongside reviews of research on other comprehensive school reform programs. The first, titled "Schoolwide reform models: What works?" was published in *Phi Delta Kappan* (a monthly journal published by the leading professional association for K–12 and university educators).[70] The second, titled *Show Me the Evidence! Proven and Promising Programs for America's Schools*, was a trade book that again targeted a wide audience.[71]

As synthesized by the project team, the results appeared remarkable. Pooling data across studies and analyzing grade-level cohorts of students, Slavin, Madden, and colleagues reported that the program showed positive, statistically significant effects for Success for All students (as compared to students in matched control schools) on every achievement measure at every grade level, 1–5. They reported that effect sizes averaged near 0.50: considered a "medium" effect size in general terms, large by the standards of educational research, and very strong by the standards of CSRQ. Extending their synthesis, they also reported that program effects increased with time-in-program, were particularly strong for at-risk students (e.g., the lowest-performing students, special education students, and bilingual and ESL students), and were linked to reductions in special education referrals. They placed particular emphasis on effect sizes for the lowest 25% of students in Success for All schools, which they reported as averaging above 1.0 for all grades— very large by all standards. Finally, for the five earliest-adopting schools, they reported that achievement differences continued into middle school (though the gap between students from Success for All and control schools did not continue to widen during middle school).

In summarizing this research, Slavin, Madden, and colleagues did not argue that the program was an unequivocal *success*.[72] They acknowledged that not all students and schools were achieving Success for All's "on grade level" goals.[73] Rather, they argued that the program was *succeeding* in making progress on a historically intractable social problem: working from the outside in to improve the achievement of large numbers of at-risk students in large numbers of chronically underperforming schools. With that, they argued that Success for All functioned as an existence-proof challenging the widely held axiom that each and every school had to invent its own way out of its own problems.

Indeed, it was not that Success for All developers were unaware of implementation research that predicted steep problems (if not inevitable failure) for ambitious, externally developed improvement initiatives. They were well aware of it. And they simply did not buy it. As argued in *Every Child, Every School*:

> The widely-held idea based on the RAND study of innovation (Berman and McLaughlin, 1978; McLaughlin, 1990) that comprehensive school reform must be invented by school staffs themselves is certainly not supported in research on Success for All and Roots and Wings. . . . The observation that these programs can be implemented and maintained over considerable time periods and can be effective in each of their replication sites certainly supports the idea that every school need not reinvent the wheel.
>
> . . . The main importance of the Success for All and Roots and Wings research is not in validating a particular model or demonstrating that disadvantaged students can learn. Rather, its greatest importance is in demonstrating that success for disadvantaged students can be routinely ensured in schools that are not exceptional or extraordinary (and were not producing great success before the program was introduced). We cannot ensure that every school has a charismatic principal or that every student has a charismatic teacher.

Nevertheless, we can ensure that every child, regardless of family background, has an opportunity to succeed in school.[74]

While the results appeared remarkable, the technical details of this research and its synthesis made it difficult for anybody other than expert researchers to evaluate such claims critically. As such, what quickly became as important as *evidence* of effectiveness was Success for All's *reputation* for effectiveness: belief that the program was, in fact, working to improve the achievement of at-risk students. Indeed, the adage that Success for All was part program and part belief system held as much in Success for All's broader environments as it did in its schools.

A reputation for effectiveness was something that the project team actively cultivated. Running the point was cofounder Robert Slavin. Already recognized as a leading researcher (in part, for developing the very methods by which the project team synthesized its research findings), Slavin served as the public face of the Success for All enterprise and the primary champion of its cause. In addition to convincing the research community of the effectiveness of Success for All, Slavin needed to convince policy makers, school staff, district officials, and the public. Doing so played not only to Slavin's strengths as a researcher. It also played to his strengths as a pitchman. As described by Lynn Olson in a 1998 *Education Week* feature on Success for All, "the spread of the program also owes as much to Slavin himself, who, despite his rumpled jackets and low-key manner, is the consummate salesman."[75]

With efforts to publicize evidence of (and to cultivate a reputation for) effectiveness, enthusiasm for Success for All began to stretch well beyond its founders. Success for All began attracting the attention of the national press. The program was featured in a 1996 ABC Nightly News segment and in 1998 feature article in *The Atlantic*, both touting the program design and its supporting research as exciting evidence of the possibility of using an external program to improve achievement for large numbers of at-risk students.[76] Success for All also attracted the attention of researchers and policy makers at the national level, including prominent mention in a 1997 report on "tried and true" improvement strategies published by the Office of Educational Research and Improvement of the U.S. Department of Education.[77] In policy environments pressing increasing numbers of chronically underperforming schools to improve, the combination of large-scale operations and evidence of effectiveness garnered legitimacy not only for Success for All but, also, for the entire comprehensive school reform movement.

GATHERING CRITICISM

Though Success for All was succeeding in developing a reputation, that reputation was not entirely positive. Gathering enthusiasm in some circles was matched with gathering criticism in others. Indeed, if the design of Success for All provided kindling for critics, then increasing bravado and growing recognition both provided the spark and fueled the flames of what would quickly become a firestorm.

One line of criticism involved potential conflicts of interest that called into question Success for All's reputation for effectiveness. This concern was voiced most publicly by Herbert Walberg and Rebecca Greenberg of the University of Illinois at Chicago in a commentary first published in *Education Week* and later reprinted in *Phi Delta Kappan*.[78] Walberg had served as an advisor to William Bennett, U.S. Secretary of Education under President George Herbert Walker Bush. Walberg would go on to become the chairman of the Heartland Institute, a conservative libertarian think tank headquartered in Chicago that advocated for free-market solutions to social and economic problems.[79] At that time, among the free-market solutions gaining currency were educational vouchers and charter schools that would both give parents choice over their children's schools and preserve the local control needed for schools to respond to market pressures. While such strategies maintained a keen focus on whole school improvement, they contrasted sharply with the notion of a new, niche market of external providers supporting the comprehensive reform of existing public schools.

In their article in the *Kappan*, Walberg and Greenberg asserted what, in their view, was a paradox: positive reports from program developers about the effectiveness of their programs, juxtaposed against continuing evidence of weak education outcomes in national and international evaluations (especially among poor and minority students). This paradox, they argued, called into question Title I as a federal program pumping billions of dollars into the improvement of education for at-risk students. This paradox, they also argued, called into question the methods and motives of program developers working under the Title I regime who regularly reported positive effects. If all of these programs worked, then why did national and international assessments continue to show little (if any) change in the achievement of U.S. students?

As a case in point, Walberg and Greenberg cited Success for All. With the possibility of political and financial gains hanging in the balance, Walberg and Greenberg argued that the Success for All project team was designing its own research in ways that favored the program, overstating positive program effects, and ignoring weak and negative program effects reported by independent researchers. Again, to Walberg and Greenberg, Success for All's claims of program effectiveness were one instance of a broader problem in educational research and evaluation:

> Government agencies, foundations, and other not-for-profits are often thought to be superior in knowledge, objectivity, and altruism. They, however, are increasingly driven by monetary and political pressures, which are not necessarily in the public or students' interest. The same government agencies and foundations that fund the programs, for example, hire evaluators, evaluate the programs themselves, or allow program developers to evaluate the programs. Having said the programs would succeed, can agency administrators easily return to Congress or their foundation's governing board to say they were wrong? Are they likely to hire independent-minded evaluators?

The principle of conflict of interest is hardly news. Aristotle warned his fellow citizens to consider the source, and the ancient Romans asked who would benefit from proposed conclusions and decisions. What is new is the pervasiveness of what we will call "the Diogenes factor" in program evaluation. According to ancient Athenian lore, Diogenes searched, with a lighted lantern, through daytime Athens for honesty. Though fabrication may be rare in educational evaluation, we can easily find selective evidence and misleading comparisons, which favor funded programs. These lead to misleading overestimates of program effectiveness.[80]

Criticism of Success for All went beyond claims of program effectiveness. Another line concern was raised in an *Education Week*, the national "paper of record" in education. In a feature article on Success for All, *Education Week's* Lynn Olson questioned whether the program's rapid rate of growth risked compromising the quality of implementation and outcomes.[81] Yet another line of concern questioned the alchemy of "professionalism by design" and framed Success for All as a top-down, bureaucratic reform effort. This concern was less a public charge and more a quiet buzz that reverberated throughout the academy, among researchers and scholars who placed a premium on teachers' knowledge and autonomy (and not external designs) as the basis for professionalization.

Growing criticism became a problem for the Success for All project team, especially criticism of research on program effectiveness. After all, the roots and identify of Success for All stretched into a leading research center at a preeminent research university. Further, both its moral high ground and its market advantage derived from the project team's commitment to effective, research-based programs. Finally, there was, in fact, a great deal of money in play. In its 1998 feature article, *The Atlantic* reported that Success for All's annual operating budget had grown to $30 million.[82]

With the stakes high and the kitty growing, Slavin responded to the criticism of Walberg and Greenberg with a letter to the editor in *Education Week* in which he argued that theirs was an ad hominem critique "outside the bounds of professional ethics." In his response, Slavin reasserted findings of research on Success for All. He also asserted that Walberg and Greenberg had, themselves, overstated weak findings on Success for All to serve their own interests.[83] Slavin argued that Walberg and Greenberg cited just two studies showing weak effects, and he proceeded to raise his own concerns about the findings of those studies. Specifically, for one study of a single South Carolina school, Slavin argued that weak effects were a consequence of the circumstances of program adoption, weak implementation, and a hurricane that severally damaged the school.[84] For a study of Success for All in Baltimore, Slavin argued that, even with the study reporting positive program effects, the concern raised by the author was that Success for All students were still not performing (on average) at grade level at the end of elementary school.[85] Slavin's response was followed by another letter to *Education Week* by CSOS researcher and Success for All associate Samuel Stringfield, who defended the interpretation of available evidence on

Success for All while calling for additional longitudinal research on all such programs.[86]

Responses to criticism of Success for All went beyond the project team and its associates to researchers with no affiliation with Success for All. In a letter to the editor of *Phi Delta Kappan*, Bruce Joyce, co-author of a leading textbook on evidence-based models of teaching, both recognized the contribution of Success for All in addressing "the great literacy problem" in the US and chided the Walberg/Greenberg critique as unwarranted and biased.[87] In a later exchange in *Phi Delta Kappan*, Walberg and Gerald Bracey, a researcher and noted watchdog of education reform, engaged in a heated debate as to whether Walberg and Greenberg deserved one of Bracey's "Rotten Apple" awards for the article in which they critiqued Success for All. Bracey asserted that "the disingenuousness with which Walberg and Greenberg slant facts and proffer untruths is breathtaking."[88] Taking exception, Walberg responded that, "even if the facts were completely on Bracey's side, such rhetoric is unacceptable in scholarly and professional writing."[89]

QUESTIONS

Despite efforts to avoid dogmatic (even vitriolic) debates that often plagued U.S. educational reform, the Success for All project team managed to stir up one of its own. With lines being drawn and sides being chosen, the safe bet was that the truth was likely lying where it often does under such circumstances: somewhere in the middle. On the one hand, Success for All appeared to be generating positive results, and there was good cause for excitement. On the other hand, the research base was ripe for scrutiny by analysts less vested in the program, and there was reason to be cautious.

To be sure, Success for All's experiences over its first decade raised questions, with the questions being asked depending on what side of the line one was standing. Enthusiasts might have asked, simply: How? How was Success for All achieving unlikely success against such long odds? Critics might have asked, instead: Why? Why, in Success for All schools, were all students, teachers, and leaders not able to use the program successfully? For those betting on the truth being somewhere in the middle, the only fair thing would be to give each group (and its questions) their due.

Notes

1. Slavin, Madden, Dolan, and Wasik (1996:230), citing Edmonds (1979:23). Emphasis in original. Roots and Wings was an expanded version of Success for All developed under the New American Schools initiative.
2. Slavin, Madden, Dolan, and Wasik (1996:xii).
3. For more on the history of Success for All and SFAF, see: Slavin (1996); Slavin, Madden, Dolan, and Wasik (1996); Slavin and Madden (2001b; 2001c); Matthews (2002); and Success for All Foundation (2008a).

4. Coleman, Campbell, Hobson, McPartland, Mood, Weinfeld, et al., (1966).
5. See: Hobbie (2001); Matthews (2002).
6. Stevens and Slavin (1995:322).
7. For example, see Slavin (1980; 1983; 1991) for syntheses of research on cooperative learning. For Success for All team members, these syntheses affirmed their confidence in the consistent effects of cooperative learning on multiple educational outcomes (affective, academic, and social) for schools in all geographic regions (urban, rural, suburban), for students in all grade levels (K-12), and for students of all ability levels. Achievement effects were found to be most consistent with cooperative learning strategies that blended team goals with individual accountability. See Slavin, Leavey, and Madden (1984) for findings from two studies that affirmed their confidence in the effects of team assisted individualization (the instructional strategy underlying Team Accelerated Instruction) on achievement outcomes. See Stevens, Madden, Slavin, and Farnish (1987) for findings from two studies on CIRC that affirmed team members' confidence in: (a) positive effects on achievement from interventions that integrate cooperative learning with strategies for student motivation, classroom management, curriculum, and metacognitive strategies; and (b) the possibility of teachers effectively implementing such interventions.
8. Stevens and Slavin (1995:322). Citation in text.
9. See Slavin (1986; 1987).
10. Success for All Foundation (2008a).
11. Slavin, Karweit, and Madden (1989:viii).
12. Slavin and Madden (1996b:ii).
13. With the 1981 reauthorization of the Elementary and Secondary Education Act, Title I was renamed Chapter 1. With the 1994 reauthorization, Chapter 1 was again renamed Title I. Throughout this book, Title I will be used to describe both Title I and Chapter 1 of ESEA over its history.
14. The figure of $4.6 billion in funding for Title I was reported by Riddle (1989:3). The percentages of districts and schools receiving Title I funding were reported by Puma (1999), citing Moskowitz, Stullich, and Deng (1993).
15. See Goertz (2001) for an analysis of the concept of "adequate yearly progress" as initially set out in the Improving America's Schools Act of 1994 and as revised later in the No Child Left Behind Act of 2001.
16. See Herdman (2002) on the "basic bargain" of accountability in exchange for autonomy.
17. From over 700 proposals, NAS initially selected eleven designs for participation in the project. Four dropped out during the demonstration phase, leaving these seven programs to begin the scale-up phase in 1995/96. See Kearns and Anderson (1996:11–13). Besides Roots and Wings (the expanded version of Success for All), the other remaining programs were: Purpose-Centered Education (originally Audrey Cohen College); ATLAS; Co-NECT; Expeditionary Learning Outward Bound; Modern Red Schoolhouse; and the National Alliance for Restructuring Education (which later became America's Choice).
18. For more on the history of New American Schools and its design teams, see: Berends, Bodilly, and Kirby (2002); Stringfield, Ross, and Smith (1996); and Kearns and Harvey (2000).
19. Burnett (1993:1).

20. For the number of Title I schoolwide programs in 1991 and 1996, see Wong and Meyer (1998:2).
21. Sherman (1999:1).
22. See Slavin, Madden, Dolan, and Wasik (1996:226) for discussion of the "on grade level" goal as central to SFAF's concept of "neverstreaming" (as an alternative to "mainstreaming") for special education students.
23. Statistics provided at the Success for All Leadership Academy Training, Columbus, OH, on 09/22/2000.
24. Statistics provided at the Success for All Leadership Academy Training, Columbus, OH, on 09/22/2000.
25. See, for example: Brophy and Good (1974); Good (1987).
26. See, for example: Canady (1988); Canady and Rettig (2000).
27. Nelson (1994).
28. This, again, is the loose coupling of schools as organizations, in which formal organizational structures have weak linkages to the work of teachers and students in classrooms. See, for example: Bidwell (1965) and Meyer and Rowan (1983).
29. On privacy, autonomy, and teacher-by-teacher "bricolage," see: Lortie (1975); Little (1990); and Huberman (1993).
30. For an historical account of the "reading wars" between proponents of phonics and whole language, see: Pearson (2004).
31. See, for example: Durkin (1979); Barr and Dreeben (1983); Barr and Sadow (1989).
32. See, for example: Rowan, Guthrie, Lee, and Guthrie (1986); Allington and Johnston (1989).
33. On the structure and leadership of schools as impediments to teachers' professional learning, see: Shedd and Bacharach (1991); Elmore (1990); and Elmore, Peterson, McCarthey (1996).
34. Regarding egalitarianism as an impediment to teacher leadership, see: Hart (1990); Conley and Levinson (1993); and Smylie and Smart (1990).
35. On weaknesses in the knowledge base of leadership and its disconnect from instruction, see: Griffiths (1979); Greenfield (1986); Evers and Lakomski (1991); Donmoyer, Imber, and Scheurich (1995); Erickson (1979); Bridges (1982); Hoy (1982); Murphy (1988); Sergiovanni (1992); and Cuban (1992).
36. Slavin, Madden, Dolan, and Wasik (1996:3).
37. Description of professional development as "Job 1" in Success for All is taken from Robert Slavin's keynote address at the Success for All New Sites Training, San Diego, CA, May, 2000.
38. For more on teacher professionalism as a mid-1980s reform initiative, see: Carnegie Forum on Education and the Economy (1986); and Holmes Group (1986). For a subsequent summary of scholarship on teacher professionalism, see: Darling-Hammond and Sykes (1999).
39. See Little (1990) for discussion of the concept of "joint work." See Shulman (1987) for discussion of "professional reasoning and action" as a mechanism for generating wisdom of practice (especially "pedagogical content knowledge" as a domain of knowledge unique to teachers).
40. Description of Success for All as a simultaneous "heart and lung transplant" is taken from notes on Robert Slavin's keynote address at the Success for All Experienced Sites Conference, New York, April, 2006. See, also, Olson (1998).

41. Descriptive analysis of Success for All as it developed over its first decade draws from the following documents, listed in chronological order: Slavin, Karweit, and Madden (1989); Wasik and Madden (1992); Wasik and Slavin (1993); Slavin (1994); Haxby, Lasaga-Flister, Madden, Slavin, Dolan, and Wasik (1995); Wasik, Bond, and Waclawiw (1995); Madden (1996); Slavin, Madden, Dolan, and Wasik (1996); Haxby, Lasaga-Flister, Madden, and Slavin (1999). Madden (1999); Madden, Slavin, Farnish, Livingston, and Calderon (1999); Wasik and Bond (1999); Madden, Wasik, and French (2000); Slavin and Madden (2001b).

42. For more on the core beliefs, see Slavin, Madden, Dolan and Wasik (1996:1–3;230).

43. See Slavin, Madden, Karweit, Dolan, and Wasik (1992), titled *Success for All: A Relentless Approach to Prevention and Early Intervention in Elementary Schools*. See, also, Slavin, Madden, Dolan, and Wasik (1996:1–4).

44. Slavin, Madden, Dolan, and Wasik (1996:8).

45. Slavin, Madden, Dolan, and Wasik (1996:12). Citation in original text.

46. See Slavin, Madden, Dolan, and Wasik (1996:5).

47. Madden, Slavin, Farnish, Livingston, Calderon (1999:1). Emphasis in original

48. Madden, Slavin, Farnish, Livingston, Calderon (1999:17–19).

49. Madden, Slavin, Farnish, Livingston, and Calderon (1999:19).

50. Wasik and Madden (1992:3–4).

51. See Slavin, Madden, Dolan, and Wasik (1996:156).

52. Slavin and Madden (1999a:11). Slavin and Madden (1996a:5).

53. Slavin, Madden, Dolan, and Wasik (1996:174).

54. Slavin, Madden, Dolan, and Wasik (1996:170).

55. Livingston, Cummings, and Madden (1996, "Monitoring Implementation," p. 1). Emphasis in original.

56. Slavin and Madden (1996b).

57. See, for example, Rowan, Camburn, and Barnes (2004:4–6). Reviewing research on the "Research-Development-Dissemination-Utilization" strategy for educational change, Rowan, Camburn, and Barnes (citing Darling-Hammond and Snyder, 1992) argue that knowledge of such difficulties first emerged in the 1960s, with evaluation studies of ambitious curriculum reforms showed implementation in schools so varied that the interventions were unrecognizable. See Dow's (1991) account of "Man: A Course of Study" for a case study exemplifying such findings. Alternatively, Rowan, Camburn, and Barnes cite the Rand Change Agent Study (Berman and McLaughlin, 1975) as the most significant of a series of large-scale studies that "came to the conclusion that planned educational programs were implemented quite variably in local settings, so much so, in fact, that many researchers began to doubt that faithful implementation of research-based practices would ever occur inside schools" (p. 5). Rowan, Camburn, and Barnes continue by citing Firestone and Corbett (1988:324), who argued that, as a result of the Rand Change Agent Study, "the proposition that centrally adopted innovations [c]ould . . . [never] . . . be implemented locally became widely accepted and publicized by academics, policymakers, and even the popular press. . .and federal funding for such efforts dropped dramatically. . .In its place emerged a 'let a thousand flowers' bloom theory [of educational change] that stressed local invention. . .and the development of a built-in 'capacity' to improve at the school or district site" (p. 5).

58. See Berman and McLaughlin (1978) on mutual adaptation, as well as McLaughlin (1991) for reflection on chief findings of the Rand change agent studies more than

a decade hence. See, also, Elmore (1979–80) on "backward mapping" as a strategy for program design and implementation. This strategy reasons *from* the behaviours that need to be enacted in order to realize policy objectives *to* the organizational and policy supports needed to enact those behaviours.

59. The characterization of "bureaucratic" and "technocratic" derives from the following: Adler and Borys (1992), and their analysis of interpretations of formal organizational controls as "coercive" versus "enabling"; Bradach (2003), who analyzes comparable interpretations in networks of non-profit organizations; Rowan (1990), and his analysis of differing interpretations of external control of instruction among teacher-advocates and teachers in schools; and Shedd and Bacharach (1991), who argue for the imperative to strengthen both bureaucratic and professional control in schools. For analysis of interpretation as central to the implementation of comprehensive school reform programs, see Datnow and Park (2009), who frame implementation as a time-dependent process of sense-making and co-construction among schools, developers, and other educational agencies.

60. See Cohen and Levinthal (1990). Arguments of absorptive capacity echo themes from the implementation literature, which hold that the success of innovations depends not only on the existing skill of implementers but, also, their willingness to incorporate innovations and engage change (e.g., McLaughlin, 1976, 1991; Pressman and Wildavsky, 1984). All echo findings in the broader literature on innovations, in which unusually skilled and willing "early adopters" demonstrate unusual capacity to incorporate and to use innovations (Rogers, 1995). In an historical analysis of the failure of educational innovation, Cohen and Ball (2007) report exactly that, with more capable and resourceful schools historically more able to incorporate and to use complex innovations.

61. For Success for All's scale of operations, see Slavin and Madden (1999b:6–7). In a report prepared for the U.S. Department of Education by the Council of Chief State School Officers, Williams, Blank, Toye, and Petermann (2007) reported Oregon as having 747 public elementary schools in SY 2002/2003.

62. See Slavin, Madden, Karweit, Livermon, and Dolan (1990) for first-year outcomes for Success for All. For internal reviews of research on Success for All over its first decade, see: Slavin, Madden, Dolan, Wasik, Ross, Smith, and Dianda (1996) and Slavin, Madden, Dolan, and Wasik (1996).

63. Slavin, Madden, Dolan, and Wasik (1996:195).

64. One of the original federally funded educational laboratories, the Southwest Regional Educational Laboratory merged with the Far West Laboratory in 1995 to form WestEd.

65. See Valentine and Cooper (2003). All effect sizes reported in this book are standardized mean differences (Cohen's d).

66. See Cohen (1988). Examples of "education-related fields" include personality, social, and clinical-psychological research. These guidelines would ultimately be adopted by the federally funded What Works Clearinghouse to evaluate the effectiveness of externally developed improvement programs. See Valentine and Cooper (2003).

67. Comprehensive School Reform Quality Center (2005:18).

68. Slavin and Fashola (1998:11).

69. See: Slavin, Madden, Dolan, and Wasik (1996); Slavin, Madden, Dolan, Wasik, Ross, Smith, and Dianda (1996).

70. Fashola and Slavin (1998).

71. Slavin and Fashola (1998).
72. See Slavin, Madden, Dolan, and Wasik (1996), Chapter 8: "Research on Success for All." In particular, see the discussion on pp. 215–216 for their challenge of what they saw as a well-established and widely held rationale for the necessity of school-based design.
73. See Slavin, Madden, Dolan, and Wasik (1996:204–205).
74. See Slavin, Madden, Dolan, and Wasik (1996:215). Citations and capitalization of "RAND" as in original.
75. Olson (1998).
76. See Lemann (1998).
77. U.S. Department of Education (1997).
78. See Walberg and Greenberg (1998; 1999), who cited weak and negative findings in evaluations of Success for All conducted by Jones, Gottfredson, and Gottfredson (1997) and Venezky (1994).
79. See Heartland Institute (2009).
80. Walberg and Greenberg (1998).
81. For example, see Olson (1998).
82. See Lemann (1998). Olson (1998) also reports a figure of $30 million, though as estimated revenues for 1998 (rather than as Success for All's operating budget).
83. See Slavin (1998).
84. See Jones, Gottfredson, and Gottfredson (1997).
85. See Venezky (1994).
86. See Stringfield (1998).
87. See Joyce (1999).
88. See Bracey (2000).
89. See Walberg (2000).

Supporting

The implementation of Success for All or Roots and Wings requires substantial change in school organization and practices. It affects curriculum, instruction, assessment, early childhood programs, Title I, special education, promotion/retention policies, parent involvement, relations with health and social services agencies, and internal school governance. It requires the active participation of every staff member in an existing staff; no Success for All or Roots and Wings school has ever been able to select staff specifically for the program. It requires dramatic changes in daily teaching methods for teachers who may have decades of experience doing something else. It requires a change in beliefs about the school's ability and responsibility to ensure the success of every child, no matter what.

How does all of this change come about? How do Success for All and Roots and Wings enter a school, solicit enthusiastic participation of school staffs, train staff in program procedures, monitor and improve implementation over time, assess progress towards desired goals, and maintain coordination among the many pieces of the program? These are extremely important questions that we have had to address as we "scale up" Success for All from a pilot program to become a replicable, reliably effective model for school change.

ROBERT SLAVIN, NANCY MADDEN, LAWRENCE DOLAN, AND BARBARA WASIK, 1996[1]

Success for All's first decade of operations was something of a puzzle. From one perspective, Success for All was improbably effective in improving achievement in large numbers of chronically underperforming schools. From another perspective, Success for All was struggling to live up to its name. The possibilities and problems began with the work of designing: work in which systems of problems begot systems of solutions, and systems of solutions begot systems of new challenges.

But the work of designing was not performed in isolation. Rather, the work of designing was performed in interaction with the work of supporting implementation. With Success for All, supporting implementation was not a straightforward process of disseminating a shrink-wrapped improvement program that could be used effectively right out of the box. Instead, supporting implementation had developers devising and enacting a strategy for replicating a complex organizational blueprint across large numbers of chronically-underperforming schools.

The strategy for supporting implementation evolved between 1987/88 and 1997/98 lock-step with the organizational blueprint, with the work of devising that strategy bearing keen resemblance—for better and for worse. On the one hand, the project team drew on research and experience to construct a system of interdependent components to support an ambitious goal: schoolwide implementation beginning Day 1 of Year 1, with implementation then refined over a three-year period. On the other hand, the resulting strategy had a familiar character. Raising the hopes of enthusiasts, it appeared to increase the odds of success. Fueling the flames of critics, it appeared to introduce more (and very steep) challenges. Chief among these critics were the very teachers whose professional practice and learning Success for All was intended to support.

As with the work of designing, these challenges again arose from the interactions among the program, schools, and environments. And, again, responsibility for managing these challenges circled back to the Success for All project team as an organization. Among members of the project team, those bearing particular responsibility were the trainers whose job it was to ensure the success of all leaders, teachers, and, especially, students.

THE PROGRAM ADOPTION PROCESS

Success for All's strategy for supporting implementation began with a comprehensive program-adoption process to be enacted prior to Year 1 implementation, a starting point soon identified as absolutely critical in external research on the implementation of comprehensive school-reform programs.[2] More than a recruiting mechanism or a sales pitch, the program adoption process was designed both to address stubborn problems of externally sponsored improvement programs and to establish initial conditions in schools and environments that favored effective implementation. Supported by explanatory materials, step-by-step directions, and direct assistance, the process served schools by establishing a firm foundation upon which to begin rebuilding. It also served the project team by reducing the risk of devoting scarce resources (and linking its reputation) to schools and environments uncommitted to deep change.

For "Success for All the Crusade," the program adoption process resembled a "come to Jesus" meeting: a deliberate intervention that brought schools face-to-face with their self-destructive habits, and that gave them the option to chose a new path. For "Success for All the Player," the program-adoption process looked like an attempt to stack the deck.

Establishing an "Attainable Vision"

At the heart of Success for All's strategy for supporting implementation was addressing head-on the most fundamental problem in chronically underperforming schools: the downward spiral of expectations and practice—disbelief in the academic potential of at-risk students, which fueled low-level instructional practice, which fueled low achievement, which fueled low expectations, ad infinitum. That is where Success for All's program adoption process sought to begin: with establishing an "attainable vision" of success as the basis for an upward, self-reinforcing spiral of improvement.[3]

The first step was for all relevant constituencies (teachers, school leaders, parents, and district personnel) to begin learning about Success for All through a combination of print and video resources and through awareness sessions conducted by Success for All staff members. As designed, these initial educational opportunities included explanations of the first principles of the program (prevention, early intervention, and relentlessness), explanation of Success for All as a systemic design for school restructuring, and review of research on program effectiveness. They were also intended to serve as a context within which to articulate expectations for student achievement, for professional practice, and for professional learning—and, with that, to immediately stem interpretations of Success for All as either a bureaucratic or technocratic intervention.

Included in this first step was the expectation that teachers and school leaders would read *Every Child, Every School: Success for All*.[4] A trade book written by cofounders Robert Slavin and Nancy Madden in collaboration with colleagues Lawrence Dolan and Barbara Wasik, *Every Child, Every School* was a resource that synthesized the Success for All philosophy, goals, design, and research base for presentation to a wide audience. The preface to the book set out clearly the beliefs, expectations, and practices that the project team sought to cultivate in schools:

> If we truly believed that every child could learn under the proper circumstances, we would be relentless in the search of those circumstances. We would use well-validated instructional methods and materials known to be capable of ensuring the success of nearly all children if used with intelligence, flexibility, and fidelity. We would involve teachers in constant, collaborative professional development activities to continually improve their capabilities to reach every child. We would frequently assess children's performance to be sure that all students are on a path that leads to success, and to be able to respond immediately if children are not making adequate progress. If children were falling behind despite excellent instruction, we would try different instructional approaches, and if necessary, we would provide them with tutors or other intensive assistance. We would involve parents in support of their children's school success; we would check to see whether vision, hearing, health, nutrition, or other nonacademic problems were holding children

back, and we would find solutions to those problems. If we truly believed that all children could learn, we would rarely, if ever, assign children to special education or long-term remedial programs that in effect lower expectations for children. If we truly believed that all schools could ensure the success of all children, then the failure of even a single child would be cause for great alarm and immediate, forceful intervention.[5]

Teachers and leaders were not expected to take it on faith that Success for All could function as a resource for fostering such beliefs, expectations, and practices. Rather, the program adoption process included the strong recommendation that school representatives visit an established Success for All school to observe the program in operation, with project team members brokering and facilitating these visits. School visits were an opportunity for teachers and leaders to further their understandings of the program, both in principle and in operation. With their own eyes, teachers and leaders could witness the possibility of people much like themselves working very differently with students just like theirs to achieve very different outcomes. The bet hedged was that, having borne witness, teachers and leaders would begin developing new expectations for student achievement and deep responsibility for improving their own practice.

Free and Informed Choice

In chronically underperforming schools, the downward spiral of expectations and practice were often matched with a problematic reality: Pressure for (and programs of) improvement were often imposed as top-down, bureaucratic directives, either by district or school administrators. To stem the risk of misinterpreting Success for All as yet another bureaucratic imposition, and to build teachers' ownership and commitment, program adoption was predicated on a positive vote by 80% of all instructional staff (classroom teachers, "specials" teachers, and supplemental teachers) on a confidential ballot. To ensure that the choice was also informed, the ballot provided to schools by Success for All also asked that teachers indicate whether they had attended awareness sessions, read recommended print resources (including *Every Child, Every School*), visited a Success for All school, and discussed program adoption with colleagues.[6]

Again, the intended result was for teachers to commit voluntarily to an extensive, long-term, and deep-reaching program of improvement—and not for school administrators, districts administrators, or anybody else to impose that expectation on them. Moving such critical decision-making authority *out* of districts and other environmental agencies and *into* schools was consistent with broader calls in the late 1980s and early 1990s for site-based and participatory management, as well as with the basic bargain of standards-based reform: accountability for student achievement in exchange for autonomy in the work of improving schools.[7]

Managed and Mediated Environments

Potentially negative effects of schools' environments went beyond the bureaucratic imposition of pressure and programs. They included such well-worn problems as unstable agendas and uncertain funding, which had schools constantly adopting new programs and quickly abandoning them as they chased the latest-and-greatest ideas for reform. They also included constraints on practice, structure, and resource allocation that impeded improvement efforts. For example, in the case of Success for All, such common constraints as union contracts and district personnel policies had the potential to limit classroom observations by school leaders and, with that, their work as on-site change agents responsible for effective implementation. As potentially problematic as the things that environmental agencies conventionally *did* do were the things that they conventionally *didn't* do: for example, provide extensive, coherent, practice-focused support for school improvement. Instead, environmental guidance for improving instructional and leadership practice was famously uncoordinated, unstable, and weak.[8]

To manage and buffer environments so as not to impede implementation, the Success for All project team collaborated with schools and districts in a formal contracting process designed to secure supportive environmental conditions over a three-year implementation window. The contracting process included specifying all materials, training, and other services to be delivered by Success for All so that (among other things) school and districts leaders understood the full breadth and depth of the program. Further, the contracting process included efforts to secure stable funding. While Success for All was designed so that it could be funded using resources earmarked for at-risk students (especially from Title I), the high costs of the program sometimes required that schools and districts agree to reallocate resources *away* from other improvement initiatives and *to* Success for All. Finally, the contracting process included efforts to secure exemption from district-level requirements for curriculum, Title I, special education, staffing, and grade-level promotion and retention—essentially, the very features of schooling that Success for All intended to restructure.

To mediate environments to support implementation, the project team incorporated newly adopting schools into the professional network of Success for All schools. This was something of an "alternative environment": a formidable and stable entity with the potential to directly support the development of both technical capabilities and a supporting culture, with members bound by Success for All as a common program of improvement. It was also intended to function as a social infrastructure supporting long-term implementation at a large scale, as it created opportunities for school-to-school mentoring over and above support provided to schools by Success for All staff members. As explained by Success for All cofounders Slavin and Madden in a report on Success for All's strategies for working at scale:

> School-to-school mentoring lets the real experts—the teachers, facilitators, and principals in successful Success for All schools—share their wisdom of

practice and hard-won experience. It gives new schools an attainable vision of what Success for All should be like. It gives staffs of new schools support when they run into problems or opposition. Mentor schools know the local situation, so they can help new schools adapt to local realities more readily than our trainers can.

Perhaps most importantly, building support networks enables school staffs to provide emotional support to one another. In an isolated Success for All school, staff members are always wondering if they're doing the right thing, if problems they perceive are temporary setbacks or serious roadblocks. Others in the district or even in the same school are often skeptical, either wondering what madness has come over the school or feeling envious about the attention and resources the school is getting. A local support network or mentoring arrangement helps school staffs withstand the inevitable pressures that come with innovation. Teachers, facilitators, and principals in Success for All schools speak a common language and share a common vision and purpose.[9]

Knowledgeable and Respected Leadership

As with environments, school leadership had long done much to impede school improvement, and little to support it. Hostility and distrust between school leaders and teachers were centuries old, owing to such issues as gender differences between (mostly male) administrators and (mostly female) teachers, tensions arising through formal authority relationships, and historical attempts by school administrators to impose principles of scientific management on what many teachers viewed as the organic work of educating children.[10] Further, conventionally, there was little opportunity in the day-to-day work of educational administrators to practice the sort of "instructional leadership" imagined by Success for All, and little knowledge in the field as a whole to support such practice.[11]

As such, an essential step in the program adoption process was to staff the central leadership role in Success for All schools: the role of reading facilitator. To sidestep historic tensions and to bring knowledge and expertise to bear, developers advised that schools staff the position with a knowledgeable, experienced, and respected teacher, preferably with a strong background in elementary reading, early childhood education, or Title I. Success for All would then be both a *teacher-selected* and a *teacher-led* improvement initiative, further stemming possibility the teachers and school leaders would interpret the program as bureaucratic and top-down. Strategically staffing the position of reading facilitator was argued to be absolutely critical to program success. As explained in *Every Child, Every School*, "the facilitator is the linchpin of the entire program; the effectiveness of the program depends to a substantial degree on his or her skills as an agent of change."[12]

A Firm Foundation

Thus, by engaging teachers, leaders, schools, and districts in an extensive pro-gram-adoption process, the intent was that neither schools nor the Success for All project team would begin implementation in the same deep hole as most exter-nally sponsored improvement efforts. Rather, by engaging in a highly prescribed and extensively supported program adoption process, the goal was for schools and the project team to begin implementation with a firm foundation for effective implementation: an attainable vision of success; free and informed choice by teachers; managed and mediated environments; and knowledgeable and respected teacher-leadership.

THE REPLICATION PROCESS

Support for implementation continued with a three-year process of replicating Success for All's organizational blueprint in newly adopting schools. The process included replicating formal features of schools: for example, new roles, structures, curricula, assessment, and other technologies. The tougher task was replicating social features of schools: for example, beliefs, norms, relationships, capabilities, and, especially, practices—the behaviors to be co-enacted by students, teachers, and leaders in the course of their day-to-day work. Still tougher was doing all of the preceding at scale, in schools and environments that offered little by way of infrastructure and much by way of challenges.

While Success for All cofounder Robert Slavin maintained a heavy hand, pri-mary responsibility for devising the replication process rested with two project team members who brought diverse experiences and expertise to bear on the work: Nancy Madden and Barbara Haxby. Madden (who cofounded Success for All with husband Robert Slavin) managed and coordinated all initial develop-ment and training operations. Madden also was the primary developer of the cur-riculum and instruction components of Success for All. Haxby, a clinical social worker with expertise in family therapy, was the primary developer of the family support component, and assisted Madden in managing and coordinating devel-opment and training operations.

As it emerged and evolved over its first decade of operations, Success for All's replication process rested on three interdependent mechanisms: *elaborating* the organizational design; *scaffolding* the intended practices; both within a deliberate *developmental sequence*. Capitalizing on the firm foundation established (in prin-ciple) through the program-adoption process, the intent was to use these mecha-nisms to initiate and sustain an upward spiral of improvement: new capabilities for instructional and leadership practice, which would lead to previously unreal-ized success by students, which would renew the school's commitment to improve-ment, which would fuel new capabilities for practice, ad infinitum. The effect, then, would not be to simply diffuse or disseminate the organizational blueprint to schools. Rather, the effect would be to *recreate* the organizational blueprint in schools, including (and especially) capabilities for instructional and leadership practice.

Elaborating

Elaborating involved embedding knowledge and information about the organizational blueprint into common materials, tools, and artifacts of schooling including books, component-specific manuals, videos, K–6 curriculum materials, student texts and workbooks, assessments, forms, manipulatives, posters, consumables, and more.[13] These tools and artifacts were designed to be moved seamlessly into schools, used immediately (and effectively) with existing capabilities, and used in more sophisticated ways as capabilities grew. They were also designed so that they could be combined in different ways to match specific needs in schools and their environments.[14] In that respect, elaborating the blueprint functioned as a mechanism for addressing challenges of knowledge transfer, absorptive capacity, and variable environments associated with externally developed improvement programs. These tools and artifacts were also designed to be reproduced en masse on a unit cost basis, improved on-going, and re-issued to schools upon improvement. In that respect, elaborating the program was also responsive to the project team's ambitions for working at scale, and to its commitment to continuous improvement.

The intent of the preceding was to support quick replication of formal and social features of schools. The tools and artifacts provided to schools not only described in detail the essential roles and structures that needed to be created. More importantly, they also included three devices that were intended to support deep, coordinated improvement in instructional and leadership practice: *routines*, *information resources*, and *supplemental guidance*. In theory, using these devices to improve practice would create the foundation for cultural transformation in the school: feelings of efficacy, commitment, and empowerment among teachers and leaders.

Routines were the essential "best practices" to be replicated across schools: conventional, recognizable patterns of interdependent actions to be enacted by teachers and leaders, individually and collaboratively.[15] A cornerstone of Success for All was to extensively "formalize" or "codify" routines: simply put, to write down in manuals and other materials exactly what it was that teachers and leaders were to do (in contrast, for example, to developing capabilities for practice by having teachers and leaders engage in sustained apprenticeships with master teachers and leaders in other schools).

Routines varied in their level of detail, ranging from step-by-step directions to narrative descriptions of courses of action. Success for All included closed routines: directions and scripts that could be enacted immediately with existing knowledge and a minimum (if any) of site-based discretion (e.g., routines for administering and scoring quarterly assessments). It included open routines: procedures for making decisions and taking action under conditions of uncertainty (e.g., in case meetings in tutoring and family support). It included learning routines: procedures to guide school-based reflection and improvement (e.g., processes for peer coaching between teachers and leaders). And it linked closed and open routines into more complex, coordinated organizational routines (e.g., routines for coordinating regular classroom instruction, tutoring, and family support into a coherent program for individual students).

Information resources were designed to capture and communicate information that was essential for analysis and coordination within the school. Because digital information technologies were not yet ubiquitous during its first decade of operations, Success for All included a paper-based information system comprised of forms, assessments, codes, and rubrics, all of which ran parallel to the school's existing records and reporting systems. Key information resources spanned every component of the program: for example, a quarterly reading assessment used both to place students into classes and to evaluate instructional effectiveness; eight-week assessment summary forms used jointly by teachers and school leaders to record, communicate, and analyze information bearing on the quarterly evaluation of students; standard forms for coordinating regular classroom instruction, tutoring, and family support; self-assessment checklists used by teachers to generate information about classroom-level implementation; and a grade level summary form used to analyze school-wide reading performance.

Supplemental guidance included information and advice about the organizational design and its implementation. This included background information: for example, discussion of the program's history, philosophy, norms, and principles; descriptions of the individual program components and their interactions; and explanations and examples of Success for All's many routines and information resources. It included discussion of implementation-essential activity that was heavily dependent on local conditions and, thus, not easily routinized: for example, creating the 90-minute reading block within school-specific scheduling constraints, or coordinating the program with district requirements. And, importantly, it included guidance for performing open routines that required discretion and judgment on the part of teachers and leaders: for example, information for leaders about grouping students and teachers for reading instruction; background knowledge for teachers on monitoring students' understandings of reading skills and strategies; and guidance for the tutoring and family support teams regarding monitoring, diagnosing, and responding to students' academic and nonacademic needs.

While the entire organizational design was extensively elaborated, one of the most distinguishing features of Success for All was its extensive elaboration of regular classroom instruction. The core components of the reading curriculum (i.e., Early Learning, Reading Roots, and Reading Wings) included sequenced units and lessons that structured K–6 reading instruction, schoolwide. Units and lessons were composed of uniquely named instructional routines, all of which were explicitly and aggressively paced to make the fullest use of the 90-minute reading block.[16] Instructional routines were complemented by interdependent routines for classroom management and conflict resolution.

Some of the instructional routines were closed: for example, literal scripts for use in direct instruction to present new letter sounds, to explain and model meta-cognitive skills, and to present reading comprehension strategies. Others were open, thus creating opportunity for flexibility and adaptation by teachers. For example, the conventional cycle of diagnostic instruction was designed to create opportunities for in-the-moment monitoring and intervention by teachers as students worked in cooperative learning teams. Further, only the "Treasure Hunt" portion of each Reading Wings unit was determined in advance: three 55-minute lesson components across Days 1, 2, and 3 of the five-day Reading Wings unit. The remainder of each unit was constructed at the teacher's discretion within a standard unit template and (in part) by selecting from a library of supplemental reading comprehension lessons, with the goal of producing an integrated instructional experience that was responsive to students' needs, to learning opportunities afforded by particular texts, and to environmental expectations for performance.

To support the informed, discretionary selection and enactment of instructional routines, Success for All also embedded information resources and supplemental guidance directly into the curriculum materials. These took several forms: for example, discussion prompts for whole group instruction; required student work products and assessments; forms and rubrics for recording information about students; general information on the curriculum's design; and specific information on reading skills and strategies.

Thus, as elaborated, individual units and lessons structured 90 minutes of direct instruction, cooperative learning tasks, independent learning tasks, and assessments for *this* particular skill or strategy, using *this* particular text, for students performing at *this* particular reading level. The entire collection of units and lessons, then, coordinated instruction across the entire K–6 reading curriculum. These instructional activities were further supported by complementary routines enacted by supplemental teachers (e.g., assessment and intervention routines enacted in tutoring and family support) and schools leaders (e.g., routines for quarterly assessment and regrouping of students).

Anchored in research and refined through experience, the bet hedged by Success for All developers was that this combination of routines, information resources, and supplemental guidance would support instances of quick success. Detailed routines would enable teachers and leaders to act on their new expectations for students and their new commitment to improvement. Amidst the blizzard of activity in the school, information resources would structure teachers' and leaders' attention and focus it on those things that mattered most to the relentless use of the program: analyzing the performance of students and teachers; coordinating activity in the school; and making strategic adaptations. And supplemental guidance would inform both the selection and enactment of routines and the analysis and use of information. Instances of success, in turn, could be used as evidence that it was possible for teachers and leaders to work very differently to achieve very different outcomes with students. With that, the intent was for the "attainable vision" fostered during program adoption to become an upward spiral of efficacy, commitment, and continuous improvement.

Scaffolding

Scaffolding consisted of an extensive, coordinated array of learning opportunities over the three-year implementation window, with both the project team and other schools functioning as key resources to support teachers' and leaders' learning.[17] One purpose was to assist teachers and leaders in understanding, acting on, and using all that was elaborated. A second purpose was to convey essential knowledge and information not easily (or not yet) elaborated: for example, tacit knowledge of the program, its history, and its use; the art and craft of practice; and disciplinary knowledge of instruction and leadership. A third purpose was to create opportunities for Success for All trainers to collaborate with schools in managing inevitable, school-specific exigencies and problems: for example, integrating Success for All with existing school systems (such as attendance systems, student records systems, and IEP processes); aligning Success for All with district and state requirements; and, importantly, managing potential interpretation of the program either as bureaucratic or technocratic.

Success for All integrated three interdependent forms of scaffolding often advanced as stand-alone learning opportunities in other external improvement programs: direct instruction, practice-based learning, and in-practice monitoring and follow-up. All were anchored squarely in the day-to-day work of instruction and leadership, used the same tools and artifacts used by teachers and leaders, and created opportunities to develop new capabilities, norms, and beliefs in schools. Success for All did not use a one-size-fits-all approach. The only standardized dimension of scaffolding was initial training prior to Year 1 implementation. Otherwise, the curriculum for professional learning was developed and adapted in response to the needs of individual teachers, leaders, and schools, primarily via collaboration between school leaders and Success for All team members.

Direct instruction took the form of conventional training sessions: initial training and New Sites Conferences that preceded Year 1 implementation; annual Experienced Sites Conferences for school leaders; and optional, school-selected training modules for experienced schools. Direct instruction functioned as an opportunity for project team members to introduce and explain the program, to explain and model instructional and leadership practice, and to distribute supplemental resources (called "participant training books") to further support implementation. Thus designed, direct instruction created opportunities for team members to bring the program to life, providing examples of how highly elaborated practices could be enacted with vitality, agency, and even personal flair. Recognizing the limited effects of direct instruction on daily practice, the learning objective was typically exposure to (not mastery of) new routines, information resources, and supplemental guidance.[18] Beyond developing technical capabilities, direct instruction also functioned as an opportunity to develop a social infrastructure to support implementation through a number of means: for example, articulating and reinforcing goals and principles; introducing and using a common vocabulary; celebrating success in order to build efficacy and commitment; and facilitating relationships among teachers, leaders, team members, and schools.

Scaffolding continued with practice-based learning: teachers and leaders actually using Success for All-provided resources to enact daily practice, learning through the experience, and cultivating new norms and relationships by collaborating in the work. Practice-based learning took conventional forms: "learning by doing" through repetition, experience, and trial-and-error; one-on-one coaching (either teacher/leader or teacher/teacher); small group learning in component team meetings; collegial learning among school leaders; and collegial interactions with schools in Success for All's professional network. Practice-based learning was highly dependent on school leaders (especially the reading facilitator) collaborating with teachers to identify and address school-specific problems of practice. As explained in *The Facilitator's Manual*, the primary manual for school leaders:

> Your leadership, as both a teacher and a learner, is essential for the success of the program. On one hand, this program is highly structured; implementation requires mastering the skills and information detailed in several manuals. Success does in fact depend on using a well-developed and highly specific curriculum and some methods proven by research in real classrooms to be particularly effective. On the other hand, many of the questions teachers ask are not answered in the manuals. A lot of the problems you encounter are products of your unique situation and are best solved by homemade remedies. For that matter, some of the ideas about making Success for All work have not yet been thought of and are awaiting to be discovered by you and your colleagues. Regular opportunities for team problem-solving help to ensure that everybody feels a part of the solution and emphasize the importance and value of shared ideas. . . .
>
> This program works best in the hands of competent teachers challenged to use their own professional judgment in deciding many important questions about implementation. As the facilitator, you must model the use of good judgment. Nothing this or any manual could possibly include eliminates the need for you to consult with teachers often, to weigh facts carefully, to read relevant research reports and review the principles embedded in the program, and to make your own, sound professional decisions. Effective implementation depends on your reflective and adaptive leadership.[19]

Scaffolding continued, finally, with in-practice monitoring and follow-up in the context of what Success for All called "implementation visits." Implementation visits were conducted by a group of three project team members, each with specialized knowledge in a specific program component (usually Reading Roots, Readings Wings, and family support). One of the team members served as a "point trainer" responsible for successful implementation and outcomes in that particular school. Given the importance of developing leaders as on-site change agents, implementation visits were structured to mirror the day-to-day work of leaders, so that trainers could model and mentor key leadership practices. As such, implementation visits included a conventional set of activities: for example, pre-visit data analysis; extensive classroom observation; observation of tutoring sessions; peer coaching in the context of instruction; and participation in component team meetings. Thus structured, implementation visits created the opportunity for Success for All team members to observe the implementation of all program components and to providing assistance to teachers and leaders in the context of their work.

Scaffolding was structured to provide extensive, initial support from project team members early in implementation and to gradually shift responsibility to schools, themselves. To support a radical break from past practice and the immediate, school-wide implementation of the program, direct instruction was most extensive in initial training over the summer preceding Year 1 implementation. Initial training was standard across schools: a week of leadership-specific training (to prepare them as change agents); three days of initial training for teachers and leaders in curriculum and instruction; and two additional days of training for teachers and leaders in both tutoring and family support. Thereafter, direct instruction consisted of annual, 3-day Experienced Sites Conferences for school leaders and optional, school-selected training modules for teachers. Like direct instruction, implementation visits were also reduced over time: 23 trainer days in Year 1, 10–12 trainer days in Year 2, and 5–8 trainer days in Year 3.[20]

With reductions in direct instruction and implementation visits over time, the primary focus of scaffolding shifted to schools' own practice-based learning, under the guidance of school leaders and with continued participation in Success for All's professional network. This supported ambitions for large-scale operations by increasing the self-sufficiency of experienced schools and freeing Success for All team members to collaborate with newly recruited schools. It also created an imperative for experienced schools to take full ownership of the program.

Developmental Sequence

Mindful both of the initially weak capabilities of schools and of the ultimate goals of professional practice and learning, elaboration and scaffolding were structured to support a two-stage developmental sequence that aimed to take teachers and leaders from *novice* to *expert* use of the program.[21]

For teachers and leaders new to Success for All, the first-order goal was novice use: using Success for All-supplied tools and artifacts consistently and conventionally, with fidelity and without deviation. The intent was for newly motivated teachers and leaders to begin working differently and effectively, schoolwide, on Day 1 of Year 1 of implementation: that is, using closed routines to enact new, coordinated forms of practice; enacting open routines as if closed (for example, as a series of steps comprising a decision-making process, with little initial expectation of making meaningful, strategic decisions); using information resources to observe, record, and communicate essential information in conventional ways (though without yet analyzing it and using it); and using supplemental guidance to inform and to reflect on their work (and not yet to guide site-specific adaptations).

Consistent, schoolwide implementation was intended to solve a set of pragmatic problems associated with externally sponsored school improvement. As a starting point, consistent implementation had the potential both to quickly displace past (and presumably ineffective) practice and to prevent a quick backslide into past practice. The combination would preserve the identity and integrity of the organizational blueprint amidst the uncertainty of early implementation. Consistency also had the potential to quickly establish what Success for All project team members described as a "high floor" under practice: new forms of coordinated instructional and leadership practice, both anchored in and validated by research and experience. The program's basis in research and experience upped the potential that this "high floor" would yield quick (and otherwise unlikely) gains in student achievement. These gains could then be used as tangible evidence supporting the claim that, by working differently and collectively, teachers and leaders in *this* school could experience new levels of success with *these* students, thereby sustaining the upward spiral of technical and cultural development.

Very importantly, consistent implementation was intended to create a social infrastructure to support collaborative, professional practice and learning—an infrastructure missing when instruction is constructed on a teacher-by-teacher basis. This infrastructure would include: shared classroom work and experience; shared vocabulary and language; and shared student work products, assessments, and observations. In a 2003 interview, Success for All cofounder Robert Slavin described a conventional "technology of instruction" as the essential foundation for school-generated learning and innovation:

> Once you begin to have a technology of instruction, it creates the potential for lasting innovations that doesn't exist when instruction is thought of as art. People have a common set of understandings about what they're trying to do and the structures that they're using to get those things done that enables progressive innovation at all levels.

Beginning in the middle of Year 1 and continuing through the third year of implementation (and thereafter, for schools electing to continue beyond the initial, three-year contract), the primary goal became expert use: using Success for All-supplied resources and newly created social infrastructure to work flexibly and adaptively in identifying and addressing the strengths and needs of individual students, teachers, and leaders in specific classrooms, schools, and districts. With developing knowledge and expertise, teachers and leaders would use combinations of information resources and supplemental guidance to guide the careful selection and performance of routines. With this, responsibility for the effectiveness of the program shifted away from knowledge and information embedded in materials and tools and toward teachers and leaders, themselves, as they assumed ownership of the program and agency in its use. In principle, the resulting success would further empower teachers and leaders, inspire new expectations, and heighten their commitment to continuous improvement.

Thus, consistency as the first-order goal was not intended to make instruction "teacher proof" or leadership "leader proof." The intent was to establish a high floor under schoolwide practice, but not a ceiling above it. The expectation that teachers and leaders would do more was inherent in the first principles of the program: the relentless pursuit of academic success for each and every student. The combination of extensive, developmentally structured elaboration and scaffolding was intended to enable the enactment of precisely those principles, by creating infrastructure to support evidence-driven, adaptive practice and evidence-driven, practice-based learning. The groundwork for the progression from novice to expert was to be laid for school leaders by Success for All trainers, in their earliest scaffolding opportunities. School leaders, in turn, would lay the groundwork for teachers. As explained in *The Facilitator's Manual*, the primary print resource for school leaders:

> Success for All's highly elaborated structure sometimes makes teachers uneasy about using their own judgment to solve instructional problems. They often comment that they are afraid to do something that will alter the program's effects. In fact, you really do want them, especially at first, to be conservative about digressing from the prescribed routines. However, at a practical level, it is impossible to provide for every eventuality of implementation, no matter how comprehensive a manual may be. Further, teachers must know from the start that their sound professional judgment is essential for program effectiveness.[22]

Upping the Odds

Again, there was an alchemy to Success for All: an external design for professional practice and professional learning that confounded what many reformers saw as antithetical approaches to improving schools. With the program adoption process as the catalyst, the replication process was intended to set in motion the series of actions and reactions by which lead (an external design for improvement) could be turned into gold (professional practice and learning)—not just in one school, but in many schools.

Understanding and appreciating these actions and reactions required moving away from widely held "either/or," "we/they," "inside/outside" understandings of strategies for school improvement: for example, strategies that either stressed external designs for improving instruction *or* that relied on the professional discretion and initiative of teachers. In Success for All's replication strategy, this was an "and" proposition, in that implementation depended both on heeding external designs for improving instruction *and* on enabling teachers' professional discretion and initiative. Indeed, in Success for All's replication process, the former (heeding external designs for improving instruction) was intended to create social infrastructure supporting the latter (teachers' professional discretion and initiative).

The unusual combination of fidelity and adaptation, in turn, rested on the inter-dependent elaboration and scaffolding of all that was intended for students, teachers, leaders, and schools. As explained by Nancy Madden, cofounder of Success for All, in a 2003 interview:

It's not just producing a book. It's not even just producing training. It's the interaction of the two that makes Success for All so complex. But that's also what we think makes it powerful. We think that's really the key to what we do, having that combination of resources.

Such extensive support may not have been necessary in stronger schools: schools with the capabilities and motivations to incorporate and use raw ideas and rough blueprints to engineer their own improvement. But Success for All was an external program targeting chronically underperforming Title I schools. Absent Success for All's replication process, these schools would have been left to find and/or devise the essential knowledge and resources needed to support a comprehensive, ambitious, and unfamiliar organizational model. They would have then have had to teach themselves how to bring that model to life and to work effectively within it. There was much in the chronic underperformance of these schools to question their capabilities and motivations to fulfill such tall orders. For these schools, the replication process was intended to up the odds of deep, lasting, schoolwide improvement.

COMPOUNDING POTENTIAL, COMPOUNDING RISK

By 1997/1998, Success for All had evolved on two interdependent levels, such that the program included both an organizational blueprint and a strategy for supporting implementation. The two, together, supported developers' ambitions for effecting deep change in large numbers of chronically underperforming schools. Indeed, the strength of the program was in its interdependencies: program adoption, elaboration, and scaffolding—all developmentally sequenced, all working in interaction both to advance a system of interdependent solutions and to manage a system of associated challenges.

Even so, Success for All's strategy for supporting implementation was hardly foolproof. Like a twelve-step recovery program or a good game plan, improving the odds of success did not obviate the risk of failure. Quite the opposite, in fact. If Success for All's strengths were in its interdependent solutions, then so, too, were its weaknesses. Each component of the strategy for supporting implementation introduced new, compounding potential for success. Yet each component also introduced new, compounding challenges that increased the risk of failure, with apples in the eyes of enthusiasts again serving as low-hanging fruit for critics.

Success for All's strategy for supporting implementation again evoked a set of complex interactions among the program, the chronically underperforming schools for which it was designed, and the environments in which the program and schools operated. Even though the strategy included efforts to reduce the demands on the project team as an organization, the result was to make the Success for All project team the fulcrum of the entire enterprise, especially the team members working as trainers. Problems had solutions, solutions had challenges, and, on the ground and in schools, the entire lot was theirs to manage.

Risks in Program Adoption

Potential risks began with the program adoption process. While essential for establishing a firm foundation for effective implementation, the Success for All project team had no formal authority over the process. Consequently, it had no formal control over tasks critical for its success: for example, supervising the voting process to ensure a free and informed choice by teachers (and, with that, their commitment to the program); hiring a knowledgeable and respected reading facilitator (the linchpin of the entire program); and establishing long-term funding. At the time of program adoption, the project team was no more than an external program provider pitching its program to schools. Even though team members provided advice, guidance, and support, the process was to be enacted by chronically underperforming schools, largely on their own and in collaboration with district officials. However, many of these schools were weak in extant capabilities, subject to high rates of staff turnover, and mired in unrest and pressure due to nonachievement. Further, many were located in large, notoriously bureaucratic districts, proximal environments in which constellations of interests constantly wrestled with their own ideas for improving schools: the district office, unions, school board members, parents, community groups, and more.

Under such conditions, there was no shortage of things that could go wrong with the program adoption process, in schools and in their environments. For example, initial investigation of Success for All required that teachers quickly learn about a complex program, the very strengths of which would likely have been beyond the knowledge and experience of teachers in most U.S. schools. The voting process required that schools steeped in internal and external politics conduct a fair vote, with principals (under pressure to improve) and districts (accustomed to top-down control) relinquishing crucial decision-making authority to teachers. Contracting required that districts accustomed to bureaucratic control (and likely pursuing their own improvement agendas) abide by their agreements and not meddle in schools. And selecting a reading facilitator was constrained by a host of issues: for example, the available candidate pool; the willingness of teachers to accept an obviously challenging position (and, due to union contracts, likely without additional compensation); the willingness of teachers to assume leadership positions amidst strong norms of egalitarianism among teachers; and district-level employment policies and hiring practices.

Even if enacted with integrity, there was the real possibility that the program-adoption process would yield unintended consequences. For example, it was entirely possible that a vote intended to unite staff could fragment it. Anything less than a consensus vote for program adoption ensured that there would be a minority of teachers who dissented, with the possibility of up to 20% participating against their wishes. It was possible that, during the contracting process, reallocating funding to Success for All from other programs could anger proponents of those programs and exacerbate political tensions with the school. And it was possible for the leadership selection process to be muddied by the usual micropolitics of schools, ranging from internal competition for the leadership positions (and, thus, winners and losers) to placement of external candidates (and, with that, teachers' distrust of outsiders filling these new and very sensitive leadership positions).

Finally, even if enacted with integrity, the positive effects of program adoption could be quickly and easily undone. For example, depending on the margin of the vote, notoriously high teacher turnover in weak schools could quickly fragment teacher solidarity, even in the short time between taking the vote in the spring and beginning implementation in the fall.[23] Further, using the contracting process to establish stable funding and to secure district support depended on environmental stability, both in external funding sources and in district agendas and leadership. Neither was a given. In that the then-average tenure of urban superintendents (2.5 years) was less than Success for All's three-year implementation window, environmental turbulence was a near certainty.[24] Finally, nothing prevented districts from exploiting newly developing capabilities in Success for All schools for their own purposes: for example, by moving key teachers and leaders out of Success for All schools and into other struggling schools. For that matter, nothing prevented teachers and leaders deciding for themselves to leverage their new capabilities to find new positions in less-challenged schools.

Thus, enacted with integrity, insight, and extensive support from the Success for All project team, the program adoption process could well yield the intended ends: informed, committed, and united instructional staff; capable and committed leadership; stable funding; and freedom from district intervention. At the same time, given challenges in schools and their environments, contrary ends were at least as likely: weakly informed, coerced, and divided instructional staff; weak and contested leadership; uncertain funding; and district-level intrusions and obstacles. A fair bet was a mix of the two, and a problem all its own: each individual school and its proximal environments their own mix of strengths and weaknesses, positioned uniquely and uncertainly to begin implementing Success for All.

Risks in Elaboration

However intended and however strategic, an extensively elaborated program (combined with a developmental sequence that stressed initial consistency and fidelity) introduced additional challenges and risks. At a minimum, extensive elaboration meant that Success for All would place tremendous logistical demands on schools. During their initial training prior to Year 1, leaders in newly adopting schools were trained in strategies for receiving, warehousing, distributing, and maintaining literally a truckful of curriculum materials, manipulatives, manuals, assessments, and other materials. Managing the lot was a tough task in a school of 250 students. It was tougher yet in a school of 500 or 1000 students.

However, these logistical demands paled in comparison to the risk that extensive elaboration could exacerbate interpretation of Success for All either as a bureaucratic, top-down reform or a technocratic, automatically effective solution. With such interpretations came the risk of teachers actively resisting the program and/or complying rotely and mechanistically.

The risk began at the very heart of Success for All's organizational blueprint: in regular classroom instruction. That instruction was elaborated *at all* exacerbated the risk of teachers interpreting Success for All either as bureaucratic and/or technocratic. Attempts to routinize instruction had long been viewed by many teachers as attempts at bureaucratic, top-down control at odds with the very essence of instruction: uncertain, dynamic, moment-to-moment interaction between teachers and students, each with individual learning styles and needs. At the same time, for other teachers (e.g., teachers facing increasing pressure to improve, new and uncertified teachers, and experienced teachers newly jarred out of past practice), a technocratic solution would have been just the ticket: a detailed, comprehensive, research-based, and research-validated program telling them precisely what to do, when to do it, and how to do it. Indeed, in a 2003 interview, Robert Slavin explained that "trying to get the balance where you have teachers not feeling like automatons but where they really are engaged with students" was among the most difficult dynamics to manage in Success for All's replication process.

As problematic as the simple fact of instructional elaboration was the particular way that Success for All's instructional elaboration had evolved over its first ten years of operations: that is, in a way that provided more specific support for novice use than for expert use. Again, Success for All provided detailed, closed routines to support consistent, novice use, going so far as to script presentation for *this* specific letter, sound, or reading strategy, in ways appropriate for students performing at *this* specific reading level, using *this* specific text. At the same time, Success for All provided open routines, information resources, and supplemental guidance to support expert, adaptive use. However, while Success for All provided these resources, it did not provide equally detailed support for using them expertly and adaptively. For example, Success for All did not include decisions trees that structured the use of *this* particular assessment to monitor likely problems associated with *this* particular reading strategy at *this* particular reading level, with *this* array of routines as possible interventions.[25]

Compounding comparatively weak elaboration of expert use was that, in materials available to teachers, the developmental sequence from novice to expert was not explicitly elaborated. The ambitions for expert use were represented in the core principles of the program, as well as in the language of "professionalism" and "adaptation" distributed throughout Success for All's many print resources. Even so, explicit representation of the intended progression from novice to expert use was simply nowhere to be found in the materials available to teachers, nor was the rationale underlying the developmental sequence.

Success for All's extensive elaboration of novice use was perfectly sensible. After all, the adage among researchers was that, in incorporating external programs, schools often did more to change programs than programs did to change schools, as teachers and leaders bent novel ideas around their existing understandings.[26] Under such conditions, spelling out the intended practices in detail and insisting on consistent implementation made great practical sense. Moreover, comparatively weak elaboration of expert use was understandable. Success for All's developers were neither omniscient nor exhaustively resourceful, thus unable to anticipate and address every eventuality of day-to-day practice across every school. Indeed, the program was still in the early stages of its evolution. Project team members were still learning how to expertly use their own creation at the same time that they were learning how to support expert use in large numbers of chronically underperforming schools. Doing so had Success for All team members depending heavily on schools to take ownership of the program, to use it relentlessly and flexibly to ensure effectiveness in local contexts, and to learn from their experiences.

Yet even though enabling ownership, agency, and adaptation were among the most central objectives of Success for All, careful attention to novice use absent commensurate attention to expert use played directly to interpretations of the program as either bureaucratic or technocratic: for example, by providing extensive support for tasky, day-to-day work, absent commensurate support for the more demanding and rewarding work of diagnosing and responding to the needs of individual students. Further, to *not* elaborate expert instructional practice in great detail and to *not* explain the developmental sequence was to not elaborate two of the most important, unfamiliar, and subtle dimensions of the program. The result was to deny teachers essential guidance for shaping their interpretation of the program as a resource for professional practice and learning—and, with that, failing to stem the possibility of teachers interpreting Success for All as bureaucratic and/or technocratic.

Thus, uncertainty that followed from the program-adoption process was compounded by uncertainty that followed from elaboration. Skeptical teachers inclined towards bureaucratic interpretations encountered resources that did much to reinforce (and little to challenge) precisely those interpretations. At the same time, earnest teachers inclined towards technocratic interpretations lacked resources for pushing their understandings and capabilities further. The result was great risk of rote, mechanistic implementation among both skeptical and earnest teachers.

Risks in Scaffolding

Circa 1997/1998, the comparatively weak elaboration of expert use of Success for All created dependence within the strategy for supporting implementation: specifically, on scaffolding as the primary context for developing knowledge of how to use available routines, information resources, and supplemental guidance to monitor and to address school-specific needs. Yet scaffolding also brought with it new challenges and risks. Scaffolding pressed teachers, leaders, and Success for All trainers into new, collaborative relationships, and it challenged them with an aggressive schedule: immediate implementation on Day 1 of Year 1; mastery of novice, consistent use by the end of Year 1; a quick transition to expert, adaptive use in Years 2 and 3; all amidst annual personnel turnover that likely guaranteed that schools would always be a mix of novice and expert users.

Much hinged on developing the capabilities of school leaders to function as on-site change agents, including their capabilities to scaffold teachers. However, the evolution of the leadership component of the program interacted with enduring weaknesses in the conventional preparation and experiences of school leaders to exacerbate the potential for adverse interpretations and misuse of the program.

Historically, Success for All's leadership component emerged last among the four primary program components (i.e., instructional organization, curriculum and instruction, supplemental services, and leadership). In the early and mid-1990s, Success for All's increasing scale of operations reduced the amount of time that project team members could devote to on-site assistance in any particular school, thus creating the need to develop school leaders as the on-site change agents responsible for (among other things) scaffolding the work of instruction. This was no small matter, for the simple reason that instructional leadership of the type required by Success for All was likely beyond the professional preparation and experience of most school leaders of the day.

Despite being the linchpin of the program, there were problems and shortcomings in the leadership component of the program. Due to its later emergence, the design of (and support for) the leadership component lagged that of the other three program components, with no one project team member as closely tied to its development as Nancy Madden and Barbara Haxby were tied to the development of curriculum and instruction, tutoring, and family support. Regarding elaboration, there was nothing like a "daily plan" for leadership that was anywhere close to teachers' lesson plans in its formalization and integration of routines. Instead, during the first decade of operations, formal elaboration of the leadership component was long on information resources: for example, quarterly assessments, forms for recording and exchanging information with teachers, and forms for gathering schoolwide achievement data. It was also long on supplemental guidance: for example, an 11-chapter volume detailing the program as a whole, each of the program components, and the functional responsibilities of the leadership team.

What the leadership component lacked was codified procedures and protocols supporting the day-to-day work of school leaders. The lack of formalized routines touched on every dimension of leadership practice. For example, the leadership component lacked routines to structure the analysis of student reading performance, either using "internal" data (e.g., quarterly summaries of student achievement) or "external" data (e.g., state assessment results). While the family support component included highly developed routines for coordinating with family and community environments, the leadership component lacked routines for coordinating with dynamic district and state standards and assessments. In contrast to "Getting Along Together" (the social-problem-solving curriculum for students), the leadership component lacked routines and guidance for resolving social problems among staff members that were likely to arise when implementing Success for All. And despite the centrality and novelty of scaffolding teachers in the use of Success for All, the leadership component did not include anything like a readily usable "curriculum for teacher learning" to support leaders in such work.

In cases where the leadership component *did* include executable routines, the routines focused primarily on the novice practice of both leaders and teachers: for example, leaders faithfully using a detailed classroom observation protocol to evaluate the consistent use of the program by teachers. The routines did not focus on the expert practice of leaders and teachers: for example, collaborative analysis and planning using student achievement data.

Attention to the novice practices of teachers and leaders was responsive to the steep challenge of quickly replicating a complex organizational model and achieving a base level of operations. However, with novice leadership practice focused squarely on ensuring consistency of implementation by teachers, there was great risk that school leaders could either inadvertently or intentionally misuse Success for All-provided resources as a sort of bureaucratic "personnel management system" to keep close tabs on teachers (rather than as resources for the formative evaluation of teachers). That, in turn, risked reinforcing the bureaucratic and/or technocratic interpretations of teachers.

The weak elaboration of leadership (and the risks that arose from weak elaboration) placed great demands on Success for All trainers to scaffold school leaders in their new roles, especially in order to convey tacit knowledge, capabilities, and practices through conversation, modeling, and mentoring. Yet, in its first decade of operations, there were shortcomings in the scaffolding of school leaders, as well. Beyond initial training prior to Year 1 implementation, Success for All provided no consistent, structured curriculum of direct instruction for school leaders. Mindful of leaders' variable learning needs and of their status as the paying customers, Success for All allowed leaders to construct their own curriculum from a menu of sessions at the annual Experienced Sites Conference, guided only by suggestions from project team members. A real risk was that leaders would string together a hodge-podge of conference sessions rather than a coherent curriculum supporting expert use.

The shortcomings of scaffolding went beyond direct instruction. Practice-based learning depended heavily on school leaders exploiting collegial learning opportunities in Success for All's developing professional network. However, this was an uncommon sort of learning for school leaders accustomed to working in isolation, in their own, geographically separated schools. Further, collegial leadership among leaders was not formally structured, depended very much on personal initiative, and assumed the existence of able and proximal schools willing to provide assistance. Finally, while implementation visits created essential opportunities for project team members to mentor school leaders, these visits declined in frequency and number over Years 2 and 3 of implementation, precisely when schools would be poised for the transition to weakly elaborated, expert use.

Again, just as no program could be exhaustively elaborated, neither could it be exhaustively scaffolded. The need for unanticipated and incidental learning was inevitable. Yet the specific *way* that Success for All's leadership component was partially elaborated and scaffolded was particularly problematic. The leadership component provided the least-specific support for work that: (a) was central to successful implementation; but (b) was likely beyond the professional preparation and experience of many school leaders. This work included analyzing data, coordinating academic programs with policy environments, developing an improvement-oriented culture, and developing teachers' professional knowledge. With available support focused primarily on novice practice, the risk was that weak support for school leadership would interact with risks in program adoption and instructional elaboration to heighten the potential for bureaucratic and/or technocratic interpretations among teachers. From that followed increased risk of active resistance and/or rote use.

Demands on the Organization

Thus, as Success for All's strategy for supporting implementation evolved over its first ten years of operations, formal elaboration and scaffolding were highly developed to support novice, consistent, and rapid replication of the organizational model and its base-level practices across large numbers of schools. At the same time, the strategy was comparatively weakly developed to support expert, locally responsive, adaptive use.

One could interpret this state of affairs (correctly) as a problem: that developers had yet to formalize artifacts and training opportunities to support high levels of use in chronically underperforming schools. One could interpret it (correctly) as evidence of the complexity and difficulty of bringing a complex, external design into schools and making it operational: that is, the challenge of simply arresting and reversing the downward spiral of expectations and capabilities, never mind the subsequent challenge of enabling ownership and agency. One could interpret it (correctly) as symptomatic of broader weaknesses in the field of education at that time: that both knowledge and technologies were weakly developed to support the sort of professional practice and learning intended by Success for All developers. And one could interpret it (correctly) as a harbinger of things to come. In fact, Success for All developers would soon come to recognize shortcomings in the formal elaboration and scaffolding of expert use and commence a program-wide development effort in response.

Regardless of the interpretation, Success for All's strategy for supporting implementation had evolved over its first decade both to increase the odds of success *and* to increase the risk of failure. Enacting the program-adoption process with insight and integrity could have reduced such risks by using a free and informed vote to ensure committed and engaged teachers. These risks could be further reduced by the selection of a knowledgeable, experienced, and respected reading facilitator, one with capabilities to see and exploit the potential in the program and to see, manage, and compensate for its shortcomings. The combination— committed teachers and knowledgeable leaders—would have been better yet. But, again, a favorable combination was just as possible as an unfavorable combination.

Responsibility for capitalizing on the odds of success and managing the risks of failure ultimately placed tremendous demands on the Success for All project team as an organization, in that it required capabilities far beyond simply designing an organizational blueprint. For example, it required capabilities to monitor multiple environments (research, policy, and commercial) to discern implications and opportunities for the program. It required capabilities to design, print, warehouse, and distribute an extensive array of material resources. It required capabilities to develop and coordinate relationships and activities within Success for All's professional network. It required capabilities to study school-level implementation and effectiveness, and to feed the findings back through the entire enterprise. And it required executive-level capabilities to manage and sustain such a complex operation in the new, dynamic, niche market of comprehensive school reform. Ironically, these increased demands on functional capabilities came despite intentional efforts to *reduce* demands on the organization: for example, by using readily reproduced artifacts to transfer knowledge into weak schools, by developing leaders as on-site change agents, and by creating potential for school-to-school support in Success for All's professional network.

Above all else, the strategy for supporting implementation required a highly capable group of Success for All team members to serve as trainers in schools. Success for All trainers were the front line managers of the program: the "teachers" in Success for All's instructionally driven support strategy, and the social conduit that linked the schools that comprised the professional network. It was trainers' responsibility to collaborate with schools to exploit the potential of the program while, at the same time, managing interdependent challenges, problems, and risks.

This was novel and knowledge-intensive work: exactly the sort widely expected of (but rarely provided by) state, local, and other governmental education agencies. This was hard work: living on the road; working across multiple schools, districts, and sometimes states; coordinating across training teams to ensure consistent support within and between schools; all within an implementation window that was shrinking exactly as teachers and leaders were advancing to the most complex, novel, and weakly elaborated use of program. Perhaps most challenging, trainers had to do all such work absent formal authority. Their only authority derived from their capacity to build trustful, productive relationships with teachers and leaders, at the same time that their very status as external experts risked effecting interpretations of Success for All as bureaucratic and/or technocratic (and, with that, effecting either active resistance and/or rote implementation).

The challenges of effecting deep change in large numbers of chronically under-performing schools could not be "designed away"—not with a complex design for comprehensive school reform, not with a complex strategy for supporting implementation, and likely not with additional layers of design. At the same time that successive layers of design increased potential for deep change, they also affected a set of accumulating and interacting challenges, problems, and risks.

This could not be a matter of infinite regress. The buck had to stop somewhere. And, in Success for All, the buck stopped at the Success for All trainers.

PROGRAM AS CLASSROOM

Thus, the Success for All project team had taken a consistent approach to the twin tasks of designing and supporting the program—an approach that appeared both rational and reasonable. Project team members carefully studied the problems to be solved in schools, as well as the problems of solving them via an externally developed design for improvement. As they did, they constructed a system of interdependent solutions: a multicomponent blueprint for comprehensive school reform, coordinated with a multicomponent strategy for supporting implementation. Anchored in research and experience, the approach supported the project team's goals for improving student achievement. Anchored heavily in reproducible materials, the development of local leadership capacity, and collaborative relations among schools, the approach supported the project team's aspirations for large-scale operations.

With that, Success for All looked to be many things, all at once. Viewed from one perspective, Success for All continued to resemble an evangelical crusade: recruiting the troubled, showing them a new way, and promising to walk that new road with them. Viewed from another perspective, Success for All continued to resemble a player in the new, high-stakes game of comprehensive school reform, placing layers of carefully calculated bets that combined to increase the odds of success.

Yet, viewed from the perspective of its support for implementation, Success for All assumed a still-different character: appropriately, that of a classroom. Indeed, in many ways, Success for All *was* a classroom: a context carefully designed as a venue for learning. But the learning that it occasioned was not only that of at-risk students. It was also that of teachers and leaders. In the metaphorical classroom that was Success for All, teachers and leaders, themselves, became students. As students, teachers and leaders were challenged with rigorous (and possibly perplexing) academic content: an externally developed program likely beyond (if not at odds with) their knowledge and experience, and rife with critical holes and disconnects. That they would even be in the position of needing Success for All suggests that these teachers and leaders were, themselves, at-risk learners, with the chronic underperformance of their schools standing as evidence of the difficulty that they had working together to incorporate and effectively use new technologies, knowledge, and capabilities. The teacher in this scenario, finally, is the

Success for All trainer, responsible for bucking the histories of these at-risk learners and ensuring their success.

Viewing Success for All as a classroom opens up new perspective on the ways in which otherwise-static designs and supports stood to shape dynamic interactions among actual people. For even with a detailed organizational blueprint and an extensive array of supports, the process of turning chronically underperforming schools into centers of professional practice and learning depended on the central human and social resources in all instructional endeavors: the will and skill of "students" (i.e., teachers and leaders in chronically underperforming schools); the knowledge and expertise of "teachers" (i.e., Success for All trainers); the relationships between the two; and their joint capacity to use available resources to develop new knowledge, skills, beliefs, and norms.

Viewing the program as a classroom places a particularly keen focus on Success for All trainers as teachers. Trainers were held to the same professional standards as the teachers and leaders that they served: responsible for preventing problems of implementation from arising in the first place; intervening early and aggressively at the first sign of problems; and working relentlessly to ensure success. In the context of direct instruction and implementation visits, trainers put a human face on the program. No matter the research, the overview volumes, and the extensive array of material resources, it was Success for All trainers who represented and animated the core ideas, principles, structures, and practices of the program. It was they who identified and attended to the learning needs of individual teachers and leaders. It was they who communicated and supported knowledge of novice and expert use. And it was they who modeled and reinforced essential norms and beliefs. Indeed, the Success for All enterprise turned on trainers' leveraging uncommon knowledge and expertise in very challenging instructional contexts.

Circa 1997/1998, the Success for All project team again pointed to research for evidence that some teachers, leaders, and trainers were successfully enacting Success for All's strategy for supporting implementation and, with that, successfully replicating the form, function, and effectiveness of Success for All's design for comprehensive school reform. A series of studies of Success for All convinced project team members that success rested on two key points: comprehensiveness and quality.[27] Regarding comprehensiveness, an internal study compared the effects of different configurations of Success for All program components on student achievement in 46 Success for All schools and 18 comparison schools in the Houston (Texas) Independent School District.[28] Findings suggested that the comprehensive implementation of the full program (as opposed to subsets of components) was critical for program effectiveness, especially in schools with larger populations of at-risk students. Regarding quality, a summary of research by project team members and affiliated researchers at the University of Memphis argued that success improving student achievement depended on the quality of program implementation as reported by Success for All trainers.[29]

Put plainly, the claim was this: When Success for All was implemented as designed and with quality, students succeeded. When it wasn't, they didn't.

And over Success for All's first decade, a small body of research that was emerging beyond the program suggested that critical to achieving high-quality implementation of an ambitious, externally developed improvement program was to do exactly as the Success for All project team had: match detailed guidance for practice with context-sensitive, practice-based professional development.[30]

Evidence and understanding of the possibility of success were not only emerging in formal research. Evidence and understanding were also emerging in the day-to-day experiences of those using the program. In the mid-1990s, when her school first began implementing Success for All, one veteran Title I reading specialist was named the reading facilitator of the school. Motivated in part by her positive experiences using the program, this reading facilitator eventually joined the Success for All project team, and she assumed responsibilities for providing assistance both to schools and to Success for All trainers.

In a 2003 interview, this reading facilitator-turned-Success for All trainer reflected on her experiences with initial training and implementation. Despite weaknesses in the elaboration and scaffolding of the leadership component of Success for All, she described herself as collaborating with her principal to quickly advance to expert use of the program, including analyzing evidence of student achievement, coordinating services to students, adding value to the program by drawing on their own knowledge, and adapting the program while still maintaining its integrity.

She attributed her shared success with her principal to a set of conditions that interacted in positive, mutually reinforcing ways to determine how they understood and used the program: for example, the unique knowledge, beliefs, and motivations that she and her principal brought to the program; their professional relationship; the resources made available to them by the program; environmental incentives to improve; and their collaboration with the early members of the Success for All project team. She recalled:

> I first came to New Sites Conference with my principal, who was an absolutely driven "type A" personality. We roomed together, because we were saving money. I won't go into the background about my school, but our school needed this program. She was a fairly new principal in that school, and we'd had like ten of them in the previous ten years. That was my first experience with Success for All, as a facilitator in the school.
>
> And we came to the conference. In those days, they didn't worry about people's physical stamina. They ran from early in the morning until 8:00 o'clock or 9:00 o'clock at night. We were just sponges, soaking it up. And when we weren't in the trainings, we were planning together how we were going to do this in our school, and what all the implications were of what we had heard.
>
> And I remember the single thing that most stressed her out was the understanding that results were what mattered, and that the data had to be managed. Now, she had already been working from her first year on getting all teachers to do more assessment, whether it was formal or informal,

a checklist or whatever, and to be more cognizant of what their students' skills really were—you know, just as good, diagnostic teaching. And I was the reading specialist in the Title I position, and we transferred over to Success for All. But she understood that this was a more high stakes kind of thing. It was a different approach to making sure the curriculum worked. Not that you have a testing piece for accountability and then a curriculum piece for what you're going to teach, but that they had to be integrated.

And that came from some of the principal sessions with Nancy Madden. And I was getting information from my facilitator trainings about how important the accuracy of the data was. That and family support were the things that most stressed her, because she understood about Success for All truly being an integrated program.

As a facilitator, from the very first day, I kept my data. I created my own database. It was extensive. Every quarter, after assessments, I would present reports to the teachers with charts and graphs. And I mean, this was in the mid-1990s. Some of that was just our own driven natures. It seemed like a natural extension for us of what the overriding directions were for how you really make this work and how you make sure you're tracking your progress.

But we didn't come up with all of that on our own. I know that the people who came and worked with us, some of the original Success for All trainers, these people came to our district, and they looked at our data with us. They looked at our assessment summary forms. They looked at our grade summary forms. . . .

I think, fairly early on, I understood that there were lots of ways to flex and be true to the intent of what the process was.

At the same time, this reading facilitator-turned-Success for All trainer recognized that the experience of program implementation varied among Success for All schools, even within her own district. She recalled that, despite having the same program resources, the same Success for All trainers, and the same district environment, differences in schools and in the people in them led to differences in how they apprehended, understood, and used Success for All. One critical difference was in understandings about the possibility of using Success for All flexibly while still being true to its intent. She explained: "I accept that not every school did that. . . I was one of four facilitators in my community, and I know that all four of us did not understand that equally well. And we had the same trainers, but we didn't have the same kinds of principals, and we didn't have the same kinds of teachers. We were four different people."

There is much to suggest that such differences in understanding and implementation where not unique to the four schools in that one, particular district. Again, for Success for All, claims of success accumulated alongside staunch criticism— not only from researchers and others in academia but, also, from some of the very teachers that Success for All aimed to serve. And the criticism of these teachers was every bit as legitimate as the accolades of others.

Perhaps the most public of the criticism from Success for All teachers came from Georgia Hedrick, a first grade teacher in a Nevada school with over 30 years of classroom experience. Leveraging the newly emerging power of the Internet, Hedrick collaborated with another Success for All teacher in 1998 to launch an on-line discussion forum called "alt-sfa." The discussion forum quickly became a venue in which Hedrick, her collaborator, and other Success for All teachers across the country exchanged information and ideas that were largely (and sharply) critical of the program, thereby giving teachers a public voice in the Success for All debate.[31] As reported by Hedrick, alt-sfa drew enough attention in cyber space to warrant contact from Robert Slavin (Success for All's cofounder) and John Hollifield (Associate Director of the Center for the Social Organization of Schools at Johns Hopkins University).

In 2000, Hedrick published an article in the *Teachers.net Gazette*, an online newsletter, in which she reflected on her experiences as a Success for All teacher in the mid- through late 1990s. This was a period roughly concurrent with the experiences of our reading facilitator-turned-Success for All trainer.

Hedrick's account suggested that her experiences with Success for All were similarly wrapped up in a set of interacting conditions: for example, her personal knowledge, beliefs, and motivations; the conditions within her school; the resources made available to her by the program; environmental pressure to improve; and the Success for All project team. Yet for Hedrick, these conditions did not interact in positive, mutually reinforcing ways. Rather, they interacted in negative, mutually destructive ways, to the point that they evoked a crisis of conscience as a professional educator.

Where our reading facilitator-turned-Success for All trainer recalled understanding and using Success for All as a resource for professional practice and learning, Hedrick wrote that she experienced Success for All's organizational design and its associated supports for implementation as directly challenging her personal philosophy, creativity, and expertise as a professional educator. That, in turn, inhibited her potential to provide her students the rich learning opportunities she felt they deserved. In her article, Hedrick recounted her early experiences with Success for All, in training sessions and in the classroom:

> I was 58 when this program came into my face. I felt like this was a joke to laugh at. Then, I realized they were serious.
>
> I thought: do the people, who built this, think that teachers are idiots? Any fool knows certain basics, like: you have to know sounds, you have to recognize letters, you have to connect these things together, you do it with pictures that make you say words, and you have to recognize what a word is.
>
> Why is this (Success for All trainer) acting as if some new element has just been discovered? Why does she act as if a miracle has just happened? A program is nothing; a child is everything. To discover the process by which a child learns is the thrill of teaching. Every child has a different process, even if ever so slightly, to learn. The fun of teaching is the discovery and the development of what is learned in this discovery.

But here is a program that is: "one size fits all." How insulting. When or if a mom put the same size clothing on all her children, some will feel bad because such clothing will not fit.

The child is everything in this teaching and learning process. The order in which you do things depends entirely on each and every child.

I thought: surely, all the teachers will laugh and guffaw at such idiocy as in this program.

When we went back to school, only one or two teachers talked badly about the program. The rest were silent. It was as if children didn't matter in this deal, just looking good, pleasing the administration mattered. Didn't they see what I saw? Was I really this alone?

There was so much talent at this school. Instead of sharing the talent, all we did was listen to some outsider telling us how to be the same way. Children were the very last consideration in this matter.

A classroom has its own culture. Now the culture and the community would be broken apart. We would be invaded by outsiders telling us exactly how to teach, as if we were first year teachers. This was a total violation of my philosophy and no one cared. No one asked. We were told to do this. No amount of outside research would change this. . . .

I couldn't do the program, lockstep. It invaded my world of creativity. It told me ways to talk that were unnatural to me. I had my puppets. I had my methods. I am able to do this on my own. . . .

I COULD NOT TEACH SFA THE WAY IT WAS WRITTEN TO BE TAUGHT. It violated my philosophy of teaching to the core.[32]

As it emerged and evolved over its first decade, that was the great puzzle of Success for All: that it could be apprehended, interpreted, and used in such completely different ways by different individuals and groups.[33] These differences held for elite researchers in the academy. These differences also held for people on the ground in schools. Success for All enabled success among some teachers, leaders, and trainers. Success for All also evoked steep criticism and incited stiff opposition among others. Further complicating the puzzle was that the explanations for how some were succeeding and why others were struggling appeared to be one in the same: Whether positive or negative, the apprehension, interpretation, and use of Success for All was bound up in complex interactions among schools (and the people in them), the program, environments, and the Success for All project team.

Sorting out the first-decade puzzle of Success for All requires pushing deeper into the dynamics of these interactions. Moreover, shifting the perspective to program-as-classroom suggests a possible, new perspective on these dynamics. Rather than asking "how?" or "why?," one drawn to an instructionally focused interpretation of Success for All might ask, simply: Who? Who were the teachers, leaders, and trainers for whom schools, the program, environments, and the organization were interacting in positive, mutually reinforcing ways? Who were those for whom these same conditions were interacting in negative, mutually destructive ways?

Probing these questions requires exploring the work of scaling up Success for All. For it was through the work of scaling up that the otherwise-arid landscape of designs and supports was populated with actual people. Indeed, probing these questions requires exploring the work of recruiting increasing numbers of teachers and leaders in schools distributed across increasing numbers of districts and states. It requires exploring the work of simultaneously recruiting proportional numbers of trainers to serve those teachers and leaders. And it requires exploring the work of creating systems to support the development and practice of trainers, in order to ensure their success as the "teachers" of at-risk "students."

Designing, supporting, and scaling up were not tasks that the project team performed serially, one after the other: designing the program; then constructing a system of supports; and, then, recruiting schools to use the program. Rather, these were tasks that the project team performed concurrently, in interaction, over Success for All's first decade of operations, all while continuously improving and adapting the program. And, as they did, the installed base of schools, the program, their environments, and the project team co-evolved in ways that, in the eyes of team members, helped to explain both possibilities and problems in the implementation and effectiveness of Success for All.

Notes

1. Slavin, Madden, Dolan, and Wasik (1996:167).
2. On the importance of program adoption to implementing comprehensive school reform programs, see: Bodilly (1998); Datnow (2000); Datnow and Stringfield (2000).
3. Slavin and Madden (1996; 1999b).
4. Slavin, Madden, Dolan, and Wasik (1996).
5. Slavin, Madden, Dolan, and Wasik (1996:xi-xii).
6. Slavin, Madden, Dolan, and Wasik (1996:193).
7. Herdman (2002).
8. For example, see: Cohen and Spillane (1991); Hess (1999).
9. Slavin and Madden (1999b:19).
10. See, for example: Lortie (1975:1-24), Larson (1977:178-207), Katz (1992); and Cohen (1985).
11. For then-current critiques on the practice and knowledge of school leadership from within the field of educational administration, see: Griffiths (1979); Greenfield (1986); Evers and Lakomski (1991); Donmoyer, Imber, and Scheurich (1995); Erickson (1979); Bridges (1982); Hoy (1982); Murphy (1988); and Sergiovanni (1992).
12. Slavin, Madden, Dolan, and Wasik (1996:170).
13. For more on elaboration, see Cohen and Ball (2007:24-26). While Cohen and Ball frame the concept primarily as adding detail and specificity to raw ideas, the concept as used here focuses on embedding knowledge in artifacts that can be easily transported without distorting the knowledge thus embedded. This usage is akin to Latour's (1986) notion "immutable mobiles." Success for All developers describe the work of producing these artifacts using such terms as "formalizing," "designing,"

"writing," and "embedding." All refer to the work of creating specific tools, manuals, videos, and other resources that function to codify, retain, and transfer the knowledge base of the program.

14. Materials, tools, and other resources could be selected and combined in different ways to meet differing needs of schools. For example, schools were given a choice among quarterly assessments for use in grades 2–6, depending on their available resources and their needs: a set of commercial, norm-referenced assessments; a Success for All-produced assessment; or criterion-referenced assessments provided with their commercial reading curriculum. As another example, in cases where schools were using district-mandated reading curricula, schools were able to select Reading Wings materials for grades 2–6 that were designed to be used in interaction with commercially published reading series and literature anthologies.

15. For more on routines as used here, see Feldman and Pentland (2003:96) and Nelson and Winter (1982:14–19).

16. See Slavin, Madden, Dolan, and Wasik (1996) for samples of curriculum materials in Reading Roots and Reading Wings as they had evolved over Success for All's first decade of operations.

17. For more on scaffolding, see: Palincsar (1986:123); Palincsar (1998); and Cohen and Ball (2007:24–27). Metaphorically, consider scaffolding as surrounding teachers and leaders with a set of intentionally structured learning opportunities, all under the guidance of Success for All trainers. Initially, this "scaffolding" supports teachers and leaders in making substantive changes in their day-to-day work. Over time, these Success for All-supported learning opportunities are removed, such that teachers and leaders gradually assume fuller responsibility for their own professional learning opportunities.

18. In May of 2000, citing Joyce and Showers (1995) and Calderon (1984), initial training for school leaders conducted in San Diego, CA included extensive discussion of research showing the limited effects of "pull out" professional development and, consequently, the need for "sustained, on-going professional development" in the context of practice.

19. Livingston, Cummings, and Madden (1996, "Role," pp. 6–7).

20. Slavin and Madden (1999b:8).

21. Beginning in 1999/2000, SFAF would eventually elaborate an eight-stage "Levels of Use" framework that made finer-grained distinctions between levels of implementation. See Chapter 4, "Continuously Improving." However, this framework did not emerge until Success for All's second decade of operations.

22. Livingston, Cummings, and Madden (1996, "Monitoring Implementation," p. 9).

23. For example, Guin (2004) reported that schools with majority populations of minority students experienced teacher turnover at twice the rate of other schools.

24. In 2003, the Council of Great City Schools (2003) reported the average tenure of GCS superintendents at 2.75 years, an increase from 2.5 years in 2001.

25. This lack of specificity was most glaring and most precipitous in Reading Wings. Not only were teachers called on either to devise or construct all but three 55-minute blocks of instruction in each five-day unit, disciplinary knowledge supporting reading comprehension instruction (the primary focus of Reading Wings) was, at that time, much more weakly developed than early reading acquisition (and likely more weakly developed yet among teachers in chronically underperforming schools).

26. For example, see Cohen and Barnes (1993) and Spillane (2004).

27. See: Nunnery, Ross, Smith, Slavin, Hunter, and Stubbs (1996); Nunnery, Slavin, Madden, Ross, Smith, Hunter, and Stubbs (1997); and Ross, Smith, Slavin, and Madden (1997).
28. See Nunnery, Slavin, Madden, Ross, Smith, Hunter, and Stubbs (1997).
29. See Ross, Smith, Slavin, and Madden (1997).
30. For research on the importance of design specificity and/or context-specific professional development for effective implementation, see: Firestone and Corbett (1988); Bodilly (1996, 1998); and Nunnery (1998). Further additional research would emerge early in Success for All's second decade, both in education (e.g., Desimone, 2002) and in broader research on organizational replication (e.g., Winter and Szulanski, 2001; Szulanski, Winter, Cappetta, and Van den Bulte, 2002).
31. See Hedrick (2000).
32. See Hedrick (2000). Grammar and emphases are as in the original text.
33. For more on the matter of interpretation, see Chapter 1, in the discussion of external programs within the section titled "Challenges, Redefined."

3

Scaling Up

Demonstrating that an effective program can be replicated successfully removes one more excuse for the continuing low achievement of disadvantaged children. When Ronald Edmonds stated that we can successfully teach all children "whenever and wherever we choose," he may indeed have been right in principle. However, practical demonstrations of this principle are still essential. To ensure the success of disadvantaged students, we must have the political commitment to do so, along with the funds and policies to back up the commitment. We must also have methods known to be effective in their original sites and replicable and effective in other sites.

Success for All requires a serious commitment to restructure elementary schools and to reconfigure the uses of Chapter 1, special education, and other funds to emphasize prevention and early intervention rather than remediation. It also requires a vote of at least 80% of teachers in favor of implementing the program. However, when a school makes such a commitment, it can succeed. The evidence summarized in this article offers practical proof that, "whenever and wherever we choose," we can successfully teach all children.

ROBERT SLAVIN, NANCY MADDEN, LAWRENCE DOLAN, BARBARA WASIK, STEPHEN ROSS, AND LANA SMITH, 1994[1]

Understanding the emergence and evolution of Success for All over its first decade (along with variability in interpretations, implementation, and effectiveness) requires exploring how the project team approached the work of scaling up: that is, of enlisting schools in the program and expanding the organization to support them. Over its history, the work of scaling up ran concurrently with the work of designing the organizational blueprint and devising supports for implementation.

By the standards of its approach to the work of designing and supporting, the project team's approach to the work of scaling up was straightforward: "whenever and wherever we choose." If schools wanted in, the project team would take them. The strategy was anchored in a combination of faith, confidence, and capabilities: faith that any school with a critical mass of willing and committed staff could be improved; confidence that the Success for All program could be used effectively in those schools; and the capabilities of project team members to serve as "teachers" for at-risk "students"—that is, for teachers and leaders in chronically under-performing schools.

Yet as Success for All closed its first decade and opened its second, this combination of faith, confidence, and capabilities would be tested. A rapidly growing base of schools, a rapidly growing organization, a still-developing program, and broader environments combined to effect a perfect storm. This was a storm in which steep, interdependent risks in the program become large-scale realities: large numbers of schools interpreting Success for All as either technocratic or bureaucratic; large numbers of schools locked into patterns of rote, mechanical implementation; far fewer schools engaged in expert, adaptive use; and what Success for All project members described as a "plateau effect" on achievement below their ambitious goals for all students. And at the very root of these problems was the Success for All organization, itself: in particular, its own trainers, and the systems supporting their work and professional development.

EMERGENCE AND CO-EVOLUTION

Exploring the work of scaling up Success for All requires delving more deeply into how the installed base of schools, the program, broader environments, and the organization emerged and co-evolved between SY 1987/88 and SY 1997/98, Success for All's first ten years of operations. This was a period in which Success for All's comprehensive design and its associated supports first emerged and matured, both as a system of solutions and as a system of challenges. Chief among the challenges were a set of signature vulnerabilities: comparatively strong support for novice, consistent use by teachers and leaders; comparatively weak support for expert, adaptive use; great risk of interpreting the program as bureaucratic and/or technocratic; and great risk of either rote, mechanistic implementation and/or out-and-out resistance. A deeper challenge, though, was this: Rather than effectively managing these vulnerabilities, Success for All's training organization emerged and co-evolved in ways that risked exacerbating them.

Early Adopters, Permissive Environments, and Social Organization

The first half of Success for All's first decade (the period from SY 1987/1988 to SY 1991/1992) was one in which support for both comprehensive school reform and standards-based reform first began to emerge in federal and state policy environments. This period also marked the first phase in Success for All's scale-up. During this period, Success for All's base of schools expanded from a single school in Baltimore to a network of 30 early-adopting elementary schools scattered throughout the country. This was a network comparable in size to a mid-sized school district, with roughly the same number of elementary schools as in the New Haven (Connecticut) Public Schools and more than the total number of schools in the Trenton (New Jersey) Public Schools.

From the beginning, Success for All targeted chronically underperforming Title I schools. While long recognized as tough contexts for reform, project team members recalled a critical mass of early adopting schools as atypical in their enthusiasm for external support, their initial capabilities, and their freedom from environmental turbulence. While far from universally strong, they recalled these schools as already having key characteristics of effective schools, including a strong sense of mission, a climate conducive to learning, and (sometimes) newly appointed principals hand-picked to lead improvement efforts. Indeed, these schools were among the first in the nation feeling the pressure for accountability, in states that were leading the charge. Freed by the "basic bargain" of accountability in exchange for autonomy, they were also among the first in the nation to forego schoolwide improvement as a "do-it-yourself" project and to enlist willingly in externally developed comprehensive school reform programs. Interviewed in 2003, an SFAF manager who had been a principal of an early Success for All school recalled:

> Back in the day, the type of principals that were picking up Success for All were people that were true leaders, because you had to go out you had to find it, you had to fight for it, you had to put it in your school. There was a day when it was truly voluntary, and so it attracted, I think, a certain kind of principal. I don't know how you want to describe it. Someone who was a little more of a maverick. The classic "early adopter". The heat seekers. The heat seekers is probably the best way to describe them. And again, I always remember, as a principal, one of the things they wanted you to do as a principal is put on your marquis, "We are a Success for All School." And I never wanted to do that as a principal, because I felt, no, we are a school in our own entity, and we use the Success for All program. So, to me, it was always the tool to accomplish what we already wanted to accomplish, because we were clear on what goals we wanted to accomplish, we were clear on the student outcomes that we wanted to accomplish, and we were looking for strategies and a methodology to make that happen.

At the very outset, these schools were served by the original Success for All project team, which operated out of the Center for the Social Organization of Schools at Johns Hopkins University. The team was composed of researchers, developers, and instructors who had participated in the research and development underlying Success for All, including developing and fielding the individual program components that would eventually be integrated into the complete, comprehensive program. Well represented in the team were knowledge and experience in classroom teaching, cooperative learning, reading instruction, "diagnostic instruction," clinical social work, and teacher education, along with knowledge and experience working as external trainers to support schools.

This was not a big organization. Memories put the number of initial team members at less than ten. Nor was it a rigid, hierarchical, formal organization. Rather, from the outset, the project team was much more a small, tightly knit social network: a collection of unusually knowledgeable and experienced colleagues working and learning within a research and development center in a research university, in close collaboration with the schools they were serving. The arrangement closely resembled what social learning theorist Etienne Wenger described as a "community of practice":

> Communities of practice are formed by people who engage in a process of collective learning in a shared domain of human endeavor: a tribe learning to survive, a band of artists seeking new forms of expression, a group of engineers working on similar problems, a clique of pupils defining their identity in the school, a network of surgeons exploring novel techniques, a gathering of first-time managers helping each other cope. In a nutshell: Communities of practice are groups of people who share a concern or a passion for something they do and learn how to do it better as they interact regularly.[2]

On the initial project team, there were no firm lines between "developers" and "trainers." Rather, trainers also had significant program development responsibilities, and program developers also had significant training responsibilities. The relationships, the work, and the learning were not formally structured. With everybody working in Baltimore, team members convened frequently to discuss their work, to solve problems, and to evaluate the use of Success for All in actual schools. Key social resources brought structure and order to the community and its work: dense, personal relationships; norms of collegiality; shared mission and values; and shared knowledge and expertise.

Just as there was not a firm line between developers and trainers, there was not a firm line between the project team and its schools. Early on, those with school-level training responsibility worked in very close contact with schools in a capacity akin to that of the reading facilitator, collaborating with early adopting teachers and leaders in the day-to-day work of using Success for All and, with that, bringing extensive knowledge and expertise to the work. At the same time, team members also tapped these early schools for two key resources. One was first-hand knowledge and expertise about the use of Success for All in actual school contexts. The second was expert users of the program. Very early in its operations, the Success for All project team began a pattern of hiring leading teachers, facilitators, and (to a lesser extent) principals into the project team, including early users with extensive education and experience in the "individualized instruction" movement of the early 1970s and the "effective schools" movement of the early and mid-1980s.

Early efforts to formally elaborate and scaffold Success for All included instances of extensive attention to expert use: for example, detailed elaboration of diagnosis and intervention in tutoring.[3] However, in the main, primary development efforts focused on a collection of issues central to initial scale up: for example, articulating the first principles of the program; elaborating intended practice in broad strokes; and integrating previously independent program components into a coherent, comprehensive school reform program.

With efforts to formalize the program in their earliest stages, Success for All's intimate, social network—its community of practice—became the locus of developing, sharing, and retaining tacit, craft knowledge of both novice and expert practice across three essential domains: instruction, leadership, and training. It also became the locus of developing, sharing, and retaining norms central to continuously improving that knowledge: for example, a deep commitment to improving achievement for at-risk students; a deep commitment to Success for All as a program of improvement; a commitment to constant tinkering and experimentation; and a commitment to formal research and evaluation both to inform and to validate the work. By all accounts, this was a learning community, drawing from the prior knowledge and experience of individuals, their extensive collaboration with schools, and their continued participation as members of the broader community of researchers. This was precisely the sort of learning community that Success for All sought to recreate in schools, and it was precisely that which supported on-going learning and improvement within the project team, itself.

Though informal at its roots, the project team quickly began to develop distinct capabilities for development and training—and, with that, distinct identities and suborganizations. While two parts of a whole, the work, knowledge, and coordination demands of development and training were qualitatively different. Some developers continued to train, and some trainers continued to develop. But a growing number of developers and trainers did one or the other.

Despite these distinct identities, both developers and trainers continued to function largely as informal communities of practice. Linking the two were program founders and project managers who actively participated both in development and training, thus enacting a sort of boundary-spanning role that linked the entire project team into a dense, social network. Much as trainers were in close, day-to-day contact with schools, this "executive nucleus" was in close, day-to-day contact with trainers, conveying tacit knowledge of the program and developing capabilities to support the program as intended. In a 2003 interview, Success for All cofounder Nancy Madden recalled the importance of such intimate contact between trainers, cofounder Robert Slavin, and herself:

> When we were really very small, Bob and I interacted with almost all the trainers all the time, doing on-going staff development and making sure all of the agendas are being taken care of. You've got to grow to make the real power of the program accessible to many kids and many schools. And in that process, our trainers had to learn how to make the program truly replicable with the full power that it has. It's a lot to replicate. It's not an easy program.

But it's not something where you just pick up a book and read out of the book. There's a lot of subtlety to the program.

Modal Schools, Meddling Environments, and Formal Organization

The second half of Success for All's first decade (the period from SY 1992/1993 to SY 1997/1998) was marked by a set of conditions that favored continued scale-up: stability in (and strengthening of) policy support for both comprehensive school reform and standards-based reform; economic growth (and, with that, public and philanthropic investment in educational reform); and Success for All's growing reputation as an effective program. However, this period also brought with it a set interdependent conditions that quickly combined to complicate the enterprise: a rapid increase in the number of Success for All schools; increased variability in their initial capabilities; increased involvement from their local environments; and a rapid increase in the size, complexity, and formality of the Success for All organization.

With ambitions and commitment to work at a large scale, Success for All cofounders leveraged agenda stability and complementary support to lead a rapid expansion in Success for All's scale of operations. From SY 1992/1993 through SY 1997/1998, the number of Success for All schools increased an astonishing 1500% over a six-year period (see Table 3.1.). This was remarkable growth measurable in state-sized chunks. Over two successive years—SY 1994/1995 and

Table 3.1 APPROXIMATE NUMBER OF SUCCESS FOR ALL AND ROOTS AND WINGS SCHOOLS: 1987–1998[*]

School Year	Schools	Gain	Percentage Gain
1987–88	1		
1988–89	6	5	500
1989–90	9	3	50
1990–91	16	7	78
1991–92	30	14	88
1992–93	50	20	67
1993–94	100	50	100
1994–95	200	100	100
1995–96	300	100	50
1996–97	480	180	60
1997–98	750	270	56

*School totals for 1987–1998 taken from Slavin and Madden (1999b:6–7).

SY 1995/1996—Success for All took on 100 new schools per year, roughly as many elementary schools as in the state of Delaware.[4] In SY 1996/1997, Success for All took on 180 new schools, roughly as many elementary schools as in either Hawaii or Alaska.[5] In SY 1997/1998, Success for All took on 270 new schools, roughly as many elementary schools as in the state of Vermont.[6] With that, the Success for All project team went from supporting a network of elementary schools roughly the size of a mid-sized district to one roughly the size of the state of Oregon.[7]

As the number of schools increased, the initial capabilities of schools and their relationships with their local environments began to shift. As recalled by project team members, expansion in the number of schools began a rapid regression to the mean, as atypical, early adopters gave way to more typical, chronically under-performing Title I schools. These were schools more suspicious of external designs and support, weaker in initial capabilities, and subject to turbulence and interference from local environments. Increasing involvement of local environments was not accidental but, instead, deliberate. During this period, the 1994 reauthorization of the federal Elementary and Secondary Education as the Improving America's Schools Act included resources and incentives for districts to provide technical assistance and support to schools to develop schoolwide improvement programs. The New American Schools initiative also began enlisting districts in the adoption and implementation of participating comprehensive school reform programs.[8] Even with increasing district involvement, project team members recalled that, in many instances, Success for All's program adoption process still functioned to ensure at least base levels of commitment and capabilities, along with some buffering from environmental turbulence. Even so, conditions in schools and environments were becoming much more complex.

The combination of environmental dynamics and a growing base of schools drove changes in the organization of the Success for All project team. During this time window, the project team moved from the long-established Center for the Social Organization of Schools to the newly founded, federally funded Center for Research on Education for Students Placed At Risk (CRESPAR), also located at Johns Hopkins University.

Concurrently, expanded funding for program development drove an increase in the size and complexity both of the development agenda and the development organization.[9] For example, besides continuing to develop and refine its core comprehensive school reform program, the Success for All project team leveraged funding from the New American Schools initiative and other (primarily private) funding to launch development of "Roots and Wings": a still-more-comprehensive program that went beyond reading to include writing, mathematics, and integrated science/social science.

With program development ubiquitous in U.S. educational environments, Success for All executives succeeded in recruiting accomplished developers to staff both new and continuing development efforts. Expansion brought with it some formalization of roles and responsibilities: for example, the creation of component-specific development teams, with certain members designated as lead developers. Even so, developers recruited during this period reported that they continued to work largely as an informal community of practice, sharing knowledge and experience and informally coordinating their work.

At the same time, the growing number of Success for All schools drove proportional increases in the size of Success for All training organization. During this period, the Success for All project team began experiencing a problem in its training organization that it was not experiencing in its development organization. Where Success for All leaders succeeded in identifying the funding and human resources needed to expand the development organization, they struggled to identify commensurate resources needed to expand the training organization. Specifically, project leaders struggled to identify a large pool of instantly expert trainers from which it could draw to support its growing base of schools. At the time, training of this sort was historically novel work, and programs and agencies simply did not yet exist to develop and credential expert trainers. Project leaders also struggled to identify a pool of funders willing to support the professional development of novice trainers.[10] While funders were willing to invest in program development, they were unwilling to invest in organizational development.

Absent environmental support, Success for All leaders elected to develop the training organization as a self-funding operation supported by fees charged to schools.[11] While serviceable, project leaders did not see this fee-for-service funding scheme as satisfactory. In SY 1992/1993, as the number of schools increased from 30 to 50, project leaders began reporting that recruiting, developing, and retaining new trainers was becoming problematic, to the point that expansion of the training organization was identified as a potential threat to (and limiting condition on) successful implementation and continued scale-up.[12] The problems increased as the number of schools and trainers increased, such that, by SY 1995/1996, project leaders were using public reports of "lessons learned" in scaling up Success for All to advocate for the environmental resources needed to support its training organization:

> The most important limitation on the broad dissemination of Success for All is our own capacity to provide high-quality professional development services to a very large number of schools. Our model requires a great deal of training and follow-up, and any equally ambitious restructuring program that intends to change the daily instructional practices of all teachers would require equally intense training. We can only add so many schools each year without overtaxing our staff's considerable energies or seeing the quality of professional development decline. As a result, we must decline to work with further schools whenever our training calendars are full.
>
> Our professional development organization is self-funding; our trainers' salaries are supported by fees we charge schools for their time. However, rapid scale-up has costs. While we are training new trainers, we must pay their salaries, fly them to observe schools or training sessions, and so on. Costs for establishing trainers in sites other than the project's home site may be particularly great, as these trainers must travel frequently to the home site. There is no source of funding for these costs. By the time a trainer is fully

operative and bringing in enough revenue to cover his or her salary, we may have spent more than $50,000.

There is a need to provide training organizations like ours with funds to scale up their operations. Ultimately such organizations must be self-funding, but they need capitalization as they begin their work and as they engage in significant expansion of their national capacity. As noted earlier, private foundations have largely fulfilled this capitalization function for some projects.

The U.S. Department of Education's National Diffusion Network (NDN) also provided small grants to "developer/demonstrators" to help them build training capacity for programs whose effectiveness had been validated by a panel of experts. However, a substantial expansion of capacity to serve thousands of schools responding to the national call for reform will require a far greater investment in existing and future training networks to build their capacity to provide quality professional development.[13]

To staff its growing training organization, Success for All founders continued a strategy that it had been using from the beginning: recruiting successful teachers and reading facilitators from Success for All schools, along with a small number of principals.[14] The strategy was prudent. Even if not expert trainers, experienced Success for All teachers and reading facilitators had at least some knowledge of (and commitment to) the program. By 1996/1997, Success for All's training organization had expanded to 31 full-time trainers and 40 part-time trainers working on a per diem basis: primarily women, either early-career (and pre-family) or late-career (and sometimes retired), thus free to take on the travel demands associated with the work of training—a demographic pattern that would continue throughout.

As they expanded the training organization, project leaders also made significant changes in its formal organization. Specifically, Success for All leaders developed a regional, geographically distributed training structure, with some trainers in Baltimore and some working out of their homes. The decision had both benefits (e.g., reduced travel costs en route to schools; the development of local knowledge and expertise) and costs (e.g., outfitting home offices; travel costs to Baltimore for meetings and training). To manage regions, project leaders introduced the role of regional manager, a complex role that included responsibilities for administration (e.g., travel, scheduling, and billing), trainers' professional development, and direct support to schools. Project leaders supported the training organization with a newly constituted "Training Institute": a team of developers and trainers charged with elaborating and scaffolding the work of trainers. This was development and training work that ran parallel to elaborating and scaffolding the work of teachers and schools leaders.

Challenges growing the in-house training organization ultimately led project leaders to begin pursuing partnerships with other organizations to provide training services to schools. Early experimentation and experience led them to quickly rule out federally funded educational laboratories, universities, states agencies, and even districts, owing to a combination of complexities: for example, geographic and funding constraints; conflicting institutional missions and identities; weak capabilities; and weak commitment to Success for All.[15] Even so, project leaders succeeded in identifying three external partners: WestEd, a government-sponsored, nonprofit regional educational laboratory that had collaborated in research on Success for All; a research group at the University of Memphis that began collaborating to support Success for All schools as early as 1989; and Education Partners, a for-profit organization newly founded in 1994 to provide professional development to reconstituted schools in San Francisco. In combination with the core training team in Baltimore, these three partners extended Success for All's regional structure: WestEd covering the southwest portion of the country; the University of Memphis team covering the southeast; Education Partners covering the northwest; and Success for All's own trainers covering the east, mid-Atlantic, and Midwest.

While a promising and practical approach to managing rapid scale up, Success for All project leaders proceeded cautiously. For example, of WestEd, project leaders acknowledged the uniqueness of a federally funded lab actually supporting a federally funded center, and of the weak incentives for labs to support programs not of their own design.[16] Of Education Partners, leaders reported that "the for-profit nature of Education Partners was initially uncomfortable to us, but apparently is not perceived as a problem by schools. It has substantial advantages in terms of capitalization and marketing expertise, but we will not know for a year or more whether this organization can significantly accelerate our pace of scale-up without compromising quality."[17]

The Success for All training organization and its external partners grew in size lock-step with the increases in schools. By SY 1997/1998, the year in which Success for All recruited 270 new schools, members of Success for All reported that one-quarter of all new hires at Johns Hopkins University, Baltimore's largest private employer, were for the Success for All project team—primarily trainers.[18] Education Partners, the largest training partner, would eventually serve over 180 schools, itself nearly as large as all of Success for All in 1994/95, and with more elementary schools than served by three state departments of education (Delaware, Hawaii, and Alaska).[19]

Thus, in period from SY 1992/1993 to SY 1997/1998, riding sustained environmental support and continued interest from schools, Success for All transformed itself from a Baltimore-based research-and-development project to a nationally distributed provider of programs and training services, with its training capacity distributed among the project team and three other (and very different) organizations. These programs and services, in turn, where in use in a state-sized network of chronically underperforming schools.

Quality and Consistency

With a rapidly growing base of more challenging schools, with local environments beginning to meddle, and with a sprawling and distributed training organization, attention remained fixed on continuing to advance Success for All's growing reputation for technical effectiveness. In a 1996 report on scaling up Success for All, cofounders Robert Slavin and Nancy Madden explained: "Quality control is a constant concern. Whatever dissemination strategy we use, constantly checking on the quality of training, implementation, and outcomes is essential. Without it, all programs fade into nothingness."[20]

In Success for All, quality began with consistency: accurate replication of the design for comprehensive school reform across a state-sized system of chronically underperforming Title I schools. With quality the problem and with consistency its solution, Success for All's strategy for supporting implementation and its strategy for supporting its own training organization evolved to mirror each other. Both were comparatively highly developed to support novice, consistent use. And both were comparatively weakly developed to support expert, adaptive use.

As a matter of strategy, Success for All already had consistency sitting at the nexus of a complex rationale for forestalling problems of implementation, reversing problems of schools, and initiating an upward spiral of improvement. Indeed, consistency was a single means to interdependent ends: preserving the integrity of the design and preventing a backslide into past practice; displacing current practice and quickly establishing a high floor under schoolwide practice; producing evidence of possibility in teachers and students, thus inspiring commitment to improve; and creating a social and technical infrastructure to support expert, adaptive use. Beyond this complex logic, research on Success for All provided straightforward evidence to support attention to consistency. When implemented consistently, comprehensively, and well, the program showed effects on students' achievement; when implemented weakly, piecemeal, and poorly, it didn't.[21]

Between SY 1992/1993 and SY 1997/1998, the general weakening in initial commitment and capabilities in schools and the growing intervention of proximal environments pushed Success for All harder in the direction of consistency. Practically speaking, more schools needed more help to get Success for All's interdependent roles, structures, technologies, and practices in place and functioning at a base level of operations—quickly. At the same time, more schools needing more help risked a classic problem of large-scale implementation: schools unclear of what exactly to do, co-opting the program, and quickly reverting to past practice. In a 2003 interview, Success for All cofounder Robert Slavin explained:

You don't want a situation in which every teacher doesn't know what the program is supposed to look like, makes up whatever they're going to do, and basically slides back into their usual practices. That's been the history of education reform since the earth cooled: wonderful ideas that worked in the first few schools, and when you try to go to your fifth or sixth schools, much less your tenth or twelfth schools, it's gone. There's no trace. It's not happening. That has been the history. The forms may remain, but the function is gone. The flag may be on the front of the school, but there's nothing inside that you can pick out. Even before Success for All, we did cooperative learning. Before that, I studied mastery learning and other things. Over and over and over again, you see the progression from a few excited people saying, "It's going to solve all my problems!" and, then, no trace among schools that think that they're implementing something.

The combination of theoretical justification, growing evidence, practical need, and past experience drove extensive elaboration and scaffolding of Success for All to support novice, consistent use at scale. Yet attention to consistency did not stop with schools. Between SY 1992/1993 and SY 1997/1998, Success for All faced exactly the same practical problem in its training organization and in its training partners as it did in schools: more newly recruited trainers needing more help to quickly support novice, consistent use across a state-size (and still-growing) base of schools. The response for its training organization and training partners was exactly as for its growing schools: to formally elaborate and scaffold novice training practice to ensure that newly recruited trainers would provide consistent support for consistent implementation in schools.

Resources for trainers mirrored those for teachers. For example, to support consistent direct instruction during in initial training, in conference sessions, and in school-based training modules, members of Success for All's Training Institute began developing what trainers called "scripts": thick binders that detailed each training session's purpose, the trainer's role, content presentation, learning tasks, assessments, and more. To support school-based monitoring and follow-up, members of Training Institute developed the Implementation Visit Report: a detailed observation and reporting protocol that provided items and rubrics for assessing whether each program component was in place structurally and being implemented faithfully, with summative reports provided to Success for All project leaders and formative reports provided to school leaders.[22] The use of extensively elaborated training resources was supported by structured professional development opportunities in which more experienced trainers presented these detailed resources to new trainers and, then, modeled their consistent use. For external training partners, attention to consistency went further, to include contracts that specified performance standards and that included allowances for direct observation of schools by Success for All project team members.[23]

As recalled by Robert Slavin in a 2003 interview, the focus on consistency within the training organization and training partners was not anchored in the same sort of complex logic that drove attention to consistency in schools. Rather, Slavin recalled the focus on consistency in training as a response to practical demands and concerns that came with large-scale implementation:

At the beginning, in the early schools, we knew these schools. We knew the people who were working in them. And I think we focused very much on quality implementation and not on what was on the walls or the time schedule or the exact adherence to the script or anything like that. We then kind of got into a scale-up phase in which we were hiring a lot of people, brand-new, training them up and sending them out. And we trained them very well; it's not that we didn't. But we fell into, not with any philosophical intention, but we fell into trying to be very, very explicit with our own trainers about we expected them to do. And we wanted to have consistency from trainer to trainer, from region to region. Because what we were terrified about, particularly once we started allowing people to not live in Baltimore, was that the program would become just anything wherever it was.

Between SY 1992/1993 and SY 1997/1998, while Success for All was devoting considerable attention and resources to novice, consistent use of the program, comparatively less attention was being devoted to formally elaborating and scaffolding expert, adaptive use, either for schools or for the training organization. Instead, knowledge and norms of expert use and of expert training continued to be developed, transferred, and retained informally, through communities of practice. Such communities were supported by Experienced Trainers Institutes and other occasional meetings that brought trainers from around the country together in one location for purposes of debriefing, training, and renewal. Even if too many and too widely distributed to meet informally around a table in Baltimore, trainers could still meet formally and occasionally in a single room. In a 2003 interview, one trainer who joined one of Success for All's new training partners in 1996 recalled the experience:

I came on board in 1996 with Education Partners. Education Partners had just become a licensed disseminator of Success for All. Education Partners didn't train us internally, because there were just three of us. I first went to Phoenix and attended the training for WestEd trainers. WestEd was another disseminator at the time as well. After that, Education Partners sent the three of us to Baltimore, and we attended SFA's training for trainers. The next week, SFA had their Experienced Trainers meeting. Everybody together, it was about thirty people. We were in a little room at Johns Hopkins University. It was a very small group. When you have a very small group, it's very likely that everybody is going to be philosophically like-minded. It's very likely that everybody will understand the program the same way.

Yet at the same time, the size, organizational distribution, and geographic distribution of training operations began to strain these communities of practice as the primary mechanism for developing, transferring, and retaining critical, expert knowledge. Success for All cofounders Slavin and Madden explained that regionally based trainers "are often isolated, working from their own homes without the informal collegial supports that are so important to our Baltimore staff. Operating far from our center, these trainers cannot routinely attend meetings or keep up easily with the latest information or developments."[24] Further, communities of practice began to develop unevenly. The number of more experienced and expert trainers was increasingly dwarfed by the number of new and inexperienced trainers, and the social ties between trainers were stretched thinner due to the newness of large numbers of trainers and to the geographic distance between them.

Gathering Clouds

From the perspective of scaling up, the period from Success for All's founding in SY 1987/1988 to SY 1997/1998 (its first decade of operation) was one of remarkable success. Indeed, Success for All succeeded in creating something that had yet to emerge in the 300+ year history of U.S. public schooling: a state-sized (and still-growing) network of schools with conventional roles, structures, technologies, and practices carefully designed to support the achievement of at-risk students; a hub organization with the commitment and capability to provide programs and technical assistance beyond those provided by the usual state and local administrative agencies; and evidence of possibility (though not inevitability) in leveraging this combination to improve student achievement in participating schools.

Yet amidst this success emerged of a set interdependent dilemmas that cut to the heart of the entire enterprise. The ultimate goal of Success for All—school-based flexibility and adaptation—was also its primary threat to early implementation. Further, addressing that threat with careful attention to consistent implementation risked projecting the program as something that its developers never intended: that is, either a shrink-wrapped, technocratic solution or a compliance-driven, bureaucratic directive. Finally, to limit adaptation during early implementation was to initially discourage that which the program ultimately sought to achieve.

Among Success for All project leaders, these were not logical conundrums to be debated but, instead, practical problems to be managed. Their means of doing so: Damn the torpedoes, full speed ahead. Over the first decade, the fundamental, first-order concern became establishing conventional usage of the program across a state-sized (and still growing) base of schools. Both the design and the training organization evolved to address that concern. Progressing to expert, adaptive use, then, became a problem to be managed by (and through) informal communities of training practice.

And, with that, clouds began to gather, as risks of adverse interpretation and misuse emerged and interacted: weak schools leveraging new funding streams to adopt a very ambitious program; declining school autonomy and increasing environmental intervention; a design for implementation formalized in ways that could easily be mistaken as a quick fix and/or a bureaucratic directive; a training organization strengthening in ways that risked promoting adverse interpretation and misuse; and a training organization weakening in ways that would enable it to manage these many, interacting risks.

EXPLODING GROWTH

As Success for All transitioned into its second decade of operations, both environments and schools continued to co-evolve. Increasing environmental support for both comprehensive school reform and standards-based reform combined with corresponding changes in recruiting dynamics to effect dramatic growth in

Success for All's installed base of schools and in its own organization. This next phase of scale-up did not occur as a comparatively glacial, decade-long swell but, instead, as an immediate, tectonic lurch. Indeed, this period was described by project team members as one of explosive growth. Success for All doubled its installed base of schools in two short years, equaling the success of the prior decade in a small fraction of the time. The organization evolved in kind. Success for All emerged from this period not just as a state-sized system of schools. It emerged as a *big* state-sized system of schools rivaling all but the largest. And at the hub of the system was not the usual state education agency but, instead, the newly independent, nonprofit Success for All Foundation.[25]

Evolving Environments and Changing Dynamics

Over SY 1998/1999 and SY 1999/2000, environments continued to evolve to support comprehensive school reform and standards-based reform (in general) and Success for All (in particular). Sponsors of the New American Schools initiative continued to gain credibility and clout as high-profile advocates of comprehensive school reform. The Improving America's Schools Act (IASA) continued to enable schools with over 50% of students in poverty to use Title I funding to pursue schoolwide improvement. State accountability systems continued to develop and evolve, such that by 1999, *Education Week's* "Quality Counts 2000" reported that all states except Iowa had standards and assessments in at least some content areas. All benefited from the gathering dot-com bubble, which fueled tax revenues, public spending, and philanthropy.

SY 1998/1999 and SY 1999/2000 also saw two dramatic changes in federal policy that occurred in rapid succession, each extending support for systemic, comprehensive school reform. In December of 1997, Congress passed the Obey-Porter Comprehensive School Reform Demonstration Act (CSRD), with funding slated to enter the system for SY 1998/1999. The initial authorization of CSRD provided $150 million per year to support comprehensive school reform through state-level competitive grants, with $145 million to go directly to schools. This funding was sufficient to provide 2,900 schools with $50,000 per year (renewable at two years) that could be combined with Title I funding to support schoolwide improvement.[26]

Beyond additional federal funding, CSRD also provided more detailed guidance for the use of that funding, including new requirements that participating programs be "based on reliable research and effective practices, and have been replicated successfully in schools with diverse characteristics." (See Table 3.2.) The legislation explicitly identified seventeen programs meeting all nine funding criteria, including Success for All and Roots and Wings (the NAS-funded version of Success for All that bundled the reading program with other content area components).[27]

CSRD was quickly followed by the Reading Excellence Act of 1998 (REA), with funding slated to enter the system for SY 1999/2000. Part of President Clinton's

Table 3.2 Obey-Porter Comprehensive School Reform Demonstration Act: Criteria for Qualifying Schoolwide Programs*

Key components of schoolwide programs under Obey-Porter CSRD included:

1. Innovative strategies and proven methods for student learning, teaching, and school management that are based on reliable research and effective practices, and have been replicated successfully in schools with diverse characteristics;

2. A comprehensive design for effective school functioning that (a) aligns the school's curriculum, technology, and professional development into a school-wide reform plan designed to enable all students to meet challenging state content and performance standards and (b) addresses needs identified through a school needs assessment;

3. High-quality and continuous teacher and staff professional development and training;

4. Measurable goals for student performance and benchmarks for meeting those goals;

5. Support by school faculty, administrators, and staff;

6. The meaningful involvement of parents and the local community in planning and implementing school improvement activities;

7. High-quality external technical support and assistance from a comprehensive school reform entity (e.g., a university or independent research organization) with experience or expertise in schoolwide reform and improvement;

8. A plan for the evaluation of the implementation of school reforms and the student results achieved;

9. Identification of how other resources (Federal, State, local, and private) available to the school will be utilized and coordinated to support and sustain the school reform effort.

*These criteria are compiled from Hale (2000) and North West Regional Education Laboratory (2001).

"America Reads" initiative, REA amended Title II of IASA to create a second, new, state-level competitive grant program to support the improvement of K–3 reading in the nation's lowest-performing elementary schools, with the express goal of on-grade-level reading achievement by the end of third grade. Like CSRD, REA provided additional funding that could be combined with funding from both Title I and CSRD to support schoolwide improvement: $260 million in FY1999 and FY2000, $241.1 million of which went to states. REA also provided additional, non-regulatory guidance for the use of federal funding. Like CSRD, REA emphasized the use of research as a criterion for federal funding: "The Act emphasize(d) strongly the importance of scientifically based reading research, including findings related to phonemic awareness, systematic phonics, fluency, and reading comprehension, in carrying out these activities."[28]

One effect of environmental dynamics was to increase the legitimacy, guidance, resources, and incentives supporting comprehensive school reform, in ways that provided direct and indirect support to Success for All. Again, Success for All was identified as one of the 17 programs meeting federal criteria for the use of CSRD funding, along with Roots and Wings. REA formalized what Success for All developers had long held as the most critical goal of the program: on-grade-level reading achievement by the end of third grade. And growing emphasis on scientifically based research in federal policy played directly to Success for All's reputation as a research-based and research-validated program.

A second effect was to change recruiting dynamics within schools, again in ways that stood to benefit Success for All. The rapid emergence of new federal policies created a mix of resources and incentives that both pushed and pulled increasing numbers of schools to pursue schoolwide improvement and to adopt comprehensive school reform programs. For earnest schools either eager to begin or already pursuing schoolwide improvement, CSRD and REA provided extensive, additional funding to act on their initiative, and Success for All stood as an established potential partner. For less-committed schools feeling increasing pressure to improve, CSRD and REA provided necessary funding, and Success for All looked to be a proven program with potential as a quick fix. For even-less committed schools practiced in the age-old strategy of tapping new funding streams absent any intention to heed associated expectations, CSRD and REA provided rich veins to tap, and Success for All was a legitimate selection unlikely to draw scrutiny.

A third effect was to change dynamics in local environments, again in ways that stood to benefit Success for All. Earlier trends accelerated. Deference to school-based decision making began to wane, the basic bargain of autonomy-for-accountability began to break down, and states and districts began to become increasingly involved in the funding, adoption, and implementation of comprehensive school reform programs. The causes were many and interacting: for example, federal accountability provisions that required intervention from states and districts; political pressure that precluded states and districts from abdicating responsibility for improving schools; and opportunities to leverage CSRD and REA funding to develop state-level and district-wide initiatives. At the district level, one strategy was to establish "home grown" comprehensive school reform programs in accordance with guidance in the Obey-Porter CSRD Act of 1997. Another strategy was to coordinate and support the selection of external designs through such means as district-level program adoptions, limiting school-level choice to a small number of programs, or providing detailed guidance for school-level selection.

In several high-profile instances, district and state intervention provided unusual support for Success for All. For example, in SY 1999/2000, the New York City Public School's Chancellor's District required over 40 its weakest elementary schools to adopt Success for All.[29] In 1998, the New Jersey State Supreme Court provided additional funding for schools in 28 of the state's poorest urban districts to adopt one of five comprehensive school reform programs over a three-year period.[30] Prior to the decision, the New Jersey Department of Education had advised the court:

Whole-school programs for elementary schools exist and are sufficiently well documented to pursue implementation. The most promising of these is the

Success for All program developed by Johns Hopkins University. As described in more detail below, this report recommends that the Success for All program, or an equivalent one, be implemented in all elementary schools of the Abbott districts. . . .

The NJDOE recommends that all elementary schools in the Abbott districts be required to implement Success for All, a model of whole school reform focused on improved student achievement. The district and school may present a convincing case as to why it should be permitted to establish an alternative research-based, whole school reform model which includes the Comer School Development Program, Accelerated Schools, the Adaptive Learning Environments Model, and the Modern Red School House. The burden of proof must rest heavily with the district and school to show convincingly that an alternative model will be equally effective and efficient, or that it is already in place and operating effectively.[31]

While changing recruiting dynamics pulled more and more schools towards Success for All, they also pulled Success for All towards more and more schools. Indeed, the incentives for Success for All to enlist new schools were as complex as the incentives for schools to adopt Success for All. CSRD and REA presented unprecedented opportunity for Success for All to act on its mission and commitment to improve education for large numbers of at-risk students. Further, Success for All faced incentives to increase its market share by enlisting as many schools as possible, lest the schools enlist with other programs. Finally, leveraging CSRD and REA to increase Success for All's scale of operation stood to heighten its profile and prestige, clearly identifying Success for All as a cutting edge program with novel capabilities to effect large-scale improvement in the nation's weakest schools.

A Dramatic Increase in Schools

The combination of rapid increases in environmental support for comprehensive school reform and consequent changes in recruiting dynamics interacted to fuel a dramatic increase in the installed base of schools. In SY 1998/1999 and SY 1999/2000, as CSRD and REA funding made its way into the system, Success for All took on 340 schools and 460 schools, respectively, with its total enrollment rocketing from 750 to 1550 in two short years.[32] Success for All added roughly as many schools per year as its total enrollments for the years SY 1995/1996 (300 schools) and SY 1996/1997 (480 schools). By 1999/2000, Success for All was serving more elementary schools than all but eight state education agencies.[33] It was operating in 48 states, from Miami to Anchorage and from Hartford to Hawaii.

It wasn't just that Success for All was succeeding in recruiting new schools. It was that existing schools weren't leaving. In contrast to the conventional cycle of program adoption-and-abandonment that had long characterized U.S. educational reform, Success for All schools were electing to continue with the program at the end of their initial, three-year contract. For a program whose primary goals included establishing a nation-wide, professional network of schools, such an unusually strong track record of retention amidst the usual, unstable agendas of schools and districts was a tremendous success. In a 2001 report on lessons learned during the scale-up of Success for All, cofounders Robert Slavin and Nancy Madden reported on the remarkable retention of Success for All schools through the CSRD and REA surge:

> An important indicator of the robustness of Success for All is the fact that of the more than 1,100 schools that have used the program for periods of 1 to 9 years, only approximately three dozen have dropped out. This usually takes place as a result of a change of principals, major funding cutbacks, or other substantial changes. Hundreds of other SFA schools have survived changes of superintendents, principals, facilitators, and other key staff, major cuts in funding, and other serious threats to program maintenance.[34]

A Dramatic Transformation of the Organization

The dramatic increase in schools was matched with a dramatic transformation of the organization. In the summer of 1998, concurrent with the initial CSRD funding entering the system, the original Success for All project team negotiated an amicable split from Johns Hopkins University to found the independent, non-profit Success for All Foundation (SFAF), headquartered just north of Johns Hopkins University in Towson, MD. As with the installed base of schools, this was an organization that quickly grew to a formidable size: as reported by executives, approximately 500 total people, 250 people working out of the Towson headquarters and 250 in its geographically distributed training operation.

Amidst changing dynamics in environments and rapid growth in schools, the first-order task became establishing the newly-founded SFAF as a going concern, an effort that required knowledge and expertise over and above that required to conduct the usual business of Success for All. Establishing formal and social structures within the organization proved not to be a problem. Establishing operating capital and revenue did.

The decision to establish SFAF was motivated by a set of interacting problems and anticipated opportunities that began coming to a head over SY 1997/1998. To start, such a large, complex enterprise had become increasingly difficult to manage under the umbrella of a research center in a research university. Further, project leaders had their eyes trained squarely on federal policy activity, and they fully anticipated that operations were soon to become even larger and more complex. Finally, in SY 1997/1998, Success for All's primary means of mitigating organizational growth—its external training partnerships—began to fail, requiring SFAF to assume responsibilities for its partners' schools.[35] The WestEd partnership failed in the spring of 1997/1998 due to problems in the consistency and quality of support to schools. The Education Partners partnership began failing soon thereafter due to a set of interacting issues: problems of consistency and quality; legal complexities that came with collaborating with a for-profit organization; and what SFAF executives saw as a moral tension between serving at-risk students and serving investors. The University of Memphis partnership eventually terminated in 2001, when the Memphis City Schools ceased implementing all comprehensive school reform programs and the University of Memphis training site was closed.

Establishing SFAF as a going concern was largely an evolutionary process. It began with establishing formal structures that extended those of the John Hopkins-based project team: a program development organization; a geographically distributed training organization; Training Institute, responsible for developing training programs for schools and trainers; a research organization in Towson responsible for on-going analysis of program effectiveness; a publications department; a conference planning department; a customer service center; and basic business units previously provided by Johns Hopkins University (e.g., financial systems, information systems, and personnel/human resources). The executive level of the organization included a core set of roles and structures: a chairman (Robert Slavin, responsible for grant writing, research, and strategy); a president (Nancy Madden, responsible for daily operations and program development); a director of implementation (Barbara Haxby, a member of the original project team and developer of the family support component); a chief financial officer (Roger Morin); and a board of directors that included Slavin, Madden, a representative from Johns Hopkins University, and two representatives from a supporting philanthropic organization.

Despite increasing size, complexity, and formalization, all involved reported that the social structure of the organization remained intact. SFAF retained its character as a tight, social organization, with extensive cross-functional participation among teams, informal coordination between teams, and (above all) a shared mission to improve schools.

Establishing SFAF as a going concern continued with capitalizing the organization. While SFAF succeeded in securing government grants and philanthropic contributions to continue program development, securing operating capital was much more difficult, owing in part to the decision to charter SFAF as a nonprofit foundation. For example, SFAF needed to secure $5 million in grants and loans from two family foundations and from the New American Schools initiative in order to have sufficient assets simply to obtain necessary lines of credit from commercial banks.[36] Slavin and Madden explained that, "even with this, we remain seriously undercapitalized for an organization of our size and rate of growth. For example, we have an annual printing bill of about $20 million, which we must pay many months before school districts begin to pay us."[37]

Despite the implications for generating capital, the decision to organize as a nonprofit was anchored in the desire to represent the organization to its members, to its schools, and to its public as deeply committed to improving education for at-risk students. Within and beyond the organization, SFAF executives recognized the imperative of maintaining and projecting commitments that had driven the Success for All project team from its inception. Slavin and Madden explained:

> One of the key issues we had to resolve early on was whether to remain as a not-for-profit organization. This was a difficult decision. On one hand, it was clear that as a for-profit we would have no problem raising capital; many venture capital firms and individuals courted us heavily. However, there were several factors that led us to strongly favor staying in the not-for-profit world if we could. One was a desire to maintain an institutional ethos that focused on what is best for children, not what is best for profits or investors. Our staff is deeply committed to children and to school reform, and we did not want to undermine this spirit in any way. Another factor related to the public perception of our efforts. Watching the hostile reception in many quarters to the Edison Project and other for-profit education reform groups, we wanted to be sure that our program was seen as having unmixed motivations. The American Federation of Teachers and, to a lesser extent, the National Education Association, have strongly supported us (and opposed Edison). We did not want to endanger support of that kind. Finally, as a practical matter, we wanted to be certain that any operating profits would go back into development, research, and quality control, not into investors or taxes.[38]

Establishing SFAF as a going concern also required establishing revenue streams to support on-going operations. For this, SFAF depended primarily on revenues generated from the sales of program materials and training services to schools. That brought with it profound implications for the organization's scale-up strategy. Revenues from both materials and training were heavily weighted towards first year schools. Schools purchased virtually all required materials in the summer preceding Year 1 implementation. Further, due largely to the extensiveness of initial training, the standard Success for All contract included 23 person-days of training in the first year of implementation, 12 in the second, and 5–8 in each subsequent year.[39] Other income from the sales of materials and training was largely at the discretion of schools: purchasing updated materials, attending annual Experienced Sites Conferences, and contracting for supplemental training modules.

With that, the newly founded SFAF succeeded in securing the operating capital and revenue streams needed to establish the organization as a going concern. But in doing so, SFAF created for itself a critical dependence: a dependence on a steady flow of new schools. With its operating capital secured by loans, and with its core revenue streams heavily dependent on new business, continued scale-up became more than a matter of acting on the core mission of the organization and raising its public profile. Continued scale-up became an organizational imperative.

Continuing Criticism

As it entered its second decade, the installed base of Success for All schools, the program, broader environments, and SFAF as an organization were co-evolving in positive and mutually reinforcing ways. Yet, as they did, criticism persisted in SFAF's environments. Consequently, at the same time that the newly founded SFAF had to mine its environments for essential resources, it also had to manage these same environments to ensure a favorable public perception. This required going beyond organizing as a nonprofit in order to maintain moral high ground. It again required taking on Success for All's critics.

In this period, some of the most dogged criticism of Success for All came from Stanley Pogrow, then a professor at the University of Arizona. Like Slavin, Pogrow was a developer of external programs that sought to improve education for at-risk students in Title I schools. In contrast to Success for All's comprehensive, school-wide approach, Pogrow developed two targeted interventions: Higher Order Thinking Skills (HOTS), which aimed to improve instruction by developing capabilities for Socratic dialogue between students and teachers in grades 4–8; and SuperMath, which aimed to motivate and to enrich students' learning experiences through computer-based learning activities. In 1998, Pogrow reported that HOTS was in use in over 3,000 schools.[40]

Beginning in October of 1998 and running through February of 2002, Pogrow and SFAF cofounder Robert Slavin engaged in a heated debate that began in the *Educational Researcher* (a monthly publication of the American Educational Research Association) and continued into *Phi Delta Kappan* (a monthly journal published by the leading professional association for K–12 and university educators). The debate was heated enough—and the stakes high enough—to eventually draw the attention of the Washington Post, which featured an article in 2002 by education writer Jay Matthews titled *Success for Some* in which he described Success for All as a "controversial method" for improving the achievement of at-risk students.[41]

Pogrow's critique picked up where the critique of Herbert Walberg and Rebecca Greenberg left off, and voiced similar concerns: for example, assertions of methodological problems in the research base on Success for All; assertions of conflicts of interest among internal and external researchers; and assertions that Slavin and colleagues overstated the program's effectiveness.[42] Indeed, Pogrow eventually went so far as to assert that careful scrutiny of the research base shows that Success for All was, in fact, a failure.[43]

The problem, Pogrow argued, was that widespread failure to recognize such concerns had mistaken understandings of Success for All's effectiveness leading to a succession of mistakes in federal and state policy, including unwarranted policy enthusiasm for comprehensive school reform, the concentration of federal funding among a small number of organizations pursuing comprehensive school reform (including SFAF), and a lack of federal funding for other promising improvement strategies (including Pogrow's own HOTS program). As argued by Pogrow:

> The issue of whether the use of Success for All (SFA) is supported by valid research is probably the most important and relevant research discussion for practitioners in recent years. The belief in the unique success of SFA has caused Congress to reshape Title I policy in favor of comprehensive

schoolwide reform models and approaches, has caused states and courts to mandate such programs, and has caused New Jersey to try to mandate the use of SFA in all high-poverty schools in the state. As SFA and its approach are increasingly favored, the choices that schools and teachers are allowed to consider to serve educationally disadvantaged students are increasingly restricted. The belief in the validity of this program has also concentrated funding from the U.S. Department of Education (ED) in the hands of a few large organizations that are deemed to be using the right approach. Thus new knowledge and program innovations are also restricted. . . .

However, if the research supporting SFA is not valid and if the program does not work, then we have been using the wrong approach to helping disadvantaged students, and they may be falling through the cracks. Indeed, the $8 billion this nation spends each year to help Title I students may be helping the more advantaged students to reap even greater benefits thereby increasing the learning gaps the funds were designed to reduce.[44]

Slavin's response to Pogrow mirrored his response to Walberg and Greenberg. Specifically, his response included reviews of a growing base of internal and external research that reported positive program effects, with particular emphasis on new research that used publicly available data and state accountability assessments to measure student achievement. It included explanations of research showing weak program effects. And it included counter-assertions that Pogrow's critique was an ad hominem attack that served Pogrow's interests as the developer of HOTS.[45]

One thing that Slavin did not do in his response was apologize for any influence that Success for All was having on federal and state policy. Rather, Slavin reasserted an established argument: Evidence of Success for All's effectiveness functioned as proof of the possibility of using externally developed programs to effect large-scale improvement in the education of at-risk students, from which followed a moral and political imperative to vigorously pursue that possibility. Slavin did not argue that evidence of effectiveness warranted a Success for All monopoly on serving Title I schools. Instead, Slavin advocated for market-like educational reform, though not as commonly understood: that is, as parents using vouchers to exercise choice among public and charter schools. Rather, Slavin argued for a different version of market-like educational reform: schools using public funding to exercise choice among providers of research-based, research-proven comprehensive school reform programs. The goal was to make what, to that point, had been a new, niche market into an institutionalized feature of the educational landscape. And the momentum, Slavin asserted to his critics, was clearly in that direction:

The CSRD grants and the Abbott decision, among other more local policy decisions along similar lines, are harbingers of genuine change in school reform. For the first time ever, serious funding is being attached to evidence of effectiveness for school change models that affect the entire school. The potential here is revolutionary. It is now possible to contemplate setting in motion a process of research, development, evaluation, and dissemination that will truly transform our schools.

What both Stanley Pogrow and Herbert Walberg seem to be afraid of is in fact coming to pass. Title I is increasingly emphasizing comprehensive reform models, especially for schoolwide projects (in which at least 50% of students qualify for federally subsidized lunches). An emphasis on evidence and comprehensiveness in Title I is anathema to Pogrow, whose HOTS program has neither. It is anathema to Walberg, who wants to destroy Title I in favor of vouchers and charters.

Yet research-based, comprehensive reform could be the salvation of millions of children in Title I schools. Instead of continuing to have Title I primarily support remedial programs or classroom aides—neither of which have much support in research—Title I schools could increasingly use programs that are well worked out, well researched, and capable of working with hundreds or thousands of schools with quality and integrity.[46]

Indeed, concurrent with the passage of both CSRD and REA, Slavin had also been strongly advocating in both policy and academic environments for the use of research as a criteria for federal funding. Slavin's challenge to program developers, policymakers, and schools was made clear in the title of a book on "proven and promising programs" co-authored with CRESPAR researcher Olatokunbo Fashola: *Show Me the Evidence![47]* Towards establishing a market for comprehensive school reform programs, the book set out criteria for assessing the effectiveness and replicability of schoolwide programs, classroom instructional programs, dropout prevention and college attendance programs, and district strategies supporting school change. Featured prominently throughout were SFAF's programs and strategies: Success for All, Roots and Wings, cooperative learning, and Cooperative Integrated Reading and Composition (the basis for the instructional component of Success for All).

As in his exchange with Walberg and Greenberg, Slavin's response to Pogrow was backed by responses from other researchers: in this case, Samuel Stringfield (a researcher in the Center for the Social Organization of Schools at Johns Hopkins University) and Steven Ross (a researcher at the University of Memphis).[48] Different from his exchange with Walberg and Greenberg, Slavin's response was matched with independent research on comprehensive school reform not conducted by associates of SFAF but, instead, by other leading research organizations with no affiliation with SFAF. This independent, external research included two reviews of comprehensive school reform published in 1999. Both aimed to provide guidance for those considering adopting comprehensive school reform programs. Both were widely cited. And both were used by Slavin to further promote the effectiveness of Success for All.[49]

Published by the American Institutes for Research, *An Educator's Guide to Schoolwide Reform* provided a *Consumer Reports*-style evaluation of 24 schoolwide programs. Reviewing available evidence and research, Success for All was one of only two programs identified as providing both strong support to schools and strong evidence of effectiveness. Published by the Thomas B. Fordham Foundation, *Better by Design? A Consumer's Guide to Schoolwide Reform* matched the reviews from the *Educator's Guide* with program descriptions and school-level vignettes from ten leading comprehensive school reform programs, each written by *New York Times Magazine* writer James Traub. While Traub's assessment of Success for All was generally favorable, it was also frank in the assessment that potential benefits gained by the specificity of Success for All came at the potential costs of the freedom and autonomy so highly valued in many U.S. schools.

This independent, external research also featured a series of reports from the Rand Corporation on the schools, programs, districts, and design teams participating in the New American Schools initiative. Rand had been commissioned to conduct longitudinal research on the entire endeavor. The result was the most rigorous, sustained, comparative analysis to date of the piloting, scale-up, implementation, and effectiveness of comprehensive school reform programs.

Rand researchers published their baseline observations and analysis of program pilots in 1995 and 1996 (respectively).[50] In 1998, Rand researchers published a formative analysis of the first two years of the scale-up phase (SY 1995/1996 and SY 1997/1998).[51] Among their findings, researchers reported that Roots and Wings (SFAF's offering) and one other program (Expeditionary Learning) showed higher levels of implementation than the other five participating programs. Researchers attributed successful scale-up to a set of interacting conditions: for example, the buy-in, structure, and climate of schools; the specificity of the designs and the associated support for implementation; favorable environmental conditions, in districts and in broader institutional arrangements; and the capabilities of the sponsoring organizations.

Findings from their study of scale-up came with what Rand researchers described as a "heavy caveat" that their sample and data collection might unfairly represent the progress made by some teams.[52] Moreover, like Traub, Rand researchers were frank in acknowledging that their findings were open to interpretation:

> From our observations, what one makes of the NAS initiative to date is open to judgment. About half the schools in our sample were making significant progress toward implementation at the end of the second year. Whether one considers this "good" or "bad" performance depends, of course, upon one's point of view and prior experience. If one is familiar with past reform efforts or with the difficulties of complex organizational change in the public sector, these results probably look quite positive. Seeing any movement at all in a two-year period, other than the adoption of a small program or adoption by some part of the school, can be considered strong progress. For those used to command-based organizations or to organizations free from the influence of local politics, these results might be frustrating, even bleak.[53]

Yet even with such caveats and qualifiers, the findings of Rand researchers continued to fuel SFAF's reputation as a provider of effective, replicable comprehensive school reform programs. And if policy trajectories continued as predicated by

Slavin, SFAF's growing reputation stood to heighten its status as a leader in what looked be an increasingly institutionalized market for comprehensive school reform programs.

The Forecast: Sunny Skies

Thus, the newly founded SFAF quickly assumed responsibility for operating a large, state-sized system of chronically underperforming schools, absent the legitimacy, capital, and/or stable funding of a state education agency and despite continued criticism in its environments. While operating at the scale of a large SEA, SFAF's core organizational capabilities were quite different. Rather than a bureaucratic agency in the executive branch of government, SFAF was the hub of an emerging professional network, with self-assumed responsibility for the on-going improvement of Success for All, support for schools, and maintenance of the professional network.

This was not only a large organization but, also, a complex organization performing an array of independently complicated and mutually dependent functions: designing programs, materials and learning opportunities; developing and operating a geographically distributed training organization; engaging in research and evaluation; publishing, warehousing, and distributing materials; all atop the usual business operations. While many external providers of educational services specialized in one of the preceding core functions, few (if any) specialized in all.

Performing such work under such conditions would appear daunting. Even so, leaders of SFAF did not see evolving environments, changing dynamics, organizational complexities, and continued criticism as gathering clouds. Rather, they saw them as a rainbow under which sat a pot of gold: legitimacy, guidance, resources, incentives, and (with the founding of SFAF) new organizational capabilities to support growing ambitions for large-scale reform.

Indeed, this was time of great optimism within SFAF, as still-greater success appeared to be on the horizon. For FY 2000, Congress increased the appropriation for CSRD by $75 million, with $50 million targeted to support comprehensive school reform in 1000 more schools. As of SY 1999/2000, SFAF executives were forecasting adding an additional 250 schools for SY 2000/2001, with the total number of schools expected to exceed 1,800.[54] Against such projections, the new, essential bet on which the entire enterprise rested—continued scale-up as a source of operating capital for the newly independent, nonprofit SFAF—appeared to be a safe one.

EXPLODING RISK

While SFAF leaders saw a rainbow, clouds continued to gather and swirl. Exploding growth was matched with exploding risk that a set of ripening conditions in schools, environments, and the SFAF training organization would trigger interpretation of the program as either technocratic or bureaucratic: a very large number of weak schools that quickly needed to advance to novice use; tremendous potential in these schools and their environments to co-opt, subvert, or undermine the program; and tremendous potential for Success for All trainers to underscore what was already an increasing emphasis on consistency. From such interpretations, then, came the potential for problems of rote, mechanistic use and/or out-and-out resistance.

Risks in Schools and Environments

The risks began in schools and their proximal environments: districts and states. From its inception, Success for All's extensive program adoption process was the primary mechanism both for ensuring favorable initial conditions in schools and for managing schools' proximal environments. During this period of explosive growth, the program adoption process became even more important, given the complex motivations within (and interactions between) schools, districts, and states. At the same time, SFAF experienced problems using its program adoption process to establish a foundation for successful implementation. Indeed, what was already a regression to the mean in the initial motivations, capabilities, and environments of newly adopting schools quickly became a rush.

The problems began with the complex motivations of newly interested schools. Some earnestly sought to engage schoolwide improvement. Some were looking for a quick fix. Some were acting out of financial opportunism. However, the sheer number of newly interested schools made it very difficult for SFAF to work closely with them to sort out these motivations. Worse yet, the sheer number made it difficult for SFAF to ensure the integrity of the 80% vote for program adoption by instructional staff. In fact, some members of SFAF recalled the vote being intentionally compromised in schools: for example, by allowing only regular classroom teachers (and not "specials" teachers in art, music, and physical education) to vote. Further, even when conducted with integrity, heavy spring-to-fall teacher transience meant that the teachers implementing the program in the fall were not the same ones who voted for it in the spring. The result, thus, was a large number of schools weakly committed to improvement (in general) and to Success for All (in particular).

Then there was the matter of the initial capabilities of newly adopting schools. Some schools that adopted Success for All during this period of explosive growth shared the atypical and maverick nature of early adopting schools.[55] Even so, in the main, those involved recalled the vast majority of newly recruited schools as representative of more modal, chronically underperforming Title I schools: weaker organizations, with higher incidents of social problems, more uncertified instructional staff, weaker knowledge of reading instruction, and more staff mobility. Many newly adopting schools had weak understandings of instruction on any level, let alone initial capabilities that would ultimately support the expert, adaptive use of Success for All. In a 2003 interview, one seasoned trainer with knowledge and experience in diagnostic, adaptive instruction recalled working with these schools:

> You go into a school, and you've got teachers who are zero to a hundred. You've got situations where more than half the teachers have just come off the streets. I mean, they didn't have credentials. They were so overwhelmed by behavioral issues, and they did not see the link between instructional design and behavioral control or management. Talk to them about analyzing data, and they tell you, "I could tell you what my data is. Yesterday, there were ten kids in my room. Today there's two, because I kicked eight out, and things are going better today. So that seems to be working."

And then there was the matter of proximal environments. While the program adoption process had long been used to manage and to buffer the proximal environments of schools, increasing district and state involvement began compromising the program adoption process.[56] Some schools were forced by districts and/or states to select a comprehensive school reform program from a short list of providers, with Success for All a clearly favored option (for example, schools in New Jersey's Abbott districts). Some schools were given no choice (for example, schools in New York's Chancellor's Districts). For these schools, program adoption was not a free and informed choice but, instead, something more akin to a blind date, an arranged marriage, or a shotgun wedding. In a 2003 interview, Nancy Madden, cofounder of Success for All, recalled:

> When we started this in the 90s, in the early 90s, we had schools beating down the door to use Success for All. So what kind of schools are these? These are self-selected schools that have more initiative, so they are generally stronger as organizations. As time went on, as the accountability pressure increased in the field, schools were being pressured to do something. And where is the data? The data is with Success for All. So they were being pressured to do Success for All. The schools that were being put into reconstitution were told, "You will be reconstituted if you don't do something. Do something. Here are your choices." There were a limited number of choices, and Success for All was one of them.

And, again, there was incentive for Success for All to look past these many problems. Given its mission of improving education for at-risk students, and given its ambitions for scale, SFAF *wanted* these schools. Given the dependence of the newly independent, nonprofit SFAF on revenues from new schools, SFAF *needed* these schools.

The result was to stack the deck—but not in SFAF's favor. Again, SFAF's strategy for supporting implementation depended heavily on establishing initial conditions favoring effective implementation: knowledge of the program; an attainable vision of success; commitment to begin a deep-reaching, long-term improvement initiative; free and informed choice by 80% of the instructional staff; knowledgeable, respected, experienced leadership; and buffered and managed environments. Yet during its period of explosive growth, changing dynamics and a compromised program adoption process resulted, instead, in conditions favoring adverse interpretation and misuse of the program: weak knowledge of the program; weak (if any) commitment to sustained, deep-reaching improvement; forced choice and/or external imposition; questionable leadership; and intrusive, hostile, and turbulent environments. And, in some cases, rather than working to stem some conditions, SFAF was complicit.

By all accounts, these conditions had already been ripening as Success for All expanded to 800 schools. They were widespread throughout the 800 schools newly recruited to the program in SY 1998–1999 and SY 1999–2000.

Risks in Expanding the Training Organization

Explosive growth, failing training partnerships, and exploding risks in schools and environments combined to put deep strains on SFAF's training organization. The training organization quickly needed to increase in size to serve 800 new schools without giving ground on its 800 existing schools. Moreover, it needed to do so under conditions of tremendous uncertainty, as SFAF did not have firm estimates of the number of new schools (and, thus, the number of needed trainers) until mid to late summer of any given year.

To serve its exploding base of schools, SFAF's training organization grew both in size and in structural complexity. Barbara Haxby, SFAF's director of implementation, estimated that SFAF increased its training staff by nearly 100% for each of the first two years of its existence, to a total of over 250 trainers by 1999/2000. The estimate of 100% growth in trainers over consecutive years meant that, in a given year, 50% of the SFAF trainers were in their first year of training, and 25% were in their second year.

Building on the existing structure of its geographically distributed training organization, SFAF organized regions and regional managers into four new, superordinate areas, each with an area office and director: east (headquartered in Maryland), midwest (headquartered in West Virginia), south (headquartered in Louisiana), and west (headquartered in Arizona). SFAF also maintained a separately managed staff of trainers specializing exclusively in family support. The resulting structure had the trappings of formal hierarchy: teams of trainers working under a school-specific point trainer; all trainers reporting to regional managers; regional managers reporting to area directors; and area directors reporting to the national director of implementation.

While SFAF recruited some new trainers from its ex-partner organizations, SFAF still had yet to identify and tap a large, reliable source of instantly expert trainers in its environments. Instead, SFAF satisfied its urgent need for trainers using its established strategy of recruiting from successful Success for All schools— mostly teachers, some reading facilitators, and very few principals or others with formal leadership education or experience.

This established strategy solved key problems. Beyond at least some familiarity with (and capacity to use) the program, trainers who left their schools to join SFAF expressed a commitment to the program and to the organization. Many had positive personal experiences using the program in schools, and they were excited to help others to learn to do the same. In a 2003 interview about the growth of the SFAF training organization, a member of SFAF's Training Institute, herself an ex-Success for All teacher and trainer, recalled the missionary spirit and vitality of new Success for All trainers:

> Everybody who works here has a missionary spirit. There's no doubt about it. For the trainers, the people who come on are people who have had a really great experience with Success for All in their school. And I believe that most of them come on for the same reasons that I did. "Boy, if I can make this dif-ference with my class, my 16 to 25 kids, and maybe 60 kids throughout the year, then I can come on, and not only can I help 60 kids, but I can touch all these teachers and their kids, and then those kids will touch other." You really get this sense that you can help more kids, because you're touching more people and helping them to understand how great this program is and how it really can transform a child's life. Because I've seen it. I've seen it happen. I've seen it in my own classroom. And then being out in the field, I've seen it in other people's classrooms, too. They've been so excited and brought data to me. "You wouldn't believe these kids! They were here and now they've gone to these heights, and these kids have passed the test! We only had 30%, and now we have 55%!" And being a part of that energy is so exciting. And so it's really about spreading the message and spreading the goods. And I think a lot of people come on because they want to do that. They really believe in it, because they saw it in their class.

While SFAF's recruiting strategy solved key problems, one key problem remained: Few newly recruited trainers had the knowledge or experience to manage steep, pressing risks of adverse interpretation and misuse in newly recruited schools and their turbulent environments. With the exception of expe-rienced trainers recruited from ex-partners, most of SFAF's newly recruited train-ers were rookies. Few had ever worked beyond their own classrooms, let alone on the road and out of a suitcase. Few had experience working as an external expert charged with the professional development of teachers and school leaders. Few had extensive knowledge and experience across the entire range of Success for All program components. And, to the extent that they were recruited from strong schools that were succeeding in the expert use of Success for All, their experiences were likely rooted in schools quite unlike those that they would be serving: schools recruited under the complex dynamics of CSRD and REA, most of which were generally weak, many of which were of mixed motivations, and many of which were working in increasingly intrusive district and state environments.

With that, SFAF's training organization began to take on the very problems that it was to solve in schools. Indeed, the more trainers SFAF recruited, the less they resembled the atypical members of the original training team, and the more they resembled the modal good teacher or reading facilitator in Success for All schools: committed to the program and its mission; comparatively strong in initial capabilities for novice use; comparatively weak in initial capabilities for expert use; and susceptible to technocratic and/or bureaucratic interpretations of the program.

Risks in Structuring Trainers' Work and Professional Development

Problems recruiting instantly expert trainers created the urgent need to structure the work and professional development of rookie trainers. The challenge mirrored that of schools: quickly establishing base-level capabilities for novice training; and, then, quickly progressing to expert training. The strategy used by SFAF mirrored that for schools: formally elaborating and scaffolding novice, consistent training; and depending on informal communities of practice to develop capabilities for expert training. The result, again, was that support for trainers mirrored that for schools: strong formal support for faithful, consistent training; and weaker formal support for responsive, adaptive training.

The most urgent need was to quickly create the capabilities for these newly recruited trainers to work as "novice trainers": trainers who could introduce, teach, model, monitor, and support Success for All faithfully, consistently, and with fidelity in any given school. The need was, in part, financial. SFAF needed to get new trainers into the field quickly and billing for their services in order cover the up-front costs of recruiting, training, and equipping them—again, potentially as high as $50,000 per trainer.[57] The need was, in part, pragmatic. The very task at hand was quickly establishing base levels of operations in hundreds of newly recruited schools. The magnitude of this task cannot be understated. In a 2003 interview, an SFAF regional manager recalled coordinating initial training for a large, urban district during the first year of CSRD funding:

> That first year, we had a massive initial training, because the district wanted everyone trained on the same three days. Every teacher, every para-professional, every principal was trained. Usually initial training is held around the last week of August, around August 27th, 28th, or 29th. We went in for three days. I brought the 16 trainers on my team, and I brought in other regions' trainers, too. A total of 55 SFA trainers trained the initial three-day training. There were approximately 1,700 participants. We started with the overview on day one. Everyone is required to attend that session. On days two and three, we trained Early Learning, Reading Roots, and Reading Wings. In that district, the day after we trained, they hired new people. There were about 200 hires after the mass initial training. That happens at every school district, as a matter of fact, and especially the big ones. So then we had to figure out, "How do we get into the schools to train these new hires?" When school starts, you cannot do a three-day initial training, so we condensed everything

into a one-day initial training for those participants. In many instances, principals could not find coverage for their teachers even for the one day sessions, so those teachers ended up attending a half day session for about two and a half hours.

Equally urgent was that trainers quickly develop capabilities for expert training. Indeed, while novice training was an "in-principle" step in trainers' professional development, there was little room for it in practice. Almost immediately, trainers needed to develop capabilities to work in some of the nation's most challenged schools on a complex set of interdependent tasks: mopping up problems that arose through the program adoption process; managing and mediating increasingly intrusive environments; and compensating for weaknesses and shortcomings in the elaboration and scaffolding of Success for All. Doing so was predicated on developing teachers' and leaders' trust in them as partners in learning and not as inspectors charged with reporting and sanctioning teachers and leaders who were not using the program "correctly."

To elaborate and scaffold novice training, SFAF continued with established strategies. It provided detailed scripts for trainers to use in direct instruction with schools. It provided detailed Implementation Visit Reports to assess the consistency of implementation in schools. And it provided professional development sessions in which more experienced trainers modeled the consistent use of training scripts and Implementation Visit Reports. While serviceable, this combination was described by several trainers as "the bare minimum" needed to provide basic support to schools at the start of trainers' first year with SFAF.

Problematic, though, was that consistent use of highly elaborated training resources risked trainers inadvertently modeling technocratic use of program resources and/or evoking bureaucratic interpretations of the program. The risk was particularly acute in trainers' usage of the Implementation Visit Report, which required that trainers make brief observations of every class, focus primarily on teachers' behaviors (and not teachers' or students' understandings), and produce summary reports focused primarily on consistency of implementation. In a 2003 interview, one SFAF staff member who had experienced the Implementation Visit process both as a principal in a Success for All school and as a field-based trainer recalled the experience:

It really was an inspection model. Come in and check, check, check, check, check, check, check, check. To me, it was so similar to the teacher evaluation systems that we were trying to abolish 20 years ago. You know, the check, check, check, check, check, check, check teacher evaluation systems.

As novice trainers then entered the field, SFAF continued to support their work and professional development with annual and regional meetings (during the school year) and with week-long Experienced Trainers Institutes (during the summer). These "pull out" professional development opportunities functioned for trainers much as Experienced Sites Conferences did for school leaders: as opportunities for exposure to (rather than mastery of) expert knowledge and practice, for renewal and commitment building, for networking and debriefing, and for learning about new developments within Success for All.

Formal support for more expert training was problematic, as well. Members of SFAF recalled that, during this period of explosive growth, the message of "consistency" was much stronger than the message of "adaptation," even in meetings for experienced trainers. In fact, they recalled one Experienced Trainers Institute in which trainers were given hats bearing the slogan from the then-current Nike advertising campaign: "Just Do It!" The message was clear: Just do the program, exactly as elaborated and scaffolded.

At the same time, the comparatively weak message of expert use fell on deaf ears, in that few newly recruited trainers had understandings and experience that would enable them to hear and understand the message of expert use. In a 2003 interview, one senior SFAF manager who shared responsibility for developing and conducting Experienced Training Institutes during this period reflected on the experience:

I don't think that, within our training cadre, the concept of diagnostic instruction was totally understood. At an Experienced Training Institute, I was talking about the cycle of instruction and diagnostic instruction. And half of the room was with me, and half the room was not.

I think you could trace it all the way back to university training with teachers. When I went through, and I've heard other people articulate this, there wasn't a lot of emphasis on diagnostic instruction. There was a lot of emphasis on best practices and using good teaching strategies. Some folks, I certainly was among them, thought that what that meant was, you use all your good things. But using all your good things is different than strategically using those good things. It's understanding that maybe I use just this particular piece and this particular piece and, then, I figure out if it's working or not and, then, I change and adapt.

But I don't think we were communicating that basic understanding. I think for the most part, we were talking about this great program and doing this great program and that it had all the best practices that you needed. And, then, we would talk about the eight week assessment summary form as a good way to look at who's above and who's below, and then you get a sense of who you have to put more energy into.

But except for exceptional trainers who had that understanding anyway, or who came out of special education or other special programs, I think that trainers were not able to make that connection to diagnostic instruction within themselves and articulate it to a school. The reading trainers come from schools, so they're teachers. They mirror that same population.

To support expert training, and to compensate for shortcomings and risks in support for novice training, SFAF's trainers continued to function as small, informal learning communities within the larger, complex, hierarchically structured training organization. Indeed, despite the formal training opportunities described above, the most poignant learning opportunities for trainers were exactly as for schools: practicing the work of training and, then, learning in and from practice via collaboration with colleagues. Yet there was no formal design for practice-based learning within these communities: for example, rotations of new trainers through more highly developed communities; established curricula to guide and support their practice-based learning; and means of monitoring trainers' development. Rather, learning opportunities continued to develop exactly as they had: informally, as novice trainers developed and leveraged personal relationships with high-level trainers, training developers, managers, and executives.

Problematic was that, during this period of explosive growth, many circumstances began to work against informal communities of practice as the primary means of developing capabilities for expert training across large numbers of new trainers: for example, the size of the training organization; the geographic distribution of trainers; the ratio of new and inexperienced trainers to established and experienced trainers; variable knowledge of expert training among leaders in the training organization (i.e., regional managers and area directors); and the lack of slack time for practice-based learning. Such communities *did* continue to develop in exceptional situations: for example, in the Chancellor's District in New York City, in which an experienced member of the SFAF executive team managed a geographically concentrated group of trainers; and in SFAF's western-most geographic area, in which area and regional managers with unusual capabilities for expert use worked to develop comparable capabilities and trainers. However, such cases were the exception, not the rule.

Though its communities of practice were becoming strained, SFAF was slow to recognize the depth of the problem. It was slower yet to develop formal structures and learning opportunities to compensate. In a 2003 interview, Barbara Haxby, SFAF's director of implementation, recalled exactly that:

> How do you target change? How do you make thoughtful adaptations in the program? How do you help schools be able to target and troubleshoot? A lot of that was happening very informally within our organization, because we were a very small staff. If there's only six of us sitting around a table, then you say, "What do you do with . . . Well, what if. . . ." It was all at that much more "sitting around a table" kind of level. When we added 70 trainers per year, we got systems for training. But what really lagged behind was the whole system for how do we monitor and how do we address implementation and issues of implementation. You can't just be about, "Is the program in place?" You've got to be looking at the outcomes. You've got to be able to shift what people are doing. You have to be able to talk to people about what their goals are.

Calculated and Managed Risk

Conditions were ripening. With past trends amplified by explosive growth, the strengths and weaknesses of systems supporting the work and professional development of trainers mirrored precisely those for teachers: strong in formal support for novice, consistent training; and weak in formal support for expert, adaptive, locally responsive training. With that, SFAF ran real risk that its own training organization was formally structured to exacerbate precisely the problem that it most needed to solve: interpretation of the program as technocratic or bureaucratic, from which would follow either rote, mechanical implementation or active resistance—all at a previously unimaginable scale.

Even if in motion for nearly a decade, even if clear in retrospect, and even if proclaimed loudly and clearly by critics in the moment, these conditions were forming under the radar of many within SFAF, obscured by unprecedented scale-up, continued evidence of effectiveness, and the potential for more. In fact, during this period, SFAF executives were actually attempting to calculate and manage such risks by determining the number of new schools that could be added per year without compromising the quality of training support provided schools.[58] Their procedure for doing so had them working backwards: first determining the number of experienced trainers available to serve as mentors to novice trainers; then determining the number of novice trainers that could be added in a given year; then using the total number of available trainers and the number of existing schools to determine the number of trainer days available for new schools; and, from that, determining the cap on new schools to be added. By this procedure, SFAF was adding no more schools per year than (per executives' estimates) could be supported with high quality training services.

Despite having detailed procedures to protect against over-recruiting, nobody involved recalled SFAF ever rejecting large numbers of schools. Environments presented unprecedented opportunity for rapid scale up, evidence of program effectiveness created a moral imperative, and SFAF's financial strategy created a real need. Amidst exploding growth and exploding risk, SFAF's approach to the work of scaling up was as it had been from the program's inception. Manifest destiny. Wherever and whenever we choose. Damn the torpedoes. Full speed ahead. Yet, in a 2003 interview, one senior SFAF trainer reflected that the writing was on the wall:

> The systems within our organization were all built around fidelity and consistency. Every single one. Our training, our communication, our documents, our reporting, our everything. Your documents, if you're not careful, can drive you, even though you don't know that's where you're going.

A PERFECT STORM

As it entered its second decade, the interdependencies among SFAF's schools, program, environments, and organization were perplexing. On the one hand, positive interactions promised sailing so smooth that critics charged SFAF as having been afforded unfair advantage in national-level education reform. On the other hand, negative interactions had conditions ripening for a perfect storm: newly adopting schools with deep weaknesses and complex motivations;

designs that had evolved to favor formal support for novice use and weak support for expert use; environments increasingly encroaching on school-level autonomy, and lacking in critical human and financial resources to support the development of a training organization; and a training organization that was constituted, formally structured, and socially structured in ways that exacerbated (rather than ameliorated) the risks of adversely interpreting and misusing the program.

With the thunderclap of explosive growth, the storm broke, and the newly independent SFAF sailed straight into it. At the same time that SFAF and others publicized positive research findings, SFAF's executives, researchers, field managers, and lead trainers were also concerned, in that they began to recognize a broad pattern of two interacting problems in schools. Internally, these were framed as problems of "process" and of "outcomes." Regarding process: Members of SFAF began observing that many schools were locked into a pattern of novice use, focused exclusively on consistency, faithfulness, and fidelity, absent attention to the learning needs of students or the effects of instructional and leadership practice on students' learning.[59] Regarding outcomes: Members of SFAF began to describing a "flatlining" phenomenon, a sort of "plateau effect" on both internal and external measures of student achievement well below the intended on-grade-level reading goals.[60] The assumed causation was that problems of process were causing problems of outcomes: that students were not learning at expected levels precisely because instructional and leadership practice were disconnected from academic needs and outcomes.

Reports of problems of process and outcomes were sufficiently widespread as to warrant extensive investigation by Nancy Madden (SFAF's president) and Barbara Haxby (SFAF's director of implementation). In a 2003 interview, Haxby recalled:

> Nancy and I did a bunch of visits to several different schools around the country. One of the things that we saw were teachers doing a really good job of instruction, and neither Nancy nor I saw sufficient evidence of people really listening to what the kids were doing at a whole bunch of different levels. We were at one school where the teacher was teaching a great 2.1 lesson in Reading Wings (second grade, first semester). Really, he's energetic, the kids are with him, and they're all talking in their teams. And you think, "Well, this looks pretty good." And we're talking to him at the end. He says, "Oh, it's the best class. I'm really enjoying it. It's great." But we said, "What do you think about your kids?" And he said, "Oh, they're fine. They'll all end up the semester on 2.2 (second grade, second semester). They're moving right along. We're going to end up right on place."
>
> Well, it was funny. Half of his class were 4th graders. And there's this sense that, "No, no, half of your class is in crisis. If they're doing this well, why aren't you strategically planning how to move those kids faster, to get them out of 2.2 and into something else? You have a huge problem in your classroom, because you've got 4th graders sitting in here. It's not OK that they're working at a 2.1 level, no matter how nicely they're doing it."

You know, but the class was really fun. It was energetic. It was spirited. And, somehow, he wasn't concentrating as much on the data showing where the kids were.

So there's this real sense that there wasn't being sufficient attention paid by teachers to what the kids were really able to do in the classroom and no tracking on whether they were getting growth. There wasn't sufficient attention to making thoughtful adaptations of the program to really hone in on the skills that the kids weren't achieving.

While Success for All was intended to quickly establish a high floor under implementation and student achievement, it appeared that the program was actually establishing a ceiling above them. As SFAF executives, developers, field managers, and lead trainers teased out the root causes, they began recognizing the underlying conditions that had been emerging and ripening for over a decade, appreciating their subtleties and importance, and understanding how they interacted to create conditions favoring adverse interpretation and misuse of Success for All.

And the deepest problems—the ones that SFAF was slowest to recognize—were those in its own training organization. An extensive focus on fidelity and consistency in the systems supporting the work and professional development of trainers effected and aggravated "technocratic" and "bureaucratic" interpretations of the program. From that came problems of process and outcomes: rote, mechanistic implementation of Success for All, with achievement flatlining at a level far below the intended success for all. In a 2003 interview, Robert Slavin recalled recognizing exactly that:

> We knew what we didn't want to have happen. We had long experience in the ways in which good ideas were undermined. We wanted to be very explicit and provide some definite guidelines. But we went too far. In practice, we went too far. Again, that was never our conceptualization. But in the process of transmitting our knowledge-base to the next level to the next level to the next level, that's what happened. It became proceduralized the further you went down the line.

Some schools and trainers were succeeding in progressing beyond novice use to more expert use of Success for All, whether due to schools' initiative and capabilities, the guidance of more able trainers, or some combination. In fact, during this period, members of SFAF recalled an "upward press" from more expert schools and trainers for additional resources and training to support adaptive, locally responsive use. And, as discussed in the next chapter, SFAF would immediately begin an expansive, deep-reaching, four-year development cycle to address these (and other) needs.

However, many other schools were struggling. The ratio of success to problems was not clear, as SFAF had no data from that time period documenting the number of schools at the novice and expert levels. Asked in 2005 to estimate the percentage retrospectively, Barbara Haxby, SFAF's director of implementation, estimated the percentage of expert schools at approximately 25%.[61] By that estimate, the number of schools progressing to expert use was roughly 400, a subsystem of schools roughly the size of small state (e.g., South Dakota). At the same time, that put the number of nonexpert schools very, very high: at roughly 1,200 schools, roughly as many elementary schools as in the state of Georgia.

Certainly, the gravity of the situation varied among struggling schools, and even struggling schools were sure to have experienced at least some success. Even so, for an organization that banked its reputation on technical effectiveness, one that aspired to professional practice and learning, and one that saw itself positioned to make historic progress in the large-scale improvement of education for at-risk students, SFAF was staring down a huge problem, with its primary mechanism for addressing it—its own training organization—the root cause.

RECAPTURING THE PROGRAM

While there was evidence that Success for All's alchemy of "professionalism by design" could work, it appeared to be highly dependent on controlled, laboratory-like conditions: an informed and committed teaching staff; able and experienced leadership; support from very knowledgeable and very experienced trainers; and environments carefully managed and mediated to support successful implementation. However, as SFAF scaled up its operations, controlled, laboratory-like conditions gave way to turbulent, interdependent conditions, with apparently favorable federal policy activity driving both positive and negative interactions among the installed base of Success for All schools, the program, educational environments, and SFAF as an organization. Such complex dynamics did not hold true only for SFAF. A Rand report on the scale-up phase of the New American Schools initiative suggested that this dynamic held true for all of the participating design teams:

> We would summarize this analysis with a reminder of the larger picture that has been painted. We found many interdependent, interconnected factors to be important in supporting implementation in the schools. . . . They include actions taken by schools, districts, states, unions, and design teams in concert with each other and in conflict with each other. . . .
> Our analysis revealed a messy organic model of change, not a deterministic one. Importantly, in the model we observed, implementation progress was not the responsibility of a single change agent or a managerial function. Rather, what we uncovered is a model in which design teams can give schools and districts no guarantees of results because results depend at least in part on inputs that schools and districts control or contribute—resources, commitment, time, and effort. Schools will succeed at this effort, in part, because they and their districts choose to, not simply because of the services teams provide.[62]

For SFAF, its approach to the work of scaling up—whenever and wherever we chose—was drawing the organization deeper and deeper into the world of U.S. public education. Predating the inception of the Success for All enterprise, SFAF's founders had committed to navigating this terrain rationally and strategically, drawing on research and past experience. Yet each day pushing into this world revealed more about it, and what it revealed about the interdependencies between schools, the program, environments, and the organization befuddled SFAF's rational, strategic approach. As SFAF persisted over time and increased in scale, it did not cross some river or crest some hill over which lay new, orderly, easily-navigable terrain. Rather, SFAF found itself pushing deeper and deeper into more twisted thickets and into new, dense forests, many of its own making.

Oddly, such steep problems and challenges did not swamp the optimism of SFAF, nor its self-assumed responsibility for solving them, nor its confidence that it *could* solve them. Instead, SFAF's optimism, commitment, and confidence swamped these problems and challenges. Rather than blaming teachers, leaders, schools, environments, or even its own trainers, SFAF executives assumed responsibility for problems of process and outcomes in Success for All schools, and they assumed responsibility for (and exercised agency in) solving them. As Nancy Madden, SFAF cofounder and president, explained in a 2003 interview:

> It was sort of surprising. We'd go into schools, and a teacher would be very pleased with how the kids were doing. We'd sit down with the kids, and we'd go over the words that they were reading or ask them what a paragraph meant, and they'd clearly be way off-base. And the teacher's not noticing this, which is sort of amazing. So, then, we had to figure, "Oh, my God, we haven't gotten there yet. We've got to get that teacher to understand what's missing. When teachers think they're doing the process really well and they don't notice that the kid isn't reading with any comprehension at all, there's something wrong."
>
> So, then, we have to go and say, "Well, how can we hit that harder? How can we get them to look at that child and really figure it out?" That's always our belief. If we do it well enough, they'll get it, and we can scaffold it for them. And it's always nice to have more experienced or more thoughtful teachers to work with. That's always a nice thing. That's when you get to feel like there's a little magic in the program. But you can't depend on that. We can't depend on that. Schools have the teachers that they have, and they can do a whole lot more than what they're doing. And the better we are at scaffolding for them and communicating and focusing and all of that, the better they will do.

This combination of optimism, commitment, and confidence combined to fuel work that had been ongoing in SFAF since the inception of Success for All: the work of continuously improving the program. Yet improving the program while working in 1,600 schools would surely be more challenging than doing so while working in one, ten, or a hundred schools. The work of improving the program would require that SFAF manage a set of complex, interdependent activities, including: acquiring the necessary financial and human resources; improving its comprehensive, integrated design and supports (with particular attention to increasing the potential for expert, adaptive use); improving the resources and professional development available to trainers (again, with particular attention to expert training practice); coordinating the dissemination of program improvements to its state-sized network of 1,600 schools and its 250-member training organization; all while proceeding to act on ambitions to increase the scale of the Success for All network and SFAF; all in turbulent, dynamic environments.

Perhaps the greatest challenge would lie in acquiring and/or producing the knowledge and expertise needed to support an improvement effort layered in complexity and novelty. Existing research and past experience were only taking SFAF so far, and learning from experience was both necessary and tremendously challenging, owing to the complex interactions among schools, the program, environments, and the organization. This was true for SFAF's development and training organizations, as they pushed further into designing and supporting expert use of the program. It was especially true of the SFAF executives charged with managing the effort. Indeed, though steeped in the work of external, design-based school improvement, improving both the program and the organization while operating at such a large scale was well beyond the knowledge and experience of SFAF's executives. Moreover, aside from other participants in New American Schools initiative, there were few (if any) comparable educational programs or organizations on which to draw for such knowledge and expertise, either public or private.

Still, what could easily be interpreted as overwhelming adversity was interpreted as overwhelming opportunity within SFAF. Though there were challenges to be met, SFAF was on a roll. Circa 1999/2000, environmental support showed no signs of weakening, with CSRD and REA slated to continue supplying additional funding for comprehensive school reform through the next scheduled reauthorization of the Elementary and Secondary Education Act in 2001. The broader economy was booming to unprecedented heights on the strength of the information technology sector, thus continuing to supply SFAF and many others involved in educational reform with the considerable funding needed to fuel their efforts. The country was at peace. It was a "dot com" world. The cyber-sky was the limit—for everybody, and for SFAF.

With that, SFAF embarked on an effort to improving its design, its supports, and its own organization, all while also seeking to expand its scale of operations. The development effort would run for four years. In a 2003 interview, SFAF cofounder and chairman Robert Slavin described the goals of the effort very succinctly: "We're trying to recapture the program. We're trying recapture the program and focus it on the things that it began with." And where it began was with the alchemy of using an external design to effect professional practice and professional learning—not under controlled, laboratory-like conditions, but whenever and wherever SFAF chose.

Notes

1. From Slavin, Madden, Dolan, Wasik, Ross, and Smith (1994), titled "'Whenever and wherever we choose': The replication of Success for All." Note that, with the 1994 reauthorization of the Elementary and Secondary Education Act, Chapter 1 returned to its original designation as Title I.
2. Wenger (2008). Also, see Wenger (1999) and Lave and Wenger (1991).
3. See Wasik and Madden (1992) for extensive, early elaboration of expert use within Success for All's tutoring component.
4. In a report prepared for the U.S. Department of Education by the Council of Chief State School Officers, Williams, Blank, Toye, and Petermann (2007) reported Delaware as having 104 public elementary schools in SY 2002/2003.
5. Williams, Blank, Toye, and Petermann (2007) reported Hawaii and Alaska as having 183 and 175 elementary schools (respectively) in SY 2002/2003.
6. Williams, Blank, Toye, and Petermann (2007) reported Vermont as having 257 elementary schools in SY 2002/2003.
7. Williams, Blank, Toye, and Petermann (2007) reported Oregon as having 747 elementary schools in SY 2002/2003.
8. See U.S. Department of Education (1994a) regarding the district role in comprehensive school reform. See Bodilly (1998:12–16) for the expansion with NAS to include districts. By the time it entered the scale up phase, NAS was advocating that districts needed a critical mass of 30% of schools participating in comprehensive school reform programs in order to warrant the development of district-level capabilities to assist them. The Memphis City Schools (NAS participant and home of Success for All's University of Memphis-based training operation) went further, to require 100% of schools to adopt comprehensive school reform programs.
9. Slavin and Madden (1996b:26; 1999b:26) reported that, for Success for All and other of the comprehensive school reform development initiatives, federal support was minimal in relation to private support. Culling from published reports, contributors instrumental in the scale-up of Success for All included: the Office of Educational Research and Improvement (development and evaluation); the Carnegie Foundation (development and evaluation); the Pew Foundation (development and evaluation); the New American Schools (assets for securing loans from banks; development and evaluation); the Ford Foundation (assets for securing loans from banks); the MacArthur Foundation (assets for securing loans from banks); and others (including the Sandler Family Foundation, the Stupski Family Foundation, the Charles A. Dana Foundation, and the Abell Foundation). See: Slavin and Madden (1996b, 1999a, 1999b, and 2000).
10. Slavin and Madden (1996b:26–27; 1999b:26–27).
11. While troublesome for Success for All project leaders, this was consistent with the goal of NAS to establish its design teams as stand-alone, fee-for-service organizations.
12. Slavin, Madden, Shaw, Mainzer, and Donnelly (1993:110).
13. Slavin and Madden (1996b:26–27).
14. Slavin and Madden (1996b:14; 1999a:v; 1999b:iii; 2001a.).
15. Slavin and Madden (1996b; 1999a; 1999b; 2001a.).
16. Slavin and Madden (1996b:9–10).
17. Slavin and Madden (1996b:11).

18. Slavin and Madden (2001c:xiii).
19. Slavin and Madden (1999b:10).
20. Slavin and Madden (1996b:24).
21. See: Nunnery, Ross, Smith, Slavin, Hunter, and Stubbs (1996); Nunnery, Slavin, Madden, Ross, Smith, Hunter, and Stubbs (1997); and Ross, Smith, Slavin, and Madden (1997).
22. The family support component had an additional, component-specific observation and reporting protocol.
23. Slavin and Madden (1996b:5).
24. Slavin and Madden (1996b:14–15).
25. At this time, SFAF also asserted its influence internationally, by initiating operations in Canada, England, Mexico, Israel, and Australia. See Slavin and Madden (2001c), which provides reports on SFAF's efforts in England, Canada, Israel, and Mexico.
26. $120 million was targeted at Title I schools, and $25 million was targeted at non-Title I schools, thereby increasing the reach of comprehensive school reform throughout the U.S. educational system.
27. The complete list of approved models under the Obey-Porter CSRD included: Accelerated Schools; America's Choice; Atlas Schools; Audrey Cohen College; Coalition of Essential Schools; Community of Learning; Co-NECT; Direct Instruction; Expeditionary Learning Outward Bound; High Schools That Work; Modern Red Schoolhouse; Paideia; Roots and Wings; School Development Program; Success for All; Talent Development High School; and Urban Learning Center. See Comprehensive Center - Region VI (2005).
28. U.S. Department of Education (1999a:4).
29. See Phenix, Siegel, Zaltsman, and Fruchter (2004).
30. The Abbott Districts were 28 of the poorest urban districts in New Jersey that had, since 1970, been locked in a legal dispute with the State of New Jersey over inequality in local school funding—inequalities that took on renewed concern in the face of increasing state-level pressure for school-level accountability. In 1998, with advice from the New Jersey Department of Education, the New Jersey Supreme Court ruled that the Abbott schools would be provided additional funding to pursue one of five comprehensive school reform programs: Success for All, Accelerated Schools; the Adaptive Learning Environments Model; the Comer School Development Program; and Modern Red School House.
31. New Jersey Department of Education (1997).
32. See Slavin and Madden (2001a:200). Note that the published table contained a mathematical error in the number of schools gained in 1998/1999. The published total was 390. The correct total was 340.
33. In a report prepared for the U.S. Department of Education by the Council of Chief State School Officers, Williams, Blank, Toye, and Petermann (2007) reported the following states as serving more that SFAF's 1550 elementary schools: California (5550); Texas (3934); Illinois (2619); New York (2521); Ohio (2208); Michigan (2139); Pennsylvania (1920); and Florida (1826).
34. Slavin and Madden (2001c:45).
35. Slavin and Madden (2001a).
36. Slavin and Madden (1999b:24).
37. Slavin and Madden (1999b:24).
38. Slavin and Madden (1999b:24).

39. Slavin and Madden (1999b:8).

40. Pogrow (1998).

41. See Mathews (2002).

42. See Pogrow (1998; 1999; 2000a; 2000b; 2002).

43. Pogrow (2002).

44. Pogrow (2000a).

45. See Slavin (1999; 2000a; 2000b; 2002b) and Slavin and Madden (2000).

46. Slavin and Madden (2000).

47. See Slavin and Fashola (1998), titled *Show me the evidence! Proven and promising programs for America's schools.*

48. See: Stringfield (2000); Ross (2000).

49. See: Herman (1999); Traub (1999).

50. See: Bodilly, Purnell, Ramsey, and Smith (1995); Bodilly (1996).

51. Bodilly (1998).

52. Bodilly (1998:59).

53. Bodilly (1998:107).

54. Slavin and Madden (2001b:6).

55. For example, researchers found that schools in the Year 1 cohort of Abbott schools in New Jersey were already actively engaged in reform, and leveraged the newly available funding to further their efforts. See Erlichson and Goertz (2002).

56. Datnow (2000).

57. Slavin and Madden (1999b:27).

58. Personal e-mail communication, Robert Slavin, 06/14/2005.

59. In an qualitative study of two schools that had been implementing Success for All for two or more years, Datnow and Castellano (2000) describe a pattern of implementation different than that described by members of SFAF and reported here (i.e., the distinction between rote, mechanical use and expert, adaptive use). In an analysis of two experienced Success for All schools, Datnow and Castellano reported that *all* teachers were making adaptations to the program, regardless of their level of support for the program. They also reported that, even while making adaptations, teachers felt that the program constrained their autonomy and creativity. Despite feeling constrained, Datnow and Castellano reported that teachers' continued support for Success for All derived from perceptions of benefits to students.

60. For a corroborating account of this "flatlining" phenomenon, see Rowan, Correnti, Miller, and Camburn (2009). In analysis of data collected contemporaneous with SFAF's reports of flatlining, Rowan et al. report that achievement gains in upper elementary grades lagged those in lower elementary grades. They attribute the lag to weakness in the elaboration and scaffolding of reading comprehension.

61. For a corroborating account of variable implementation in Success for All schools, see Rowan and Correnti (2009). In an analysis of logs of instructional practice collected between 2000 and 2004, Rowan and Correnti (pp. 64–66) report 57% of Success for All schools (18 of 28) had 70% or more of teachers working with a regime of procedural control (i.e., conformity to highly-specified instructional routines). They also report 24 of 28 schools as having between roughly 2% and 20% of teachers working within a regime of professional control (i.e., using expert authority). Note: The estimates of 2% and 20% are taken from interpretations of the stacked bar graphs on p. 66.

62. Bodilly (1998:108–112).

4

Continuously Improving

Programs need to constantly be learning from schools themselves and from research, and then incorporating new ideas into new materials. This enables innovative educators to feel as though they are constantly growing and contributing to an endless development process. Continuing development is also necessary to respond to new standards, new assessments, and new objectives adopted by states and districts. In addition, continuing evaluation of program outcomes, if positive, contributes to a sense that a program is progressing and is justifying the efforts necessary to implement it.

ROBERT SLAVIN AND NANCY MADDEN, 1996A[1]

For the newly founded SFAF, success brought problems. Beginning in 1999, concurrent with a rapid doubling of its installed base of schools, SFAF began recognizing widespread patterns of rote, mechanistic implementation and of lower-than-desired student achievement. With that, SFAF found itself staring down a steep and novel challenge: formalizing support for expert use of the program and, then, rapidly rippling program improvements through a 250-member training organization and through more than 1,500 schools.

SFAF needed to do so quickly. Its schools were working within a three-year implementation window, and their success (and Success for All's reputation for effectiveness) hung in the balance. The urgency was heightened by what SFAF executives forecasted to be another wave of federal policy support for continued scale-up: the pending reauthorization of the federal Elementary and Secondary Education Act as the No Child Left Behind Act. Urgency was matched with uncertainty. There were no "how to" manuals laying out knowledge and methods to guide such work. Indeed, the effort depended on SFAF's capabilities to rapidly produce and use the knowledge needed to support and sustain the enterprise.

From SY 1999/2000 to SY 2002/2003, SFAF set about the work of continuously improving the effectiveness of the program while maintaining (and seeking to expand) its installed base of schools. The effort was marked by SFAF's characteristic interdependence: the development agenda, organization, and process evolving and emerging in interaction with SFAF's ambitions and history, its programs, its schools, and their environments. The effort was marked by SFAF's characteristic combination of the rational and the organic: developers (like trainers) working within both formal structures and social relationships to leverage research and experience, all towards the goals of improving effectiveness and increasing scale. And the effort was marked by the characteristic emergence of new problems, both within the Success for All enterprise and in its interactions with its environments.

The results were remarkable. By the close of its 1999–2003 development cycle, SFAF's interdependent development agenda, organization, and process had combined to drive a revolution in the program that appeared both to increase potential for expert use and to position the organization for a new round of explosive growth. Yet at the same time, a new set of interdependent problems combined to drive a most unexpected reversal of fortune. SFAF found itself struggling not only with new challenges in its program, its schools, and its own organization. It also found itself struggling to draw essential resources from its environments, including new schools, consequent revenue, and external funding.

By the close of its 1999–2003 development cycle, rather than have reached a new zenith of effectiveness and scale, SFAF found itself living in a very strange place and on a very fine edge, with the continued viability of the Success for All enterprise hanging in the balance.

THE DEVELOPMENT AGENDA

Central to SFAF's approach to the work of continuous improvement was managing a dynamic development agenda: an informal "to do" list describing on-going and emerging efforts to improve the program. Beginning in 1999/2000 (immediately upon recognition of problems of process and outcomes) and continuing through 2002/2003 (the first year that NCLB was making its way through the system), SFAF's explosive growth in schools and in its training organization was matched with an exploding agenda for further developing and improving the program.

SFAF was a rational actor in what appeared to be rationalizing environments. Even so, SFAF's development agenda did not take shape in a classic, rational way: that is, through a comprehensiveness analysis of all available information, an exhaustive review of all possible improvement initiatives, and the selection of some optimal set of improvement initiatives that would maximize both effectiveness and opportunity for growth. Rather, SFAF's development agenda emerged in ways that mirrored the very policymaking processes on which it depended: as a sort of "muddling through" more incremental and evolutionary than classically rational, as SFAF adapted its ideas and plans for improvement in response to its ambitions, its history, and, especially, its environments.[2]

SFAF's 1999–2003 development agenda emerged at the intersection of two streams of influences. The first stream ran through the Success for All enterprise, itself: the organization, its program, and its network of schools. Consistent with its long-held commitment to continuous improvement, SFAF began its 1999–2003 development cycle already engaged in planned and previously funded improvement activity spanning virtually every component of the program: the curriculum components (Early Learning, Reading Roots, and Reading Wings); tutoring: family support; and leadership. In response to increasing recognition and understanding of problems of process and outcomes in Success for All schools, this ongoing development activity was both redirected and expanded to address those problems. The focus was squarely on improving resources and learning opportunities to support teachers, leaders, and trainers in the expert use of the program (both novice users needing to master expert use and expert users wanting more).

The second stream of influences ran from beyond the Success for All enterprise: from U.S. educational environments, and from still-broader political, economic, and social environments. Three such influences bore heavily on SFAF's development agenda. The first was plentiful funding to support development activity. In contrast to its struggles securing funding for its training organization, SFAF had a long history of securing funding to support development activity, as funders saw program development (rather than organizational development) as a legitimate use of their resources. As it began its 1999–2003 development cycle, there was much such funding to be had, with the broader economy booming on the strength of activity in the information technology sector (and, with it, the grants economy that fueled research and development in education). The second was emerging knowledge, technologies, and other resources with potential to support expert use of the program: for example, rapidly evolving research on early reading, new research on instructional leadership and on "data use," commercial assessments, and new information technologies. The third was continued educational reform activity in state and federal policy environments, including state-level efforts to devise the primary instruments of standards-based reform: curriculum standards, performance standards, and accountability assessments.

These streams of influences were constantly flowing, and they were constantly reshaping themselves—not randomly, but in cycles: for example, the annual school year as a cycle, public and private funding cycles, electoral cycles, and policy cycles. Of particular interest to SFAF was the periodic reauthorization of the federal Elementary and Secondary Education Act (ESEA). As SFAF embarked on its 1999–2003 development cycle, policy environments were buzzing with activity surrounding the reauthorization of ESEA. And with long-term viability as important as near-term effectiveness, SFAF was looking out over the horizon, with a keen eye on what had long been its North Star.

As with earlier federal policy initiatives, activity surrounding the reauthorization of ESEA provided hope for renewed support for comprehensive school reform (in general) and for Success for All (specifically). Regarding general support, the New American Schools (NAS) initiative continued to garner legitimacy and influence, with its proponents advocating for formally incorporating the Obey-Porter CSRD into ESEA. In 2001, Chester E. Finn, president of the Thomas B. Fordham Institute, described NAS as having transitioned from "revolutionary outsider to beltway insider," and as instrumental in advancing the cause of comprehensive school reform.[3] As Finn observed, "With billions of federal dollars subsidizing its advance, the strategy known as whole-school reform is a fixture of the U.S. education landscape. NAS did a great deal to bring that situation about."[4] Regarding specific support, in congressional testimony on the reauthorization of ESEA in 1999, U.S. Secretary of Education Richard Riley cited Success for All as a "proven reform model that struggling schools can adopt—often with the help of federal funds—'right out of the box.'"[5] Indeed, over the period preceding the reauthorization, SFAF was actively seeking to influence federal policy activity, with cofounder and chairman Robert Slavin advocating widely for using of Title I of ESEA as "an engine of reform" to support comprehensive, research-based, and research-validated programs.[6]

With SFAF executives, developers, and trainers all sitting at the intersection of these two streams, the resulting development agenda did not emerge as a detailed set of top-down marching orders: a coherent plan for a next, improved, integrated version of the program (as in the style of a software upgrade). Rather, it emerged as set of shared understanding of SFAF's development priorities.

With an eye on improving expert use, improving student outcomes, and increasing the scale of operations, these priorities did not focus on improving the fundamental design for school restructuring. Little in SFAF's research or experience gave its members pause to question the organizational blueprint for comprehensive school reform. Nor did the agenda focus primarily on addressing deep problems in the SFAF training organization: for example, improving strategies for recruiting new trainers, or strengthening the practice-based learning of trainers. At the beginning of the 1999–2003 development cycle, the depth of such problems had yet to be fully recognized and understood within SFAF.

Instead, the development priorities focused primarily on improving two things. The first was Success for All's supports for implementation: the coordinated materials, tools, and learning opportunities provided to schools. The second was the formal supports for the work and professional development of trainers (rather than the social supports provided through communities of training practice).

These shared priorities directed and coordinated improvement activity across the full complement of program components: instructional organization; curriculum and instruction; supplemental services (i.e., tutoring and family support); and school leadership. Guided by shared priorities, actionable sub-agendas were established at the level of the individual improvement initiative: for example, incorporating commercial assessments to support quarterly analysis and regrouping; completely rewriting all primary curriculum components; developing new supports for school leadership; supporting schools in aligning the program with state standards; incorporating information technologies; and improving the supplemental services components (along with their coordination with both instruction and leadership).

These sub-agendas were managed and coordinated informally and jointly by teams of developers and SFAF executives, their specifics evolving and adapting with streams of influences from within and beyond the SFAF enterprise. In fact, a joke in SFAF was that these sub-agendas could evolve quickly on any given day based on who rode the elevator together that morning and how many floors they rode it. This sort of expansive, dynamic agenda management was enabled by ample funding for development that supported program-spanning development initiatives, that created slack for experimentation and adaptation, and that reduced efficiency as a primary managerial concern.

Thus, with the way that SFAF approached the work of continuous improvement, the development agenda was many things at once. It was both reactive and proactive, addressing past problems and future opportunities. It was both rational and organic, with key goals for development managed socially. It was diffuse, owing to the many problems to be solved in schools, the comprehensiveness of the design and its supports, and ample funding for improvement. It was dynamic, as the agenda ebbed and flowed with changing understandings, ambitions, and influences.

The development agenda was also decidedly evolutionary. The agenda for improving Success for All formed largely within (and at the margins of) established, fundamental parameters of the program: for example, the existing program components; extensive elaboration as a way of recreating usable knowledge in schools at scale; extensive scaffolding via direct instruction, practice-based learning, and in-practice support; and supporting trainers using this same combination of elaboration and scaffolding.[7] To be sure, the agenda included important efforts to extend the boundaries of the program: for example, efforts to continue horizontal expansion into other K–6 content areas, and efforts to initiate vertical expansion into pre-K and middle school reading. Even so, the agenda for improving Success for All did much more to chart evolutionary improvement within (and at the margins of) existing parameters than it did to reconstruct those parameters, themselves.

THE DEVELOPMENT ORGANIZATION

Within SFAF's approach to the work of continuous improvement, a dynamic development *agenda* was matched by a dynamic development *organization* that shouldered the day-to-day work of improving the program. Just as scaling up its base of schools drove growth in the training organization, scaling up the development agenda drove growth in the development organization. While knowledge and technologies were emerging to support the development agenda, SFAF's environments were hardly a parts bin from which developers could quickly cobble to improve the program. Rather, the work of continuous, program-wide improvement required that SFAF expand its internal capabilities to create, revise, and adapt its many materials, tools, and scaffolding opportunities.

The expansion of the development organization mirrored the expansion of the development agenda; it also mirrored the expansion of the training organization. The expansion was largely evolutionary in nature, with SFAF building on a well-developed foundation (rather than starting from scratch). Further, the expansion blended the rational and the organic. While the development organization evolved to feature more complex formal structures, its core capabilities continued to rest in informal communities of practice.

Again, the original Success for All project team began as a university-based group with extensive knowledge and experience in program development, training, and research, uniquely positioned at an intersection between academic, educational, and policy networks. Thus positioned, the original project team worked as an informal community of practice, able to quickly identify, incorporate, process, produce, and use knowledge and information bearing on their work.

Over the 1990s, with the success of its comprehensive school reform program and with funding from NAS to expand into additional content areas, the development agenda continued to expand and, with it, the development team. And, as it did, the project team succeeded in identifying and recruiting knowledgeable and experienced developers, as such work was ubiquitous in the reform-rich environments of U.S. public education. While this growth was matched with some formalization of roles and responsibilities, developers of that period reported that they continued to work in informal communities of practice: social networks within which they collaborated to share knowledge and information, to coordinate their activities, and to perform their work.

Between SY 1999/2000 and 2002/2003, as the development agenda and organization continued to grow, those earlier trajectories held. SFAF succeeded in drawing from its environments and its own network to recruit knowledgeable and experienced developers, thus incorporating their expertise into the development organization and (by virtue of their professional associations and memberships) expanding the development network. SFAF also recruited seasoned teachers and leaders from Success for All schools and districts both as full-time members and as adjuncts, bringing with them knowledge and experience in the expert use of the program. And SFAF developed key partnerships with external developers, including commercial assessment providers, external media production firms, and university-based development and research organizations.[8]

As with the training organization, increasing size and complexity brought with it increased formalization. For example, developers were organized into component-specific and function-specific teams, some pre-existing and others newly constituted: Early Learning, Reading Roots, Reading Wings, tutoring, family support, leadership, Training Institute, alignment, media development, and software development. Roles were differentiated within teams: senior staff charged with overseeing and coordinating projects; mid-level staff charged with a combination of managerial, design, and production responsibilities; base-level staff charged with responsibility for producing program and training materials; and boundary-spanning roles that had some developers continuing to hold formal responsibilities in the training organization. And formal systems were established for generating, communicating, and retaining information useful to developers: for example, reports from schools (e.g., Implementation Visit Reports, quarterly assessment results, and curriculum-based assessment results); state assessment results; and research reports produced both by SFAF's internal research department and by external researchers.

Despite such formalization, those involved reported that the development organization functioned exactly as it always had: as a collection of communities of practice. All involved reported extensive, informal participation, interaction, and collaboration spanning teams and spanning levels within teams. Freed from rigid structures, developers were able to devise, coordinate, and respond to rapid shifts in the development agenda, constrained loosely by such broad goals as supporting expert use the program, improving student outcomes, and adapting the program to changing environments. The combination energized developers and fueled their collaboration. In a 2003 interview, one seasoned developer explained that SFAF's communities of development practice actually mitigated problems that she had experienced in an earlier position at another organization in which development activity was organized more formally:

> That's one of the things that I marvel at. Where I worked before, collaboration was not as easy. When I came in, I was always on the defensive, expecting people to be engaged in turf battles and wanting to stake out ownership of ideas and people. I was kind of stunned at the way people work with each other here. It's much more collaborative. People are much more inclined to get to agreement and consensus and to work towards that and to have that as a goal, rather than to stake out turf and to be more competitive. Everybody here is on the same team. And another place where I worked, it was like a curriculum team, then a school team, and then an administrative team, and all those teams were sometimes more in competition then alignment.

These informal relationships stretched far beyond the development organization and into the training organization, the Success for All network of schools, and broader environments. As had always been the case in Success for All, some developers continued to train, and some trainers continued to develop (including area and regional managers within the training organization). Further, developers were in constant contact with trainers and with schools, both formally (e.g., via program pilots in schools, and as "downstream consumers" of Implementation Visit Reports) and informally (e.g., via interactions at conferences, via phone, and via email). Finally, many were active participants in (and collaborators with) professional organizations and associations in their individual areas of expertise.

As a consequence, SFAF developers lived under a waterfall of constantly flowing knowledge and information about existing problems, about potential solutions, about emerging research and technologies, and about environmental contexts. Some of this knowledge and information was formalized into white papers and research proposals and circulated among developers. However, the vast majority of knowledge and information was informal, anecdotal, and unrecorded. It was retained and indexed in the minds of individuals and in their collaborative ways of working. It was shared and transferred via personal interactions, thus highly dependent on a collective sense of "who knows what," and on relationships between those having and those needing knowledge and information. And its meaning was constantly negotiated and renegotiated by all involved.

All of these informal interdependencies made for formidable coordination challenges. Yet within the development organization, work was not coordinated and managed via formal methods of project management, nor even by tight, formal control of the agenda. Rather, true to its historical roots, and consistent with its means of managing its dynamic development agenda, coordination among developers was largely informal. One informal, coordinative mechanism was as described immediately above: dense, informal interactions among developers, complemented by norms of agreement and consensus. A second was the active participation of SFAF executives in the day-to-day work of development and training, which allowed them to establish and coordinate agendas, to allocate resources to development initiatives, and to facilitate coordination by brokering relationships. A third was the Success for All program itself. The established program functioned as a template around with developers described themselves as "tinkering" and "fiddling."

Much as with schools, the preceding placed a premium on newly recruited developers buying into the program and understanding that they were to work within its constraints. In a 2003, one developer explained that SFAF cofounder and President Nancy Madden took care to ensure that newly recruited developers shared that understanding:

> Nancy [Madden] has always been careful that whoever comes in, particularly in reading, that they recognize the Success for All stance, and that they recognize that Success for All way of doing things. In general, in a working sense, it's to let people know not to expect to come in and creatively go off on your own, in your own direction, and have complete leeway to do that. And also to recognize that there is significant detail. There is a process already established, and there will always be a significant level of detail. There will always be certain elements that are represented in this program, such as direct instruction, such as phonics, such as directing teachers what to do. There are certain elements of instruction. There's a process of instruction. There is an approach to instruction. All of those things, a template for that, literally and figuratively, has been established. And so it's to let people know that you can't come in and just ignore that template and go off and develop what you want to develop, if it differs significantly from that template.

As these communities of development practice emerged and evolved, their work continued to be motivated and supported by key, enabling conditions: for example, physical proximity (most developers worked at SFAF's Towson headquarters, and those who didn't work at the headquarters traveled there frequently); slack time and resources (owing to ample funding for program development); the shared language of the Success for All program; long-established (and deeply-valued) personal relationships; functional interdependence among the program components on which all were working; cross-team responsibilities within the development organization (both formal and informal); and members who continued to have both development and training responsibilities. Most important were norms, values, and practices linked by developers both to SFAF's founders and to its roots as an organization: deep (almost religious) commitment to the mission of improving the academic achievement of historically disadvantaged children; to-the-bone pragmatism; vigilant attention to the research literature; constant experimentation; and constant evaluation of effectiveness. Chief among these was great tolerance for informality over formality. As explained by Barbara Haxby, SFAF's director of implementation and a member of the original project team:

> It has to do with kind of the history of the organization. It's always been such an academic group that sort of morphed into an organization and, as such, I think real, definite hierarchical labeling of people has never been what we've been very comfortable with. So consequently, we all have very strange titles that reflect only part of what we think the person does.

Thus, even with SFAF and its broader environments advocating for rationality in educational reform, the SFAF development organization (like the development agenda) continued to evolve organically. In some ways, it evolved to capitalize on key resources readily available in U.S. educational environments: specifically, a large pool of experienced and capable developers, and ample funding for program development. In other ways, it evolved to compensate for weaknesses of U.S. educational environments: specifically, a lack of readily available and readily usable knowledge and technologies with which to quickly improve the program. Indeed, as much as a knowledge-*consuming* organization, the development organization evolved as a knowledge-*producing* organization, staffed and informally structured to quickly fashion a waterfall of constantly flowing knowledge, experience, and information into new understandings, tools, and methods for improving implementation, outcomes, and scale.

THE DEVELOPMENT PROCESS

The third, interdependent dimension of SFAF's approach to continuous improvement was the development process, itself: the set of activities by which members of the development organization moved ideas from the development agenda (SFAF's figurative "to do" list) and into its designs, its supports for schools, and its supports for trainers. The development process included a critical point of coordination: a point at which the development organization released program improvements to the training organization, which was then responsible for supporting their effective use in the installed base of schools. School-level use, in turn, fed back into the development agenda, organization, and process. With that, SFAF's development process drew the work of designing, supporting, and scaling up into a process of on-going reflection, reconsideration, and adaptation of the program, its ends, and its means. In doing so, the development process leveraged the full range of resources spanning SFAF's networks, its programs, its environments, and its own organization.

As enacted during its 1999–2003 development cycle, SFAF's development process was much less a classic "research-and-development" process and much more a pragmatic, collaborative method for producing and codifying practical knowledge in usable, replicable form. As developers worked to improve Success for All, they did not organize and coordinate their work as a progression through an established sequence of steps: problems/needs definition; basic and applied research; development; commercialization; diffusion; and, ultimately, adoption and use.[9] The work was not compartmentalized and arranged nearly so neatly.

Rather, developers engaged in a collection of simultaneous, interdependent, and loosely coordinated activities distributed across SFAF's many development teams: using the program in schools; acquiring, pooling, and interpreting knowledge and information; formalizing and piloting promising improvements; disseminating improvements through the installed base of schools; and using research to evaluate overall program effectiveness. All of these tasks were performed continuously, in interaction, over the entire 1999–2003 development cycle.

Working in this complex, interdependent way reversed the usual order of things. This wasn't so much "research-and-development" as it was "development-and-research," as new, practical knowledge emerged and evolved from the continuous, collaborative improvement efforts of SFAF developers, trainers, leaders, and teachers.[10] Understandings of problems, needs, and opportunities emerged *from* the work of large-scale use of the program (not in advance of it), and functioned to inform SFAF's dynamic agenda-management process. The majority of new knowledge about how to improve the program emerged through the work of formalizing, piloting, and disseminating program improvements, largely via processes of collaborative, experiential learning (and not in advance of such tasks, via basic and applied research). Trainers, school leaders, and teachers were active participants in the development process, and not the downstream benefactors of it.

By way of organizational epistemology, the development organization was not dogmatic in its approach to the work of development but, instead pragmatic. While developers were vigilant in leveraging research when available, they were equality vigilant in leveraging widely distributed, experiential learning. In a 2003 interview, in a moment of candor that belied SFAF's public face of rationality, cofounder and President Robert Slavin acknowledged just that:

We don't know what we're doing. We're making this up. We don't have a final answer. We have to be learning from the experience. You'd be crazy to be working in all these schools all over the place and not learning from them to gradually move toward something better.

With that, SFAF's development process mirrored key characteristics of its development agenda and organization. The development process was adapted to SFAF's environments. In environments pressing for effectiveness but thin on knowledge, SFAF used the development process to produce its own. The development process was more organic and social than it was classically rational, as developers collaborated to explore new paths, reconciled their experiences, and agreed to exploit those that seemed most promising. And the development process was decidedly evolutionary, with developers, trainers, leaders, and teachers leveraging their experiences to make incremental improvements within (and at) the established parameters of the program.[11] Active use in schools functioned as a source of variation in understandings and practices. Acquiring, pooling, and analyzing functioned as mechanisms for selecting favorable understandings and practices (and for culling unfavorable ones). Formalizing and piloting functioned as mechanisms for codifying and retaining favorable adaptations. And disseminating functioned as a mechanism for replicating favorable adaptations through the installed base of schools.

Active Use

Integral to SFAF's development process was on-going use of the Success for All program by students, teachers, school leaders, and trainers: an ever-churning source of knowledge and information from 1,500+ schools spanning 48 states. Large-scale use functioned as a source of knowledge and information about problems: about the specific difficulties experienced by students, teachers, leaders, and trainers as they sought to enact the program as intended, at both the novice and expert levels. Large-scale use functioned as a source of potential solutions. Indeed, as designed, expert use of Success for All was, itself, a process of systematic, distributed experiential learning involving analysis, experimentation, and reflection. And large-scale use functioned as a source of information about dynamic, evolving environments: alone (for example, specific district and state environments); as they interacted with each other (for example, as districts interpreted and acted upon state and federal policies); and as they bore on the design and use of Success for All in schools.

Acquiring, Pooling, and Analyzing

Concurrent with large-scale use, SFAF developers constantly acquired, pooled, and analyzed new information and knowledge: as generated and reported formally within SFAF; as generated via participation in personal and professional networks; as generated via interaction with the Success for All teachers and leaders; and, especially, as generated through interaction with SFAF trainers. It was through these processes of acquiring, pooling, and analyzing that tacit understandings were made explicit and explicit understandings were shared.

Especially important was the constant flow of knowledge and information from SFAF trainers. The core work of trainers included collaborating with teachers, leaders, and other trainers to analyze information about implementation and outcomes on a classroom-by-classroom, school-by-school, region-by-region, and area-by-area basis. Some of the resulting knowledge and information was recorded and reported formally: for example, in Implementation Visit Reports. Much was retained and transferred informally, through personal interactions. Indeed, trainers functioned as a sort of social conduit of knowledge and information in the Success for All network, connecting schools to each other, to the development organization, and to SFAF executives. In a 2003 interview, Robert Slavin described the contributions of trainers as a sort of informal, widely distributed qualitative research that complemented the formal, disciplined research of the SFAF research department:

> Since we're not doing a lot of our own qualitative research, we get our wisdom of practice from the trainers, themselves, who are doing their own little qualitative research, in a sense. They're not qualitative researchers. But, in a way, they're doing a form of qualitative research all the time to characterize what's happening. And we pay close attention to our trainers, particularly with the new programs, where we're thinking about new initiatives, to understand from them what they're learning out there. We very much feel the terror of going around changing stuff all over America. We can't see it. We don't know what's happening, ourselves, on a day-to-day basis in all these many, many schools and all these different places. But, on the other hand, we have eyes and ears in these places who are very capable and intelligent people. And so rather than imposing an idea that there are researchers, and then there are trainers, and they're not the same people, we take our own trainers very seriously and want to hear their experience and be able to incorporate their experience into some sort of a progressive change process. And, to me, it's hard to imagine that you'd do things any other way.

Formalizing and Piloting

New knowledge and information fed what most approached a moment of invention within the development process: that point at which developers devised and tested new print resources, classroom materials, videos, software, training materials, and other tools. SFAF developers described this as a process of "formalizing" best practice, "writing" materials, and "embedding" new knowledge and ideas in tools and materials. In some cases, this had SFAF developers readily incorporating new knowledge and technologies into the program: for example, the findings and language of the National Reading Panel; commercial assessments and reporting systems; and increasingly affordable, stable, and ubiquitous information technologies.[12] In most cases, this was the point at which informal knowledge and information were formally codified and retained in usable form in Success for All's standard array of supports: in manuals, materials, and other tools for use in schools, and in scripts, booklets, and other materials used by trainers in formal scaffolding opportunities.

Concurrent with formalizing program improvements, developers also piloted them in schools. In some cases (e.g., when required as a condition for external funding), piloting included formal, summative evaluation of the effectiveness of a given program improvement. However, in the main, piloting was largely an informal, formative process by which lead developers and trainers tested individual program improvements for "proof-of-concept" in actual schools prior to large-scale replication (and, if necessary, made any required revisions). In a 2003 interview, one experienced SFAF developer with responsibility for preparing supports for trainers summarized the process:

What happens is, we get comments and feedback from both schools and trainers, or more research shows that another approach is more effective. It builds up until, one day we determine that it's time to rewrite a piece. A development team is identified. Who takes part depends on the component, but Nancy (Madden) oversees all of the teams. She meets with the writing team to discuss what needs to be written. The writers begin to write and then they meet with her again and review what's been written. Often they'll ask other people to review the materials and provide comments, ask questions and the like. When our department gets involved, we share our opinions as well. That's particularly helpful because we've all worked in Success for All schools in the field and know what is likely to work, and what's not. And it just sort of morphs into this on-going process. Each item is revised and revised and revised based on internal feedback and feedback from talented trainers and even feedback from teachers.

Disseminating and Using

Every year, the combination of publication deadlines, SFAF's annual scaffolding cycle, and the new school year drove divergent, exploratory development activity to a point of convergence. At this time, program improvement efforts were drawn to a temporary close and disseminated through the training organization and the installed base of schools.[13] Dissemination was not structured so that program improvements were queued up, coordinated, integrated, and released as new, "shrink-wrapped" versions of Success for All, in the style of software releases: for example, "Success for All v. 3.0." Rather, program improvements were released more in the style of software bug fixes: immediately and independently, on a fix-by-fix basis. This improvement-by-improvement dissemination strategy was responsive to multiple concerns: the impossibility of expecting all schools to re-purchase a completely revised program every year; pressure shared by SFAF and its schools to quickly improve implementation and student achievement; and SFAF's commitment to helping as many students as possible, as quickly as possible. These concerns combined to create great urgency in SFAF's dissemination process. Explained one SFAF developer: "There's always sort of an eagerness here, that if we think it's going to work, get it out there and let them start using it. There's always an eagerness. If we think it's going to work, get it out there!"

SFAF had two primary means of disseminating program improvements. One was through the sale and distribution of new and revised materials: a sort of immediate, large-scale broadcasting of program improvements. Another was through Success for All's conventional scaffolding opportunities, especially annual Experienced Sites Conferences (for schools) and annual Experienced Trainers Institutes (for trainers). These scaffolding opportunities functioned as opportunities to share additional information and knowledge about program improvements beyond that formally codified in program resources, both informally (e.g., verbally, through discussion) and formally (e.g., via booklets and copies of overheads used in scaffolding sessions). They also created opportunities for trainers, leaders, and (sometimes) teachers to practice using program improvements, though within the constraints of 1.5 hour to 3 hour off-site training sessions, thus usually with the goal of exposure to (rather than mastery of) those improvements.

Dissemination, in turn, triggered active use in schools—first at the novice/consistent level, and then at the expert/adaptive level. This was active use *at scale*: not via collaboration among lead developers, lead trainers, and able schools in the controlled context of a pilot; but via collaboration among modal trainers, leaders, and teachers in uncontrolled contexts. Indeed, it was at this point that environments were reintroduced into the development process. Variability in specific schools and their local environments, in turn, triggered another layer of widely distributed, experiential learning, as trainers, leaders and teachers began to experience (and learn to manage) the interaction between program improvements, school contexts, and environmental challenges. In a 2004 interview, Barbara Haxby, SFAF's director of implementation, explained:

So you get this very clean result in pilot. And somehow you assume that, if that's effective, you can put it at scale. But, in the dynamics of going to scale, there are a whole lot of other factors that all of a sudden have equal weight compared to the effectiveness of curriculum. Superintendent turnover, district support, power of principals in school leadership, teacher turnover, basic school climate issues, environmental instabilities, longitudinal questions of what happens over time. You've got teachers turning over every single year. You've got superintendents coming in brand new and wanting to bring their own stuff with them. You've got the personal dynamics that happen in some schools, people who don't like each other. You get into all that messy stuff. And when you're at scale, you have to take care of those kinds of things, too, if you're going to create change. A wonderful curriculum, in and of itself, or any other structure, whether it is effective or not often depends on all these other things. And I think one of the lessons of learning at scale is to say, "We've got to learn some things about how to create conditions where even something that's got a great research base can be nurtured and grown." These are things you can learn about. I'm not sure that's just chaos and unknowable. You can learn about them. Because when you're at scale, that's the kind of stuff that you worry about each and every day, much more so than the mechanics of the program.

The Role of Research

Research played several important roles in the SFAF development process. In some cases, external research functioned as an input to the work of developers, as they recognized existing or new findings and incorporated them into their improvement efforts. In other cases, developers did a sort of "bench check" in which they squared their ideas for program improvements with the research literature, both to get a sense of the likely effectiveness of the program improvements and to legitimate the program improvements as having a basis in research.

The most systematic role of research was in the work of SFAF's internal research department. The work of the research department did not include fine-grained, qualitative analyses of program implementation. Again, informal, qualitative research was the province of trainers. Rather, the research took four primary forms: funded studies of program effectiveness for the program as a whole (most often using a matched comparison design); formal evaluation of component-specific program improvements as required by funders; periodic meta-analyses and syntheses of both internal and external research on Success for All; and annual production of state-by-state "Reports of Program Effectiveness" (ROPEs) using student outcomes on state accountability assessments. Indeed, if the mantra of SFAF's development organization was "Get it out there!" then the mantra of SFAF's research department was "Does it work?"

Again, the work by the research department did not directly inform the work of the development organization. Developers did much more to leverage their own experiential learning than they did findings from internal research efforts. Rather, findings from internal research efforts were used most prominently by SFAF executives to monitor and manage development and training operations, to rally continued commitment and enthusiasm among Success for All schools, and to demonstrate publicly the effectiveness of the program.

Vitality and Complexity

Thus, rather than a tidy sequence of compartmentalized tasks, the SFAF development process consisted of a set of continuous, interdependent learning activities. While the process drew on research when possible, it drew most heavily on the experience of using the Success for All program in schools. These activities were supported by unusual capabilities for learning in the SFAF development organization: seasoned developers organized into communities of practice; freed to experiment by slack time and resources; motivated by a shared mission; informally managed and coordinated; and driven to consensus. They were supported by unusual capabilities in the SFAF training organization to provide a steady flow of knowledge and information about interactions between the program, schools, and their environments. And they were supported by an unusual role for chronically underperforming schools: not as the downstream recipients of packaged solutions but, instead, as active participants in a novel process for producing, validating, and formalizing practical knowledge in usable, replicable form.

Those involved described the SFAF development process as making for a dynamic and invigorating (if sometimes-chaotic) work environment. The vitality derived, in part, from the sheer ambition of the 1999–2003 development cycle. While SFAF had long engaged in the work of continuous improvement, never had development efforts been so expansive, nor had the training organization or the installed base of schools with which developers were to coordinate. The scope and scale were new for most all involved. The vitality derived, in part, from the close collaboration among developers, the sense of urgency and mission behind the development efforts, and the constant learning of all involved.

And the vitality derived, in part, from close interaction with SFAF cofounders and chief executives Nancy Madden and Robert Slavin. Though by all accounts a large organization, SFAF was still described by its members as a Mom and Pop shop. All involved described drawing enthusiasm and energy from their steadfast commitment to the mission of the organization. Explained one SFAF developer, in a 2003 interview:

It is really energizing to work here. It is for me, doing what I do. It's energizing, because there is such a clear vision. There's such a clear goal. And I can tolerate the messiness of the organization sometimes, because the goal is there. But I think Nancy (Madden)'s vision and the style of managing makes everything you do seem really important. Everything seems really important, because she takes it that way. I practically never found a level of detail that Nancy, if I took it to her and wanted her feedback, would say, "Oh, just figure it out." Even though I could, she's keenly interested in thinking it over. And she often takes things to a level of detail that I never would. Some of that is good. Some of it, I don't agree with. But I do think that, by her style of management, she does energize. She and Bob (Slavin) both probably energize people and galvanize them around this mission. I feel that what I do is used better, more effectively, more directly, and so I can see the consequences of my work in positive ways, which is very energizing for me.

If the development environment was energizing for developers, it was also tough on the SFAF executives responsible for managing the enterprise. Much as research-proven effectiveness was a hallmark of Success for All, so, too, was the identity of Success for All as an integrated suite of program components and, thus, an alternative to conventional, targeted approaches to school reform. Yet norms of continuous, distributed experimentation and improvement made for steep challenges of coordination and integration. The imperative for SFAF executives, thus, was to ensure that the many products of the development process were stitched together into a single, coherent, comprehensive program. In a 2003 interview, SFAF President Nancy Madden explained that coordination and integration were among the steepest challenges that came with SFAF's approach to the work of continuous improvement:

> We're not standing still. We want to keep getting better. You have to keep moving people along. As the thinking develops, and as the problem-solving strategies get implemented, you have to implement them with a lot of people. All those people have to be on the same page, and they are all contributing to the page at the same time. And possibly the most unmanageable part of all of this is that we encourage that. We want people to be taking what they see, finding the nuggets—again, not just changing to do something different, but finding the pieces that will really make a real improvement. And when we see those things, then we say, "Well, you know what, we can do that one, and it's going to have an impact." And so, then, we've got to make sure that that then gets played out in all of the different ways it's got to be played out to be an integrated part of the whole.

REVOLUTION VIA EVOLUTION

As enacted during its 1999–2003 development cycle, the work of continuous improvement in SFAF rested on interdependent, simultaneous, distributed, and largely evolutionary activity: managing the development agenda; growing, structuring, and managing the development organization; and enacting the development process. Over this four-year period, this combination of evolutionary activity drove a revolution in the Success for All program. The blueprint for school restructuring remained largely intact, its core components and the relations among them readily identifiable. Yet working to the rhythm of the annual school year, a rapid succession of incremental improvements transformed a program highly adapted to support large-scale, novice use into one packed with new potential to support large-scale, expert use. At the same time, these incremental improvements were designed to position the program to exploit what SFAF executives anticipated to be opportunities for continued scale up under the No Child Left Behind Act of 2001.

The 1999–2003 development cycle began almost jubilantly, and it proceeded with even higher expectations. Already supporting an installed base of 1,500+ schools, and with additional funding from the Obey-Porter Comprehensive School Reform Demonstration Act and the Reading Excellence Act slated to enter the system through 2002, members of SFAF saw growth to over 2,000 schools as just over the horizon, and practically inevitable. With new support from No Child Left Behind of 2001, SFAF executives forecasted the possibility of growing to over 3,000 schools. In that SFAF's financial strategy depended heavily on revenue from new business, new potential for large-scale growth brought with it new potential for the long-term viability of the Success for All enterprise.

1999/2000: Fundamental Framing

SFAF's 1999–2003 development cycle began with activity at the extremes of the program: leadership, historically the component that provided the weakest support for expert use; and tutoring, historically the component that provided the most support for expert use. These improvements marked a sea change in the Success for All enterprise, in that they gave common language to ambitions for expert use that had long been on the minds of key members of SFAF but that all had struggled to communicate.

In 1999/2000, SFAF constituted a new leadership development team charged with improving the linchpin (but historically weak) leadership component. Balancing program goals for grade-level reading performance with state accountability requirements, the effort focused on formalizing a process for working backwards from state assessment results, quarterly assessment results, and other information resources to develop grade-by-grade, classroom-by-classroom, student-by-student goals and plans for improvement. This effort yielded a set of key program improvements: for example, data analysis routines; the incorporation of commercial formative assessments for quarterly regrouping and analysis; and a new leadership manual formalizing key practices of expert Success for All leaders.[14] All were drawn together into a new scaffolding initiative called "Leadership Academy," which was developed and piloted in New York City's Chancellor's District. Working on a monthly basis with leadership teams from geographically concentrated schools, Leadership Academy was designed as an opportunity for developers to support the use of new resources, to facilitate the construction of local support networks, and to collaborate with principals and facilitators on school-specific analysis and problem solving.

Arguably the most important contributions of the leadership development team were three frameworks that, for the first time, formally codified the developmental sequence from novice to expert use, thus giving language to Success for All's aspirations for professional practice and learning.[15] "The Change Process" described a general sequence of steps through which all schools could expect to progress in transitioning from novice to expert use. Drawn from the Concerns-Based Adoption Model, "Stages of Concern" provided language that framed the individual-level experience of progressing from novice to expert. Also drawn from the Concerns-Based Adoption Model, "Levels of Use" detailed an eight-stage progression from novice, individual use to expert, collective use of Success for All, with the leap from "routine" to "refined" use marking the transition from novice to expert (see Table 4.1, below). Indeed, the very notion of "Levels of Use" effected a subtle—but critical—shift in agency. As framed formally for schools, Success for All went from being a program that teachers and leaders were expected to *implement* to being a tool for them to *use* in solving problems of student achievement.

Concurrently, the curriculum development team revised the tutoring component to improve support for expert use, with the primary goal of strengthening the relationship between assessment, goal setting, and intervention. As with the leadership component, a central contribution was new language framing expert

Table 4.1 Success for All: Levels of Use Framework*

Levels of Use (LoU) of the Success for All Program

The Levels of Use component of the Concerns-Based Adoption Model (CBAM) identifies eight distinct levels of the change process. School leaders can use these levels to determine the extent to which teachers and school are implementing the SFA program. Educators who can accurately assess where individuals or schools are in relation to these levels can provide the support necessary to encourage schools to progress to the next levels. The chart below outlines how the Levels of Use might be described in a Success for All school.

Level	Description	Examples
Level O: **Non-use**	Schools have little or no knowledge of SFA, no involvement with it, and are doing nothing toward becoming involved.	• Schools and teachers who have not been exposed to SFA.
Level I: **Orientation**	Individuals or schools have acquired or are acquiring information about SFA and/or have explored its value and requirements.	• Awareness sessions have been conducted with the school staff. • Visitations to SFA schools have occurred. • Individuals and schools have examined the research related to SFA.
Level II: **Preparation**	Schools are preparing for their first use of SFA. All requirements for implementation have been met, and a specific date to begin has been determined.	• An 80% vote has been secured. • Principal and facilitator have attended the New Leaders Conference. • Teachers at the school have been trained. • Materials have been organized and classrooms prepared.
Level III: **Mechanical Use**	Teachers are implementing SFA for the first time. Focus is on mastery of the instructional tasks of the program. These attempts often result in disjointed, awkward, and superficial instruction. This level coincides with the storming stage of the Tuckman change model. Teachers and schools often experience discomfort during this stage due to the stress of trying to master new materials. A high level of support for teachers is vital at this stage.	• Teachers experience difficulty with teaching all components within the 90 minute reading period (pacing). • Teachers often refer to the teaching manuals during lessons. • Transitions between activities are slow.

Table 4.1 Success for All: Levels of Use Framework* (Cont'd)

Level	Description	Examples
Level IVa: Routine	Teachers' capacity to teach SFA has stabilized. Focus remains on the teaching process rather than the consequences of the program on student achievement. Teachers and schools often feel a certain amount of relief at this level; the discomfort of the mechanical level of implementation has passed. School leaders need to make sure that a school does not stabilize at the routine level. Routine levels of instruction may feel more comfortable but do not guarantee student achievement. It is not until teachers begin to "own," use, and adapt the instructional process to thoughtfully advance student achievement that real, substantive, and long-lasting academic gains are realized. Schools can get "stuck" at this phase and fail to reach the higher levels of use that are synonymous with high achievement and success for all.	• Teachers can complete all lesson components within the allotted time. • Routines have been established that reduce the amount of time teachers spend on lesson preparation.
Level IVb: Refined	Teachers focus on the connection between instruction (process) and student achievement (results). Teachers are able to adjust instruction to meet the needs of individual students. This level of use is necessary to attain powerful gains for students. In schools with high teacher turnover, all teachers may not reach refinement at the same time. It is the responsibility of school leaders to assess each teacher's progress toward this goal and to provide the supports needed for each teacher to attain refinement.	• Teachers make professional decisions within the SFA framework and research base. • Teachers use student achievement data to determine effectiveness of instruction. • Teachers understand the rational behind various program components and are able to emphasize different instructional strategies based on individual student needs. • Teachers accelerate instruction when appropriate.

(Continued)

Table 4.1 SUCCESS FOR ALL: LEVELS OF USE FRAMEWORK* (CONT'D)

Level	Description	Examples
Level V: Integration	Level at which teachers skilled in teaching SFA are combining their own efforts with the efforts of other skilled teacher to achieve a collective impact on student achievement. This is also the stage at which a whole-school reform effort finally connects all the elements so that a school can attain the full synergy possible in comprehensive reform. Now, not only is every component at a level of refinement, but all the components function seamlessly together to promote grade-level performance for every student.	• Teachers skilled in the use of SFA consult with one another to share effective instructional strategies. • Schools encourage collaboration among skilled SFA teachers by creating structure to promote team learning. • Tutors communicate regularly with teachers to develop seamless connections between tutoring and classroom instruction. • Family Support personnel collaborate with teachers to develop both preventive and early intervention plans that are targeted to student achievement. • School and community resources are fully aligned with the school's SFA goals.
Level VI: Renewal	The level at which schools seek major ways to improve the implementation of SFA across all parts of the school community, with an emphasis on increasing the reading achievement of all students. This is the stage where change becomes self-sustaining. Structures have been put into place so that the "program" is now how the school does business, and the business is to promote high growth for student through the thoughtful engagement of all school personnel.	• Staff and community examine student achievement data on a continuous basis and engage in problem solving and decision-making processes aimed at improving implementation. • A culture of mutual accountability exists among school staff and community members.

*From *Success for All Leadership Guide*, (pp. 1.6–1.8), by the Success for All Foundation (2002a). Reprinted with permission.

tutoring practices. Specifically, the language focused on describing options available to teachers for in-the-moment diagnosis-and-response. "Teaching and modeling" described supplemental direct instruction in a particular skill or strategy in response to evidence of non-understanding and misuse by students. "Prompting and reinforcing" described strategic questioning, prompting, and encouragement to probe and to improve students' use of skills and strategies. Much as "routine use" and "refined use" soon became conventional language characterizing the leap from novice to expert use, "teaching and modeling" and "prompting and reinforcing" soon became conventional language characterizing the leap from simply *implementing* the Success for All cycle of diagnostic instruction to actually *using* the cycle of diagnostic instruction adaptively to identify and to address students' immediate needs.

There was nothing particularly profound about this new language and these new frameworks. The framework and language incorporated into the leadership component had been in circulation for years. Even so, with the Success for All enterprise super-saturated in adverse interpretations and misuse, this new language and these frameworks acted as seeds that both crystallized understandings of those problems and provided a means of clearly communicating long-held intentions for expert use.

2000/2001: Rapid Diffusion

Momentum gathered over SY 2000/2001. In March of 2001, Slavin and Madden published a second edition of their earlier trade book on Success for All, *Every Child, Every School*, though with its titled updated to reflect the scale of the program: *One Million Children: Success for All*.[16] The book featured an updated review of research on Success for All that echoed earlier reviews, with a reported average effect size of 0.50 in grade levels 1–5, and with reported effect sizes for the lowest 25% of students ranging from 1.03 (first grade) to 1.68 (fourth grade).[17]

Throughout the year, earlier development initiatives also continued. Leadership Academy was expanded to six sites, and the revised tutoring component was released to all schools. Concurrently, key ideas and language from these initiatives began to diffuse throughout the Success for All enterprise, as developers and trainers began working both to manage interpretation of the program as bureaucratic and/or technocratic and to improve support for expert use across the conventional array of scaffolding opportunities.

To improve direct instruction for newly-recruited schools, initial training for teachers and leaders was adapted to incorporate new frameworks and language developed within the leadership initiative. The intent was to immediately dispel the notion of Success for All as either "bureaucratic" or "technocratic" and to locate power and responsibility squarely with leaders and teachers. With the "Levels of Use" framework, teachers and leaders were immediately presented with clear descriptions of the ultimate goals for individual and collective practice: refinement, integration, and renewal. They were also immediately presented with the central challenge of Success for All: first mastering mechanical and routine use and, then, bridging the gap from "routine" to "refined" use by shifting their focus from their own performance to students' performance. With complementary discussion of "The Change Process" and "Stages of Concern," issues of stress, affect, motivation, and commitment were presented immediately, framed consistently, and given language to be shared by teachers, leaders, and trainers.

To improve direct instruction for experienced schools, developers created 19 new sessions for SFAF's annual Experienced Sites Conferences focused on both novice and expert use of all program components. These included new sessions in leadership and tutoring that drew from on-going improvement efforts. Importantly, these also included the introduction of two sessions focused on laying a foundation for expert use in regular classroom instruction: "Observing, Informing, and Performing in Reading Roots" and "Observing, Informing, and Performing in Reading Wings." Both sessions drew from the improvements in the leadership component to frame expectations for teachers' performance as a progression from "routine" to "refined" use of the program. Both sessions provided routines for monitoring students' use of reading skills and strategies, framed using Yeta Goodman's notions of "kidwatching."[18] And both sessions drew from the tutoring component to frame subsequent intervention in terms of "teaching and modeling" and "prompting and reinforcing" the use of skills and strategies.

Improved support via direct instruction was matched with improved support for practice-based learning and in-practice follow-up. For example, a team of SFAF developers produced state-by-state resources documenting the alignment between the Success for All curriculum and individual state standards, along with routines, forms, and guidance for mapping backwards from state assessment results to plans for classroom intervention and professional development. These resources were intended to be used collaboratively by teachers and leaders in component team meetings, as well as by leaders and trainers in implementation visits. At the same time, another team of developers revised the standard Implementation Visit Report. Developers eliminated the requirement that trainers conduct a comprehensive, "check-check-check" survey of implementation, and they increased guidance for observing the substance of instructional interactions among students and teachers (again, with an eye on the progression from "routine" to "refined" use of the program).

2001/2002: Tightening Linkages and Anticipating Environments

By 2001/2002, what had started two years earlier as a trickle of improvements in two program components became a torrent spanning the entire program. Early efforts continued: the release of Leadership Academy to all schools, supported by its own cohort of specially-selected trainers and by a new, web-based information system; the doubling of new and revised Experienced Sites Conference sessions (from 19 to 38), the majority of which addressed issues of expert use;

and continued revisions to the implementation visit process to focus on the progression from "routine" to "refined" use. Complementing the preceding were three key initiatives focused keenly on both technical effectiveness and increasing the scale of operations: an initiative to more tightly link trainers and leaders; an initiative to more tightly link leaders and teachers; and an initiative to more tightly link the entire enterprise with anticipated changes in policy environments.

To more tightly link the work of SFAF trainers and school leaders, developers devised the Goal Focused Improvement Process. Initially piloted in 2001/2002 in one of SFAF's four geographic training areas, the Goal Focused Improvement Process sought to integrate SFAF's rapidly-expanding routines, information resources, and guidance into a conventional, continuous improvement process for leaders and trainers. The process included: identifying school-level goals; analyzing "internal" and "external" data; prioritizing areas of concern and identifying the root causes of problems; and devising and monitoring interventions. Embedded within the Goal Focused Improvement Process were additional routines and guidance for mapping backwards from state assessment results both to classroom-specific interventions and to priorities for teachers' professional development, thus providing the additional advantage of linking the work of trainers and leaders more tightly with environmental expectations for performance.

To more tightly link the work of schools leaders and teachers, developers devised the "Building Better Readers" series: a school-based curriculum for teachers' professional development designed to support both existing curriculum components and curriculum revisions anticipated for SY 2002/2003. Building Better Readers focused on developing foundational knowledge of four core reading comprehension strategies: clarification, summarization, questioning, and prediction. It also included tools and methods for assessing students' use of these strategies, for collaboratively analyzing formal and informal assessments, and for intervening in response to misuse or weak use. Building Better Readers included primary source materials, materials for direct instruction, self-study guides, guidance for structuring collaborative component team meetings, DVD and other media resources, and assessments.

To more tightly link the entire enterprise to its environments, SFAF began adapting its development agenda and process to respond to what many at the time were calling the most aggressive federal educational reform policy to date: the reauthorization of the Elementary and Secondary Education Act as the No Child Left Behind Act of 2001 (NCLB).

Since the founding of Success for All, SFAF executives had been seeking to influence policy, research, and other environments to secure support, with a particular focus on advancing the twin causes of research and rationality in educational reform.[19] Things appeared to break SFAF's way, with NCLB both reinforcing the agenda for rational, systemic reform and changing the rules. Rather than a radical, monolithic policy, NCLB was its own bundle of evolutionary, incremental policy and program changes that promised to interact and invigorate reform activity throughout the system—not just in chronically underperforming schools, but in all schools, districts, and states. These changes ran the gamut: for example, federal goals for 100% of students performing on standard by SY 2013/2014; revised provisions for holding school, districts, and states accountable for adequate yearly progress towards those goals; new provisions for disaggregating student performance by historically underperforming subgroups; new resources to enlist districts and states in providing technical assistance to struggling schools; a reduction in the poverty threshold allowing schools to pursue schoolwide improvement using Title I funds (from 50% to 40%); new provisions for teacher licensure; and more.

The biggest payoff for SFAF appeared to be in support for research-based and research-validated comprehensive school reform. NCLB formally incorporated and adapted the two federal policies that had driven SFAF's explosive growth: the Obey-Porter Comprehensive School Reform Demonstration Act (which evolved into Comprehensive School Reform, or CSR); and the Reading Excellence Act (which evolved into Reading First). At the same time, NCLB further formalized guidance for qualifying external programs, with increased attention to programs both based on and validated by "scientifically-based research"—a phrase used famously 111 times in the legislation. For example, Comprehensive School Reform expanded Obey-Porter's nine criteria for qualifying programs to eleven, including new criteria directly addressing the research basis of programs (see Table 4.2, below).

Research was especially central to the rhetoric of Reading First, which drew directly from the findings of the National Reading Panel to specify five core dimensions central to success in primary reading: phonemic awareness, phonics, vocabulary development, reading fluency (including oral reading skills), and reading comprehension strategies. Per the federal guidance for Reading First:

> Quite simply, Reading First focuses on what works, and will support proven methods of early reading instruction in classrooms. The program provides assistance to States and districts in selecting or developing effective instructional materials, programs, learning systems and strategies to implement methods that have been proven to teach reading. Reading First also provides assistance for the selection and administration of screening, diagnostic and classroom-based instructional reading assessments with proven validity and reliability, in order to measure where students are and monitor their progress. Taken together, the complementary research-based programs, practices and tools required by Reading First will give teachers across the nation the skills and support they need to teach all children to read fluently by the end of third grade.[20]

The rhetoric of rationality was complemented by the parallel emergence of an administrative infrastructure that appeared to support research-based, research-validated comprehensive school reform. For example, with the Education Sciences and Reform Act of 2002, the Department of Education's Office of Educational Research and Improvement was reorganized into two new organizations: the Institute of Education Sciences and the Office of Innovation and Improvement.

Table 4.2 No Child Left Behind Act: Criteria for
Qualifying Schoolwide Programs*

Key components of comprehensive school reform programs under NCLB included:

1. Employs proven strategies and proven methods for student learning, teaching, and school management that are based on scientifically based research and effective practices and have been replicated successfully in schools;

2. Integrates a comprehensive design for effective school functioning, including instruction, assessment, classroom management, professional development, parental involvement, and school management, that aligns the school's curriculum, technology, and professional development into a comprehensive school reform plan for schoolwide change designed to enable all students to meet challenging State content and student academic achievement standards and addresses needs identified through a school needs assessment;

3. Provides high quality and continuous teacher and staff professional development;

4. Includes measurable goals for student academic achievement and benchmarks for meeting such goals;

5. Is supported by teachers, principals, administrators, school personnel staff, and other professional staff;

6. Provides support for teachers, principals, administrators, and other school staff;

7. Provides for the meaningful involvement of parents and the local community in planning, implementing, and evaluating school improvement activities consistent with section 1118;

8. Uses high quality external technical support and assistance from an entity that has experience and expertise in schoolwide reform and improvement, which may include an institution of higher education;

9. Includes a plan for the annual evaluation of the implementation of school reforms and the student results achieved;

10. Identifies other resources, including Federal, State, local, and private resources, that shall be used to coordinate services that will support and sustain the comprehensive school reform effort; and

11. (A) Has been found, through scientifically based research to significantly improve the academic achievement of students participating in such program as compared to students in schools who have not participated in such program; or (B) has been found to have strong evidence that such program will significantly improve the academic achievement of participating children.

*U.S. Department of Education, 2005, Sec. 1602.

By all appearances, the aim was to create federal infrastructure to support a system-wide emphasis on the use of science in educational reform. Concurrently, federally funded, quasi-governmental organizations were developing capabilities to evaluate comprehensive school reform programs and other programs for rigorous evidence of effectiveness: for example, the University of Oregon's Reading First Center, the National Clearinghouse on Comprehensive School Reform, and the What Works Clearinghouse.

SFAF's dynamic development agenda and process, its fluid development organization, and its long-established capabilities for (and commitment to) research supported a quick response. Responding to NCLB's emphasis on scientifically based research, SFAF sought to set the standard by designing a randomized field trial of Success for All, the closest that SFAF or any other provider had ever come to conducting a controlled experiment evaluating the effectiveness of a comprehensive school reform program. At the same time, SFAF drew quickly from existing and newly developing resources to package a version of Success for All targeted directly at districts and schools received federal funding under Reading First.[21] Called "Success for All–Reading First," promotional literature described the program as "precisely aligned with the requirements of this new legislation."[22] A promotional booklet describing the program to prospective schools explained further:

> To align Success for All with the requirements of Reading First, we have created a new program, Success for All–Reading First, which is designed to meet these requirements. It builds on the programs, practices, and training capabilities established over the years by the nonprofit Success for All Foundation.
>
> Success for All–Reading First is not merely an element of Success for All. Every aspect of the classroom program for grades K–3 has been examined in light of the Reading First guidelines and in light of changing state and national standards for practice and content. Many new elements are being introduced in Success for All–Reading First to strengthen the alignment with Reading First guidelines, and to improve professional development, assessment, curriculum, and other elements.[23]

2002/2003: The Core Curriculum Components

For 2002/2003, earlier development initiatives continued. These efforts spanned all components and operations: for example, a complete redesign of initial training for school leaders; a complete revision to the primary leadership manual to align it with on-going program improvements; a new release of Success for All's web-based information system; the continued piloting and release of strategy-specific components in the Building Better Readers series; initiation of a second revision to tutoring in which all tools and resources would be incorporated into a multimedia software package; reconceptualization of the family support team as the "solutions team," including efforts to more tightly coordinate academic and nonacademic services for students; an extended pilot of the Goal Focused Improvement Process throughout the training organization; the release of 27 new or revised Experienced Sites Conference sessions (along with associated participant training books); and the initial fielding of SFAF's randomized study of program effectiveness.

At the same time, SFAF put the figurative capstone on its 1999–2003 development cycle by completing revisions to the core Success for All curriculum components. Early Learning was redesigned and re-released as KinderCorner. Reading Roots was released as "Reading Roots Third Edition," which included a new phonics sub-component called "FastTrack Phonics." And Reading Wings was updated to include new "Targeted Treasure Hunts" focused on the same, four core comprehension strategies as the Building Better Readers series: clarification, summarization, questioning, and prediction. All had been under revision during the entire development cycle, though they were under a much longer development timeline due to the time and cost of updating such extensively elaborated materials and due to their sensitivity as the coordinative center of the entire program.

Across the components, the overall design for curriculum and instruction remained intact: continued focus on cognitive skills and strategies; continued use of cooperative learning and the cycle of instruction; continued use of highly elaborated units and lessons; and increased attention to embedding supplemental guidance in the core curriculum materials. Within this framework, developers sought to accomplish multiple goals at the same time. One goal was to increase support for expert use in regular classroom instruction: for example, by strengthening informal and formal assessments and their use for adapting instruction; by adopting conventional language of expert use across curriculum components (e.g., "diagnostic instruction," "teaching and modeling," and "prompting and reinforcing"); and by embedding video and DVD technology into classroom instruction to model expert use by teachers and students. A second goal was to further adapt the program to environments: for example, by aligning intended outcomes with standards and assessment of key states, and by incorporating the increasingly ubiquitous language from the findings of the National Reading Panel. A third goal was to address sundry needs that had been recognized over time: for example, improving aesthetics and "ease of use"; improving coordination and transitions between the different levels of the reading curriculum; and incorporating additional writing instruction into the reading curriculum.

Reprise: Recapturing the Program

If the goal of SFAF's 1999–2003 development cycle was to recapture the program, there was much to suggest that SFAF was well on its way. In four quick years, while continuing to support its installed base of schools, the SFAF development organization used incremental, component-by-component improvements to completely re-engineer Success for All. Collectively, these program improvements appeared to position Success for All strongly in response to past problems of "process" and "outcomes" by vastly increasing support for more expert use of the program. While revisions to the core curriculum components functioned as a figurative capstone on the 1999/2000–2002/2003 development cycle, development efforts would actually continue, with (among other things) a particular focus on improving guidance for school-specific interventions. Even so, by the end of 2002/2003, all of the above-described program improvements were available in some form to the full network of Success for All schools.

The 1999–2003 development cycle also appeared to position the Success for All enterprise very strongly in response to NCLB, two of its flagship programs (Comprehensive School Reform and Reading First), and its increased attention to scientifically based research in educational reform. Indeed, in the view of SFAF's executives, the still-growing research base on Success for All was a key, potential source of competitive advantage in NCLB-effected environments.

To help secure that advantage, SFAF began posting research on Success for All on its web site. Two studies were featured particularly prominently. Both were led by University of Wisconsin researcher Geoffrey Borman.[24] Both were published in leading, peer-reviewed journals concurrent with the close of the 1999–2003 development cycle. And both bore good news, for comprehensive school reform (in general) and for Success for All (in particular).

In 2002, Borman and Gina Hughes, a Johns Hopkins University researcher, published a study of the long-term achievement effects and the cost effectiveness of Success for All in *Educational Evaluation and Policy Analysis*, a journal of the American Educational Research Association. In the study, Borman and Hughes used data provided by the Baltimore City Public School System for the years 1986/1987 to 1998/1999 to compare students who attended five of the original Success for All schools in Baltimore to students who attended matched comparison schools as they progressed to middle school and high school. Borman and Hughes reported that their results indicated that "Success for All students complete eighth grade at a younger age, with better achievement outcomes, fewer special education placements, and less frequent retentions in grade at a cost that is essentially the same as that allocated to educating their control-group counterparts."[25] Further, they reported that "the replicable educational practices of prevention and early intervention, as modeled by Success for All, are more educationally effective, and equally expensive, relative to the traditional remedial educational practices of retention and special education."[26]

In 2003, Borman and colleagues published in the *Review of Educational Research* (another journal of the American Educational Research Association) what, to that point, was the most extensive meta-analysis of the effects of comprehensive school reform programs on student achievement: a 100+ page review of the results of 232 studies of 29 comprehensive school reform programs. While they acknowledge weaknesses in the amount and quality of available research, and while they reported that effect sizes varied tremendously, Borman and colleagues argued that "the overall effects of CSR are statistically significant, meaningful, and appear to be greater than the effects of other interventions that have been designed to serve similar purposes and student and school populations."[27]

Further, Borman and colleagues observed that, even though conventional funding covered a three-year implementation window, achievement gains improved dramatically as schools exceeded that window. Specifically, schools that had implemented comprehensive school reform programs for five years or more showed achievement effects two times the overall average effect size of 0.15. Schools that had implemented programs for seven or more years showed gains 2.5 times greater than the overall average effect size. And schools that had implemented programs for eight to fourteen years showed gains 3.3 times greater than the overall average effect size.[28]

More importantly for SFAF, Borman and colleagues identified Success for All and two other programs (Direct Instruction and the School Development Program) as having the strongest evidence of effectiveness, with Success for All reported as having an overall effect size of 0.18 and an effect size of 0.08 in third-party research.[29] To be sure, the difference between the overall effect size (which included SFAF's own research) and the effect size for third-party research was eye-catching. So, too, were the difference between the effect sizes reported by Borman and colleagues and the +0.50 effect sizes reported by SFAF.[30] While recognizing the potential for bias, Borman and colleagues argued that the explanation more likely rested in developers either: (a) deciding not to publish weak findings; and/or (b) studying high-quality implementation in order to best learn how their programs work in practice.[31] To guide interpretation, Borman and colleagues drew on conventional sources to suggest that an effect size of 0.20 be interpreted as generally small, though representative of positive effect sizes in education-related fields. They also suggested that, in education and related fields, modest effect sizes (i.e., between 0.10 and 0.20) should not be interpreted as trivial.[32]

From the perspective of SFAF, that both studies showed positive findings was clear. With an extensively revised program and new evidence of effectiveness, the stage appeared to be set for another rapid increase in scale. That was a view held by SFAF's executives. That was also a view held by many others, as well. For example, in a 2003 book on leadership in comprehensive school reform programs, researchers Joseph Murphy (of Vanderbilt University) and Amanda Datnow (then of the Ontario Institute for Studies in Education at the University of Toronto) made exactly that point:

> The market for CSR models is quite an active one; it has been estimated that more than $1 billion was spent by local school improvement services by the year 2001 (New American Schools, n.d.)
>
> Overall, we now find that the scaling up of CSR models is occurring at an unprecedented rate, affecting thousands of schools in the United State and elsewhere. . . . Considering that the number of schools implementing CSR models is estimated at 6,000 (Educational Quality Institute, n.d.), these schools comprise 6.5% of the approximately 92,000 public schools in the United States. . . .

There is considerable evidence to suggest that the CSR movement will continue to grow and thrive in the next few years. Congress has continued to support CSRD, an increasing amount of research is being conducted on the implementation and effects of CSR (and hence our knowledge base has increased), and the reform models are maturing and design teams are becoming more adept at working with schools. There is still much to be learned from the CSR movement and its implications for school improvement and for leadership.[33]

NEW PROBLEMS WITHIN, NEW PROBLEMS BEYOND

SFAF's revolution was not the same type of abrupt, seismic event as federally education policy: a bundle of evolutionary, interdependent policy and program improvements enacted on a given day, with the stroke of a pen. Rather, it was a series of waves that swelled over the course of the 1999–2003 development cycle and that lifted the entire enterprise. As those waves swelled, the Success for All enterprise began to look less and less like the fragmented, technically-weak system of U.S. public education and more and more like the coherent professional network long sought by SFAF founders.

Yet as waves of success swelled, a new set of interdependent and deeply perplexing problems began swirling beneath them. And, oddly, at the same time it was evolving in ways that *differentiated* itself from U.S. educational environments, the Success for All enterprise was also evolving in ways that *resembled* U.S. educational environments. Much as with explosive growth its training organization, SFAF's development agenda, organization, and process interacted over the course of the 1999–2003 development cycle to recreate enduring problems of U.S. educational reform within the Success for All enterprise, including some of the very problems that SFAF had initially set out to solve. By no means had the Success for All enterprise suddenly devolved into a dysfunctional urban school district. Even so, for those who have studied such districts (or, more problematic for SFAF, for teachers and leaders actually working in them), the problems would have been familiar: a steady supply of rapidly churning and weakly integrated improvement initiatives; incoherence, faddism, and distrust in schools; and a potential-rich program that exceeded capabilities for effective use in schools.

At the same time that new problems began emerging within the Success for All enterprise, new problems began emerging beyond. Broader stability gave way to profound turbulence, and environments that had long been supportive of SFAF turned unexpectedly hostile. As its 1999–2003 development cycle progressed, despite projections for continued growth, SFAF found itself struggling to secure both the contributions needed to support its continuing development efforts and the revenues needed to sustain the enterprise.

Just as with the emergence of new potential within the Success for All enterprise, these new problems were not effected in one, turbulent moment. They, too, emerged, interacted, and compounded over the 1999–2003 development cycle.

As members of SFAF began recognizing them, early enthusiasm evolved to grave concern. In some ways, SFAF found itself sailing out of one perfect storm and straight into another, this one more furious than the one before it. In other ways, SFAF found itself someplace altogether different: living on some complex and ever-turbulent edge, staring down a combination of interdependent problems and solutions within and beyond the Success for All enterprise, its continued viability hanging in the balance.

Churning and Weakly-Integrated Improvement Initiatives

Within the SFAF enterprise, the problems began with the development agenda, organization, and process interacting to recreate a version of the uncoordinated reform blizzard constantly howling in the broader environments of U.S. public education. Spanning the 1999–2003 development cycle, developers worked urgently to improve both the elaboration and scaffolding of every program component, with improvements readied for release on at least an annual basis (and sometimes more frequently than that). While the intent was to rapidly address pressing problems and to seize new opportunities, an unintended consequence was that SFAF's prolific development organization produced a torrent of constantly churning program improvements. The number of new and revised sessions at annual Experienced Sites Conferences was dizzying in and of itself: 19 new or revised sessions in 2001; 38 new or revised sessions in 2002; and 27 new or revised sessions in 2003. Over this same period, the Success for All Materials Catalog (the standard document detailing products and services available to schools) evolved from a thin newsletter to a 50+ page booklet.

Much as the rapid scale-up of the installed base of schools overwhelmed the historic informality of SFAF's training organization, so, too, did the rapid scale-up of development activity overwhelm the historic informality of SFAF's development organization. Developers struggled to coordinate these many, complex, and fast-paced improvement initiatives informally among themselves. Further, the number, complexity, and pace made it increasingly difficult for SFAF executives to be as intimately involved in all aspects of the day-to-day work and, thus, more difficult for them to informally coordinate it. Consequently, from 1999–2003, what from a bird's eye view appeared to be an orderly progression of program improvements appeared much less orderly for those on the ground. In a 2003 interview, one SFAF developer expressed the frustration of many:

> Somebody gets an idea, we're rolling it out the door the next day, without any real thought as to how it's going to effect this, this, or this. All this stuff comes rolling out. . . . Its just like, every day, I walk in, and I think, "What's new this week?" I love our organization, but whoever is there last at any given meeting is the one who seems to make the decision. "Okay, this is how it's going to happen." But you can walk out in the hallway and talk to another person, and somebody else can change that decision.

Problems of coordination in the development organization led to what members of SFAF described as problems of integration: that is, problems linking separately improved components into a comprehensive, coherent, improved program.
Program improvements simply were not fitting together as tightly as developers
intended and as schools needed. Integration was particularly problematic within
the leadership component. SFAF had a dedicated leadership team charged with
improving support for school leaders. At the same time, virtually every other program improvement from every other development team had implications for
school leaders, from aligning the program with environments to scaffolding
teachers in the use of new curriculum improvements. While these many program
improvements had potential to interact to support a more expert version of leadership practice, the lack of coordination among developers resulted in a lack of
explicit linkages between program improvements, as well as a lack of shared
understandings about how the entire lot could work in interaction.

Problems of constantly churning and weakly integrated program improvements were not recognized immediately. Instead, members of SFAF began to recognize them midway through the 1999–2003 development cycle, as development
initiatives expanded, efforts to field them grew, and experiences and frustrations
accumulated. Yet stopping these problems at their source by slowing the number
and pace of improvement initiatives did not present itself as an option to SFAF.
Continuous, program-wide improvement was among the core commitments and
capabilities of SFAF, work historically supported by a steady stream of public and
private funding. Thus, it continued.

Incoherence, Faddism, and Distrust in Schools

Constantly churning and weakly integrated program improvements began to
interact with complex, school-level dynamics to recreate within the Success for
All enterprise versions of the incoherence, faddism, and distrust so characteristic
of chronically underperforming schools. The problems began with SFAF's urgent
dissemination process, which effected a level of incoherence in schools even
beyond that effected by problems of design-level integration. Again, a rallying cry
among SFAF executives and developers was, "Get it out there!" And, again, rather
than issuing complete, revised versions of Success for All in the style of software
releases (e.g., "Success for All v. 3.0"), program improvements were urgently
"gotten out there" much more in the style of software "bug fixes" and "patches," on
an improvement-by-improvement basis (sometimes annually, sometimes more
frequently).[34] Thus, while newly enlisting schools received a complete, up-to-date
version of Success for All, all other Success for All schools were always working
with some combination of existing and improved program components.

Incoherence was exacerbated by a sort of faddism. Working as an external provider on a voluntary basis, SFAF had no formal authority over which schools
elected to adopt which new-and-improved program components. Though developers and trainers provided guidance, their voluntary relationship with schools

gave them no formal authority over such decisions. Rather, such decisions were intentionally delegated to schools, themselves: in deference to their status as the paying customers; in an effort not to effect interpretations of SFAF as a bureaucratic, controlling outsider; and to cultivate schools' ownership and motivation. The result, thus, was individual schools working within existing understandings, preferences, and budget constraints to sample from SFAF's ever-expanding catalog of materials and scaffolding opportunities: a veritable shopping mall of hot, new school improvement resources and services.[35] Some schools aggressively pursued the latest and greatest, no matter their needs. Others rode out this year's model in anticipation of next year's model. Still others did a little of both.

Problems of incoherence and faddism were matched with problems maintaining trustful relationships with schools. Working as an external provider, SFAF always had to maintain a soft touch, actively working to support implementation without breeching the trust or autonomy of schools. The work of continuous improvement complicated that challenge, with SFAF sitting between a rock and a hard place. On the one hand, members of SFAF reported that some schools pushed for continuous improvement, both as a sign of SFAF's commitment to them and because they drew motivation from participating in a dynamic, forward-moving enterprise. On the other hand, members of SFAF reported that other schools interpreted continuous improvement as a sign that SFAF was floundering. Exacerbating that perception was the fact that, with problems both in coordinating and disseminating program improvements, SFAF sometimes did flounder. In a 2003 interview, one member of SFAF with joint responsibility for development and training explained the consequences:

When you're out in the field, there's nothing worse than principals mad at you because they ordered materials and they didn't get them. Or the revisions are not quite done, and they're trying to order materials now, because they have their funding, but they don't know if Reading Roots Third Edition will be ready in time. There's nothing worse than that. There's nothing more destructive in terms of the way that we maintain ourselves. Word of mouth between schools is, "Yeah, they're a good program, but they don't have their act together." And people in the field deal with that, and Customer Relations deals with that. Developers don't always deal with that.

The Paradox of Potential and Practice

Among the most surprising of the problems that SFAF recreated within its own enterprise was the paradox of potential and practice: The more potential that the development organization packed into the program, the more difficult it was to put that potential into practice in weak schools.

With the program improvements released during its 1999–2003 development cycle, SFAF was pushing its schools to make a fundamental transition. Teachers and principals locked into mutually reinforcing interpretations of Success for

All as bureaucratic and/or technocratic (and, consequently, into mutually-reinforcing patterns of mechanistic use) were being challenged to understand and to use the program fundamentally differently: that is, as a resource for professional practice and learning. However, the more support for expert use that developers layered into the program, the harder and farther they pushed teachers and leaders beyond existing understandings and ways of working.

While SFAF's new materials, tools, and resources were developed with careful attention to ease of use, and while SFAF's new scaffolding opportunities were developed with the intent of supporting quick use in practice, none of these supports was designed to be effective without the extensive involvement of SFAF trainers. Indeed, SFAF's 1999–2003 development process pushed SFAF trainers to think and to work just as differently as it did teachers and leaders. Further, absent solutions to problems of integration, coordination, and dissemination within the development organization, those became problems for trainers to solve on the ground, in their work with schools. Understanding how to leverage program improvements simply at a rudimentary level grew to be increasingly problematic as the number and pace of improvement initiatives expanded, never mind integrating the different program improvements to support expert use in schools.

And that was the rub. As the development organization worked urgently to pack new potential into the program, it pushed hardest on what, going into the 1999–2003 development cycle, had been SFAF Achilles' heel: its training organization, many members of which were, themselves, locked into adverse interpretations and misuse of the program. Yet awareness of the breadth and depth of problems in the training organization was not shared equally among members of SFAF *in advance* of the 1999–2003 development cycle. Rather, shared awareness emerged and sharpened *over the course of* the 1999–2003 development cycle. This awareness emerged as trainers began attempting to use new resources and new scaffolding opportunities to support expert use in schools, and as SFAF executives, managers, and developers began recognizing their struggles doing so.

During its 1999–2003 development cycle, absent deep understanding of the extent of problems in the training organization, SFAF approached improving the professional development of trainers exactly as it approached improving the program as a whole: that is, via incremental, evolutionary improvement. SFAF continued to work within existing constraints: for example, a lack of external funding to support the development of the training organization; the inability to stop development activity and re-allocate earmarked funding to the training organization; and the inability to take trainers "off line" and out of the field to engage in extended professional learning opportunities. As such, SFAF continued to support trainers' professional development with the same, formal structures: via direct instruction in the context of annual conferences and periodic meetings, with a primary focus on exposure to SFAF's many, new program improvements (rather than mastery of them). And SFAF continued to rely on informal communities of training practice to develop capabilities for expert training practice.

Familiar results followed. More expert trainers participating in stronger communities of practice were more able to capitalize on program improvements.

More novice trainers participating in weaker communities of practice struggled, often incorporating new language and ideas (especially the distinction between "routine" and "refined" use of Success for All) without changing their day-to-day work. Uneven progress developing trainers' capabilities to exploit new potential in the program, in turn, became a limiting condition on developing schools' capabilities to exploit that new potential. Some in SFAF drew the line right down the middle, with two of four geographic training areas progressing to more expert use and with two continuing to struggle.

As members of SFAF began recognizing the challenges both of expert training and of developing expert trainers, SFAF initiated immediate efforts to respond. For example, in SY 2001/2002, SFAF revised first-year professional development for new trainers to include the analysis of data from actual Success for All schools, with the goal of immediately beginning to develop their capabilities to identify problems of implementation and effectiveness—in September, before they ever conducted their first Implementation Visit. To support collaboration and integration among trainers, SFAF incorporated its previously independent family support training team into the full training organization, and it began aggressive efforts to "cross-train" trainers to ensure that all were equally prepared to support all program components. And one of SFAF's geographic training areas used early pilot work on the Goal Focused Improvement Process to learn more about communities of practice as a context for developing capabilities for expert training.

Lessons learned from these early efforts suggested steep challenges, most notably the pilot work on the Goal Focused Improvement Process. The pilot, itself, was something of a best case scenario: an expert regional manager (a National Board Certified teacher with a master's degree in organizational development) in SFAF's most progressive, geographic training area, working with approximately 10 trainers to support 100 schools, under the guidance of an area manager who also served as one of the lead developers. Recalling her experiences, the regional manager reported that it required three years of intensive collaboration among her team to advance to expert use of the Goal Focused Implementation Process. En route, she experienced 50% attrition among her team, in part because of trainers self-selecting out of the organization due to the challenges in the work. With this best case scenario as a lower bound, developing expert trainers under the guidance of the modal regional manager in the modal geographic training area was shaping up to be a very long-term proposition.

Thus, SFAF found itself facing the same paradox of potential and practice that had long frustrated other ambitious, external educational reformers. It was a matter of organizational physics: of potential and kinetic energy. SFAF developers were winding and winding and winding a spring that packed potential into the program. However, the spring's release mechanism—its training organization—was stressed entering the 1999–2003 development cycle, and it began to seize up as the cycle progressed. This release mechanism was not a simple trip switch. Rather, the release mechanism was a complex, geographically distributed, self-funding, hard-working group of very committed people without the plan, the opportunity, or the slack to support collegial, practice-based learning. With that, new potential remained tightly coiled in the program, and not in motion and in practice in schools.

Of all that members SFAF reported learning through the 1999–2003 development cycle, problems and complexities in the professional development of trainers appeared to be most surprising, both for experienced members of SFAF and for developers newly recruited to the effort. Whether a veteran or a rookie, none had ever managed so extensive a program improvement effort in interaction with such a large training organization and such a large installed base of schools. Explained one newly recruited developer, in a 2003 interview:

> This work environment is a new experience for me, working with hundreds of trainers in the field and disseminating information to thousands of schools. That's the type of infrastructure for this size of an organization, and it is new for me. I'm the type of person who's an action person. I usually do something, I get it done, I do the next step, and it all happens very smoothly. I've just learned, oh, but we're dealing with hundreds of people now. Hundreds of people who learn very different ways, have very different styles of learning, have different needs, have different backgrounds, and they're just not all going to get this at the same time and in the same way. That's been a learning experience for me, and I think a valuable one, because that's just the real world.

Hostile Environments

Enduring problems of reform within the Success for All enterprise began interacting with an equally enduring problem beyond: Broader environments quickly turned hostile.[36] SFAF's 1999–2003 development cycle began concurrent with a series of abrupt, seismic events in broader economic, political, and social environments. Economic growth, political stability, and domestic security that SFAF had enjoyed over its history quickly gave way to profound turbulence. Early in 2000, the very thing that had driven the economic prosperity of the late 1990s—the "dot com" bubble—burst. Following quickly was the 2000 presidential election, among the most contentious and controversial in the nation's history. For an enterprise that had gained its full momentum largely within the administration of a single Democratic president, the 2000 election marked an abrupt transition. Square in the middle of SFAF's 1990/2000–2002/2003 development cycle came the terrorist attacks of 9/11/2001. Resulting turbulence stretched clear through the 1999–2003 development cycle to the invasion of Iraq in March of 2003.

Shocks and aftershocks ramified through U.S. educational environments. Money began drying up everywhere. Philanthropic contributions began to decline with the rapid fall in over-valued investment portfolios. States, districts, and schools that had reaped the benefits of the roaring '90s suddenly found themselves squeezed. With new pressure from NCLB to increase achievement, the challenge to states, districts, and schools was to do much more with much less.

Indeed, many critics decried NCLB as an unfunded mandate, arguing that the work required of states, districts, and schools far exceeded federally provided resources.

Shocks and aftershocks ramified through the Success for All enterprise. The 9/11 terrorist attacks dealt yet another blow to SFAF's ever-stressed training organization. Several years earlier, one of SFAF's most experienced teams of trainers had been relocated to Manhattan to serve New York City's Chancellor's District. Its members were distributed throughout the city and in schools at the time of the attacks. At the very same time, all of SFAF's newly recruited trainers for that year (many ex-teachers fresh out of their own classroom) were gathered for initial professional development in Tyson's Corners, Virginia, within a few short miles of the Pentagon at the time of the attack. Other trainers were distributed throughout the country, conducting their first implementation visits of the new school year. All struggled to travel home to their families—and, for the years following, to travel at all.

To match new strain on the training organization, declining philanthropic contributions began to erode the funding available to support SFAF's expansive development agenda. Uncertainty in state and local funding meant that schools had fewer resources with which to purchase SFAF's newly revised materials and training services, thus stemming a key source of revenue. And uncertainty in state and local funding interacted with SFAF's loosely coordinated dissemination process to create a drain on SFAF's hard-won operating capital. Long printing timelines, uncertain demand for new materials and training sessions, and ever-churning development had SFAF incurring large costs for obsolete program materials on an annual basis (costs estimated by one SFAF executive to be in the millions of dollars).

Still worse was a rapid decline in SFAF's primary source of operating capital: revenues from new business. Rather than beginning the climb to 3,000+ schools over its 1999–2003 development cycle, SFAF executives began recognizing an unfamiliar and unanticipated phenomenon: a rapid decrease in the rate of growth in 2000/2001 (from 42% to 3%) and, then, the actual loss of schools for 2001/2002 and 2002/2003 (at a rate of roughly 4% per year).[37] SFAF lost experienced schools: in some cases, school-by-school; in other cases, en masse, as districts that had coordinated the adoption of Success for All and other comprehensive school reform programs dropped them (including New York City's Chancellor's District, in the winter of 2003).[38] Worse yet, SFAF struggled to recruit new schools. By 2002/2003, the end of its development cycle, the installed based had declined to 1,480 schools—still more than supported by all but nine state education agencies, and more than SFAF served at the time of the organization's founding in SY 1998/1999.[39] Even so, for an organization heavily dependent on generating operating capital through new business, this was very bad news.

Reductions in funding, revenue, and the installed based of schools led to an unanticipated contraction in SFAF as an organization. Rather than growing to provide more support to more schools, SFAF found itself needing to lay off developers, trainers, and administrative staff, the first reductions in force in the history of Success for All. Exhaustion and uncertainty had others leaving voluntarily. SFAF's historically informal (and slack-rich) development organization began to face new incentives to manage the development process more efficiently, against scarce resources—at the same time that it was discovering the need to urgently address problems of integration and to urgently support the practice-based learning of trainers. Amidst new policy expectations for adequate yearly progress and the strain of life on the road in post-9/11 environments, SFAF's already stressed trainers faced new pressure to improve achievement in order to retain existing schools, and they faced new incentives to recruit new schools in order to save their own jobs.

For a young organization still viewed by its members as a Mom and Pop shop, the impact of unexpectedly hostile environments struck a deep blow in the combination of confidence, camaraderie, and missionary zeal that had long supported the work of the organization. Particularly frustrating to all involved was that SFAF was experiencing these new problems with its environments despite the success of its 1999–2003 development cycle, both in packing new potential into the program and in strategically aligning it with NCLB's Reading First program. Just as frustrating was that SFAF was experiencing these problems despite what appeared to be a strengthening in policy (and other) support for the still-nascent, niche market for research-based, research-validated comprehensive school reform programs.

However, whether the comprehensive school reform market was strengthening or weakening was actually emerging as a very open question. Concurrent with the close of the 1999–2003 development cycle, a new line of criticism was beginning to develop in SFAF's environments: criticism not of Success for All, in particular, but of comprehensive school reform, in general. Where SFAF cited the review of research by Borman and colleagues as continued evidence of possibility, others cited the overall effect size of 0.15 as evidence that comprehensive school reform was yielding weak returns on very formidable investments, and weaker yet when considering that the overall effect size for third party research was only 0.09.[40] By this logic, Success for All appeared to be the happy exception, not the disappointing rule.

One such critic was University of Michigan historian Jeffrey Mirel. In 2001 and 2002, Mirel published two reports on the history of the New American Schools.[41] Arguing that the history of NAS was one of "unrequited promise," Mirel was critical of the participating designs as more evolutionary than "break the mold," of achievement effects as weak, and of NAS garnering formidable political influence amidst questionable evidence of effectiveness (thereby echoing the earlier criticisms of Stanley Pogrow).

Just as problematic was the ten year report on the New American Schools initiative published in 2002 by Rand researchers Mark Berends, Susan Bodilly, and Sheila Nataraj Kirby.[42] Their report framed whole school reform as challenging-yet-promising. Over their period of study, the challenges were formidable: for example, the participating designs were under constant development; achieving uniformly high levels of implementation in schools proved difficult; environments complicated implementation; and design team capacity in the sponsoring organizations proved to be variable.[43] Those challenges notwithstanding, they also reported that approximately 50% of schools implementing NAS designs demonstrated achievement gains relative to comparison groups.[44]

Consistent with the findings of Borman and colleagues, Berends and colleagues qualified their report by observing that implementation appeared to be improving over time, and that it may have been premature to expect robust achievement results across all schools in the six year window structured by NAS. However, recognizing little tolerance for complex, long-term reform, they concluded their report with a cautionary note regarding expectations for externally designed whole school reform:

> Currently, many schools throughout the country are attempting whole-school reform requiring significant changes in teacher and administrator behaviors using the federal funding provided by such programs as Title I and the CSRD program. RAND's program of studies of NAS has identified the conditions needed to make these efforts successful including: teacher support and sense of teacher efficacy; strong and specific principal leadership abilities; clear communication and ongoing assistance on the part of design developers; and stable leadership resources, and support from districts.
>
> The RAND analyses indicate these conditions are not common in the districts and schools undertaking CSRD. . . .
>
> We anticipate continuing conflicts between whole-school design or model adoption and district and schools contexts as well as political pressures rushing schools and external assistance providers into partnerships that are not well thought through. If districts continue in this manner, the outcome will be neither short-term gains nor long-term success. Expectations regarding the ability of schools to make meaningful changes with the assistance of externally developed designs in this fragmented and unsupportive environment are not likely to be met. This may well lead policymakers to abandon what could be a promising vehicle for whole-school reform without having given it a chance.[45]

Losing the Organization

With SFAF, so much depended on one's perspective. From one vantage point, its 1999–2003 development cycle appeared to have SFAF recapturing the program. From another, its 1999–2003 development cycle appeared to have SFAF losing the organization: the organization of its developments efforts, resulting in problems of ever-churning and weakly integrated program coherence; the organization of its cornerstone program, with problems of incoherence and faddism in schools; the organization of its training operations, with new potential in the program exceeding trainers' capabilities to exploit that potential; and the SFAF organization, itself, as environments turned unexpectedly hostile.

That all of this was happening was becoming increasingly clear. Why it was happening was not. Apprehending and understanding the array of interdependent problems both within and beyond the Success for All enterprise would have challenged executives and executive staff in even the most professionally managed organizations. Yet SFAF continued to be managed by educational researchers and developers, themselves supported by thin executive-level staff. Indeed, SFAF did not have a formal operations department to tease out the complex problems within the Success for All enterprise, nor did it have a formal "marketing department" or "policy department" that monitored and interpreted environments. Again, much such work was conducted informally among executives, developers, trainers, school leaders, and teachers. However, echoing problems in development and training, profound turbulence over the course of the 1999–2003 development cycle swamped SFAF's informal means of monitoring and interpreting interdependent activity within and beyond the enterprise—and, with that, its abilities to apprehend and understand interdependent problems bearing on it.

Just as with SFAF's program improvements, these new problems had been emerging, evolving, interacting, and compounding over the course of the 1999–2003 development cycle. As the cycle drew to a close, these new problems reached a fevered pitch. SFAF was under great stress. Cracks began to show in its members' resolve. Trainers were overwhelmed. Developers were exasperated. Executives were bewildered. One SFAF staff member spoke for all: "It seems like we're always raging against the machine."

LIVING ON THE EDGE

Over the 1990s and into the new millennium, as SFAF worked to design, support, scale up, and improve its comprehensive school reform program, students of complex systems began wrestling with a notion that they called "the edge of chaos."[46] This notion was used to describe complex systems that had evolved to teeter on some fine point between predictability and randomness. At issue was what happens to such systems over time, as small changes in key variables drive abrupt transitions from one phase in the system's existence to another. One wrinkle in scholars' debates focused on the capabilities of entities living on this edge. Some argued that the edge of chaos was a place of maximum evolution. They argued that, through natural selection processes, entities that survived there "evolved to evolve" by developing unusual capabilities to process large volumes of information and to adapt quickly and strategically. Some questioned the argument of the edge of chaos as a place of maximum evolution. Others questioned whether some place like "the edge of chaos" really existed at all.

While scholars debated, the theoretical notion of "the edge of chaos" evolved into a general metaphor describing the challenge of existing in some space between predictability and randomness. To the chagrin of some, the metaphor grew legs, and it began to travel. The metaphor made its way into research and practical writing on business strategy. Scholars and analysts appropriated the notion to describe "creative disorganization" as a legitimate and adaptive (if inefficient) managerial strategy under particular conditions (and a stark contrast to conventional methods of rational management).[47] A variant of the metaphor made its way into research on innovation. Scholars leveraged the notion to frame the innovation process as a journey down a river that oscillated between divergent, random, chaotic flows and convergent, orderly, periodic flows. For managers, they described the most acute problems as sitting at the point of transition between convergent and divergent flows: the fulcrum between predictability and randomness, and a point of choice between rational and "pluralistic" management strategies.[48] The metaphor even made its way into popular literature, with a novel titled *The Edge of Chaos* using the notion to frame a fundamental human condition in the new millennium: a need for constant learning and change in order to stem a life of hopeless predictability, though at risk of effecting a life of disorder and instability.[49]

Whether real or imaginary, fact or fiction, the notion of "the edge of chaos" appeared to describe perfectly the place where SFAF and its enterprise lived, and what it took to survive there. SFAF and its installed base of schools lived at the interstices of three complex, interdependent systems: SFAF's self-constructed network of schools; the broader system of U.S. public education; and the still-broader economic, political, and social system. In some ways, in the early 2000s, these systems were mired in order and predictability, each reinforcing the other: Success for All schools, mired in rote, mechanistic use of the program; the deeply institutionalized U.S. educational system, mired in sub-standard performance and non-improvement; and the broader system, mired in an industrial economy and political partisanship. In other ways, these systems were in the throes of great change, each reinforcing the other in a push for some new, rational order, and at a rapid rate when cast against history: the Success for All enterprise, driving systematic experimentation and evidence-based decision making into classrooms, schools, external programs, and policy; the U.S. educational system, driving systemic reform through the use of research and accountability; and still-broader environments, in which the Information Revolution fueled a global economy and a populist enlightenment.

These were dynamic systems. They were prone to abrupt, seismic changes at their most fundamental levels, followed by shocks and aftershocks within and between: for example, in Success for All, with the introduction of new, simple language describing expert use that captured fundamental ambitions and fueled rapid development; in the U.S. educational system, with a bundle of evolutionary, interdependent changes in policies and programs enacted at a moment with the stroke of a pen; and in the broader economic, political, and social systems, as bubbles burst, towers crumbled, and all watched in shock and awe. Yet these changes were not entirely random. Key elements of these systems moved in predictable (if uncoordinated) cycles that functioned to synchronize activity within and between actors: the school year; policy cycles; funding cycles; economic cycles; and electoral cycles.

Working amidst abrupt shocks and within predictable cycles, these systems and the entities in them responded. They did not do so using a shared set of rules, such that each was responding in known and predictable ways to each other. Indeed, though rhetoric, intentions, and possibilities for rationality ran through all three systems, movement over time within and between systems was far more evolutionary than it was classically rational, as all simultaneously processed circumstances, made meaning, and charted their way forwards. Actor by actor, the great bulk of activity appeared to more of the "successive limited comparisons" variety than the "step back, consider, evaluate, and choose the optimal alternative" variety.

This was SFAF's world: the interstices of three complex, interdependent, adapting systems. This world was certainly not what some described as "empty": a world of predictable parts neatly arranged, such that one could easily improve the world by isolating a given part, plucking it out, studying it, improving it, and re-inserting it. Nor was this world an apocalyptic anarchy, with all its parts strewn here and there, each acting in its own self-interest, absent any recognition of, deference to, or responsibility for the collective. Rather, this was a sort of "full world" in which parts, problems, solutions, and challenges were moving and interacting with each other, within and between, in regular cycles, punctuated by occasional, abrupt changes in the fundamentals. Indeed, at its very core, the vision of Success for All was predicated on this very fullness: the deep faith that, somehow, the gentlest of movements—little children in classrooms learning together in new ways—could stir up a storm of equality, prosperity, and hope.

Living at the nexus of these three systems, SFAF had evolved to evolve, constantly adding new organizational capabilities both in response to (and to compensate for) its environments. These capabilities combined to support an approach to the work of continuous improvement that blended capabilities for exploiting what research had to offer with an unusual, pragmatic epistemology for producing new knowledge from experience. SFAF had evolved to include mechanisms that kept it flooded with information and knowledge from within its own system, from the broader system of U.S. public education, and from the still-broader economic, political and social system. It had evolved to include mechanisms for rapidly processing that information and knowledge, making shared meaning of it, and codifying it. It had evolved to include mechanisms for rapidly adapting its program and its organization. It had evolved to include mechanisms for replicating favorable adaptations across its installed base of schools. And it had evolved to include mechanisms with which to influence, manage, and buffer environmental disturbances, all in an effort to secure conditions favoring its effectiveness and survival.

Over its history, SFAF had succeeded in leveraging these capabilities to understand and to manage key interdependencies within its own enterprise: among its schools, program, and organization. SFAF had also succeeded in leveraging these capabilities to manage key interdependencies with its environments: among organizations and interests both in the broader system of U.S. public education and in the still-broader economic, political, and social system. Yet, at the close of its 1999–2003 development cycle, SFAF was staring down two steep challenges. On the one hand, SFAF was evolving so fast, along so many dimensions all at once, that it began to recreate within its own enterprise many of the very problems that it had originally set out to solve. On the other hand, SFAF was not evolving fast enough.

Well into its second decade of operations, and even with all of its unusual capabilities for learning, SFAF was *still* developing the knowledge, programs, and capabilities needed to effectively support large-scale, comprehensive school reform. At the same time, experiences surrounding the passage, early implementation, and administration of NCLB had SFAF deeply concerned. Billions of dollars in federal funding were entering the system in apparent support for systemic, comprehensive, schoolwide reform, with billions more slated for each of the next five years. Yet problems retaining and recruiting schools had SFAF worried about a weakening in the comprehensive school reform market. How, exactly, states, districts, and schools were using this funding simply was not clear. In 2003, one member of SFAF with joint responsibilities for development and training expressed the worries of many:

> I think our organization is just coming to understand whole school reform through this development process, as well as data-driven instruction and implementation. I think we're *still* trying to understand whole school reform. And it might be gone by the time we understand it.

Sustaining the enterprise by maintaining its strategic, precarious position at the nexus of these three, complex, interdependent systems would surely require continued, rapid evolution: perhaps within the niche market for comprehensive school reform; perhaps to transform the enterprise and to position it for entry into some new market niche. And with rapid evolution shaping up as a near-certainty, so, too, were new challenges. On the one hand, rapid evolution risked continuing to effect and to exacerbate the classic problems of U.S. educational reform that were emerging within the SFAF enterprise. On the other hand, SFAF's capabilities for rapid evolution were eroding. With declines in contributions and revenues, slack was quickly evaporating, and SFAF's long-held tolerance for "creative disorganization" was being matched with urgent need for rational management. The size and complexity of the operation—the installed base of schools, the program, the development and training organizations, and their environments—were all pushing in this same direction. Camaraderie was being tested, and confidence was waning.

If responsibility for packing potential into the program rested with the development organization, and if responsibility for implementation rested with the training organization, then responsibility for evolving the strategic vision and charting a course that would sustain the enterprise rested with SFAF executives. Such work had been on-going over the history of Success for All, and highly confounded with work of continuous improvement, though always under the tight control of SFAF executives. Problems that emerged over SFAF's 1999–2003 development cycle took work that had long been taken for granted in SFAF and yanked it to the fore.

The work of sustaining the enterprise was shaping up to be as challenging as any that SFAF had yet faced. The work would require building new executive capabilities commensurate with the complexity of activity within and beyond the enterprise. It would require developing the capability to discriminate between "creative disorganization" and simple disorganization. It would require striking a balance between budding ideas like "pluralistic leadership" and plain, old-fashioned rational management. Above all else, it would require incorporating and producing the executive-level knowledge needed to pull it all off. This last challenge was shaping up to be the most difficult of the bunch. All of this, at a moment when leading scholars were still struggling simply to conceptualize the fundamental condition that appeared to be at hand, and while other leading scholars and analysts were just beginning to produce the practical knowledge needed to manage it.

Much like the schools it sought to serve, SFAF had arrived at its own moment of reckoning. For SFAF the missionary, the moment had come to save thyself. Either that, or call off the revival, roll up the tent, and move on. For SFAF the player, the moment had come to pull an ace out of its sleeve. Either that, or fold 'em, walk away from the table, and hit the buffet. For SFAF the organization, the moment had come to see clearly the complex, full world in which it lived, and to evolve rapidly in response. Either that, or succumb.

Such was SFAF's surreal life at the interstices of these three complex, interdependent, adaptive systems: a place aptly described as the edge of chaos.

Notes

1. Slavin and Madden (1996a: 7).
2. Lindblom (1959).
3. Finn's comments about the transition from revolutionary outsider to beltway insider appear in his foreword to a report by University of Michigan historian Jeffrey Mirel titled, *The Evolution of New American Schools: From Revolution to Mainstream.* See Mirel (2001:iii). Mirel's report is ultimately critical of NAS, and raises questions as to its implementation, effectiveness, and influence. Taking up Mirel's critique, Finn's foreword raises such questions, also. The Mirel/Finn critique is taken up at a later point in this chapter, in discussion of criticism of the New American Schools and comprehensive school reform that arose late in SFAF's 1999–2003 development cycle.
4. Again, Finn's comments appear in his foreword to Mirel (2001:iv). Per the preceding note, Finn's comments couched a critique of NAS, given its influence on U.S. education reform. That critique is taken up later in this chapter.
5. U.S. Department of Education (1999b).
6. See Slavin (2001) on Title I as the "engine of reform" in U.S. schools.
7. For single and double loop learning, see Argyris and Schön (1974; 1978).
8. For example: Scholastic, from which SFAF incorporated the Scholastic Reading Inventory for use in quarterly assessment; Riverside Publishing, from which SFAF incorporated the Gates-MacGinitie Reading Assessments for this same purpose; the Center for the Study of Learning and Performance at Concordia University in

Quebec, which functioned as a key collaborator in improving the tutoring components; and the National Organization for Research at the University of Chicago,
which functioned as a collaborator in conducting SFAF's randomized field trial.

9. See Rogers (1995:131–160) for a widely-cited rendering of the conventional
research-development-diffusion model of innovation development.

10. For a corroborating account of the SFAF development process, see Park and
Datnow (2008).

11. For analyses of innovation development consistent with the approach used within
SFAF, see: Zollo and Winter (2002); Winter and Szulanski (2001); Van de Ven, Polley,
Garud, and Venkataraman (1999); Van de Ven, Angle, and Poole (2000); March
(1996); and Gibbons, Limonges, Nowotny, Schwartzman, Scott, and Trow (1994).

12. The National Reading Panel was convened in 1997 at the request of the U.S. Congress
by the National Institute of Child Health and Human Development. The charge to
the Panel was to evaluate available research in order to assess the effectiveness of
different approaches to teaching children to read. The Panel published its findings
in April of 2000. See National Reading Panel (2000).

13. This characterization of innovation involving "divergent" and "convergent" learning
derives from Van de Ven, Polley, Garud, and Venkataraman (1999). See, especially,
pp. 181–214. See, also, March (1996).

14. Allen, Halbreich, Kozolvsky, Morgan, Payton, and Rolewski (1999).

15. See Tuckman (1965) and Hord, Rutherford, Huling-Austin, and Hall (1987).

16. Slavin and Madden (2001b).

17. Slavin and Madden (2001b:278).

18. These Experienced Sites Conference sessions drew from Wilde (1996).

19. See Slavin (2001) and Slavin (2002a).

20. U.S. Department of Education (2002:7).

21. At the same time, SFAF packaged a second offering, "SFA—Early Reading First,"
addressing the pre-K "Early Reading First" component of NCLB.

22. Success for All Foundation (2002b).

23. Success for All Foundation (2002c:1).

24. In that critics had long taken exception with research conducted by associates of
Success for All, it is important both to acknowledge Borman's relationship with SFAF
and to acknowledge the outlets for the research by Borman cited here (and elsewhere
in this manuscript). Like earlier researchers at the University of Memphis, Borman
was both an external researcher and an associate of Robert Slavin. In 2002 and 2003,
Borman was an assistant professor at the University of Wisconsin and senior
researcher for the Consortium of Policy Research in Education, a group of leading
research universities whose members collaborated in studying education reform,
policy, and finance as they bear on student learning. In 2001, Borman also collaborated with Robert Slavin and Samuel Stringfield (a researcher and associate of Slavin
at Johns Hopkins University) in editing a book on the history and politics of Title I
(Borman, Stringfield, and Slavin, 2001). For further reference, see, also, Borman's
work with Jerome D'Agostino on a meta-analysis of federal evaluation results on the
effects of Title I on student achievement (Borman and D'Agostino, 1996). Borman
would go on to direct Success for All's national randomized field trial. To stem critics'
skepticism of research by associates of SFAF, note that all of the research on Success
for All by Borman that is cited here (and elsewhere in this manuscript) was published
in peer reviewed journals of the American Educational Research Association.

25. Borman and Hughes (2002:256).
26. Borman and Hughes (2002:256).
27. Borman, Hewes, Overman, and Brown (2003:164).
28. Borman, Hewes, Overman, and Brown (2003:153).
29. Borman, Hewes, Overman, and Brown (2003:161).
30. As a general matter, Borman, Hewes, Overman, and Brown (2003) found that developers' own research was more favorable to their programs than was third party research. Borman et al. (p. 164) report a high-end estimated effect size of 0.15 when considering all studies and a low-end estimated effect size of 0.09 when considering only third-party studies.
31. See Borman, Hewes, Overman, and Brown (2003:167).
32. See Borman, Hewes, Overman, and Brown (2003:164).
33. Murphy and Datnow (2003:15).
34. Some such bundling was done at the component and sub-component level: for example, Reading Roots Third Edition. However, such bundling was not done for the program as a whole. Moreover, when such bundling was done at the component level, it was done amidst continued bug-fixing for those schools unable to purchase the revised, bundled component.
35. The "shopping mall" metaphor derives from Powell, Farrar, and Cohen (1985).
36. See Rowan (2002), on the population ecology of the school improvement industry, and on educational environments as hostile to innovators in marginal market niches.
37. Per personal email from Robert Slavin on 06/14/2005, school totals and percentage gains for 2000–2005 are as follows: 1600 (+3%) for 2000/2001; 1540 (−3.75%) for 2001/2002; 1480 (−3.9%) for 2002/2003; 1400 (−5.4%) for 2003/2004; and 1300 (−5.4%) for 2004/2005.
38. The loss of New York City's Chancellor's District was particularly stinging for SFAF. One point of concern was that SFAF had devoted considerable development and training resources to the Chancellor's District under very trying circumstances. A second point of concern was with the programs that replaced Success for All: "Month by Month Phonics (from Carson-Dellosa Publishing Company in Greensboro, N.C.); and the New York City Passport program (newly developed specifically for New York City by Voyager Expanded Learning of Dallas, TX). SFAF executives saw these programs as maintaining a primary focus on low-level phonics instruction (the primary focus of Success for All's first grade component, Reading Roots) and as paying comparatively scant attention to reading comprehension (the primary focus of Success for All's grade 2–6 component, Reading Wings). See Traub (2003). A third point of concern was that, in the analysis of SFAF executives, the new approach lacked anything like Success for All's base of research providing evidence of effectiveness, either in general or New York City. SFAF researchers had produced two reports showing positive effects of Success for All, both in the Chancellor's District and in the broader New York City public schools (Success for All Foundation, 2008c; 2008d). An evaluation published in 2004 by a team of researchers from New York University corroborated SFAF's findings of gains in elementary reading in the Chancellor's District (Phenix, Siegel, Zaltsman, and Fruthter, 2004). Acknowledging that their study design did not enable them to explain the specific causes of those gains, they concluded: "It is important to reiterate that the Chancellor's District took over some of the city's least well-resourced

schools serving the city's poorest and academically lowest performing students. By developing, mandating and implementing a comprehensive set of organizational, curricular, instructional and personnel changes, the Chancellor's District significantly improved the reading outcomes of the students in those schools, in three years of focused effort. This is not a small accomplishment" (p. 27).

39. In a report prepared for the U.S. Department of Education by the Council of Chief State School Officers, Williams, Blank, Toye, and Petermann (2007) reported the following states as serving more that SFAF's 1480 elementary schools: California (5550); Texas (3934); Illinois (2619); New York (2521); Ohio (2208); Michigan (2139); Pennsylvania (1920); Florida (1826); and New Jersey (1520).

40. Borman, Hewes, Overman, and Brown (2003:164) report a high-end estimated effect size of 0.15 when considering all studies and a low-end estimated effect size of 0.09 when considering only third-party studies.

41. See Mirel (2001; 2002).

42. Berends, Bodilly, and Kirby (2002).

43. Berends, Bodilly, and Kirby (2002:xxx–xxxiv).

44. Berends, Bodilly, and Kirby (2002:xxxiv–xxxv).

45. Berends, Bodilly, and Kirby (151–153).

46. See, for example: Lewin (1999); Waldrop (1992).

47. For example, see Brown and Eisenhardt (1998).

48. Van de Ven, Polley, Garud, and Venkatamaran (1999). Van de Ven et al. reference chaos theory explicitly as their orienting framework.

49. McCorduck (2007).

5

Sustaining

Let's stay focused on the core of what we do best. Let's make sure the organization can go on and on and on after Bob (Slavin) and Nancy (Madden) aren't involved any more. Let's make sure that this thing is still chugging down the track, helping kids, 20 years, 30 years down the road. They've done a heck of a job. They've been around 15 years. They've already outlasted most everybody else, other than big, old, traditional publishing companies. So they've got a heck of a head start. There's no reason why they can't keep it up.

MARK GRITTON, CHIEF OPERATING OFFICER, SFAF, APRIL, 2003

s SFAF headed out of its 1999–2003 development cycle, sustaining the enterprise quickly became the paramount concern of SFAF executives: evolving the vision for the enterprise and charting a course that would keep it viable in its complex, evolving environments. Surely, technical effectiveness remained an uncompromised priority for SFAF executives, as did solving problems in the program, schools, and the organization that had emerged over its 1999–2003 development cycle. However, amidst the uncertainty surrounding the passage of the No Child Left Behind Act of 2001, and with its viability threatened by declines in schools, revenues, and philanthropic contributions, the work of sustaining the enterprise became the first-order concern.

This was work as challenging as any embraced by SFAF, in that it required executives to see, understand, and somehow manage complexity that many either can't or don't. SFAF executives needed to examine the interdependent parts, problems, solutions, and challenges within and beyond SFAF's own enterprise. They needed to develop some set of shared understandings about what had happened, what was happening, and what was about to happen. And they needed to make tough decisions aimed at sustaining and, possibly, expanding the enterprise, absent any certainty about where those decisions would ultimately lead.

Beginning in 2003 (as developers were capping the 1999–2003 development cycle) and stretching until 2008, SFAF executives began the task. Their efforts ultimately lead them to devise and enact a strategy that took SFAF far beyond comprehensive school reform and deep into integrated, large-scale reform in all corners of the U.S. system of public education.

This new strategy succeeded in keeping SFAF viable for the duration of NCLB— and, with that, its programs, its network, and its cause. Yet the strategy did not appear to have steered SFAF into some safe, stable niche that it could comfortably occupy for 20 to 30 years. Rather, just as SFAF's new strategy was coming to fruition, pressure was building for yet another abrupt, seismic shift in federal education policy—and, with that, renewed demands on the capabilities of SFAF's executives to see, understand, and manage complexity.

EVOLVING TO EVOLVE

Over its history, problems and opportunities within and beyond the Success for All enterprise drove the evolution of SFAF as an organization: for example, the expansion of the training organization through the 1990s; the founding of SFAF as an organization in 1997/1998; and the expansion of the development organization in the early 2000s. Evolution of SFAF as an organization, in turn, drove evolution of the enterprise.

Continuing that pattern, SFAF's 2003–2008 development cycle began with the evolution of SFAF's organizational capabilities: this time, at the executive level, with the addition of new capabilities to interpret (and to respond to) uncertainty within and beyond the enterprise. With that, SFAF also continued its pattern of reproducing key tensions of its environment within the enterprise, itself: this time, matching the organization's strong, deeply ingrained pull towards divergence, experimentation, and informality with a new pull towards convergence, rationality, and formality.

In 2002, SFAF succeeded in recruiting two key executives: a chief operating officer and a marketing director, both with extensive experience in corporate America. The expansion of SFAF's executive capabilities went further, to include the creation of an internal policy shop, the enlistment of a consultant with executive experience in commercial publishing, and increased advice from SFAF's Board of Directors (including two philanthropists with over four decades of experience leading a large scale, for-profit replication enterprise). All complemented SFAF's existing executive structure: Robert Slavin as chairman; Nancy Madden as president; Barbara Haxby as SFAF's long-serving director of implementation; Roger Morin as chief financial officer; and Bette Chambers, a long-time collaborator and expert in early childhood education from Concordia University who joined SFAF as the lead developer of its pre-K, kindergarten, and tutoring components.

Central to the expansion of the executive rank was the hiring of Mark Gritton as chief operating officer in February, 2002. Gritton brought with him knowledge and experience managing organizations much larger than SFAF. Prior to joining SFAF, Gritton had served as chief executive officer of Brinks, Inc., a security organization with annual revenues over $3 billion. Prior to that, Gritton served as chief operating officer of Deluxe, Inc., a nationwide supplier of printing and other services to the banking industry with sales of over $1 billion. Gritton had also served in an advisory capacity to two start-up firms in the information technology sector.

As COO, Gritton described his charge as twofold: first, to develop a coherent strategy that would keep SFAF sustainable amidst changes in its environment; and, second, to align SFAF's operations with that strategy (which included addressing accumulating problems within and between SFAF's development and training organizations). In a 2003 interview, Gritton explained that the combination of strategizing and aligning was the key to long-term sustainability:

> I spent 30 years in corporate America, running big companies. There are two significant challenges that any business faces. The first is one of strategy, to make sure that you're on the right approach and that you're producing something or manufacturing something or providing a service that is strategically sustainable. That's number one. Number two, the second hardest thing about business is making sure that: one, all of the functions that are required to support that business are working well, and by that I mean information technology, marketing, finance, whatever; and number two, that they're not just working independent of one another, but that they're working in unison, they're working as a well-oiled, coordinated machine. And you would be surprised how infrequently that occurs. Many companies, many CEOs, spend a lot of time thinking about strategy, and they don't recognize that the pieces and parts of their organization really aren't working in sync the way they need to. Or, they get very operating-oriented, and then they worry about that, and they forget the strategy. So it's getting the two married, that is the real key to business. You can't be sustainable with one and not the other.

To support the work of strategizing and aligning, SFAF hired a marketing director in September of 2003. Like SFAF's new COO, SFAF's new marketing director brought extensive knowledge and experience from the business sector to SFAF: over 20 years of experience in a national financial services group, which included supporting a nationwide, nonprofit organization in developing a for-profit division. She described her charge to be facilitating a fundamental shift in SFAF's approach to program development and improvement: a shift away from a "if you build it, they will come" approach; and a shift toward a customer-centered approach that placed a premium on what existing and potential customers needed and valued. That, in her view, required complementing SFAF's historically informal means of monitoring and interpreting activity within and beyond the enterprise with more formal, systematic methods of learning: about customers; about competitors; and about what SFAF needed to do to differentiate itself from its competitors. In a 2003 interview, she explained:

> Marketing allows us to be more consistent. It formalizes learning about competitors and customers in a way that it hadn't been formalized before.

Learning occurred kind of through serendipity, because we have an extremely collaborative environment. This is a fabulously collaborative environment. So someone would talk to someone who would go, oh, that's a great idea. And if they thought about it, it'd get incorporated, or they'd put it over here to be considered for the next iteration. What we want to do is make that be a consistent, formal part of how we look at making change. I think this allows us to be more consistent, and it formalizes it in a way that it hadn't been formalized before, by making it an ongoing component for product reengineering and redesign.

SFAF's new executives expressed tremendous admiration for the existing organization, its culture of experimentation and collaboration, and, above all else, its commitment to the core mission of improving the academic achievement of at-risk students. As SFAF's new marketing director explained in a 2003 interview: "SFA is driven by a total and complete dedication to reaching children. Coming out of a corporate environment into this environment is like going into the ninth ring of heaven, because this is an organization totally driven by an altruistic mission."

At the same time, SFAF's new executives recognized a need to introduce structure and discipline alongside SFAF's social, mission-driven organization. On strong advice from two key members of SFAF's Board of Directors, they shared the view that SFAF's long-term sustainability needed to begin with reining in SFAF's expansive, divergent development initiatives. Instead, they argued for a convergent approach that began with adopting a narrow (rather than a broad) strategy. Doing so would enable SFAF to concentrate scarce resources behind that strategy, to develop core capabilities (including training capabilities) to support that strategy, and to manage internal operations more effectively and efficiently.

Towards more effective and efficient management, Mark Gritton, SFAF's new COO, articulated a strong need to introduce formal methods of project management to ensure that all initiatives were managed carefully against tight budget constraints and ambitious delivery dates, that they were coordinated with each other, and that they were aligned with the organization's strategy. In a 2003 interview, he explained:

The motives of people here are more pure than you would find in most for-profit companies. They're more mission-driven here. The sense of mission certainly motivates. It most assuredly keeps everybody working even in the face of confusion, because they feel so good about what they're doing. It doesn't always clarify and coordinate specific components. It doesn't work that way. But it most assuredly puts a commonality of purpose over everything. So I suppose you probably don't see the same level of frustrations that you might see in a for-profit company, where someone says, "Why am I working the weekend when I know all this is going to do is give a big bonus to that guy in the corner office" kind of a thing. Real or not, people tend to think that way at times. But it doesn't exist here, ever. Nothing like that exists here.

There's more of a purity of purpose. But that in and of itself doesn't necessarily sync up or coordinate activities. You still have to work at that, just like you would in any business or any organization. You still run the risk of having people run in seven different directions if you're not careful. You've got to make sure that's all working together.

Bringing business acumen to bear while preserving the benefits of SFAF's mission-driven, collaborative, informal organization would be no simple matter. To start, it was beyond the direct of experience of SFAF's newly recruited executives. While SFAF's newly recruited executives had extensive knowledge and experience in organizations orders of magnitude larger than SFAF, with revenues in the billions of dollars, neither had direct experience transforming the operations and culture of a large-scale, mission-driven educational reform enterprise moving in interaction with such complex environments. Further, SFAF was already an organization that had intentionally rejected a more corporate identity. At the time of its founding, SFAF executives intentionally rejected the option of incorporating as a for-profit organization. Instead, they elected to incorporate as a nonprofit organization, in part due to a strong desire to sustain the public identity of SFAF as a mission-driven organization. Likewise, SFAF's new marketing director explained that her official title was actually "director of outreach," precisely because of concerns within SFAF of signaling an overly corporate image to its schools and environments. Finally, SFAF had already attempted to incorporate and leverage comparable executive capabilities and failed. Beginning as early as 2000, with advice from its Board of Directors, SFAF set about recruiting a chief operating officer and marketing director. While candidates were hired in each position, members of SFAF explained that there were problems of "fit" within SFAF and, consequently, retention.

Thus, SFAF's expanded executive team created new potential to understand and address problems within and beyond the SFAF enterprise: in the complex interactions between its schools, designs, environments, and organization. At the same time, expanding the executive team created fundamental tensions among executives between convergence and divergence, exploitation and exploration, and order and disorder. Managing these tensions and capitalizing on the potential would require learning to work in new ways, from the executive suite to the shop floor. SFAF's newly recruited executives would need to learn to finesse the introduction of new ideas, language, and practices into a historically resistant organization. Reciprocally, members of SFAF's long-established executive nucleus would need to learn to collaborate with new colleagues, to embrace and value what they brought to the table, and to collaborate in leading SFAF developers and trainers in more disciplined ways of working. SFAF developers and trainers, in turn, would need to learn to work in more coordinated ways, under a more complex and less-familial executive team that aimed to discipline historically informal (and highly valued) ways of working. Moreover, they would need to do so without compromising the collaborative learning that had so long sustained SFAF.

Among some members of the organization, the concern was less with "organizing out" experimentation and creativity through the introduction of formal project management. The concern was more with successfully introducing more disciplined ways of working into a historically informal organization. In a 2003 interview, Barbara Haxby, SFAF's director of implementation, explained:

> I don't think Success for All has a big problem coming up with new ideas and being more than happy to think of all kinds of new ways to go find new things to do. . . . I worry more about the other end. I worry more that we have to be able to create a disciplined approach to change and be able to have it tighten down so it doesn't become overwhelming to schools or trainers. I really don't spend as much time worrying that we won't have another great idea, because I think that's pretty hard-wired into this organization, to always be looking for new things to do. I mean, to me, creating a disciplined approach is much more where we struggle.

SEEING AND INTERPRETING

Over 2002/2003, SFAF executives took on the work of seeing and interpreting the complexity underlying two key matters: how schools, districts, and states were interpreting and acting on No Child Left Behind; and why they were not selecting Success for All under two of its primary programs, Comprehensive School Reform and Reading First.[1] Such understandings would then inform the development of a new strategy with which to align the program and the organization. SFAF's approach to the work was a characteristic blend of the rational and the organic. It leveraged new executive capabilities to formally analyze market and policy dynamics. It continued to exploit its established capabilities for acquiring, pooling, and analyzing informal information. And it continued to interpret all of this information through the lens of federal policy, with a keen eye on understanding how apparently evolutionary changes in federal policy were effecting system-wide turbulence.

This was urgent work. New federal funding began entering the system only months after NCLB was signed into law in January of 2002, and decisions were being made quickly, across all 50 states. SFAF was working at a lag, having already experienced a net loss of 60 schools over two successive years (and, with that, declines in vital revenue). This was also difficult work. The interpretations and actions of schools, districts, and states were bound up with a constellation of newly founded organizations providing guidance and oversight: the U.S. Department of Education and its newly founded Institute for Education Sciences; review panels that included representatives of the U.S. Department of Education, the National Institute for Literacy, the National Research Council, and the National Institute for Child Health and Human Development; the federally funded Center for Comprehensive School Reform; technical assistance centers at the University of Oregon, Florida State University, and the University of Texas at Austin; and more.

It wasn't only funding streams and policy environments that had changed under NCLB. So too had the competitive landscape. SFAF had long been a privileged member of a subset of comprehensive school reform providers protected from competition by federal policy. These providers had been accorded special status, in part to buoy early attempts to devise and field research-based and research-validated programs. However, the initial analysis by SFAF's new marketing director suggested a new reality. In a 2003 interview, she explained: "I did a competitor scan. Beyond the handful of organizations that were involved in comprehensive school reform, my initial scan found that the market was highly fragmented, that everybody was trying to play in this game, from school districts to for-profits to not-for-profits."

By March of 2003, SFAF executives began developing the interpretation that problems recruiting and retaining schools under NCLB were resulting from concurrent, interdependent dynamics throughout the formal system: in schools, districts, states, and federal agencies. None of these dynamics were new; all had been building for over a decade. However, under NCLB, the analysis of SFAF executives was that these dynamics amplified and interacted in ways that effected both a contraction in the market for comprehensive school reform programs and the emergence of what SFAF Chairman Robert Slavin described as the "district coherence" market: programs and services supporting district-driven improvement efforts under NCLB.[2] In the interpretation of executives, this was a market for which SFAF was weakly adapted. Much to their surprise, this was also a market in which commercial publishers appeared to be flourishing.

School Dynamics

SFAF executives reported that a trend that they had begun recognizing as early as the mid-1990s accelerated rapidly under NCLB: increases in the number of (and variability in) schools pursuing external assistance for school improvement. Some of these schools were as forecasted by SFAF executives: chronically underperforming schools with large numbers of students failing to achieve at state-specified standards, thus in need of sweeping, comprehensive school reform. However, many of these schools were much less impacted than those historically served by SFAF. Indeed, many were stronger schools not in need of sweeping reform but, instead, in need of specific improvement efforts targeting the needs of specific subpopulations of students.

Increases in the number and variability of schools seeking external assistance were attributed to the tightening of accountability requirements under NCLB, resulting in more (and more variable) schools being identified as in need of improvement. For example, NCLB required annual assessment of students in reading and mathematics in grades 3 through 8 and at one grade in high school— in many states, an increase over existing regimens that required assessment at one grade level in elementary, middle, and high school. Further, NCLB sought to hold all schools accountable for adequate yearly progress towards the national goal of 100% of students performing at state-specified standards by SY 2013/2014. Finally, under NCLB, adequate yearly progress would not be measured solely based on the overall average student achievement. Rather, adequate yearly progress would also be measured based on the average performance of subgroups of students historically at risk of academic failure: for example, economically disadvantaged students; students from specific racial and ethnic groups; students with disabilities; and students with limited English proficiency.

For SFAF, this was both good news and bad news. It was good news, in that the pool of potential schools from which to recruit expanded considerably under NCLB, as more schools risked being identified as failing to meet accountability requirements. It was bad news, in that SFAF did not have programs and services with which to target the full range of potential schools. Certainly, SFAF's existing comprehensive school reform program (Success for All) and its NCLB-specific derivative (SFA—Reading First) were suitable for use in the most impacted schools. However, SFAF had no programs or services with which to address specific, targeted needs in stronger schools. In fact, SFAF had long resisted "unbundling" its comprehensive school reform program into components that could implemented selectively in schools, in part due to research that raised questions about the effectiveness of anything less than schoolwide implementation of the full program.

Thus, the analysis of SFAF executives was that the school-level market for external improvement services was growing. Even so, having only a tightly integrated, comprehensive program, and lacking a catalog of independent components that could be tailored to the needs of individual schools, they recognized that SFAF was unprepared to exploit this growing market.

District Dynamics

At the same time that they were recognizing a larger (and more variable) pool of potential schools with which to work, SFAF executives reported the acceleration of a second trend that they had begun recognizing as early as the mid-1990s: a shift in decision making from schools to districts. In their analysis, the shift was driven by new incentives and resources under NCLB to enlist districts in the work of school improvement: for example, requirements that states strengthen district-level accountability for student achievement; and funding within NCLB's $1 billion per year Reading First program to develop district-level capabilities to assist schools. And that was the rub. In the analysis of SFAF executives, the structure of Reading First interacted with the variable needs of schools to drive districts *away* from SFAF's comprehensive school reform programs and *toward* the growth market for which SFAF had no offering: component-based programs for schools.

Reading First provided districts with resources to develop their capabilities to assist schools in improving their K–3 reading programs. Consistent with comprehensive school reform, Reading First maintained a systemic approach to improvement, in that it provided funding for improvement plans featuring three interdependent components: a K–3 reading curriculum; assessment systems; and professional development. The components, themselves, would come from publishers and vendors, and would meet specific criteria—most importantly, that the K–3 reading curriculum met federal criteria for a research-based program. Districts would then develop capabilities to support curriculum, assessment, and professional development in schools throughout the district. Indeed, under Reading First, districts were to perform work very similar to that performed by SFAF: integrating program components into coherent solutions for schools, and developing internal capabilities to assist with implementation.

SFAF executives reported that districts receiving Reading First funding were using it in one of two primary ways. One option was for districts to pursue the district-wide selection of a single comprehensive school reform program and, then, use Reading First funding to develop district-level capabilities to support program implementation. Because of the potential to pool funding streams, this option was most viable in districts with large numbers of schools that also qualified for funding under NCLB's Comprehensive School Reform program. For districts with fewer schools qualifying for Comprehensive School Reform funding, a second option was to use Reading First funding to develop a backbone, district-wide improvement strategy that included curriculum, assessment, and professional development. Districts could then use other, supplemental funding (including Comprehensive School Reform funding) to provide additional support to the weakest schools.[3]

In the analysis of SFAF executives, the vast majority of districts that received Reading First funding elected to pursue a version of the second option. They described this second option as a "district coherence" strategy, in that it enabled districts to devise and support a coherent, district-wide improvement strategy while, at the same time, varying additional support with the specific needs of individual schools. The effect of the district coherence strategy, thus, was to amplify the school-level trend towards component-based (rather than integrated) solutions that could be tailored to meet the specific needs of schools. SFAF executives reported instances where the potential existed for district-wide adoption of its comprehensive school reform program, and they reported instances where chronically weak schools in non-Reading First districts continued to express interest in its comprehensive school reform program. Even so, they recognized district coherence as the primary growth market under NCLB.

For an organization whose financial strategy depended heavily on new business, tapping growth in the district coherence market was essential. Yet this was a market that SFAF was unprepared to tap. In a 2004 interview, Mark Gritton, SFAF's COO recalled:

> Historically, we were organized and dealt almost exclusively on a school by school basis, with site based decision making. So what little marketing we did, what little selling we did, really came from our existing field people dealing site by site. And over the last couple, three years or however long its taken, more and more of that has swung to the districts. And I think

No Child Left Behind pushed the pendulum even faster, because the whole need for having coherent plans for districts lead to the centralization of decisions. I think the pendulum was swinging that way anyway. No Child Left Behind came in and swung it even faster. And we weren't prepared for it. We weren't organized, nor were our programs perceived as programs that were applicable across districts. They were seen primarily as comprehensive, intensive, total school reform programs that were really meant for the poorest and the worst of the schools. And other than maybe some large urban districts, any other given district might have one or two of those schools. But certainly the majority of the schools in the district aren't perceived to need that level of intensity, that level of comprehensiveness. And so that started to shut us out.

State Dynamics

Under NCLB, SFAF executives reported acceleration of a third trend that they had been recognizing since the mid-1990s: increased involvement of state education agencies in the work of improving student achievement. New resources and incentives for states mirrored those for districts: for example, state-level accountability incentives for adequate yearly progress; and funding to develop capabilities to support schools and districts in their efforts to improve student achievement. Under NCLB, a key responsibility of states was to work within federal guidance to approve providers of curriculum, assessment, and professional development with which districts could contract in constructing Reading First plans. The effect, essentially, was for states to regulate the district coherence market by determining which providers could (and could not) participate. While this created the possibility to winnow out ineffective providers and to admit effective providers, the analysis of SFAF executives was that state-level decision making did more to reinforce the status quo than to advance the cause of reform—and, with that, to further marginalize Success for All.

In identifying qualifying Reading First providers, one key function of state education agencies was to identify reading programs that were anchored in scientifically based reading research. In the analysis of SFAF executives, this was a point that appeared to favor Success for All. More favorable yet was that federal guidance provided to states by the U.S. Department of Education bundled discussion of scientifically based reading research with a host of other program features that closely mirrored those of Success for All's long-established and well-tested blueprint for school restructuring. Indeed, the resemblance was uncanny. In many ways, it appeared that federal policy had morphed into something that closely resembled Success for All:

A high-quality reading program that is based on scientifically based research must include instructional content based on the five essential components of reading instruction integrated into a coherent instructional design. A coherent design includes explicit instructional strategies that address students' specific strengths and weaknesses, coordinated instructional sequences, ample practice opportunities and aligned student materials, and may include the use of targeted, scientifically based instructional strategies as appropriate. The design should also consider the allocation of time, including a protected, uninterrupted block of time for reading instruction of more than 90 minutes per day. A high-quality reading program also includes assessment strategies for diagnosing student needs and measuring progress, as well as a professional development plan that ensures teachers have the skills and support necessary to implement the program effectively and to meet the reading needs of individual students.[4]

Problematic was that few state education agencies had the capabilities to analyze the scientific basis of externally developed reading programs. These were administrative agencies of state governments, not independent research-and-evaluation laboratories. Pressed for quick action, SFAF executives reported that many state departments of education were relying on established textbook adoption processes to identify qualifying reading programs. Further, rather than engaging in deep investigation of reading programs, SFAF executives reported that many states were doing little more than ensuring that reading programs complied with federal criteria for scientifically based programs.

Despite what executives saw as advantages afforded to Success for All by federal guidance, their analysis was that state-level decision making was creating an additional source of problems for SFAF. First, SFAF had neither the financial nor the organizational resources to navigate 50 independent, state-level adoption processes to advocate that its programs satisfied federal criteria for scientifically based reading programs. Second, absent such advocacy, SFAF executives reported that states did not recognize the reading components of Success for All as a stand-alone reading program that could be readily evaluated in the context of conventional textbook adoption processes. In fact, SFA—Reading First bundled curriculum, leadership, the 90-minute reading block, quarterly assessment and regrouping, and professional development into a comprehensive, coherent package that targeted all three components of Reading First. SFAF did not extract and represent the curriculum components to states (or to anybody else) as a stand-alone reading program. However, in a 2004 interview, COO Mark Gritton explained that it was stand-alone reading programs on which states were most keenly focused:

> Even though primarily what we did was reading or literacy focused, Success for All wasn't necessarily seen as a core reading program. It was seen as a comprehensive school reform program. And last spring, as monies were starting to be put into the system and as people were starting to make choices against Reading First, there was really an enormous movement toward what was perceived to be core reading programs. And, in many cases, it was just simply textbook companies. So we found ourselves, I'm sure, like others who

weren't really defined and seen as a core reading program. So we were caught on the sidelines watching all this happen, trying to get in there as much as we could and say, "Don't forget us!" Because what we really do is teach kids how to read. We don't just sell textbooks. But that momentum was really swinging fast. People had to put plans together. States had to put plans together, and there was such a strong incentive for states to get their plans approved that, in many cases, they took the easy way out. And we were sort of shut out. We were standing on the sidelines, almost beyond our control. Comprehensive school reform is still out there, but everything is so overshadowed by Reading First that we got lost in the dust.

While such state-level dynamics played to weaknesses of SFAF, they played to the strengths of conventional, commercial publishers. In the analysis of SFAF executives, the largest commercial publishers had rich financial resources and highly developed organizational infrastructure that allowed them to quickly navigate adoption processes across all 50 states. Their products were easily recognized by states as stand-alone "reading programs." And, much to the frustration and amazement of SFAF executives, commercial publishers were succeeding in demonstrating to states that their reading programs satisfied federal requirements for research-based programs.

Thus, at the same time that SFAF was struggling to navigate complex state dynamics, SFAF executives reported that commercial textbook publishers were succeeding. Though the aim of Reading First was deep, system-wide reform, the result of state-level administration of Reading First was, in the analysis of SFAF executives, to reify the status quo. State-level approval processes were rebranding conventional, commercially published curricula as "scientifically based reading programs" while, at the same time, eliminating Success for All from consideration. Rather than legitimating Success for All for participation in the growing district coherence markets, Success for All was being ruled out. Explained Robert Slavin, in March of 2003:

What's happening is that the five largest basals in America are getting all of the money and everything else is being ignored. The concept of scientifically based practice was that states were supposed to designate programs one way or another that would be based on scientifically based reading research. Well, you might imagine, stepping aside and being fair, that in such a circumstance you'd expect that Direct Instruction, Success for All, and maybe Open Court would be favored in some form as recipients of this money. Exactly the opposite is taking place. Open Court is doing fine, but the big ones are Harcourt, Scott-Foresman, Macmillan—the usual basals. We don't lobby or advocate. The states have set up review processes to review materials and see whether they're scientifically-based, and so we've certainly fully participated in that. We're just not big enough or savvy enough to go around trying to lobby individual states. But it's shocking. I mean it's really, genuinely shocking. What is happening is 180 degrees different from the intention, this mentioning

111 times of scientifically based reading research. It's basals. In fact, if anything, what's happening right now is a transition to basals from anything that uses novels or trade books or any innovative programs or anything else. Four states approved Direct Instruction. Three states approved Success for All among the places that are making those approvals. Excuse me. What did we intend to do here? If you look at the patterns, you'd say this is not about scientifically based research. This is about large basal companies with multi-million dollar advertising and lobbying budgets.

Federal Dynamics

A fourth problem for SFAF was in federal guidance and oversight of interdependent state, district, and school dynamics. Especially problematic was federal guidance and oversight regarding the scientific basis of reading programs within state-level Reading First plans.

Attention to the use of research in educational reform had been making its way into federal policy at least since the Improving America's Schools Act of 1994 (and, actually, for the entire period following World War II). It was clearly evident in both the Obey-Porter CSRD legislation of 1998 and the Reading Excellence Act of 1999. NCLB picked up the mantle, with its 111 mentions of "scientifically based" research. However, in the analysis of SFAF executives, federal guidance for evaluating the scientific basis of reading programs was thin, and its oversight of state-level Reading First plans was questionable. The combination of thin guidance and questionable oversight began to erode what had long been SFAF's claim to moral high ground and a source of competitive advantage: Success for All's strong basis in research and its strong record of research-proven effectiveness.

The problems began with federal guidance to states for evaluating the scientific basis of reading programs under Reading First. While the rhetoric of "scientifically based reading research" was invoked throughout NCLB, the actual criteria were, in the eyes of SFAF executives, quite minimal. In Reading First, the focus was on the use of scientifically based research to evaluate the *basis* of reading programs: that is, to ensure that, in constructing the program, developers drew from research identifying effective methods for improving reading achievement. While NCLB and its associated guidance established clear criteria for research-based reading programs (i.e., that they address phonemic awareness, phonics, fluency, vocabulary, and comprehension), the analysis of SFAF executives was that these criteria were: a) weighted heavily towards low-level reading skills and away from the cognitive skills and strategies supporting reading comprehension; and b) present in some form in virtually all available reading programs, thus of little use in discriminating one from the other.

At the same time, neither NCLB nor its associated federal guidance included provisions requiring that reading programs under Reading First be evaluated for their research-proven *effectiveness*: that is, for evidence of scientifically based research demonstrating that the program could actually be used to improve student achievement replicably across schools.[5] For example, while federal guidance for Reading First included criteria for evaluating the individual components of reading programs, nowhere did it the address evaluating the actual effectiveness of the program as a whole.[6] While guidance for NCLB's Comprehensive School Reform program had been expanded to include criteria for evaluating program effectiveness, those same criteria had not made their way into the guidance for Reading First. Under such a scheme, providers of reading programs bore little accountability for the effectiveness of their programs. Rather, accountability for effectiveness rested entirely with users of their programs.

Thin guidance was matched with questionable oversight—not only in the opinion of SFAF executives but, also, in the opinion of others, as well. Again, the administrative apparatus guiding and overseeing the writing of states' Reading First applications was just coming into existence with the passage of NCLB: an emergent, dynamic, trans-organizational network that included government agencies, quasi-governmental organizations, and nongovernmental organizations, all coordinated by the U.S. Department of Education.

The public face of this network and its members was one of rigor, research, and science. For example, in November of 2002, under the Education Sciences Reform Act, the Department of Education's Office of Educational Research and Improvement was restructured as the Institute of Education Sciences and the Office of Innovation and Improvement. As explained by educational historian Diane Ravitch, the reorganization "signaling the Bush administration's commitment to both scientifically based research and continuous innovation within education."[7]

However, as others saw it, the signal out of this network was that states' Reading First applications were more likely to be approved if states did exactly as SFAF executives observed them doing: favoring particular, conventional, commercially published reading programs, and not other alternatives. For example, in May of 2002, five short months after the passage of NCLB, *Education Week* reported:

Lawmakers, reading experts, and publishers are urging the Department of Education to clarify reading requirements under the "No Child Left Behind Act" of 2001, amid widespread perceptions that a small number of commercial programs will win favor while other popular approaches might be discouraged or spurned.

In recent letters to Secretary of Education Rod Paige and at a congressional hearing last week, policymakers and reading organizations raised concerns that state education officials are getting the message that they can improve their chances of receiving their share of $900 million in Reading First money by ordering school districts to use particular products and materials."[8]

Under Reading First, the lack of rigorous federal guidance and oversight for the scientific basis and effectiveness of reading programs created tremendous problems for SFAF. SFAF had long staked its identity and reputation on the research basis and research-proven effectiveness of its cornerstone program, Success for All. Indeed, in 2003, SFAF was in the throes of a national randomized field trial of

Success for All that was intended to demonstrate its commitment to satisfying the highest standards for research-proven effectiveness. Yet despite policy language and an administrative apparatus that signaled a commitment to research and innovation, requirements for research-proven effectiveness was nowhere to be found, either in the policy as written or the policy as administered. With that, the resulting "reform" looked suspiciously like the status quo, at least in the analysis of SFAF executives. Conventional commercial publishers appeared to be gaining quick access to the emergent, growing district coherence market, and SFAF was struggling to gain entry.

Yet Again—Revolution via Evolution

Evolutionary and abrupt changes in a cornerstone federal policy had triggered a revolution in the market for externally sponsored educational improvement services. Key policy provisions that already enjoyed currency were incorporated and expanded within NCLB, and signed into law with the stroke of a pen: an emphasis on comprehensive school reform; an emphasis on systemic improvement in K–3 reading; requirements for adequate yearly progress; attention to research; and more. These evolutionary and abrupt federal policy changes amplified and accelerated interdependent trends in schools, districts, and states. Working within their established capabilities, schools, districts, and states quickly devised systemic plans for improvement. Yet they did so in ways that SFAF did not fully anticipate. The old growth market of comprehensive school reform weakened, and the new growth market of "district coherence" quickly emerged.

All of this spelled trouble for SFAF. Absent rigorous federal guidance and oversight of the district coherence market, SFAF went from being the prized entry on a short list of federally favored, nonprofit comprehensive school reform providers to barely existent on state-generated lists of programs qualifying for Reading First funding. With that, SFAF went from being the shining star of comprehensive school reform to a marginal player in a new market populated by institutionalized commercial publishers with annual revenues in the billions of dollars.

That this could happen—and happen so fast—was surprising to SFAF's new COO, Mark Gritton. As he began his work with SFAF, what Gritton described as most surprising and challenging was not bringing business acumen to bear in a historically informal education reform organization (i.e., SFAF). Rather, what he described as most surprising and most challenging were the environments of U.S. public education. While SFAF's founders and core executives had been wrestling with these environments for their entire careers, all of this was new to Gritton. In a 2004 interview, Gritton explained:

> The principals, the tenets, the basic beliefs and fundamentals of "managing and leading and business," it's all the same. It's probably been the same since people bartered 5,000 years ago. Not much has changed there. And a nonprofit needs the same level of focus and discipline and organization and

leadership as does a big for-profit company. So that's totally transferable, completely transferable. The world of education—that's not a "market" I knew anything about. All of the federal regulations and the politics that get played out. And the jealousies that seem to exist out there, the "my program is better then your program" kind of thing. All of that was completely new to me. That whole part has been one gigantic, new learning experience. I thought some of the markets that I did business in for 30 years were competitive. I've never seen anything like this. I've never seen anything like this. People just simply can't put that stuff aside and think about kids. They just can't, for whatever reason. It's amazing.

Following the passage of NCLB, SFAF's initial interpretation of system-wide activity was provisional—very much conjecture and not at all established fact. SFAF executives were struggling to identify general trends across highly variable and deeply particular activity in schools, districts, states, federal agencies, and more. Even though corroborating evidence was emerging concurrently, whether their initial interpretations were on the mark was still very much an open question.[9] Further, elements of the account seemed potentially incorrect and/or somewhat incredible, even to SFAF executives: specifically, anomalies in federal guidance and oversight of Reading First. Finally, at the same time that SFAF executives were seeing and interpreting its system-wide effects, NCLB was running into a wall of opposition from districts, states, interest groups, and academics—opposition that would ultimately bear on both its political support and its administration.[10]

Yet uncertainty could not be a barrier to action. SFAF was already working at a lag. Unable to anticipate the effects of NCLB, SFAF had to watch activity play out over 2002/2002 and 2003/2004 in order to see and interpret patterns of problems, and it had to quickly play catch up. No matter the uncertainty, the rapid pace of environmental dynamics and their immediate consequences for SFAF demanded immediate, urgent action.

STRATEGIZING AND ADAPTING

As it pushed through the quagmire of activity that immediately followed the passage of NCLB, SFAF arrived at what looked to be a fork in the road: a choice between continuing down the path to comprehensive school reform or beginning down the path to district coherence. Neither path was certain. Resources were running thin. Continued viability hung in the balance.

Over SY 2002/2003, at the same time that they were monitoring and interpreting system-wide activity, SFAF executives began charting their way forward. Rather than veering this way or that, their strategy was to pursue both paths at once. SFAF executives decided to continue to market and support Success for All as a comprehensive school reform program for use in chronically underperforming, Title I schools. At the same time, they decided to expand into the emerging district coherence market by targeting states, districts, and less-impacted schools.

Their rationale was straightforward. SFAF was deeply committed to comprehensive school reform as a research-validated approach to improving education for large numbers of at-risk students, and SFAF was deeply committed to the schools that had joined the cause. At the same time, the district coherence market opened up opportunity both to reach more at-risk students and, importantly, to generate essential revenue from new business,

Strategizing was the easy part. The hard part was then adapting the entire enterprise to support this new, two-pronged strategy. These efforts proceeded from SY 2002/2003 to SY 2007/2008. They echoed now now-familiar themes. From one perspective, these efforts were evolutionary: natural "next steps" in the development of Success for All and SFAF. Throughout the history of Success for All, its leaders had explored collaborating with districts and states on an ad hoc basis to support school-level change. Much of their early work with districts and states had proven sufficiently frustrating that, in the mid-1990s, executives ruled out the possibility. Even so, members of SFAF viewed some of these district experiences as successes: Hartford, CT; Lawrence, MA; Longbranch, NJ; Galveston, TX; and even New York City's Chancellor's District. In pursuing its new strategy, SFAF was poised to leverage positive experience in these districts as the basis for continued exploration and learning.

From another perspective, SFAF's efforts were revolutionary, in that they required deep change at the very foundation of the enterprise. This new, two-pronged strategy broadened conceptions of the customers/clients to be served—not just weak schools, but less-impacted schools, districts, and states. It expanded the range of programs and services to be offered—not just comprehensive programs, but program components to be integrated with existing systems in educational organizations of all types. It created new dependencies on environments—not just for financial and other resources, but for the legitimacy and opportunity to compete in emerging markets. And, to support and to manage all of the preceding, it created novel demands on the capabilities and culture of SFAF as an organization. In the spring of 2003, an SFAF manager reflected on the scope of required change:

> It's a different way of thinking. Very different. Very, very different. Internally, in terms of materials. But, more importantly, it changes our culture. How do we talk to people? If you listen to Success for All people talk with schools, we talk the language of urban, Title I, low SES schools. We don't talk the language of mid-range schools or high-end schools. . . . If we want to be appealing to a broader spectrum of schools, we have to change our language, we have to change our artifacts, we have to change our materials, we have to change everything. Most important is our language. It's not just about a materials change. It's a cultural change, and everything that goes with it.

SFAF found itself in the same situation as the schools that it had long sought to serve: needing to fundamentally reform its core practices, technologies, and culture, with its continued viability hanging in the balance. Such fundamental change has long been daunting for organizations, in general and in education. Many organizations (and most educational reforms) fail.[11] SFAF's odds appeared particularly slim. SFAF was beginning its efforts with a full menu of both old and new problems. These included artifacts of the 1999–2003 development cycle that SFAF executives were just beginning to fully understand: for example, problems of integration in its design; problems of program fragmentation in schools; problems of coordination, capabilities, and culture in its development and training organizations; and problems raising both operating and development capital. Further, SFAF pursued its 2003–2008 development cycle amidst continued environmental uncertainty: for example, system-wide efforts to respond to (and to resist) NCLB; contentious federal and state level politics spanning three election cycles (2004, 2006, and 2008); an economy that both recovered and fell back into recession; and war abroad.

Against long odds, SFAF rallied. From SY 2002/2003 through SY 2007/2008, SFAF proceeded with efforts to adapt the enterprise to support its new, two-pronged strategy. This was a development cycle every bit as ambitious as its 1999–2003 development cycle (if not more), one that drew hard on SFAF's capabilities for designing, supporting, scaling up, and continuously improving.

In the view of members of SFAF, it was also a success. By 2008, SFAF had negotiated a fundamental transformation in its clients, designs, environmental relationships, and organization, transforming itself from a narrow provider of comprehensive school reform programs to one that also had a large-scale foothold in the district coherence market. And far beyond transforming its culture, SFAF was in the throes of attempting to refashion both its identity and its role as an organization: not as a champion and provider of comprehensive school reform programs, but as an arbiter and broker of research-based and research-validated external reform programs.

Retaining and Recruiting Clients

SFAF's work began with retaining and recruiting clients in two distinct markets: the comprehensive school reform market and the district coherence market. To stabilize the installed base of schools using its comprehensive school reform program, SFAF did two things: It marketed directly to schools; and it continued to pursue opportunities for large-scale, district-coordinated adoptions. While long dependent on new business in this market as its primary source of operating capital, a combination of organizational and financial structuring had reduced costs and spending within SFAF. Consequently, stabilizing (rather than growing) its installed base of schools became a viable option.[12] Doing so would yield returns along several key dimensions: for example, continuing to act on its belief in comprehensive school reform as the most effective means of improving chronically underperforming schools; continuing to demonstrate commitment to its installed base of schools; continuing to leverage its installed base as a source of legitimacy and influence; and continuing to leverage its experienced schools as partners in program improvement.

Between 2003 and 2008, SFAF succeeded. After continued declines through SY 2004/2005, membership stabilized at 1200 schools for three successive years (SY 2005/2006 through 2007/2008).[13] As SFAF stabilized its installed base, the average time-in-program rose to over eight years (almost triple the original contract length of three years).[14]

At the same time, SFAF began efforts to make headway into the district coherence market by aggressively recruiting states, districts, less-impacted elementary schools, and even middle schools as collaborators in improving student achievement. In doing so, SFAF sought to gain leverage on the interdependent understandings and relationships that were functioning to exclude SFAF from the district coherence market. For example, by recruiting states, SFAF sought to gain (and maintain) access to districts and schools. By recruiting districts, SFAF sought both to gain (and maintain) access to schools; it also sought to develop district-level capabilities to support school-level improvement. And by recruiting new types of schools, SFAF sought to reach even more at-risk students. Collaboration with states, districts, and new types of schools, in turn, stood to create multiple, new revenue streams for SFAF.

Again, between 2003 and 2008, SFAF succeeded. In five years, SFAF attained a scale of operations in the district coherence market rivaling its scale of operations in the comprehensive school reform market, all while continuing to support its installed base of 1,200 schools. In February of 2008, executives reported that SFAF (in collaboration with the Center for Data Driven Reform in Education, a new organization founded by SFAF Chairman Robert Slavin) was collaborating with seven state education agencies, over 380 districts, and over 2,500 less-impacted elementary schools.[15] SFAF developed a particularly strong partnership with the Pennsylvania Department of Education that created opportunity to work simultaneously at the state, intermediate, district, and school levels. The partnership functioned as a key resource for generating new business; it also provided SFAF with a critical context in which to learn about providing state-level designs and supports.

Refining and Devising Designs and Supports

At the same time that SFAF worked to retain and recruit clients, it worked to refine and devise the designs and supports needed to serve them.

Efforts to improve and to integrate its comprehensive school reform program followed directly from SFAF's earlier, 1999–2003 development cycle. SFAF continued to refine and devise supports for its instructional components, including: support for diagnosing and addressing problems with lower-level reading skills at higher grade levels; support for differentiating instruction in Success for All classrooms; and resources and training for small-group (as opposed to one-on-one) tutoring. SFAF complemented these efforts with three initiatives that built on Success for All's Goal Focused Improvement Process to better integrate leadership both with instruction and with environmental expectations for improvement.

One involved the creation of 4Sight Benchmark Assessments: quarterly assessments designed to mirror precisely the content, question format, and scoring of specific state accountability assessments, thus providing schools both formative and predictive information correlated directly to state assessments.[16] Another involved the redesign of Success for All's core information system as the web-based Member Center, which included capabilities for organizing and analyzing 4Sight Benchmark Assessment results and other program-specific information. Yet another was the creation of new "Implementation Self Assessment Guides" to guide school-level analysis and intervention.

Efforts to improve and to integrate its comprehensive school reform program functioned as a springboard for new resources and learning opportunities with which to support districts and states. These efforts focused on three core tasks: summative evaluation of student outcomes; formative evaluation of school operations; and the identification and adoption of research-based and research-validated interventions and solutions—not only from SFAF but, also, from other providers.[17] For districts, designs and supports took the form of a program called the Data Driven District model. A derivative of the school-level Goal Focused Improvement Process, the Data Driven District model was a meta-routine that coordinated analysis of school-level data, goal setting, improvement planning, resource allocation, systems development, and implementation analysis.[18] The model was supported by the use of 4Sight Benchmark Assessments and the web-based Member Center information system, and it was scaffolded by a combination of consulting and coaching from staff members from SFAF and the Center for Data Driven Reform in Education (CDDRE). In cases where districts wanted to develop additional capacity to support program implementation in schools, SFAF provided additional assistance on an ad hoc basis. For states, SFAF and CDDRE staff members drew on school-level and district-level resources to provide ad hoc consulting services on a state-by-state basis.

SFAF also drew from past and on-going development efforts to devise a menu of components that could be used to target specific needs in less-impacted schools. The components supported three distinct strategies that provided different combinations of materials and training. The first strategy (called Success360) bundled material resources with direct instruction and in-practice support to address a wide variety of school-specific needs: for example, complete preschool and kindergarten programs; beginning reading (Grade 1); intermediate reading (grades 2–5); middle school reading (grades 6–8); basic phonics (grades K–1); advanced phonics (grades 2–8); reading comprehension; tutoring; after school programs; writing/language arts (K–8); mathematics (K–6); English language development; classroom management; attendance; parental involvement; family and community outreach; and school-level leadership. The second strategy bundled material resources (i.e., 4Sight Benchmark Assessments and the Member Center information system) with new, less-extensive forms of support, including an on-line help system, a customer support line, and (in some instances) assistance from districts and states. The third strategy had the SFAF training organization providing schools with "pull out" professional development in core instructional strategies (e.g., diagnostic instruction and cooperative learning). To support the use of those strategies in practice, schools either drew on existing capabilities within the school or the district, or they contracted for additional in-practice support from SFAF trainers (at cost).

With that, SFAF's approach to revising and devising designs and supports included attempts to leverage economies of scale in new ways. Specifically, SFAF expanded beyond a "program" orientation to a include "product" orientation: providing resources or services that could be reproduced easily, distributed cheaply, and used effectively in districts and less-impacted schools with assistance far short of extensive, practice-based support from SFAF trainers (e.g., a customer service line, on-line help, embedded DVD-based training, or district/state support). This product orientation had the advantage of creating new potential for large-scale operations and new potential sources of revenue, though without requiring commensurate, costly, and uncertain expansion of SFAF's training organization. The combination of increased revenues and lower costs, in turn, addressed the very problem that was most threatening SFAF's continued viability: a lack of operating capital. SFAF's 4Sight Benchmark Assessments and the Member Center information system represented initial movement towards this product orientation. By 2007/2008, SFAF had additional products nearing release that supported reading instruction, instructional strategies instruction, and tutoring, including one ("Furry Phonics") available publicly through Amazon.com.

The bulk of SFAF's new business in the district coherence market succeeded in leveraging this product-oriented approach. In 2008, SFAF executives reported that 330 districts and over 2,200 schools were using 4Sight Benchmark Assessments and the Member Center information system (many in Pennsylvania). An additional 50 schools (all in Pennsylvania) were receiving large-scale, pull-out "strategies" training from SFAF. Far fewer states, districts, and schools were pursuing options that drew heavily on SFAF's training organization, including: three states that sought ad hoc consulting from SFAF; 59 districts that were participating in the pilot of the Data Driven District model (which also included a formal evaluation of the model's effectiveness); and 208 schools that were using Success 360 components.

Managing and Mediating Environments

SFAF's efforts to adapt the enterprise to support its new, two-pronged strategy continued with efforts to manage and mediate environments. These efforts actually began with reconceptualizing clients. By doing so, SFAF stretched the boundaries of the enterprise to include organizations that had long been sources of uncertainty and problems (i.e., states and districts) and to include other organizations that it simply had not yet tried to reach (i.e., less-impacted schools). Even so, fundamental sources of uncertainty remained, especially in the federal policy environments to which SFAF had so long (and so strongly) oriented. As such, at the same time that it was transforming its clients, designs, and supports, SFAF began aggressive efforts to secure conditions beyond the Success for All enterprise to support activity within it.

The first wrinkle in SFAF's efforts to manage and mediate environments was to influence the administration of NCLB's billion-dollar-per-year Reading First program in order to secure opportunities for entry into the district coherence market. They did so by making two bold moves. In May of 2005, SFAF formally requested that the Inspector General of the U.S. Department of Education investigate the administration of Reading First. In June of 2005, SFAF filed a request with the Department of Education under the Freedom of Information Act seeking evidence with which to conduct its own investigation. SFAF was soon joined in requesting an investigation by two other program providers: the Reading Recovery Council of North America and Dr. Cupp's Readers and Journal Writers.

Indeed, over 2005, concerns with the administration of Reading First began to accumulate well beyond SFAF. For example, in June of 2005, the Center on Education Policy released a report showing a pattern of "remarkable consistency" across state Reading First applications, with states either submitting or (upon review) revising applications that included instruments published by affiliates of the College of Education at the University of Oregon (a site of one of the federally funded technical assistance centers for Reading First).[19] Also in June of 2005, Gerald Bracey, professor at George Mason University and noted educational reform watchdog, published a policy brief asserting that NCLB "enriches many private companies and individuals, especially those close to President George W. Bush and his family."[20] And in September of 2005, *Education Week* reporter Kathleen Kennedy Manzo published the results of a comprehensive investigation of Reading First in which she asserted that "close oversight of the $1 billion-a-year program has allowed a handful of commercial reading programs, assessments, and consultants to reap much of that money, while others have been shut out of the competition."[21]

In September of 2005, amidst growing concern and evidence, the U.S. Senate requested that the Government Accountability Office initiate its own investigation. In a blistering reported released in September of 2006, the Inspector General confirmed the interpretation of SFAF executives and many others:

Specifically, we found that the Department (of Education): Developed an application package that obscured the requirements of the statute; Took action with respect to the expert review panel process that was contrary to the balanced panel composition envisioned by Congress; Intervened to release an assessment review document without the permission of the entity that contracted for its development; Intervened to influence a State's selection of reading programs; and Intervened to influence reading programs being used by local educational agencies (LEAs) after the application process was completed. These actions demonstrate that the program officials failed to maintain a control environment that exemplifies management integrity and accountability.[22]

That was only the beginning. The Inspector General subsequently issued five additional reports expanding on these findings, along with comprehensive recommendations for overhauling the administration of Reading First. Corroborating reports from the Government Accountability Office and the Senate Health, Education, Labor, and Pension Committee were released in March and May of 2007 (respectively) that revealed suspect practices in the government's university-based technical assistance centers, as well.[23] On April 20, 2007, the U.S. House of Representatives Education and Labor Committee began its own hearings on the administration of Reading First.[24] That same day, the Office of the Inspector General referred a subset of its findings to the U.S. Justice Department for criminal investigation.[25]

For SFAF, the findings of multiple investigations into the administration of Reading First served as vindication, in that what just two years earlier had been "in the interpretation of SFAF executives" was now supported by the evidence and interpretation of many others. Though the findings did not provide SFAF with any financial recourse, they created new potential for SFAF to get more even-handed treatment in state and district adoption processes. They also served as moral victories for SFAF and as morale boosts for all in the organization.

However, these victories did not come without a cost. Requesting an investigation into the administration of Reading First not only put SFAF at odds with members of the sitting presidential administration. It also located SFAF at the dead center of a heated national debate. Unlike earlier debates, this debate was not about whether Success for All worked (or didn't), or whether comprehensive school reform worked (or didn't). Rather, investigation of Reading First was situated squarely in the broader, polarized, red/blue political landscape of the day. Those on the left cited Reading First as further evidence of broader corruption and mismanagement within the Bush administration. Those on the right (as well as those implicated) defended the administration of Reading First, and they challenged its investigation as the product of an over-zealous Inspector General, over-zealous Democrats, and disgruntled program providers (Slavin chief among them).[26] Indeed, Sol Stern, a senior fellow at the Manhattan Institute for Policy Research, noted that the Inspector General failed to find evidence that the Department of Education acted specifically against Success for All.[27]

A different point was drawn from the ruckus by Marc Dean Millot, who had served as the chief operating officer of the New American Schools initiative from 1997 to 2002. Millot argued that problems with Reading First were predictable, and consistent with a transition to market-like education reform in which public schools increasingly purchase improvement programs from private sector providers. In a December, 2006 commentary in *Education Week*, Millot argued:

> The legislative framework political leaders established aims at compelling public schools to purchase new, innovative programs from the private sector. But in the process, policymakers unwittingly took aim at deeply entrenched purchasing relationships involving school districts, federal and state education agencies, large multinational publishing firms, and an expert class of

consultants in academia and the think tanks. Elected officials failed to change the rules of that game. Instead, they left the making of their new market to this syndicate.

It was a bit much to ask a state-managed monopoly, its favored providers, and their coterie of advisers to open the market to competition based on the merits. That the new market would continue to favor insider relationships and inside deals is hardly surprising. Nor are the results. . .

We need legislation designed to produce clear decision criteria—arrived at openly—on education programs eligible for government funding. We need laws that mandate a rational basis for government contract decisions on charters and programs, and we need it reduced to writing. These reforms will encourage the best providers to rise to the top.[28]

The second wrinkle in SFAF's efforts to manage and mediate environments was to establish precisely the type of market regulation advocated by Millot—not via legislation but, instead, under its own roof. In 2007, in collaboration with the Center for Data Driven Reform in Education, SFAF established the Best Evidence Encyclopedia (or BEE). The BEE was a publicly accessible web site designed to serve two purposes. The first purpose of the BEE was to support states, districts, and schools in identifying evidence-based and evidence-proven programs. This support was provided in the form syntheses of research on program effectiveness in mathematics, reading, and comprehensive school reform produced by SFAF researchers and others.[29] Some of these syntheses were published in peer-reviewed journals; others were unpublished but externally reviewed. Recognizing the perils of being alone on the front lines of education reform, the second purpose of the BEE was to identify and promote a community of program developers aspiring to produce and scale-up evidence-based and evidence-proven improvement programs.

While the federally funded What Works Clearinghouse was developing contemporaneously to serve much the same purposes as the BEE, critics (including SFAF executives) took exception with its management.[30] While that further motivated SFAF executives in developing the BEE, they reported that doing so further exacerbated tensions between SFAF and political appointees in the federal Department of Education.

The third wrinkle in SFAF's efforts to manage and mediate environments involved continuing to conduct and publicize research demonstrating that its programs and services met the very criteria for "evidence-based" and "evidence proven" that SFAF was so actively promoting with the BEE. Regarding offerings in the district coherence market, SFAF (in collaboration with CDDRE) initiated a federally funded, randomized study of its Data Driven District model, and it initiated and publicized research on the effectiveness of specific components (e.g., tutoring, pre-K, middle school) and of strategies within components (e.g., embedded multi-media).[31]

Regarding its offering in the comprehensive school reform market, University of Wisconsin researcher Geoffrey Borman and a team of SFAF researchers published a series of articles reporting on the outcomes of its randomized field trial of Success for All.[32] Again, the randomized field trial was SFAF's attempt to meet the highest possible standards for evidence of program effectiveness. And, in their interpretation, they did, with the program showing positive, statistically significant effects in word attack (with an effect size of 0.33), word identification (with an effect size of 0.22), and passage comprehension (with an effect size of 0.21). Though lower than the +0.50 effect sizes that SFAF had long reported in earlier research syntheses, the effects were still larger than those identified in the earlier meta-analysis of Borman and colleagues. In summary, the research team argued that results from the randomized field trial validated the strategy of improving student achievement by embedding an intensive, multi-year approach to literacy instruction within a broader program of comprehensive school reform.

At least three external studies provided further evidence to support the point. The first was another *Consumer Reports*-style review conducted by the federally funded Comprehensive School Reform Quality Center (CSRQ) that identified Success for All as one of only two programs having moderately strong evidence of positive overall effects on student achievement.[33] Though this was second-highest possible rating, no programs were rated higher. The second (also conducted by CSRQ) was the national longitudinal evaluation of comprehensive school reform, one summary of which reported straightforwardly: "Success for All improves student achievement."[34] The third (conducted by the Consortium for Policy Research in Education) was a longitudinal, mixed methods study of three leading comprehensive school reform programs that reported positive, statistically significant program effects on leadership practice, instructional practice, and student achievement in those curricular areas for which Success for All was both highly elaborated and highly scaffolded.[35]

Over the course of the 2003–2008 development cycle, SFAF's efforts to generate and publicize research on program effectiveness continued to evoke recognition and enthusiasm, in education and beyond. For example, in 2005, Success for All was one of four programs featured in a two-hour PBS special on large-scale educational reform produced by Pulitzer Prize and Emmy Award-winning journalist Hedrick Smith.[36] In 2008, SFAF's final report on its randomized field trial was awarded the Palmer O. Johnson Award by the American Educational Research Association (AERA) as the best article published in an AERA journal in 2007. Also in 2008, Success for All was identified by the nonprofit, nonpartisan, Congressional-reviewed Coalition for Evidence-Based Policy as one of only two social programs targeting children ages 0–6 that met its "Top Tier" evidence of effectiveness.[37]

Managing and Expanding the Organization

All of the preceding placed tremendous demands on SFAF as an organization. Gaining and maintaining traction in two related (but very different) markets appeared to have SFAF working at cross purposes: for example, integrating its comprehensive school reform program while simultaneously "dis-integrating" the program into components and products; instituting more formal control over its development organization while urgently experimenting to develop new program offerings; and alleviating the strain on trainers while asking that they begin serving new types of clients in very different ways.

Despite steep and competing demands, SFAF again made progress both managing and expanding the organization. Fundamental to supporting large-scale activity in two markets were efforts by SFAF executives to improve the financial position of the organization through a combination of organizational and financial restructuring. SFAF executives dramatically reduced the size of the organization by 60%, from 500 to 200 people. They terminated what they viewed as nonessential development activities (e.g., in social studies, science, and Spanish-language reading programs) and reallocated those resources to more critical development initiatives. They reduced administrative and personnel costs by restructuring SFAF's training organization. They established a more favorable payment schedule by restructuring loans that SFAF had secured to support its founding in 1998. And, again, they structured SFAF's entry into the district coherence market in ways that created new revenue streams without making complementary (and costly) demands on the training organization. By 2006/2007, SFAF executives reported that the organization was operating in the black.

Within its development organization, SFAF executives sought to introduce roles and structures to support more disciplined project management while, at the same time, preserving capabilities for exploratory, experimental, divergent learning. The development organization continued to function as an informal social network, with extensive collaboration among developers and with tight ties to trainers and schools. To discipline and coordinate development activity, SFAF executives structured a weekly Operations Meeting in which newly identified project leaders from each initiative met with SFAF executives, members of the training organization, and key staff to share information, to coordinate work, and to evaluate decisions against resource and funding constraints. While modest by conventional business standards, these efforts represented a very large step for the historically informal SFAF, requiring the development of new understandings and new practices for all involved.

With a reprieve from a 15-year press to expand the size of the training organization, SFAF used the 2003–2008 development cycle to develop the capabilities of the training organization. This was done, in part, through a combination of attrition, lay offs, retention, and recruiting. Managers reported that attrition and cuts early in the 2003–2008 development cycle reduced the number of weaker and less experienced trainers, and that new trainers hired late in the cycle were (on average) stronger than those hired a decade earlier. SFAF also succeeded in retaining a nucleus of stronger trainers such that, by 2007/2008, executives reported that the majority of trainers had from five to ten years of experience. Much was accomplished via extensive efforts to improve and to manage the professional development of trainers: for example, shifting the focus of professional development from "training the program" to working as consultants and coaches in classrooms, schools, and districts; introducing individual reflection and collaborative learning through web-based self-study, portfolios, and case studies; and introducing formal systems to certify and track trainers' capabilities and effectiveness.

To further expand its capabilities, manage its environments, and secure its financial position, SFAF began collaborating with three other organizations that were founded and/or directed by SFAF executives and in which key SFAF staff members held joint appointments. More than partner organizations, SFAF cofounder and chairman Robert Slavin described them as integral parts of the Success for All enterprise, and instrumental in pursuing the shared mission of improving the academic achievement of at-risk students through research-based, research-proven reform.

In SY 2004/2005, Slavin secured a $10 million, five-year grant from the U.S. Department of Education's Institute for Education Sciences to establish the Center for Data Driven Reform in Education (CDDRE). CDDRE functioned as SFAF's partner in working with states and districts. In SY 2006/2007, CDDRE and SFAF's research operations were reorganized as a subunit within the newly founded, federally funded Center for Research and Reform in Education (CRRE) at Johns Hopkins University. CRRE was also directed by Slavin, and it also collaborated with SFAF in developing, supporting, and researching pre-K–8 reading programs.[38] And, for SY 2007/2008, Slavin was named director of the newly founded Institute for Effective Education at the University of York in the United Kingdom, an organization that had "a single-minded focus on developing, evaluating, and disseminating effective programmes and promoting evidence-based policies" in the United Kingdom.[39] The SFAF/IEE collaboration supported the efforts of SFAF executives both to promote the cause of evidence-based educational reform and to reshape SFAF's public identity around that cause. Following the investigations into Reading First, it also provided SFAF co-founders Slavin and Nancy Madden with sanctuary from partisan political turmoil in the US that was complicating the management of SFAF.

Among these three organizations, SFAF's new relationship with the Institute for Effective Education at the University of York was especially important. The IEE was just being established in SY 2007/2008, and its relationship with SFAF still developing. Even so, expanding the reach of SFAF executives beyond CRRE and CDDRE to include IEE appeared to mark the beginning of a new chapter in the history of SFAF as an organization. SFAF executives anticipated that IEE would eventually contract with SFAF to develop programs and services. No longer would SFAF be working solely as a provider of programs and training to "end user" organizations within the formal educational governance structure. If ambitions held, it would be serving as a secondary provider of programs and training services to another, primary provider (IEE). And, with that, SFAF created new opportunity to turn what had long been a problem for SFAF (i.e., its excess development capacity) into an advantage (i.e., yet another new source of revenue).

From Embattled to Emboldened

Over its 2003–2008 development cycle, SFAF did not embrace business acumen. It defied it. In 2003, a strong, shared belief among SFAF's newly recruited executives and key members of its board of directors was that the continued viability of SFAF depended on a sort of convergence. While mindful of constraints imposed by the mission and history of the organization, decades of business experience still had them convinced that SFAF needed to narrow its focus and to coordinate its activities to exploit its core capabilities (primarily in pre-K through middle school reading), to reduce the breadth and pace of development activity, and to create a buffer between development and training that would allow the training organization to "catch up." Yet the path that SFAF ultimately followed was anything but convergent. Instead, the system-level dynamics to which SFAF was responding pulled the enterprise in new, divergent directions: towards new, more diverse clients, programs, and services; towards new and more complicated interactions with the broader system of U.S. public education; and towards more diverse and distributed organizational capabilities.

From one perspective, SFAF's efforts over its 2003–2008 development cycle appeared predictably evolutionary. In collaboration with its new partners, SFAF had worked aggressively, concurrently, and sometimes at cross purposes to construct and improve designs and supports, to secure supporting environmental conditions, and to evolve and its expand its own capabilities. The product of these efforts was a bundle of incremental, interdependent "next steps" in clients, programs, the organization, and its environmental relationships that created vast, new potential to act on SFAF's long-established mission of improving the achievement of at-risk students.

From another perspective, SFAF's efforts appeared revolutionary. As SFAF was devising and acting on its two-pronged strategy, a new sort of "meta-strategy" had begun to emerge. This meta-strategy included recrafting the organization's public identity in order to support its entry into the district coherence market: specifically, by shifting away from a tight identification with the cause of comprehensive school reform and toward a more general identification with the cause of evidence-driven reform in education.[40]

But this meta-strategy went much further, with SFAF executives imagining a fundamentally different (and unprecedented) role for the organization. Beyond being a champion and preeminent provider of research-based and research-validated programs, SFAF executives began imagining (and recrafting) SFAF as both an arbiter and broker of such programs. By using the Best Evidence Encyclopedia to identify research-based and research-proven programs, and by using the Data Driven District model to link states, districts, and schools to these programs, SFAF sought to bring a rationality to program approval and adoption that simply had not existed amidst the turbulence that surrounded the passage of NCLB.[41]

Pursuit of this meta-strategy was, in some ways, quixotic: a romantic, chivalrous, almost-foolish quest for an unattainable ideal. It was, in other ways, prudent.

SFAF executives were well aware of other organizations that were seeking to shape values and perceptions in educational reform, both public and private, in the United States and abroad: a sort of "market of market regulators" in which SFAF sought a presence.[42] And it was, in every way, revolutionary. In the history of U.S. public education, one would be pressed to find another non-public organization that had advanced such a grand vision for reform, with such extensive infrastructure and capabilities for acting simultaneously in the interdependent roles of champion, arbiter, broker, and provider.

SFAF had begun its 2003–2008 development cycle embattled. SFAF ended the cycle emboldened. By the end of its 2003–2008 development cycle, SFAF was not simply sustaining itself. It appeared poised to thrive. One key gauge of SFAF's success had held steady: research on program effectiveness, newly strengthened (in the interpretation of SFAF executives) by findings from its randomized field trial. A gauge that had been dropping had stabilized: the 1,200 schools using its comprehensive school reform program. Another gauge that had long red-lined—the number of schools mired in weak implementation and weak outcomes—had flipped. Anecdotally, members of SFAF reported that 75% of schools using its comprehensive school reform program were making adequate yearly progress, while only 25% were still mired in weak implementation and weak outcomes. Still-other gauges that were showing zeroes or near-zeroes just five years earlier (e.g., the number of states, districts, and less-impacted schools served) were showing unthinkable numbers: 7 states, 380+ districts, and 2,500+ less-impacted schools. And, from a sustainability perspective, the most important gauge—the financial bottom line—showed that SFAF was in the black.

That was not the end of it. Work on all of these initiatives was on-going at the close of SFAF's 2003–2008 development cycle, and it would proceed beyond. For example, in 2008, SFAF's new, product-oriented approach to designing and supporting improvements (and, with it, new sources of revenue) was just coming to fruition, with new offerings slated for sale beginning in SY 2008/2009, and others projected for the years following. CDDRE's Data-Driven District model was being repackaged as a new commercial program called Raising the Bar, with responsibility for development and support shifting from CDDRE to SFAF. The SFAF training organization was engaged in yet another reorganization, shifting from a geographic organization to a cross-functional organization to better address interdependent problems in schools. And researchers were working urgently to produce the research syntheses that functioned as the core content for the Best Evidence Encyclopedia.

Indeed, all of this was more a new beginning than a fait accompli. Yet in the eyes of many in SFAF, from the executive level to the rank and file, what mattered most was not whether SFAF was an unqualified and unequivocal success. What mattered most was that SFAF was again succeeding. By the end of the 2003–2008 development cycle, the two-pronged strategy chosen by SFAF executives appeared to be paying off, and its new meta-strategy was promising more. From the perspective of many, the quagmire that had been threatening SFAF's viability was behind them, and the upward climb to long-term sustainability had begun.

THE MORE THINGS CHANGE. . .

Yet the more things change, the more they stay the same. From one perspective, by the close of the 2003–2008 development cycle, SFAF had arrived at a very different place, in terms of the make-up of its enterprise (i.e., its clients, designs and supports, environmental relationships, and organizational structure and capabilities), its core identity, and its prospects for sustainability. From another perspective, SFAF found itself standing in a spot that looking remarkably like the one on which it was standing at the close of its 1999–2003 development cycle. Stubborn problems persisted within the Success for All enterprise, amplified by the new scale and breadth of the Success for All enterprise. Certain uncertainty loomed beyond, in educational and broader environments. And, with that, sustainability remained the preeminent concern.

Responsibility for sustaining the enterprise rested where it always had: with SFAF executives. But as SFAF ended its 2003–2008 development cycle, the executive ranks were, themselves, in the throes of transition. SFAF's co-founders were stepping back, and new leaders within the organization began to assume responsibility for the perpetual work of sustaining the enterprise.

Persistent Problems Within

Within the Success for All enterprise, problems began with the development organization and the pressure put on it by the need for new materials and resources, both to serve more diverse clients and to generate much needed revenue. Unlike the exuberance that sustained its members during 1999–2003 development cycle, developers worked under great strain during the 2003–2008 development cycle. The strain derived, in part, from the challenge of engaging urgent, extensive development work amidst declining financial resources and reductions in development staff. The strain derived, in part, from demands on the technical knowledge of developers, who were producing fundamentally new types of resources for use in schools, districts, and states. And the strain derived, in part, from demands on developers' understandings. Initially, many did not fully understand what was driving changes and urgency in their work, and many struggled to connect their efforts to that which had sustained them (and the entire organization) for so long: the core mission of improving the achievement of at-risk students. In a 2004 interview, one developer spoke for many:

> People are struggling right now, because we've changed so much in response to policy, the big changes being Success360 and the 4Sight Benchmark Assessments. Now we're going to offer these little components, and offer a kind of service that we haven't offered before and a kind of product marketing that we haven't offered before. And I think we're right at the transition point now where everyone sort of understands that we're doing these new things, but I don't think most people know what that means. And I feel like

timelines are changing. Stuff needs to be done even faster, and promises are being made. And people are saying, "What's going on?" But I think they don't understand the pressure. . . . We're asking people to operate really differently. Suddenly, it's like we're sort of a publishing house.

So, well, okay. You know what I feel like? I feel like there's this bus, and it's going down the street. And we've missed it, and we're running to catch it. And we're not really sure where it's going, but we know we need to get on it. That's kind of what we feel like. "Oh, my God hurry! I don't know if it's going to go anywhere, but I think we're supposed to be on it!"

The problems continued with the training organization. While SFAF made progress developing capabilities in its training organization, trainers still continued to experience tremendous pressure. Mirroring the very environments in which they worked, some of the pressure came with the addition of new, internal systems for holding trainers accountable for improving student achievement. Some of the pressure came with working in stronger schools, and from needing to integrate stand-alone program components into schools' on-going operations. Much of the pressure came with working beyond the school, itself. Historically, SFAF's new clients—states and districts—were administrative agencies of government, not partners in systemic, rational reform. As one member of SFAF explained, to collaborate with states and districts was to negotiate no less than a paradigm shift. Such work, in turn, placed a premium on trainers being able to engage in extended, site-based analysis, consulting, and coaching—not just in schools, but at all levels of the system. For a training organization comprised primarily of ex-teachers (many of whom, one SFAF manager noted, would probably have been intimidated going into their own principal's office), developing the capabilities to work as consultants in collaboration with superintendents was no small matter.

New pressure on its development and training organizations complicated the challenges faced by SFAF executives in coordinating and managing their operations. Despite efforts to do so, progress was slow, and problems remained. For example, even with efforts to certify trainers, it was not until SY 2006/2007 that SFAF actually began to build information systems that allowed it to track the professional knowledge and capabilities of trainers (and, thus, to develop and leverage those capabilities more strategically). Further, with its rush of new materials and tools over the entire 2003–2008 development cycle, SFAF never succeeded in creating a buffer between its development and training organizations, nor in developing formal coordination and control over the dissemination of program improvements to clients. Finally, efforts to coordinate work among SFAF's many development teams were slow to come to fruition. While SFAF succeeded in creating roles and structures to support improved project management, key development initiatives continued to be coordinated informally. In a 2004 interview, one SFAF developer described the challenge of coordinating work on 4Sight Benchmark Assessments, the cornerstone of SFAF's entry into the district coherence market:

Everyone's working on these timelines. Everyone's hearing something different. We need to get the people who are printing the tests, the people who are delivering the tests, the trainers, the researchers, every piece of it at one table so we can sit down, understand what we're doing, how we're doing it, what the schedule is. And that is really hard to do. And, again, we can't get everyone. We tried to have this formal way of communicating and getting it all out in the open and getting it done, and that was not possible. There are these people doing the data piece on the Benchmarks, and they are working the best they can on their timeline. And then there are these developers who are developing the Benchmarks, and they're working the best they can on their timeline. And then you've got the training piece and getting trainers up and ready to help people use the Benchmarks. And the publications department is printing these Benchmarks, bazillions of them. Everyone's doing the very best they can in their little orbs, but we never understand what's going on. The timeline is insane, because we're responding to this market demand. And sometimes I feel like we just don't even have enough time.

Then there was the matter of revenues and contributions. Throughout its 2003–2008 development cycle, SFAF struggled to generate capital to supports its new strategy, due both to failed federal grant applications and to failed attempts to generate capital from non-public sources.[43] While nobody provided evidence, several in SFAF speculated that its struggles securing federal grants were linked to contentious relationships with members of the Bush administration both preceding and following investigations into the administration of Reading First. SFAF's struggles securing funding became so dire that, by 2006, it was teetering on the brink of bankruptcy. It was only with loan restructuring in 2006 and new revenues in 2006/2007 and 2007/2008 (largely from its new product-oriented approach to programs and services) that SFAF regained solid financial footing.

But, again, SFAF was hardly out of the woods. Its new approaches to leveraging economies of scale to increase revenues were just coming to fruition at the close of SFAF's 2003–2008 development cycle, and SFAF had yet to accumulate the reserves needed to weather fluctuations in revenues and philanthropic contributions. At the same time, the federal grant supporting CDDRE was set to expire in SY 2008/2009 (hence, CDDRE shifting its responsibilities to SFAF), and SFAF executives were working to secure federal funding to support a new center (the specifics of which were still unsettled at the close of SY 2007/2008). Consequently, despite having made progress stabilizing its financial situation, SFAF remained vulnerable to quick shifts in the demand for its products and services, to shifts in federal funding priorities, and to uncertainty in broader economic environments.

Finally, a problem that had hung over the Success for All enterprise throughout its entire existence became even more pressing: providing convincing evidence that its programs and services were technically effective in improving student achievement. Given SFAF's role as a champion, arbiter, broker, and provider of research-based and research-proven programs, the problem was paramount. Yet, at the end of its 2003–2008 development cycle, this was very much an open issue. For example, while SFAF was engaged in a randomized field trial of its Data-Driven District model, results were still pending at the close of SY 2007/2008—and, with that, evidence with which to support claims that the centerpiece of its district coherence strategy was technically effective. Indeed, at the close its 2003–2008 development cycle, the legitimacy of the Data-Driven District model derived not from its research-proven effectiveness but more from SFAF's reputation as a champion and provider of research-proven programs.[44]

Further, despite two decades of research, questions still hung over SFAF's comprehensive school reform program. In contrast to what SFAF executives saw as positive findings from the randomized field trial of Success for All, the federal Institute of Education Sciences' What Works Clearinghouse published a meta-analysis of research on Success for All that found potentially positive effects on alphabetics and general reading achievement but mixed effects on comprehension.[45] Further, research cited by SFAF as evidence of effectiveness could well have been interpreted by critics as much more equivocal. Consider the two studies released in 2005 and 2006 by the Comprehensive School Reform Quality Center. Again, one study put plainly that "Success for All improves student achievement."[46] However, with much less certainty, the other study reported that, "in sum, a large body of evidence suggests that SFA has a positive impact on student achievement some of the time."[47]

All of these problems remained unresolved at the end of the 2003–2008 development cycle. In 2008, SFAF executives, managers, and developers confirmed that the development organization was still struggling to discipline its work. Indeed, one member of SFAF described the continued approach to development as more "knee jerk" than planful. The training organization was still working to enable and support communities of training practice. Coordination between development and training continued to be problematic—described by one member of SFAF as "very, very awkward." Members of SFAF reported that they were still learning to work productively within the context of its standing operations meetings, and that formal information systems were still lagging in relation to the information needs of executives, managers, developers, and trainers. SFAF was still working to capitalize on new, potential revenue streams. And SFAF was still seeking to secure contributions to support the enterprise.

All of these problems aside, perhaps the biggest was this: The more comprehensive its programs and services, the larger and more expansive the scale of operations, and the more committed to continuous improvement, the more that critics could argue that the Success for All enterprise was taking on characteristics of the very system that it sought to displace. New efforts to leverage economies of scale (e.g., providing products and training, absent in-practice support) could be argued to be no different than the usual, targeted, and often-ineffective educational reform initiatives. Indeed, rather than insulating SFAF from competition with commercial providers, its new, product-oriented approach had SFAF in direct competition with them. With its product-oriented approach, SFAF's installed base of users could be argued to look less like a coherent professional network and more like the usual amalgamation of educational organizations, the majority of which retained the bulk of their own, core technologies and capabilities. The once-coherent hub of the enterprise could now be portrayed as a constellation of soft money organizations, with agendas and operations highly susceptible to shifts in external funding priorities. SFAF's attempt to assert itself as champion, arbiter, broker, and provider could be argued to be rife with conflicts of interest, thus setting the stage for corruption and abuses. And the entire enterprise could be argued to rest as much on its legitimacy as it did evidence of effectiveness.

It may be the case that this was a matter of degree: that, even though confronting such issues, the Success for All enterprise was in nowhere near the dire straights of (for example) many large, urban school districts, and that SFAF's long track record of making good on public confidence should alleviate concerns. If so, then a key challenge faced by SFAF executives was to make that case.

Certain Uncertainty Beyond

Despite efforts to manage and mediate environments, problems within the Success for All enterprise were matched with problems beyond. Even with efforts to cultivate a favorable image, SFAF continued to face persistent—and vehement—public criticism. During SFAF's 2003–2008 development cycle, one of SFAF's most prominent critics was Jonathan Kozol, acclaimed author and activist, and a leading advocate for improving the education and life opportunities of children of poverty. In his 2005 book, *Shame of the Nation: The Restoration of Apartheid Schooling in America*, Kozol criticized Success for All as subjecting children of poverty to an intellectually thin and overly regimented education that reinforced their place in society.[48] In September of 2005, Harper's Magazine ran an article adapted from the book that chided Success for All as a "drill-based literacy method" and "scripted method of instruction."[49] Kozol's criticism fostered yet another heated volley in *Phi Delta Kappan* on the merits of Success for All, this time between Kozol and Slavin.[50] In this exchange, Kozol landed the final blow:

> SFA, to state the matter bluntly, is a bottom feeder. It goes to where the misery and hyper-segregation are the most extreme. It is an apartheid course of study for an apartheid schooling system, promising embattled school officials it will let them do an end run around inequality and racial sequestration. We have been hearing false promises like this since 1896 when *Plessy v. Ferguson* was handed down. In this respect, the advocates for SFA help mightily to reinforce and deepen the divisions of our social order rather than confront them. Segregated education is the oldest failed experiment in U.S. social history. Shame on Mr. Slavin for pretending he can "fix" this by indoctrinating children of minorities in a noncritical and acquiescent mode of intellection. This is training for subordination and not education for democracy.[51]

However stinging, problems arising from public criticism paled in relation to those arising from uncertainty in educational and broader environments. SFAF's district coherence strategy had the enterprise stitched into more corners of the formal system of U.S. public education than ever before, thus newly vulnerable to uncertainty in states and districts. Over its history, such relationships had proven unpredictable and perilous. Indeed, working with districts and states, turbulence—not stability—was the status quo. Relationships could come crashing down in a heartbeat for any number of reasons, resulting in decreases in essential revenues, surpluses in costly training capabilities, and hard hits to internal morale. For SFAF, a particular point of vulnerability was SFAF's work in Pennsylvania. While functioning both as a source of revenue and as fertile context for experiential learning, SFAF executives acknowledge that their work in Pennsylvania (and, thus, their revenues and learning opportunities) could be altered dramatically with turbulence in state-level leadership.

Equally problematic was uncertainty in the administration of NCLB. Comprehensive School Reform—among the pivotal federal education policies of the 1990s, and an apparently central program within NCLB—withered and died. Federal funding for Comprehensive School Reform was eliminated from the 2006 federal budget, and $205 million in federal funding vanished.[52] Late in 2006, the federally funded Comprehensive School Reform Quality Center, which had been operated since 2003 by the American Institutes for Research, ceased operations.[53] It wasn't only federal support for comprehensive school reform that disappeared. So, too, did the patron of the movement. In May of 2004, New American Schools announced a merger with the American Institutes for Research, to be completed in 2005.[54] With that, the intent was to leverage the capabilities of NAS to form a consulting division within AIR to work with schools, districts, and states: in essence, a competitor of SFAF in the district coherence market, rather than a champion of SFAF and other providers in the comprehensive school reform market.

Uncertainty in the administration of Comprehensive School Reform was matched with uncertainty in the administration of Reading First. The findings of the Inspector General did not translate into an immediate increase in state-level approvals of Reading First grants that included Success for All programs and services. Instead, findings from the Inspector General actually undermined political support for Reading First and, with that, its funding. On December 26, 2007, President Bush signed a budget in which Congress slashed funding for Reading First by roughly one-third, from $1 Billion in FY 2007 to $393 Million in FY 2008. In 2008, Congress completely eliminated funding for Reading First for FY 2009. Gone, thus, was the very funding stream that SFAF executives had seen as driving the emergence of the district coherence market.

Uncertainty in the administration of NCLB was matched with uncertainty in its reauthorization. Congressional hearings on the reauthorization of NCLB had begun in earnest in the spring of 2006, with reauthorization slated for fall of 2007. However, Congressional leaders were unable to build consensus around a revised version of the legislation within that timeframe, and the reauthorization process began to stall. By the fall of 2007, the politics of reauthorization had become confounded with the politics of the 2008 elections, with many Democrats running explicitly against NCLB as it had been reauthorized and administered under the Bush administration. Policymakers, academics, and the media began forecasting that the reauthorization would not be completed until well after the 2008 presidential election.

Amidst the political uncertainty surrounding the reauthorization, SFAF extended its efforts to manage and to mediate environments by advocating an agenda that (in the analysis of SFAF executives) would secure support for research-based and research-proven educational reform. Key elements of the agenda included: guidance and requirements for the selection of research-validated programs (including a competitive grant program that would give preferential treatment for the use of research-validated programs by states, districts, and schools); additional funding for program evaluation at the state, district, and school levels; and additional funding to support decision making and intervention at the school level. SFAF focused particularly keenly on the Proven Programs for the Future of Education Act and the Education Research and Development to Improve Achievement Act: two pieces of federal legislation introduced in the fall of 2007 that had potential to strengthen federal policy support for the development, adoption, and implementation of evidence-based and (especially) evidence-proven programs. Much as the Obey-Porter CSRD Act and the Reading Excellence Act had shaped NCLB, SFAF executives hoped that these two acts would shape the reauthorization of NCLB.[55]

However, SFAF was but one small voice in a noisy and chaotic conversation that included virtually every conceivable interest group: academics; policy shops; think tanks; commissions; publishers; blue ribbon committees; program providers; professional associations; teachers' unions; bureaucrats; courts; and more. Very large voices soon to enter the conversation were those of President Barack Obama and his administration, the members of which had their own understandings of (and ambitions for) educational reform. The entire lot mixed with emerging (and equivocal) evidence of changes in student achievement under NCLB: some negative, some positive.[56]

Even with so many voices, so many interests, and such equivocal findings in play, a familiar pattern seemed to be holding: a pattern of evolutionary movement along established dimensions. Key parameters of NCLB were holding up, and functioning to structure debate: for example, strengthening existing standards and accountability systems in states; shifting from "status models" to "growth models" in measuring changes in student achievement; expanding assessment to include other content areas (possibly science); increasing the number of required assessments in high schools; relaxing NCLB's emphasis on randomized and experimental studies and including other rigorous, systematic methods of program evaluation; going beyond requirements for teacher quality to include requirements for leader quality; and others. These changes were bound up with discussions of the overall level of funding, its distribution among various programs, and its distribution to states, districts, and schools.

Yet even if evolutionary patterns held, the entire lot stood to effect yet another abrupt, seismic event: the reauthorized NCLB as a large bundle of evolutionary, interdependent policy and program improvements, signed into law on a given day with the stroke of a pen. While profound implications for SFAF were certain, the specifics of those implications defied prediction. Considering that the effects of the reauthorization would be confounded with additional turbulence in educational environments (e.g., active pursuit of other reform strategies, including charter schools) and broader economic, political, and social environments only made matters worse.

Much more predictable, though, was the process that these changes would effect, at least if SFAF's prior experiences held. Likely pressed to quickly apply for new funding, states, districts, and schools would immediately begin interpreting and acting on the reauthorized NCLB, highly constrained by their current values, understandings, capabilities, and relationships. Technologies and knowledge would continue to emerge to support their efforts. SFAF would again be operating at a lag, feverishly working formally and informally to see and understand patterns throughout this interdependent, system-wide activity. At the same time, SFAF would be working to devise strategies both for adapting to and for shaping that activity—though complicated by the increasingly sprawling nature of the Success for All enterprise. SFAF would need to evolve to evolve, either stretching or contracting its organizational capabilities in order to adapt the enterprise. It would need to leverage a combination of research and experience to inform those adaptations. The result would be another revolution via evolution, though with problems persisting within and beyond the enterprise.

How all of this would play out was anybody's guess.

The Executive Imperative

Over its 2003/2008 development cycle, SFAF executives succeeded in evolving the enterprise to maintain its position at that odd edge of the full world of U.S. public education, with the institutionalized order on the one side and reform-minded disorder on the other. Sitting at that edge, the Success for All enterprise had the appearance of a massive infrastructure supporting a massive vision for systemic, rational reform, all tightly coordinated with federal policy. Sitting at that edge, the Success for All enterprise also had the appearance of a house of cards sitting on a federal fault line. And with the reauthorization of NCLB looming, pressure on the fault line was building. A seismic event was imminent, with aftershocks to follows in states, districts, and schools. For better or worse, profound implications for the Success for All enterprise were certain. For better or worse, understanding those implications and evolving the enterprise in response would be a tremendous challenge.

The more sprawling the scope and scale of the Success for All enterprise, and the more (and different) ways that it experienced system-wide turbulence, the greater the executive imperative to read these many interdependencies, to evolve SFAF's strategic vision, and to chart the course that would sustain the enterprise. As SFAF entered its 2003–2008 development cycle, SFAF had developed complex capabilities among its executive team to act on just that imperative. Moving well beyond SFAF as a Mom and Pop shop, the executive team had expanded into a federation of seasoned advocates, researchers, developers, trainers, corporate leaders, and analysts who shared the commitment to keep Success for All chugging down the track, helping kids, 20 years, 30 years down the road.

Yet the executive level of SFAF was no more immune to problems, questions, and uncertainty than any other dimension of the enterprise. While its 2003–2008 development cycle began with a newly expanded executive team, SFAF did not retain its newly recruited executives for the duration of the cycle. By the end of 2006, all of SFAF's newly recruited executives and their staff had left the organization. SFAF also lost the majority of its Board of Directors, including two philanthropists who had provided SFAF with both funding and business expertise.

By SY 2007/2008, SFAF appeared to be in the beginning stages of its first executive transition. Cofounders Robert Slavin and Nancy Madden (along with Bette Chambers, who had joined the executive team preceding the 2003–2008 development cycle) were devoting increasing time and attention to the newly founded Institute for Education Excellence at the University of York, with their remaining time and attention split between SFAF and CRRE. Another key SFAF executive (Barbara Haxby, director of implementation, who had been with Success for All since the late 1980s) reduced her appointment to less than half time.

In the latter stages of the 2003–2008 development cycle, as newly recruited and long-serving executives transitioned out of the organization, new executive staff members transitioned in: most promoted from within SFAF; several recruited from beyond; and some retained as external consultants and advisors. Many had worked in collaboration with SFAF executives for years, and they had accumulated considerable knowledge of (and experience with) managing the complex, interdependent work of designing, supporting, scaling up, and continuously improving. Yet none had ever shouldered primary responsibility for precisely the work at hand: developing the vision and charting the course that would sustain a sprawling, nonprofit, geographically and organizationally distributed educational reform enterprise, one that functioned in interaction with even more complex environments. But, then, again, the number of people in the U.S. who *did* have such knowledge and experience were very few and very far between.

Thus, at the close of its 2003–2008 development cycle, SFAF's executive expertise was thinner than at the start of the cycle. This, at precisely the moment when pressure was building for another seismic policy event, and when the challenges involved in sustaining the enterprise were the greatest in SFAF's history.

Questions hung over the enterprise as it had evolved over its 2003–2008 development cycle. Questions hung over its future. All bore on its continued viability. Were its new program offerings effective in improving student achievement? Would SFAF's new program offerings find clients in their intended markets, and would SFAF succeed in establishing stable (and formidable) revenue streams? Would SFAF executives succeed in addressing persistent problems of coherence and capabilities within their own organizations? What changes would the reauthorization of NCLB bring, especially given an inevitable change in presidential administrations? What would it take for SFAF to evolve its enterprise in response? Would SFAF further increase its reach or, possibly, pull back? Would it continue to bundle resources with expensive, in-practice training support, or would it swing more strongly to a "product" orientation? If it swung to a production orientation, would SFAF succeed in devising alternative supports for effective use?

And, above all else, would the meta-agenda of systemic, rational reform remain stable and viable long enough for SFAF to answer these questions?

With all of this, SFAF again faced the challenge of evolving to evolve. This time, the challenge centered on transferring the most fundamental knowledge and experience from one generation of executives to another: that which supported the work of sustaining the enterprise. Whether new executive capabilities would develop to be strong enough, quickly enough to steer the enterprise through the inevitable turbulence following the reauthorization of NCLB was not clear. Just as unclear were the processes by which these new executive capabilities would develop: for example, through the continued mentorship SFAF's founding executives; through the continued incorporation of expertise from beyond SFAF; through collaboration with other organizations and executives facing comparable challenges; or through some combination. As important as capabilities were connections, and the matter of new executives developing the same sorts of relationships with key policy makers and researchers as those of SFAF's founders. In that sense, the stalling of the reauthorization of NCLB again worked to SFAF's advantage, as it created opportunity to develop new executive capabilities and connections under comparatively less-turbulent conditions.

Among the new executive staff members, primary responsibility for managing the day-to-day operations of SFAF (and of CDDRE) increasingly fell on the shoulders of a newly appointed chief operating officer, GwenCarol Holmes. A public school teacher and principal with a doctorate in educational administration, Holmes had come up through the ranks of the Success for All enterprise, having served as a principal in a Success for All school and in multiple development, training, and management positions within SFAF and CDDRE.

Through years of collaboration, Holmes had garnered the respect of many within SFAF. She was described by colleagues as very knowledgeable of the Success for All enterprise, and her experience in SFAF and CDDRE gave her sharp perspective on problems and needs within and beyond.

In contrast to characterizations of SFAF's founding executives as Mom and Pop, one member of SFAF described Holmes as an "agent provocateur": somebody working from within to incite positive changes, including those that challenged some of the central tenets of the enterprise. Indeed, in a 2008 interview, Holmes set out an ambitious agenda: for example, expanding beyond cooperative learning to feature programs that had other, research-proven practices at their center; moving from a geographically organized training organization to an expertise-organized training organization, to enable rapid response to specific problems of clients; addressing enduring problems of coordination between development and training; developing formal, internal information systems to support improved decision making; developing a marketing team that could both generate leads *and* close the deal; continuing to recraft the identity of SFAF around the principles of research-based and (especially) research-proven programs; and, reminiscent of New American schools, cultivating a critical mass of what she described as "competitors" who could join SFAF in elevating and stabilizing the cause.

Though Holmes described much as needing to change, she was equally clear that at least one thing needed to stay the same: the core commitment and mission of the organization to improve education for at-risk students. Acting on that mission required sustaining the enterprise. And, in collaboration with other members of SFAF's executive staff, that responsibility was becoming hers to shoulder. In a 2008 interview, she explained:

> In my first year sitting in this chair, that's been the big burden, this question of sustainability. And even before I had any idea that I would ever sit in this chair, I would harass Bob (Slavin) and Nancy (Madden) about this. And nobody wants to talk about it, because basically you're talking about your own demise. But we want this to outlive all of us. And all of us are getting to that age in life where we're starting to think, "How have I contributed to this world? If my life's work is to improve education for children in poverty, can you even tell I was here? How do you insure that this foundation goes forward and continues to be an advocate for these children. . .?"

TIME CAPSULE: ADVICE AND PREDICTIONS

SY 2007/2008 was a year of transition for SFAF, the end of one chapter in the life of the organization and the beginning of another. SY 2007/2008 marked the beginning of SFAF's third decade of operations—almost unthinkable, given its origins as a university-based research-and-development project, and the fact that most such initiatives evaporate in a few short years. With the founding of the Institute for Effective Education and the beginnings of an executive transition, SY 2007/2008 marked both the beginning of the end of SFAF's efforts to steer through the turbulence that followed NCLB and SFAF's early positioning for the turbulence that would follows its reauthorization.

SFAF's 2003–2008 development cycle had been very hard on all members of the organization, from the shop floor through the executive suite. Yet as SY 2007/2008 wound down, the confusion with which the cycle had begun and the strain (even desperation) experienced in its midst were lifting. There was a palpable air of relief about the organization. Confidence was returning.

Members of SFAF had no delusions of smooth sailing. Indeed, the notion of "turnaround schools" would soon capture reformers' fancy. A previously unthinkable national standards movement would soon gather. States would soon be racing to the top. And the federal government would soon be investing in innovation. All of this activity would occur against the backdrop of historic economic collapse and rabid partisan politics.

But that was all in the future. For the moment, members of SFAF saw the 2003–2008 development cycle as having the organization well positioned to continue to pursue its core mission of improving the education and achievement of at-risk students.

In the summer preceding the SY 2007/2008, to celebrate SFAF's transition from its second to its third decade of operations, members of the organization prepared a time capsule in which they placed artifacts and messages. The time capsule was to be sealed and, then, opened at some signature date in the organization's future. The time capsule was a treasure chest about the size of a bread box. There was great hope in this simple act: the expectation of viability and success that would have SFAF colleagues gathered around the table some years down the road, and the anticipation of the laughs and memories that would come with opening the time capsule and sharing its contents.

True to character, somebody in SFAF actually elaborated the task of including messages in the time capsule! Labeled "A Time Capsule Message to the Future," that somebody had created a simple, one-page form with which members of SFAF could send a message to the colleagues who they imagined gathered around that table some years down the road. The form included a "from" line to record the sender's name. It included a "to" line to indicate to whom the message was being sent. The body of the form asked the sender for "words of advice and predictions." The form closed with lines for the senders' signatures.

After so many pages, you, reader, now know as much about SFAF's history up to that point in time as did most of SFAF's members—possibly more. You have seen fullness and complexity in U.S. public education, and the problems and possibilities of deep, lasting reform. In that time will have passed since this writing, you will also inevitably know what became of SFAF.

Conjuring up only what you learned from the preceding pages, and putting yourself back in the summer of 2007, what would you have written on your time capsule message to the future? What would have been your advice and predictions? To whom would you have sent them? Finally, who would you imagine sitting around that table twenty years hence, celebrating SFAF's fortieth anniversary as a community of developers, trainers, researchers, staff members, and executives committed to the cause of academic success for all children?

Notes

1. The approach of SFAF executives to the work of interpreting system-wide response to NCLB was consistent with the work of "enacting environments" as described by Pfeffer and Salancik (1979): a sort of strategic environmental analysis to guide decision making within the organization.
2. See Slavin (2003).
3. An option that had been available to schools since provisions for "schoolwide programs" were initially incorporated into Title I in 1978 was that of designing their own comprehensive school reform programs. This option was carried directly into NCLB. For example, Section 1606 of Comprehensive School Reform under Title I of NCLB detailed the local use of funds. The list of the eleven criteria for comprehensive school reform programs closed with a "special rule" (U.S. Department of Education, 2005): "(b) SPECIAL RULE- A school that receives funds to develop a comprehensive school reform program shall not be limited to using nationally

available approaches, but may develop the school's own comprehensive school reform program for schoolwide change as described in subsection (a)." Subsection (a) referred to the subsection of Section 1606 describing the eleven criteria for comprehensive school reform programs set out in NCLB (see Table 4.2). Consequently, rather than selecting single, integrated designs for comprehensive school reform, districts were able to compose self-designed plans for comprehensive school reform: a) built around Reading First-funded backbone systems for curriculum, assessment, and professional development; and b) satisfying the eleven criteria for comprehensive school reform as set out under Section 1606, subsection (a).

4. U.S. Department of Education (2002:6)

5. Non-federal guidance did include mention of program effectiveness. For example, the first stage of guidance in Simmons and Kame'enui's widely circulated "consumer's guide" to K–3 reading programs (2003:3) began by going beyond federal guidance to recommend attention to the research-proven effectiveness of reading programs. However, evidence of effectiveness was not required as a condition for federal funding.

6. U.S. Department of Education (2002).

7. Ravitch (2005).

8. Manzo and Washington (2002).

9. Research and reports would quickly emerge to support the interpretations of SFAF executives. The first year analysis of Comprehensive School Reform under NCLB documented a school-level phenomenon consistent with SFAF's interpretation of Comprehensive School Reform being subordinated to Reading First: large numbers of schools engaged in the elements of comprehensive school reform, absent adoption of an integrated design for comprehensive school reform (Tushnet, Flaherty, and Smith, 2004). Independent analysis documented variability in the capacity of SEAs to enact their responsibilities under NCLB (e.g., McLure, 2005). Research on the New American Schools initiative described novel programs being apprehended by districts and schools through old understandings, in the context of highly institutionalized organizational forms, routines, and processes, and consequently compromised (Berends, Bodilly, and Kirby, 2002). Researchers identified a "small clique of inside policy entrepreneurs" who had unusual influence on the design and administration of Reading First (Miskel and Song, 2004). And *Education Week* ran a years-long series of reports raising questions (e.g., Manzo and Washington, 2002; Manzo, 2004, 2005a; 2005b; 2007).

10. For example, with concern over NCLB as a collection of underfunded mandates, both Utah and Vermont engaged in serious debate about turning down funding from NCLB. Underscoring state-by-state opposition was the February, 2005 release by the National Conference of State Legislatures outlining a series of concerns with (and recommendations for) continued administration of NCLB (National Conference of State Legislatures, 2005). In April of 2005, the National Education Association sued the federal government on behalf of school districts in nine states in opposition to NCLB (National Education Association, 2005). Running aside was an academic literature that had sprung up in opposition to both NCLB and Reading First (e.g., Allington, 2002; Meier and Wood, 2004; Garan, 2002, 2004).

11. Organizational transformation of this sort involves characteristic and steep problems: for example, securing necessary capital; transforming boundaries and capabilities to target new markets and generate new sources of revenue; securing necessary

political support; and maintaining the resolve of the organization (Aldrich, 1999:163–194). For more on the challenges of organizational transformation in education, see: Rowan (2002), on the population ecology of the school improvement industry; and Tyack and Tobin (1994), on reformers simply burning out.

12. By SY 2005/2006, COO Mark Gritton reported in a personal communication (June 09, 2006) that SFAF was sustainable on revenues from only 60–70 newly-recruited schools per year.

13. See Slavin and Madden (2007) for reports of stabilization at 1200 schools.

14. Reported by Robert Slavin at the Success for All Experienced Sites Conference, San Antonio, TX, February 18, 2008.

15. Personal communication, GwenCarol Holmes, Chief Operating Officer, SFAF. February 26, 2008.

16. In October of 2008, 4Sight Benchmark Assessments were available for 20 states. See Success for All Foundation (2008b).

17. Working through the Center for Data Driven Reform in Education (CDDRE), SFAF originally enlisted other program providers as key partners: America's Choice, the National Institute for Direct Instruction, Modern Red Schoolhouse, Co-NECT, Howard University Talent Quest, the University of Memphis, and the University of Wisconsin.

18. Center for Data Driven Reform in Education (2007b; 2007c). Note that, for the SY 2008/2009, SFAF renamed the Data Driven District model as Raising the Bar. See Center for Data Driven Reform in Education (2008a).

19. See Center on Education Policy (2005). The first of the two instruments identified in the report was the Dynamic Indicators of Basic Early Literacy Skills (DIBELS), co-authored by University of Oregon professors Ruth Kaminski and Roland Good and published by the Institute for the Development of Educational Achievement at the University of Oregon. See https://dibels.uoregon.edu/. The second was *A Consumer's Guide to Evaluating a Core Reading Program Grades K-3: A Critical Elements Analysis*, co-authored by University of Oregon professors Deborah Simmons and Edward Kame'enui in 2003 and published by the National Center to Improve the Tools of Education at the University of Oregon.

20. See Bracey (2005:i).

21. Manzo (2005, September 7:1).

22. U.S. Department of Education, Office of Inspector General (2006:2).

23. U.S. Government Accountability Office (2007).

24. Manzo (2007, April 25:26).

25. For reports from the New York Times and Washington Post, see Schemo (2007, April 21) and Paley (2007, April 21). Ironically, two days earlier, the New York Times, the Washington Post, and virtually every other media outlet in the U.S. reported on the testimony of Attorney General Alberto Gonzales before the U.S. Senate regarding his role in the firing of U.S. attorneys under the Bush administration, an event that had the Justice Department embroiled in its own turbulence and that would ultimately lead to the resignation of Gonzales in August of 2007.

26. See, for example, Stern (2008). Also, on March 10, 2008, the Thomas B. Fordham Institute, in a letter to the Integrity Committee of the President's Council on Integrity and Efficiency, requested an investigation into John P. Higgins, Jr., the Inspector General who conducted the investigation into Reading First, on charges of capriciousness and bias.

27. See Stern (2008:6).
28. Millot (2006:30).
29. In collaboration with CDDRE, SFAF also distributed a "user friendly" 3x5 card that set out four essential criteria for evaluating the effectiveness of any program: "Has this program been: 1. Evaluated in comparison to a randomly assigned or matched control group; 2. In studies of at least one semester, involving multiple schools; 3. Found to improve achievement significantly better than the control treatment; and 4. Published in a peer-reviewed research journal?" See Center for Data Driven Reform in Education (2007a).
30. See, for example, Schoenfeld (2006).
31. For the CDDRE research design for the Data Driven District model, see Center for Data Driven Reform in Education (2008b). Final results were not expected until Winter, 2009/2010. For evaluations of individual components, see: Chambers, Cheung, Madden, Slavin, and Gifford (2006); Chambers, Abrami, Tucker, Slavin, Madden, Cheung, and Gifford (2005); and Cheung and Slavin (2005).
32. See: Borman, Slavin, Cheung, Chamberlain, Madden, and Chambers (2005a; 2005b; 2007).
33. Comprehensive School Reform Quality Center (2005).
34. Aladjem and Borman (2006:9).
35. See: Camburn, Rowan, and Taylor (2003); Correnti, 2007; Correnti and Rowan, 2007; Rowan and Miller, 2007; and Rowan, Correnti, Miller, and Camburn (2009a; 2009b).
36. For information, see: http://www.pbs.org/makingschoolswork/index.html.
37. Coalition for Evidence Based Policy (2008:1).
38. See Center for Research and Reform in Education (2008a; 2008b).
39. See Institute for Effective Education (2008a; 2008b).
40. See, for example: Slavin (2002a; 2005).
41. Slavin (2008).
42. Slavin (2008).
43. In this period, SFAF's initial home and continuing research partner, the Center for Research on the Education for Students Placed at Risk at Johns Hopkins University, lost its federal funding in 2004 and was forced to dissolve.
44. Following the completion of this study of SFAF but preceding its publication, two reports were released that raised questions about the effectiveness of two of SFAF's stand-alone components. In May of 2009, researchers from Mathematica Policy Research, Inc. who conducted a randomized study of the first-year effects of supplemental reading comprehension interventions on fifth grade students reported negative, statistically significant effects for SFAF's program offering (Reading for Knowledge). SFAF president Robert Slavin questioned the findings on methodological grounds. In September of 2009, researchers from MDRC who conducted a randomized study of the effectiveness of after-school programs in reading and mathematics reported no statistically significant effects for SFAF's program offering in reading (Adventure Island). In contrast to the Mathematica study, SFAF did not dispute the findings and made the decision not to disseminate Adventure Island. For the two studies, see: Institute for Education Sciences (2009a; 2009b). For SFAF's response, see: Zehr (2009a; 2009b).
45. What Works Clearinghouse (2007).
46. Aladjem and Borman (2006:9).

47. Comprehensive School Reform Quality Center (2005:220–221).
48. See Kozol (2005c).
49. See Kozol (2005b:53;50).
50. See: Kozol (2005a; 2006); Slavin (2006).
51. Kozol (2006:626).
52. U.S. Department of Education (2008a).
53. Comprehensive School Reform Quality Center (2008).
54. New American Schools (2005a; 2005b).
55. See Viadaro (2007).
56. For example, see: U.S. Department of Education (2008b); Center on Education Policy (2008; 2009).

6

Seeing

That, then, is my story of SFAF, and its 20+ year effort to improve education for millions of at-risk students attending thousands of schools across the United States. The story is something of a rabbit hole, in that it takes us from one world to another: from an empty, hierarchical world of largely independent components to a full, complex world of interdependent parts, problems, solutions, and challenges.

In this full world, many of the things that we think we know about educational reform have changed, and many of the things that we wish were true about educational reform simply are not. This is not a world of straight, determined paths along which all march upward to the beat of adequate yearly progress. It is a world of blind curves, forked roads, dead ends, spiraling climbs, and steep falls, with possible paths from ambitions to ends yet to be discovered, explored, and paved smooth. This is not a world of research-and-development: a world in which people know and, thus, do. It is a world of development-and-research: a world in which people do and, thus, know. This is a world in which bad cops are good cops: a world in which reformers don't handcuff schools with routines and procedures but, instead, liberate them. And this is a world in which the problem is a key component of the solution: a world in which underperforming schools collaborate with program developers, researchers, policymakers, and others to develop the knowledge needed to ensure academic equity and excellence among children.

Reading about such a place is one thing; seeing it with one's own eyes is quite another. The remaining task, then, is to make more transparent the matter of seeing: that is, the matter of learning to apprehend fullness and complexity in the system of U.S. public education and in the work of improving it. I address this task in three steps: with a reprise that brings into sharper relief an analytic framework that emerges from the story of SFAF; with an argument about what the story of SFAF implies for developing new understandings of educational reform; and with thoughts on new understandings and continued learning as the basis for renewal.

REPRISE

Analytical complexity: Analytically, the complexity of SFAF's attempt at effective, large-scale, sustainable educational reform was anchored in the interdependence among the four big parts of its self-constructed system: its clients (students, teachers, and leaders in schools, districts, and states); its programs (its designs for improvement and supports for implementation); its own organization (especially its development, training, research, and executive operations); and the environments in which all operated. Each of these parts was a source of problems: undesirable states of affairs or levels of performance that required attention in order to improve student achievement. Each of these parts became targets of solutions: designs and supports for moving to more desirable states of affairs or levels of performance. And each of these solutions yielded new challenges: unanticipated outcomes that required subsequent attention. These parts, problems, solutions, and challenges did not exist independently of each other. Rather, they moved in complex, interdependent relationships.

Practical complexity: SFAF did not have perfect knowledge of these parts, problems, solutions, and challenges in advance of beginning large scale operations. Rather, SFAF produced, accumulated, and refined such knowledge largely via experience, as it engaged the practical work of effective, large-scale, sustainable educational reform. In the case of SFAF, this work included five core tasks: devising designs and supports to improve capabilities and coordination within and among clients; scaling up both the professional network of clients and SFAF as its hub organization; continuously improving designs and supports to improve effectiveness and increase scale; and sustaining the enterprise by monitoring activity within and beyond, making strategic choices about new directions and opportunities, and aligning the enterprise with those choices. Rather than independent and sequential, these functional tasks were again interdependent, their performance concurrent and confounded.

Ambitions vs. Infrastructure: Over its 20+ year history, the latter (practical complexity) drew SFAF deeper and deeper into the former (analytic complexity). This descent began with the original, fundamental ambitions of SFAF's founders: the goal of improving the academic achievement and life possibilities of at-risk students. Founders and members of SFAF viewed these students as if they were their own children: as exceptional in every way; as capable of mastering the same skills and knowledge at the same levels as all other students; and as deserving of schools capable of enabling exactly that. Yet SFAF's founders and members recognized that at-risk students arrive at school with unique sets of interdependent risk factors that complicate reaching their full potential. From that followed SFAF's first principles of professional educational practice: prevent those risk factors from manifesting themselves in low achievement; intervene early and aggressively at the first sign of problems; and relentlessly evaluate and adapt academic and non-academic services to ensure students' success. These principles were to be enacted reflectively and collaboratively by teachers and leaders, such that the practice of serving at-risk students became a context for building practical knowledge about ensuring their success.

SFAF's ambitions lead directly to a fundamental discovery: the lack of educational infrastructure in schools and their environments to support ambitions for student achievement, professional practice, and professional learning. SFAF's earliest efforts to improve the achievement of at-risk students focused on building positive interdependence between students in cooperative learning teams: in part, to improve motivation and social dynamics; and, in part, to create possibilities for teachers to assess and remediate as students worked together. Yet SFAF's founding members quickly recognized that the success of cooperative learning was greatly limited by at least two things: the availability of curriculum materials to support student collaboration; and the capabilities of teachers to enact their role in instruction. Subsequent attempts to address those matters revealed weaknesses in broader school conditions that limited the work and learning of both students and teachers. Addressing those, in turn, revealed weaknesses in broader community and district conditions, and addressing those revealed weaknesses in broader state and federal conditions.

Indeed, over its 20+ year history, at no point did SFAF identify a reliable infrastructure among institutionalized educational organizations that could support deep, coordinated change in professional practice, professional learning, and student achievement. Pockets of strength, yes; but a reliable infrastructure, no. Instead, at every turn, SFAF discovered exactly the circumstances that motivated systemic reform as a policy movement: a sort of negative interdependence, with more and more problems interacting not only to undermine learning, teaching, and leadership but, also, to undermine efforts to improve them.

Clients: The combination of high ambitions and weak infrastructure drove an evolution in SFAF's clients: the individuals that SFAF intended to serve, and the organizations in which they resided. Over its history, SFAF was crystal clear in its commitment to serve one, primary group of clients: at-risk students. With at-risk students the primary focus, SFAF gradually began to serve more and more clients in order to reach them. The client base expanded to serve more types of people: teachers, school leaders, and district and state leaders. It also expanded to serve more types of organizations: chronically underperforming schools, stronger schools, and local and state education agencies.

This expansion in clients wasn't driven only by the combination of high ambitions and weak infrastructure. It was also driven by evolving motivations and needs within SFAF: for example, its commitment to systemic solutions, large scale operations, and demonstrable effectiveness; its need to establish new revenue streams to fund its operations; its desire to secure environmental conditions supporting the effectiveness and sustainability of the enterprise; and its profound sense of agency—the simple belief that it *could* serve more (and more diverse) clients. It was further driven by a combination of stability and evolution in policy environments. This stability rested in a 40+ year federal policy agenda focused on improving education for at-risk students. This evolution mirrored that of SFAF's clients, with the federal policy focus expanding beyond chronically underperforming schools to include stronger schools, districts, and states.

Programs: SFAF's programs co-evolved in interaction with its clients, to include designs and supports for building educational infrastructure in and among schools, districts, and states. SFAF began with something historically absent in the broader system of U.S. public education: a replicable technology of instruction, anchored in research and refined through years of experience. Originally focused on K–6 reading, this technology targeted simultaneous, interdependent change in the student role, the teacher role, academic content, curriculum materials, learning tasks, assessments, sequencing, and pacing. Over time, this instructional technology was complemented by (and coordinated with) a comprehensive, schoolwide program that included designs for scheduling, instructional grouping, tutoring, supplemental services, and leadership. Classroom and schoolwide designs functioned as models for coordinated expansion into other content areas, types of schools, levels of schooling, and educational organizations.

Mindful of initially weak capabilities and initially weak infrastructure, designs for changes in the day-to-day work of students, teachers, and leaders always included coordinated resources, learning opportunities, and (with only a few important exceptions) practice-based support from trainers. Implementation was always anchored in a developmental progression from novice, consistent use to expert, adaptive use. Over its history, this developmental sequence, itself, progressed from a tacit set of understandings to an explicit, formal framework detailing levels of use of the program. This framework, in turn, was intended to shape fundamental interpretations of SFAF's programs: not as bureaucratic or technocratic interventions; but as resources supporting professional practice and learning.

Environments: As its clients and programs co-evolved, they created a complex set of interdependencies between the Success for All enterprise and its environments. At the same time that SFAF was working to build educational infrastructure in schools and their environments, U.S. educational environments were evolving on their own, and in ways intended to establish exactly that which SFAF sought to establish: robust educational infrastructure. This emerging infrastructure included policies and other institutional arrangements that set standards for student performance and that legitimized specific approaches to improvement. It included key resource endowments, including funding streams, research, technologies, and human resources. It included market functions, with policy-driven resources and incentives stimulating a supply of (and demand for) usable, effective programs. And it included proprietary and commercial activity, with a critical mass of program providers working to design and support systemic, large-scale, effective improvement programs.[1]

Two things followed. One was the need for SFAF to coordinate its efforts with this parallel infrastructure-building activity. Another was the possibility of SFAF drawing on this activity to support its own efforts. Over its history, SFAF sought to do both. Both proved problematic. One issue was the simple fact that this activity was emergent, and every bit as incoherent, fragmented, and ever-churning as the usual reform activity in institutionalized educational environments. A second issue was that, in the main, emerging resource endowments were weakly developed in relation to SFAF's resource needs, especially along three key dimensions: funding to support the development of SFAF as an organization; readily usable knowledge and technologies to support development activity; and trainers who could immediately provide expert assistance to schools. A third issue was that, even with comparative stability in the federal agenda, evolutionary changes in federal policy functioned as a source of continued turbulence throughout this parallel infrastructure-building activity, thereby exacerbating the uncertainty faced by SFAF.

Organization: Clients, programs, environments, and all of their associated interdependencies combined to have profound implications for SFAF as an organization: its size, its functional capabilities, its financial structure, its geographic distribution, its formal structure, and its social structure. While SFAF retained the culture and character of a mission-driven organization, it became much more. It became a professional development, training, and research operation. It also became a political advocate, lobbyist, and operator. Most profound were the demands that interdependencies in clients, programs, and environments placed on SFAF for constant, urgent learning and evolution. While such evolution and learning included absorbing and using new knowledge (in the form of research, technologies, and people), the amount of readily usable knowledge in SFAF's environments paled in relation to its needs. As such, the essential capability of SFAF rested in *producing* the system of knowledge needed to pursue its ambitions.

Belying its self-constructed image as a champion of research-based and research-validated reform, SFAF did not produce usable knowledge by engaging in a sequential process of research, development, and diffusion. Rather, SFAF operated as loosely structured hub of a professional network, with connections to thousands of schools, hundreds of districts, and tens of states. SFAF leveraged this professional network to engage in a set of simultaneous, distributed learning processes, all in interaction with each other, and all in collaboration with its clients. These learning processes included: actually using the program in and with schools; acquiring, pooling, and interpreting knowledge and information; formalizing and piloting promising improvements; disseminating improvements through the installed base of clients; and using research to evaluate overall program effectiveness. As these learning processes continuously churned, alone and in interaction, some of the knowledge thus produced was made explicit, both formalized and retained in materials, assessments, software, and other artifacts. Other knowledge remained tacit, and retained in the minds of individuals and in their communities of practice. Artifacts, individuals, and communities of practice, in turn, functioned as interdependent mechanisms for moving new knowledge throughout SFAF's professional network.

Indeed, SFAF's professional network functioned as a key resource, both for SFAF and for its schools: an alternative, SFAF-constructed environment, the members of which were bound both by shared commitment to improving the achievement of at-risk students and by a common, conventional program to support collaborative practice and learning. At the same time that SFAF functioned as the hub of this network, SFAF also sat outside the formal system of U.S. public education, as an independent, nonprofit foundation. Moreover, members of SFAF's professional network were not bound to it by a formal charter anchored in law. Rather, they remained card-carrying members of the formal system of U.S. public education, in voluntary relationships with SFAF and its professional network.

Working outside the formal system and at the hub of a voluntary professional network, SFAF operated at a disadvantage. SFAF worked without formal authority over (and access to) schools, districts, or states, and constantly had to work to expand and to retain membership in the network. Further, SFAF worked without the legitimacy and stable funding of institutionalized educational organizations, such as local and state education agencies. Consequently, SFAF's survival was always a focus of conscious efforts, as SFAF needed to constantly evolve in its turbid environments to secure the legitimacy, resources, and clients needed to remain viable over time.

Strengths begot weaknesses: Over SFAF's history, as clients, programs, environments, the organization, and all of their associated interdependencies moved in interaction with each other, SFAF faced a fundamental paradox: While every problem had a solution, every solution had a problem. SFAF worked diligently to recognize and to address interdependent problems among its clients, programs, environments, and organization. Doing so had SFAF cultivating many sources of strength to support its ambitions for students. Yet each source of strength also became a source of weaknesses and vulnerability.

A consequence of this "strengths-begot-weaknesses" paradox was that SFAF's attempts to match systems of problems with systems of solutions yielded systems of new challenges that greatly complicated its work. Chief among those challenges was this: The more SFAF did to support effective, large-scale, sustainable education reform, the more SFAF reproduced some of the most stubborn problems of U.S. educational reform within its own system. These problems included: misunderstandings of externally sponsored reform as either technocratic or bureaucratic (and not professional); implementation as rote and mechanical (and not flexible and adaptive); problems of program churn, fragmentation, and integration; problems of incoherence, faddism, and distrust in schools; problems of program potential exceeding support for practice; and problems of fleeting environmental support. Moreover, as it evolved, a looming problem was that the entire enterprise was becoming so sprawling and diverse as to raise questions about the possibility of its constant, urgent evolution. More than an indictment of SFAF, this is testimony to the ease and quickness with which such problems manifest themselves in educational reform initiatives, and to the resilience of such problems once manifest.

Even if clear after the fact, one overarching challenge for SFAF was that all of these problems and challenges were very hard to see or to predict in advance. Even while keeping a steady eye on the implementation literature, SFAF discovered the vast majority of them (and understood their full importance) only by engaging the work of systemic, large scale, sustainable educational reform, and by learning from that experience. A second overarching challenge for SFAF was that, even when predicted, and even when clearly recognized and addressed, these problems and challenges were very hard to avoid. Indeed, deciding *not* to act on specific problems risked entirely different systems of challenges. For example, *not* expanding the client base left classroom-level improvement initiatives vulnerable to enduring problems in schools, districts, and states that routinely undermined implementation. *Not* providing extensive support for novice users left open real risk that teachers and leaders would co-opt programs and quickly regress to past practice. *Not* collaborating with external partners to reduce the burden on SFAF meant struggling to generate the scarce capital needed to further expand the size, complexity, and capabilities of the organization. And so on. Damned if you do. Damned if you don't.

All of the preceding greatly complicated that which SFAF most sought to achieve: academic equity and excellence in children. To be sure, SFAF succeeded in compiling a body of internal and external research showing the possibility of progress towards these goals, and across a great number of schools. Even so, never mind its critics, the members of SFAF, themselves, would be the first to admit that all of their efforts still left them far short of their altruistic goal of academic success for all students.

Demands on executives: Responsibility for managing the entire lot of interdependent parts, problems, solutions, and challenges rested with SFAF's executives. SFAF's executives were not omniscient heads sitting atop a hierarchically-structured enterprise, exercising principles of rational management to guide a sequential research-and-development process by which knowledge was produced and, then, diffused to weak schools. Rather, they were the hub of the hub of a professional network: their own community of executive practice, engaged in all aspects of the day-to-day work, and learning their way through right alongside everybody else.

Even if not omniscient, SFAF's executives brought unique capabilities to their work and to the enterprise, including uncommonly strong beliefs, values, knowledge, experience, relationships, and reputations. These capabilities supported the performance of functional responsibilities that were uniquely theirs: for example, raising essential funding; structuring and managing the organization; maintaining the public face of the organization; advocating and lobbying throughout the education system; and more. Chief among their responsibilities was managing and coordinating constant, urgent, interdependent learning and evolution. This learning and evolution were distributed throughout the enterprise: among developers, trainers, teachers, and leaders, all of whom had different capabilities, different ways and rates of learning, different motivations for learning, and different opportunities to learn. Indeed, the sustainability of the enterprise depended on precisely such learning and on precisely such evolution.

One could imagine a time in the future when key improvements throughout the system of U.S. public education would interact in positively reinforcing ways to reduce the complexity and uncertainty faced by SFAF: for example, the development of robust, stable, and coordinated educational infrastructure in schools, districts, states, and federal agencies; the development of a commercial sector that included large numbers of components and programs shown by research to be effective in improving student achievement; and the development of new understandings of professionalism in education, and the roles of universities, professional associations, and external program providers in developing and improving professional practice and learning. Under such conditions, one could imagine

SFAF targeting weaknesses in student performance by working with a narrower band of more willing clients, providing more strategically focused programs, drawing heavily on its environments for critical resources, and greatly reducing the size and complexity of its organization. Freed from uncertainty and turbulence, one could imagine SFAF's executives being more able to draw on readily available knowledge of rational management and research-and-development to structure and manage the work of the organization.

But that time didn't appear to be coming any time soon. Until then, the analytic challenge continued to be that of developing understandings of the complex interdependencies among SFAF's clients, programs, environments, and organization, given SFAF's ambitions for improvement. The practical challenge continued to be that of engaging the work of large-scale educational reform as the context for devising those understandings: designing, supporting, scaling up, continuously improving, and sustaining. SFAF's primary strength continued to be its commitment to take on these challenges. SFAF's primary weakness continued to be exactly the same.

REFORM

Looking beyond SFAF, neither its ambitions nor its work appears to be unique. In the US, educational reform is ubiquitous activity. This includes populist educational reform: public discourse through which individuals, organizations, and groups form and re-form their ideas and understandings of public education. This includes professional reform: actions taken by individuals, organizations, and groups with specific responsibility for (and presumed expertise in) improving public education. Among both populist and professional reformers, more and more share the ambitions of rich intellectual engagement and high standards of success for all students. In acting on those ambitions, more and more professional reformers are engaging the practical work of systemic improvement, both in public organizations (e.g., local, regional, and state education agencies) and nonpublic organizations (e.g., comprehensive school reform providers, charter management organizations, and education management organizations).

What does the story of SFAF foretell for all of this reform activity? What do the experiences of a preeminent reformer predict for others who take up the cause of large-scale, sustainable educational reform?

My conjecture is this: The experiences of these many reformers will mirror those of SFAF. From their ambitions and their practical work will follow the analytic challenge of discerning, understanding, and managing complex interdependencies among clients, programs, sponsoring organizations, and broader environments. This, I maintain, is the reformer's condition in the full world of U.S. public education: the ability to imagine a better, future world; a willingness to work doggedly toward it; yet facing endemic complexity. The reformer's condition is the fundamental philosophical, practical, and political problem that emerges from the story of SFAF.

My confidence in this conjecture is strengthened by the observation that its premises have roots well beyond SFAF. For example, time-dependent interactions among clients, programs, environments, and sponsoring organizations run thick through longitudinal research on comprehensive school reform conducted by researchers at the Rand Corporation.[2] That the work of systemic improvement does not proceed according to conventional models of research-development-diffusion but, instead, as a set of simultaneous, interdependent functional responsibilities is among the key findings of Rand researchers in their summary of self-reports from the developers of thirteen leading large-scale reform efforts.[3] And that, in U.S. public education, systems of solutions and systems of problems continuously emerge, persist, and interact to drive a constant press for reform is what had historian Diane Ravitch describing the period of educational reform from 1945–1980 as *The Troubled Crusade*.[4]

If that, then, is the reformer's condition, the tragic flaw shared by our many reformers is this: Most fail to understand that, even with noble ambitions and dogged work, failing to see, confront, and manage endemic complexity undermines the possibility for deep, lasting reform. Perhaps the root cause is exactly as Herbert Simon said: Because the systems that reformers seek to improve are complex without being hierarchic, they escape observation and understanding.[5] Perhaps it is that we are simply not taught how to "see" complexity. From kindergarten through graduate school, the time spent learning to tease out and to confront complexity pales in comparison to the time spent learning to use rational methods to simplify and to solve problems. Perhaps it is that, for many, seeing complexity simply is not an option: for example, elected officials and appointed leaders who, by virtue of their circumstances and their own promises, must minimize complexity and demonstrate methods of rational management, all in hopes of maintaining confidence and delivering quick results.

No matter the underlying causes, failing to see complexity in U.S. public education risks deluding ourselves into thinking that the work of solving educational problems is just like the work of solving more ordinary problems: that is, amenable to conventional, rational methods of problem solving. And when the problems remain unsolved (as they have, even after a half century of educational reform), we are much quicker to deride the system of U.S. public education for not conforming to our methods of solving its problems than we are to adapt our problem solving methods to its complexity.

If our ambition is academic success for all students, then we need to reform our understanding of educational reform. Educational reformers, both populist and professional, need to see the world of U.S. public education and the work of improving it fundamentally differently. That is the moral of the story.

RENEWAL

From the moral of the story followed the purpose of the book: to help more people learn to see complexity in U.S. public education and in the work of improving it.

After all, to "see" complexity in U.S. public education is to see differently. Yet "seeing differently" is not as straightforward as taking off one pair of glasses and putting on another. Rather, people need *to learn* to see differently. People need to break down and dismantle highly developed understandings, and they need to acquire the knowledge and skill to perceive and to understand very familiar activity in very different ways. That has been the pedagogy of this book: chipping away at deeply held assumptions and understandings of hierarchy and rationality that many bring to educational reform; building, in their place, an understanding of education as a complex, nonhierarchical system, and the work of improving it as concurrent and confounded; and developing this framework of clients, programs, organizations, and environments as one device for finding deep structure amidst apparent chaos.

Reflecting on the book in light of its purpose, my expectation is not that a book that argues away silver bullets will somehow change everything. Rather, my hope is that the book will function as a catalyst for renewal: that the story of SFAF and its analytic framework will motivate and enable continued learning among communities of educational reformers, and that their continued learning will bring new vitality and richness to educational reform. Toward that end, I conclude by proposing a curriculum of sorts: a set of differentiated learning tasks for different groups of educational reformers.

For populist educational reformers, the learning task is to continue talking, with the story of SFAF serving as something substantive and meaningful to talk about. Indeed, the story of SFAF has potential to function as a shared text that can both stimulate and anchor discourse through which individuals, organizations, and groups form and re-form ideas and understandings about education and its improvement. Indeed, there is no shortage of questions to be drawn from the story that would serve as challenging grist for collective conversation, with the potential to use the framework that emerges from the story to push these conversations in new directions.

- Consider the story, in general. Given the knowledge and experiences of participants in the conversation, do the themes of "interdependence" and "complexity" resonate, or are they overstated when compared to the experiences of the group?
- Consider the case of SFAF, in particular. What might SFAF have done differently at key points in its history to reduce (rather than to exacerbate) complexity in its clients, programs, environmental relationships, and organization (alone and in interaction)? How might those decisions have affected the trajectory of the Success for All enterprise over time?
- Consider the implications. What does this framework of clients, programs, environments, and organizations imply or suggest about other, more immediate systemic reform initiatives? For example, what are the implications for local, school-level efforts to replicate an instructional practice across content areas and classrooms? For district-level and

state-level efforts to do the same across schools? Or for externally
sponsored efforts such as charter school networks, which seek to develop
systems of schools anchored in common values, practices, and structures?

For professional reformers, the learning tasks vary among researchers, policymakers, and practicing reformers. For researchers in education and in other academic fields and disciplines, one learning task is to continue investigating the
potentially historic transformation of U.S. public education: that is, this slow-but-
persistent push for systemic, rational reform, with the new egalitarian ideal of all
students mastering the same, rich academic content at the same, high standards.[6]
In taking on this task, the framework that emerges from the story of SFAF suggests advantage in integrating macro and micro perspectives. For example, it suggests advantage to describing and explaining how system-level activity is playing
out in the day-to-day work of teachers, leaders, and external change agents, and in
describing and explaining how the day-to-day work of teachers, leaders, and
external change agents feeds back onto system-level activity. Further, the framework suggests advantage in continuing to develop and to use conceptual frameworks and research methods that examine interdependent observations within
networks (rather than independent observations within hierarchies).

Another learning task for researchers is to collectively consider their possible
roles in the type of practice-based, organizationally distributed knowledge production processes that we saw in the story of SFAF. One potential role is to serve
in a capacity similar to SFAF's research organization, continuously monitoring
program implementation and effectiveness using rigorous research methods.
Another potential role is to serve in a capacity similar to SFAF's trainers, constantly engaged in field-based action research in order to engage, understand, and
evaluate context-specific implementation and adaptation. Yet another potential
role is to serve as I did, as a sort of embedded observer. Working from that vantage
point, researchers could produce comparative case studies of other systemic,
large-scale, long-term improvement initiatives. They could also conduct more
focused research on topics and issues that appear central to such efforts. Taken
chapter-by-chapter, the story of SFAF suggests candidates for more focused
research:

- Chapter 1 suggests a need to deepen understanding of professional
  practice in organizational contexts, with a particular emphasis on the
  simultaneous need for consistency (in order to establish coherence and
  coordination among professionals) and discretion (in order to respond
  to the needs of students and the expectations of environments).
- Chapter 2 suggests a need to further explore strategies for replicating
  organizational designs that feature interdependent professional practices,
  with a particular focus on the use of formal routines as mechanisms for
  retaining and transferring practical knowledge in usable form.
- Chapter 3 suggests the need to develop understanding of how to manage
  the development, support, and scale-up of systemic improvement

initiatives, with a particular focus on the co-evolution of improvement initiatives, their sponsoring organizations, and broader environmental supports.

- Chapter 4 suggests a need to conceptualize and explore alternative methods of knowledge production that have potential to yield practical knowledge at a rate much faster than scientifically based research, with a particular focus on the formal structures, social structures, and executive leadership that support distributed, collaborative learning within networks.

- Chapter 5 suggests the need to explore the role of education policy in effecting conditions that motivate and constrain system-wide improvement, with a particular focus on the sensitivity of system-wide activity to even subtle changes in federal education policy, and with a particular focus on the work of executives in interpreting those changes and adapting to them.

For policymakers seeking to contribute to this potentially historic transformation of U.S. public education, the learning task lies in devising means to manage the tension between education politics and education policy. Education politics encourages and rewards individual leaders who promise to use the tools of government to make and advance policies that will rapidly effect their particular vision of improvement. Yet both the story of SFAF and the framework that emerges from it suggest that doing so simply is not possible. In the U.S., education policymaking is complex activity that occurs at multiple loci within the system (local, regional, state, and federal) and that involves interactions among multiple actors (elected officials, political appointees, career civil servants, lobbyists, and interest groups). Both policymaking and the resulting policy play out in interaction within a broader web of activity in which schools, non-governmental agencies, and other organizations establish and act on their own agendas. Consequently, the effects of policy on research, program development, and practice are both mediated and enabled by a wide range of interdependent activities that emerges and co-evolves over long periods of time. Likewise, the effects of research on policy, program development, and practice, and the effects of practice on policy, program development, and research. Policymaking does more to occasion such dynamics than to determine them.

Thus framed, policymakers need to develop both capabilities and courage to do a number of uncommon things: for example, teach the electorate about the complexity of educational policy and reform, and about the false promise of rapid results; shift the political conversation away from short-term silver bullets and towards long-term infrastructure building; craft (and sell) a platform of incremental improvement in education policy that heeds the wisdom of existing education policies but that continues to push them smartly at the margins; devise and legitimate intermediate measures of success that are reasonable, challenging, and attainable; and build political and operational coalitions around such understandings. Above all else, there is a need for those in elected positions to take seriously the learning required of actors and organizations throughout the system to think, act, and interact in new ways, and for them to respond in kind by engaging in such learning, themselves. This could begin with a simple change in perspective: for example, by looking at the policy process not as a political battle between competing interest groups but, instead, as a collaborative learning process among communities of policymakers.

Before dismissing such propositions as naïve and far fetched, consider the New American Schools initiative. To be sure, NAS had its problems, including structuring the effort using sequential models of innovation development-and-diffusion and assuming that the participating programs could be brought to fruition in a five-to-seven-year time window. Even so, as a policymaking effort, NAS featured many of the characteristics set out immediately above: policymakers, researchers, program developers, and practicing educators engaged in a collaborative, sustained, learning-focused enterprise.

For practitioners of educational reform (i.e., those responsible for devising and enacting improvement programs), the learning task is not to mimic SFAF. To be sure, there is much in the story of SFAF to inform other educational improvement initiatives. After all, at the time of this writing, SFAF had been mapping the world of public education for 20+ years. Even so, there is much to the route that SFAF chose for itself that sets it apart as a very unique case: such distinguishing features as SFAF's state-sized professional network, its comprehensive programs, its expansive environmental relationships, and its unusual hub organization. Even though educational reformers are increasingly advancing systemic solutions to systemic problems, few work at the scope and scale of SFAF, or have the resources or ambitions to do so. While their reform efforts may be systemic by historical standards, they are likely partial by the standards of SFAF. Further, even for those with sufficient resources and lofty ambitions, retracing SFAF's steps risks encountering SFAF's challenges, obstacles, and threats, none the least of which was establishing evidence of effectiveness.

For practicing reformers, the challenge is to mind the ground gained by SFAF while seeking their own path. In doing so, one learning task is to exploit the analytic perspective that emerges from the story of SFAF, with practitioners doing explicitly what SFAF did tacitly: enacting a formal method of evaluating and re-evaluating the critical interdependencies on which such enterprises appear to rest. This method need not be complicated and overbearing. Indeed, groups of practicing reformers could gain remarkable insight on the complexity of their own reform initiatives by collaboratively brainstorming five categories of questions:

1. *Concerning ambitions and infrastructure:* What skills, knowledge, beliefs, and values do we seek to develop in students? What are the implications for practice: that is, for what teachers and leaders need to *do* and to *know* in order to cultivate those outcomes in students? What are the implications for norms: that is, for what teachers and leaders need to *believe* and to *value* in order to pursue those outcomes? In light of our ambitions and their implications, what strengths and weaknesses do we

see in the current capabilities of teachers and leaders (school, district, and state) that have potential to support and/or undermine our efforts? What strengths and weaknesses do we see in educational infrastructure with potential either to support or to undermine our efforts?

2. *Concerning clients:* Given analysis of ambitions and initial conditions, who do we select as our clients: that is, the individuals or organizations who will be the immediate focus of our improvement efforts? How can we cultivate their willingness to participate and their trust in us as partners in improvement? What candidate clients are we intentionally excluding? How might our inattention to them bear on realizing our ambitions?

3. *Concerning programs:* Given analysis of ambitions and clients, and given the obvious impossibility of addressing all of the weaknesses within and between them, what programs will we develop? That is, what designs or blueprints will we construct that map out interdependent improvements in norms, structures, technologies, knowledge, and practice within and between clients? What supports will we construct to actually build that design or blueprint in each of our clients, by way of coordinated resources (e.g., materials, tools, and routines) and learning opportunities (e.g., for direct instruction and practice-based learning)? How can we structure these supports so that they enable higher levels of performance for both novice and expert clients? Given that we can't do it all, what must we depend on clients to do on their own? In what ways does that leave our program vulnerable?

4. *Concerning environments:* How do key elements of our own environments (e.g., policies, standards for performance, funding opportunities, knowledge resources, technologies, human resources, and incentives for improvement) potentially support or undermine our ambitions, our clients, and our programs? How can we help our clients to leverage, manage, and mediate their proximal environments: that is, the people, organizations, and other external interests with which they routinely interact? How can we leverage environments to support our own work? How can we influence broader environments to support our efforts? How can we buffer and manage that which we can't influence? What can we *not* influence in broader environments, and how does that leave our clients, program, and organization vulnerable?

5. *Concerning organization:* What do analyses of ambitions, clients, programs, and environments imply for our own organization? What financial resources do we need, how will we acquire them, and how will manage uncertainty in them? What capabilities do we need to support development, training, evaluation, and other essential tasks? What combination of formal and social structures will support the pace at which we need to work, the coordination and integration of our work, our analysis of (and relationships with) broader environments, and our on-going learning and improvement? What does all of the preceding imply for the capabilities and commitments of our leadership team?

A second learning task is exploratory in nature: engaging the practical work and learning from experience, mindful of how SFAF engaged the work and of what it learned from the experience. After all, the preceding analysis is not intended to reveal a direct path to success but, instead, the complexity likely to be encountered en route. Further, no matter how comprehensive and thoughtful, any such analysis will likely yield only a partial understanding of that complexity. Neither those five categories nor the specific questions within them are exhaustive, and the answers to many of the questions may well be, simply, "We really don't know yet." Thus, the task becomes holding such an analysis as provisional, engaging the practical work, and adapting ambitions, understandings, and capabilities in light of experience. Drawing on the story of SFAF, the practical work includes a core set of tasks to be engaged simultaneously, in interaction: designing coordinated solutions; devising supports for implementation; scaling up; continuously improving to increase effectiveness; and adapting and evolving to sustain the enterprise in dynamic environments.

In engaging this work, the story of SFAF predicts a set of likely experiences. Practicing reformers can expect to experience this as time-dependent activity. The development and alignment of ambitions, understandings, and capabilities will not be immediate but, instead, emergent and evolutionary. Further, practicing reformers can expect to experience a constant draw to do more. New understandings and capabilities will interact with commitment, aspirations, and agency to drive an expansion in the enterprise. As the enterprise evolves and grows, practicing reformers can expect to experience an interplay between the informal and the formal, and between the formal and the social. Understandings and capabilities that initially existed informally, in the minds and actions of individuals, will gradually be formalized and routinized using materials, tools, and other media. This formalization will support the propagation of understanding and capabilities and, with that, the potential to incorporate more people into the work and the learning. And as understandings and capabilities improve and mature among them, practicing reformers can expect to experience parallel improvement and maturation in clients, such that clients become full partners and collaborators in the enterprise.

That is a powerful image: practicing reformers and their clients collaborating to develop the understandings and capabilities needed to solve systems of interdependent problems undermining the academic success of students. Now, imagine if practicing reformers and their clients were also working in collaboration with policymakers who were dutifully studying their efforts and, themselves, learning to collaborate to refine the policies needed to effect conditions supporting success. Imagine if researchers were dutifully studying the interdependent efforts of practicing reformers, clients, and policymakers, describing their efforts in order to raise them to the level of collective consciousness, analyzing them both empathetically and critically to identify strengths and weaknesses, and offering this combination of information and knowledge for collective reflection and use. Imagine if populist reformers had access to the efforts of professional educational reformers of all types, analyzed their joint efforts empathetically and critically, and reflected on their own ambitions for educational improvement in light of what they and others were learning about the problems and possibilities of improving student achievement.

That is the image that I want you to take from this book: an image not of educational reformers learning to hone that one, incisive innovation that slices through the complexity and changes everything; but, instead, an image of a community of educational reformers learning to see the world of education and the work of improving it fundamentally differently. That is not a portrait of educational reform as it is. Rather, that is a vision of what educational reform could be.

Notes

1. This framing draws from the concept of a "community industrial infrastructure" for innovation as described by Van de Ven, Polley, and Venkataraman (1999).
2. See Berends, Bodilly, and Kirby (2002).
3. See Glennan, Bodilly, Galegher, and Kerr (2004).
4. See Ravitch (1983).
5. See Simon (1996:207).
6. Reference to the egalitarian ideal of U.S. public schooling draws from Cusick (1983).

My Learning

While writing a conventional appendix detailing my research methods, two reviewers of early drafts of this manuscript passed along questions and suggestions that gave me pause. After reading a draft of the concluding chapter, Simona Goldin, a dear friend and colleague, asked: If "seeing complexity" is as difficult as I argue in my conclusion, then how did I learn to see it? Good question. After reading drafts of several chapters, an anonymous reviewer asked: How independent is (the author)? Why should we care about his approach and what he says? Also good questions. This second reviewer went on to suggest that such questions might best be addressed in a less-conventional appendix in which I discussed how I came to study Success for All, the challenges that I encountered in my work, and decisions that I made about issues of data collection, analysis, and interpretation. Heeding that advice, the following is a narrative account of my work on Success for All and the Success for All Foundation (SFAF).

FOUNDATIONS AND OPPORTUNITIES

As I thought about the questions posed above, I came to understand that my study and story of SFAF were informed heavily by the full range of my prior academic and professional learning. Bear with me as I do some reconstructing.

Analyzing and Designing Systems

As an undergraduate at Wayne State University in the early 1980s, I majored in computer science and minored in political science: an odd combination at the time, but one that allowed me to study both innovation and institutions (the juxtaposition of which I found fascinating). From 1981 until 1991, I worked as a programmer and a systems analyst in higher education, health care, and the automotive industries in southeastern Michigan. All of my work was on the development and maintenance of large, backbone, mainframe-based systems that supported the core operations of organizations: for example, student records, patient records, accounting, budgeting, and engineering.

While working as a systems analyst, I learned methods and lessons that informed my work on SFAF. Specifically, I learned to participate as a member of a team that examined complex activities, to talk to people about their contributions, to represent understandings back to them in the form of information systems, and to work together over time to improve those systems. I also learned about formal design methodologies as a way to structure our collaborative work, the complexity of design work, and the looseness between highly rational design methodologies and the work of design as actually performed.

This combination of academic and professional experience laid the foundation for the disposition that I adopted in learning about SFAF. As a systems analyst, I learned to be deferential toward "users," to see their work through their eyes, and to value their knowledge and perspective. I also learned that my role included questioning and challenging their understandings, as well as introducing understandings of my own for their consideration. This disposition ultimately took the form of the "strengths-as-weaknesses" dialectic described in the introduction as one means of maintaining a balanced perspective in organizational analysis. However, the seeds of this disposition were sewn from academic and professional experience years removed from my study of SFAF.

This combination of academic and professional experience also laid the foundation for my interpreting Success for All as a resource for professional practice and learning. The 1980s were a period of rapid evolution in corporate computing. At the same time that they were developing backbone systems, the organizations in which I worked were also pushing increasingly cost-permissive minicomputers and microcomputers into the user community. The aim was to combine the resources of the large, backbone systems with more flexible, user-controlled technologies for purposes of decision support and knowledge management, all closer to the actual point of service or work. Conventions in core operations, in turn, enabled widely distributed decision making and learning to feed back into the broader operations of the organization.

With that, I began to understand the fuller power of computing arising from the two working in harmony: simultaneous centralization and decentralization. I also began to understand a backbone system absent distributed computing as a partial resource, and distributed computing absent a backbone system to hold it all together as exactly the same.

Teaching High School

While working as a systems analyst, I continued to pursue my interest in political science by completing a master's degree in public policy at The University of Michigan in 1987. A required course in organizational studies and an elective course in computers-in-organizations (both taught by Professor Michael D. Cohen) introduced me to the literature on organizational studies, thus beginning a process by which I made richer sense of my work and experiences as a systems analyst.

From a career perspective, more important was that my masters work began my segue into public education. Immediately on the heels of the publication of *A Nation at Risk* in 1983, education policy was a hot topic.[1] Under the guidance of Professors Janet Weiss and John Chamberlin, it quickly became the focus of my elective coursework. Drawn by the need to experience education reform from a classroom perspective, and after much discussion with those close to me, I returned to Wayne State University for my certification as a high school mathematics and computer science teacher.

After completing my student teaching in 1991, I landed a position in a forward-thinking high school mathematics department, one that was wrestling with the curriculum and evaluation standards recently released by the National Council of Teachers of Mathematics (NCTM). Under the leadership of Valerie Mills, a very insightful chairperson, members of the department had decided to adopt a rigorous, detailed mathematics curriculum coordinated closely with the NCTM standards: the University of Chicago School Mathematics Project (UCSMP). Heeding guidance provided in the materials, the fundamental agreement was that all teachers would use the curriculum consistently, as detailed by its designers in teachers manuals and other resources.

Immediately, my experience as a systems analyst began framing my experience as a teacher. To begin, I maintained the same sympathetic-yet-critical disposition with my students as I had with my users, seeking to appreciate them and their understandings while also seeking to develop them and their understandings.

I also recognized that, when used consistently, the UCSMP curriculum functioned much as a central, backbone information system, in that it established conventional structures, resources, and language across all classrooms (e.g., for pacing, sequencing, content representation, in-class tasks, homework, and assessment). Those conventions, in turn, supported professional collaboration, decision making, and learning within the mathematics department. Because members of the mathematics department were doing the same work, using the same resources, speaking the same language, and generating the same information, we used much of our time out of the classroom to discuss substantive issues of instructional practice and student achievement. The potential power of a "backbone curriculum" was underscored when I began to collaborate regularly with Aileen Ryan, my own high school mathematics teacher in a town 30 miles away, when her department adopted the UCSMP curriculum and began using it consistently.

Throughout my experiences in information systems and in the classroom, there were times when I was frustrated by the obvious constraints of centralized, backbone systems, and there were other times when I was uncomfortable exercising discretion and looked for more detailed guidance. I saw the same frustrations in others. Still, my experiences enabled me to further understand and appreciate the possible synergy between simultaneous centralization and decentralization, and between conventions and discretion.

Pursuing the Doctorate

During my third year in the classroom, I applied to the doctoral program in educational foundations and policy in the School of Education at The University of Michigan. I was accepted, and I was awarded a fellowship funded by the Spencer Foundation that allowed me to begin studying full time in the fall of 1994. I focused my coursework on organizational studies, education reform, and education policy, with deliberate efforts to understand the influence of organization, reform, and policy on instructional and leadership practice. An education policy class with Professor David K. Cohen in the fall of 1994 proved particularly pivotal, as it had class members studying Goals 2000 and the 1994 reauthorization of the Elementary and Secondary Education Act concurrent with the Republican Revolution—a fascinating set of circumstances that drew me even deeper into federal education policy and politics.

Capitalizing on my background in computer science and mathematics, all but one of my research methods courses focused on quantitative methods, including courses in hierarchical linear modeling and structural equation modeling. However, a visit to The University of Michigan by Harvard University psychologist Jerome Bruner during my first year heightened my interest in qualitative research. The visit was in the context of a Spencer Seminar co-chaired by Professors Annemarie Palincsar and David K. Cohen. In preparation for the visit, we read a chapter from *Actual Minds, Possible Worlds* in which Bruner contrasts two modes of inquiry. I was particularly taken by the following passage:

> Let me begin by setting out my argument as baldly as possible, better to examine its basis and consequences. It is this. There are two modes of cognitive functioning, two modes of thought, each providing distinctive ways of ordering experience, of constructing reality. The two (though complementary) are irreducible to one another. Efforts to reduce one mode to the other or to ignore one at the expense of the other inevitably fail to capture the rich diversity of thought.
>
> Each of the ways of knowing, moreover, has operating principles of its own and its own criteria for well-formedness. A good story and a well-formed argument are different natural kinds. Both can be used as means of convincing another. Yet what they convince *of* is fundamentally different: arguments convince one of their truth, stories of their lifelikeness. The one verifies by eventual appeal to procedures for establishing formal and empirical proof. The other establishes not truth but verisimilitude.[2]

With that, I became keenly interested in the use of narrative in qualitative research. Early in my first year, I had the opportunity to pursue my interest. A project team lead by Professors Magdalene Lampert and Deborah Ball was developing a hypermedia system for exploring classroom practice as the basis for teachers' professional development, and I was given the opportunity to study their work. Heeding my new interest, I experimented with rendering my final report as a narrative account of professors and graduate students as they learned to engage the sort of large-scale, systems development that only a decade earlier had been the province of specially trained experts (such as systems analysts. . .!).

This experience served as my point of entre into the ideas underlying "teaching for understanding," and into challenges involved in developing and using complex resources to support teachers' professional practice and learning. It also gave me an opportunity to develop capabilities as a qualitative researcher through self-study, practice, and reflection. (Though I had taken a graduate course in philosophical issues in qualitative research, the bulk of my training and experience in field-based inquiry was as a systems analyst.) And it gave me an opportunity to practice my chops as a writer. (I had had only one writing teacher in my life, the incredible Patricia Arrick, but that was in high school.)

The Study of Instructional Improvement

In the fall of 1996, a team of graduate students (including myself) began working with three faculty members (Professors Deborah Ball, Brian Rowan, and David K. Cohen) on their efforts to design and field the Study of Instructional Improvement (SII). SII was a large-scale, longitudinal, mixed methods study of three leading comprehensive school reform programs that emerged and went to scale in the late 1980s and 1990s, and that continue large-scale operations at the time of this writing: Success for All, America's Choice, and the Accelerated Schools Project. While all three focused directly on issues of instruction and instructional improvement, each had a distinct approach, thus opening up the potential for rich comparisons among them. Organized under the Consortium for Policy Research in Education (CPRE), SII expanded to include researchers in the School of Education and the Institute for Social Research at The University of Michigan, Washington D.C.-based Policy Studies Associates, and others.

SII was composed of three complementary components. The first (a quantitative component that combined conventional surveys with innovative instructional logs) focused primarily on measuring changes in instructional practice, leadership practice, and their effects on student achievement in 115 schools (roughly 30 schools per program plus 26 matched control schools). The second (a case study component) focused primarily on program implementation in 12 schools (three schools per program plus three matched control schools). The third (another case study component) focused on understanding the three comprehensive school reform programs, their sponsoring organizations, and the evolution of the programs and organizations over time. My study of SFAF was conducted within this second case study component. Primary data collection for all three components ran from 2000–2004. For the third component, extended data collection ran into 2010.

SII began with preliminary research, sampling, instrument development, and researcher training that ran from 1996 to 2000. The earliest work was in a several-semester seminar in which project members reviewed a pool of comprehensive school reform programs being considered for participation in SII. The first program reviewed was Success for All. Among those in the seminar, the reaction to Success for All mirrored critical perspective then common in the academic community: that is, concern with its strong attention to early reading and (at the time) its comparatively weak attention to reading comprehension; aversion to its specificity; and critical questions about SFAF's internally conducted research on program effectiveness.

As minority voices in the group, Angus Mairs (an early SII team member) and I wrote a memo dated November 4, 1996—in essence, my first written analysis of Success for All. Drawing from design documents, curriculum materials, and summaries of research, and drawing on my prior training and experience in systems analysis, we made an argument paralleling my experiences with "backbone systems" both as a systems analyst and a teacher: specifically, that Success for All could be interpreted as establishing an infrastructure (especially information systems) to support coordination, decision making, and learning among teachers. Indeed, it was the synergy and tension between simultaneous centralization and decentralization that most piqued my curiosity about Success for All. In a memo dated September 14, 1997, early in the second year of our seminar, Joshua Glazer (an SII team member) and I drew on additional sources to begin developing this perspective more formally:

> While SFA does create an image of schools as rational and bureaucratic, it is interesting that, in doing so, it also creates opportunities for "professional community" to develop. By using the buy-in process to identify agreement (or at least a willingness to agree) on such things as the goals and technology of instruction and, then, designing an organization to support the given goals and technology, SFA greatly reduces the cognitive demands placed on teachers. Freed from the performance of institutional and managerial functions, teachers can concentrate on the demands of technical work. A common technology (curriculum, pedagogy, evaluation tools) enables formative evaluation by the program facilitator and perhaps even their peers in the grade level support teams. This is all speculative, of course, but it is still interesting to mull over.

After this initial analysis and some further courtship, Success for All was selected for participation in SII. At that point, responsibility for continued, preliminary research fell to several different SII team members, including Ruben Carriedo, Matthew Janger, and James Taylor. Their work was largely exploratory in nature, and focused primarily on understanding the program's "theory of action," the design for school restructuring, and the history and evolution of the organization. Between 1996 and 1999, SII team members assembled a considerable body of data: for example, a complete library of program materials; internal articles, research, and reports; external evaluations and criticism; field notes from visits to a Success for All school; notes and analyses from interviews with teachers and leaders in that school; notes and analyses from meetings with SFAF executives and staff members; and much more. (During this period, I conducted observations and interviews in schools implementing the Accelerated Schools Project.)

In September of 1998, I put a temporary stop to my doctoral studies to become a full-time researcher on SII. In April of 1999, I co-authored a paper with SII co-principal investigator Brian Rowan in which we summarized and framed the educational reform agenda of the 1990s as centered on the simultaneous improvement of schools as rational, natural, and open systems—a framework that served as the basis of my "systems interpretation" of comprehensive school reform.[3] In December of 1999, motivated in part by my continued interest in its blend of centralization and decentralization, I assumed primary responsibility for studying the design and organization of Success for All. Again, I worked in the third component of SII, with David K. Cohen as the principal investigator. My responsibilities also included drawing on what I was learning about Success for All to assist in developing surveys, observation protocols, and interview protocols for the other two components of SII.

Between January and August of 2000, I completed a comprehensive, 190 page technical report summarizing all preliminary data on Success for All collected to that point. The report was prepared in collaboration with SII researchers Karen Gates and Joshua Glazer, who were preparing parallel reports on the Accelerated Schools Project and America's Choice (respectively). In analyzing the data, six analytic categories emerged that captured key issues of design and organization across programs: theory of intervention; instructional design; support for enactment/implementation; recruiting schools; scaling up; and designing, managing, and improving the intervening organization. We identified 27 major sub-categories within these six primary categories. We used these categories and subcategories, in turn, to structure our initial evaluations.

WATCHING, ASKING, AND READING

By the end of our preliminary research, I had developed an array of theoretical understandings, research skills, and practical experiences that enabled me to engage in deep, comparative investigation of reform activity spanning instruction, leadership, organization, and policy. With colleagues, I had also developed a framework to guide continued investigation of Success for All, along with a keen sense of an issue that would eventually become a primary focus of Chapters 1 through 3 of this manuscript: that is, the potential for differing interpretations of Success for All as bureaucratic, technocratic, and professional.

Learning about the complexity of Success for All, then, required jumping into the enterprise feet-first and with eyes wide open. In 2000, I did just that. Informally, I would describe myself as learning by watching, asking, and reading. Formally, I would describe myself as learning through participant-observation, interviews, and the collection of documents and artifacts.

Participant-Observation

I began my formal study of Success for All with a very open charge: to learn as much as possible about the program and the organization over the period of SII's data collection. In the spring of 2000, I decided that I would begin by engaging as a participant-observer in the very same training events as teachers and leaders in Success for All schools, beginning with initial training prior to Year 1 implementation and continuing with the standard training for experienced schools. My hunch (which bore out) was that participant-observation in training events would be an efficient means of data collection in that it would enable me to do a number of things at once: experience and learn about the program in the same way as teachers and leaders; immediately talk to teachers and leaders about their interpretations and understandings; learn about tacit dimensions of the program not made explicit in materials; and observe the work of trainers (and immediately discuss it with them). Training events held in schools (as opposed off-site conference facilities) also provided opportunities to observe Success for All as enacted in schools and classrooms.

My participant-observation ran from May of 2000 to January of 2010, and included 30 one-to-six-day training events spread over 73 contact days. In SY 2000/2001, I attended all training for new schools, once-per-month Leadership Academy sessions, and the annual Experienced Sites Conferences. In SY 2001/2002, I attended initial training for SFAF's mathematics program, additional Leadership Academy sessions, and the Experienced Sites Conference. From SY 2002/2003–SY 2009/2010, I attended annual Experienced Sites Conferences. Up to 2007/2008, these conferences functioned as a primary venue for data collection. Thereafter, the provided opportunities to maintain observation of SFAF while completing my analysis. At two points (June of 2002 and June of 2004), I repeated the week-long initial training for school leaders to chart the ongoing evolution of the program.

In addition to the preceding, I engaged as a participant-observer in four training events for Success for All trainers, for an additional seven contact days: training for newly hired trainers prior to their first Implementation Visits (September, 2001); an area meeting for experienced trainers (June, 2002); a national meeting for experienced trainers (June, 2008); and a national meeting for trainers supporting districts and states (June, 2008). These training events provided opportunity to observe how Success for All was presented by SFAF executives and developers to the training organization, to observe the resources supporting trainers' work, and to immediately discuss with trainers their understandings of the program.

Throughout, I used consistent procedures for generating field notes. Each day of each Success for All training event is subdivided into 90–120-minute sessions. For each individual session, I took field notes by hand, and I collected all materials distributed to participants. Afterwards, I synthesized my handwritten notes and the associated materials into a session-specific field note that included standard components: the purpose of the session; background information; room layout; descriptions of trainers and participants; materials, the chronology of activities;

the content covered; and notes and observations (e.g., as related to our analytic categories, as expressed in informal conversations, as related to observations made in other sessions, and as newly emerging). For the event as a whole, I produced a cover report that summarized the session-specific field notes. Beginning in 2004, as I began observing patterns and redundancy, I stopped recording detailed notes on the chronology and content of individual sessions and, instead, included references to printed agendas and materials. At that point, my primary focus shifted to capturing what appeared to be the "news" in each session.

Two categories of events proved particularly useful: Experiences Sites Conferences and initial training for schools leaders. Experienced Sites Conferences brought together many different actors (e.g., school leaders, teachers, trainers, developers, researchers, and SFAF executives) on an annual basis. The keynote session always included something of a "state of the program" speech by SFAF Chairman Robert Slavin that provided a summary of activity in schools, the program, policy environments, and the organization. Conference programs provided detailed information about all sessions. Further, individual sessions were clearly marked as revised or new, such that repeated observations of Experienced Sites Conferences over time proved useful for tracking the evolution of program components. Finally, individual sessions became the basis for school-level training modules, thus providing insight on supplemental, school-based scaffolding for teachers and leaders. With Experienced Sites Conferences as a foundation, repeated observations of initial training for new leaders then provided evidence of the evolution the program as a whole, as developers and trainers pulled from the full range of on-going improvement activity to present an integrated, coherent version of Success for All to new schools.

Interviews

The first two years of participant-observation (from 2000 to 2002) were particularly fascinating, in that I had plunged into the Success for All enterprise amidst the enthusiasm of unprecedented scale-up (detailed in Chapter 3), the energy of the 1999–2003 development cycle (detailed in Chapter 4), and profound environmental turbulence (detailed in Chapters 3 and 4). At that point, I recognized that my work on Success for All had potential as a stand-alone study of education reform. In January of 2003, I approached Nancy Madden, SFAF's cofounder and president, with the idea of maintaining my participant-observation while, at the same time, expanding my data collection to include interviews with a broad range of SFAF staff members. I explained that the goal was to better understand the work of launching and sustaining large-scale, external improvement programs for low-performing schools in the turbulent environments of U.S. public education. Nancy was excited by the idea, and she welcomed the interviews.

In the spring of 2003, I identified an interview pool of 22 people who I had come to know or recognize through participant-observation. To gain a wide perspective, I selected interview subjects based on multiple criteria: for example, their tenure within Success for All (which ranged from the time of its founding to one year); their formal roles and responsibilities (which included executives, researchers, managers, developers, trainers, and support staff); what I knew of their informal relationships; and their potential to speak to the work of SFAF from multiple perspectives (e.g., as ex-Success for All teachers and leaders who later joined SFAF). In 2004, one interview subject left SFAF. I did not pursue a follow-up interview. Instead, I interviewed a staff member who had joined SFAF in SY 2003/2004.

I began by conducting 62 interviews in three waves: 22 in the spring of 2003; 22 in the spring of 2004; and 18 in the summer of 2005. My procedures for the first two waves differed from my procedures for the third wave. Among the first two waves, I conducted 34 interviews face to face and ten via phone. I tape recorded and transcribed 36 of the interviews. Eight interview subjects requested that I not tape record the interviews. I took handwritten notes during and immediately after each interview. I then drew on my notes to write a memo about each interview. These memos again included standard components: for example, a summary of potential coding categories and emerging themes; a summary of notes and observations; and a list of follow-up tasks. At the completion of each wave and as a segue to more formal analysis, I then summarized the interview-specific memos into a comprehensive report. For the convenience of my interview subjects and myself, I conducted the third wave of interviews via email correspondence and (when necessary) follow-up phone conversations. I documented these interviews using the email correspondence, itself, along with interview-specific and summary memos as just described.

The three waves of interviews were structured in a baseline/extend/confirm sequence. The 2003 interviews were semi-structured, with general questions in three categories: personal role/background; program developments since 2000 (and their history and motivation); and reflections on the experience of working in SFAF (including prospects for the future). The 2004 interviews were also semi-structured, and designed both to continue conversations from the 2003 interviews and to review interpretations that had emerged from them. The 2005 interviews were designed both to confirm particular points of interpretation, to review with participants any quotes that I planned to attribute to them, and to secure their consent to use the quotes in future publications.

This preceding point about the opportunity to review quotes was a condition of my informed consent procedures that was intended to protect individuals whose identities might either be easily inferred or made explicit in my writing. The procedures were devised in collaboration with The University of Michigan's Institutional Review Board and SFAF president Nancy Madden. In reviewing quotes, several interview subjects did correct my interpretations of their comments. Additionally, several corrected grammatical errors and transcription decisions (e.g., deleting utterances such as "um" and "hmmm"). Otherwise, none asked either to amend or to retract their comments. Only four of my interview respondents requested anonymity. However, in the end, I decided only to identify the SFAF executives who maintained the public face of the organization.

My concern was that identifying others might inadvertently complicate their relationships with teachers and leaders in schools, their relationships with colleagues in SFAF, and their standing in positions beyond SFAF. The cost was the lost opportunity to include biographical information that would surely have enriched the story.

Initially, I had expected my data collection (including my interviews) to end concurrent with the close of SII data collection in 2004. However, as detailed in Chapters 4 and 5, it was at precisely that time that SFAF encountered recruiting problems under No Child Left Behind and, then, requested the investigation of Reading First. As such, I elected to extend my data collection and to continue conducting interviews.

In 2005 and 2006, I conducted four phone interviews with subjects from my interview pool who had left SFAF, to understand the conditions of their departure and to hear their reflections on their experiences. However, between 2005 and 2008, my primary focus became SFAF executives, as the most critical activity at the time was in sustaining the enterprise. In this period, I met with SFAF executives twice annually: once informally, at Experienced Sites Conferences; and once formally, at SFAF's headquarters in Towson, MD. I also met with Robert Slavin and Nancy Madden once in 2007 in Ann Arbor, MI, as they attended a conference. In total, I conducted 11 additional interviews with SFAF executives, each between one and two hours long. Due to the sensitive nature of the topics under conversation, I did not record these interviews. Instead, I took notes during and after the interviews, and I produced a summary memo for each interview.

Documents and Artifacts

Building on our preliminary research on SII, I continued to collect a wide range of documents and artifacts concurrent with my participant-observation and interviewing. I developed an extensive library of program materials that provide rich historical perspective on Success for All and SFAF. The library includes three editions of the SFAF-published trade book detailing the origins of the program, the design components (including sample curriculum materials), and research on Success for All: *Every Child, Every School* (published in 1996), *One Million Children* (published in 2001), and *Two Million Children* (published in 2009). It includes five editions of the primary leadership manual, which lays out the whole program for internal use (1996, 2000, 2002, 2004, and 2006). It includes the primary manuals and associated materials for all program components at three intervals (1996, 2000, and 2004), as well as samples of materials at other time points. It includes collections of "participant training books" from Success for All training events that mark the evolution of the program over time. It includes annual conference brochures and materials catalogs, which also mark the evolution of the program. And it includes many, many other materials: for example, videos, CDs, DVDs, forms, trainers' materials, promotional literature, and much more.

Beyond program materials, I developed a separate library of documents and artifacts about Success for All and the broader environments in which it emerged and developed. The library includes research on Success for All as conducted by SFAF and by external researchers. It includes research on comprehensive school reform, as published in journals, research centers, policy shops, think tanks, and more. It includes media accounts and critiques of Success for All (along with responses from SFAF). It includes government documents: for example, testimony before congress; key pieces of legislation; committee reports; guidance and regulations; and results of investigations. And it includes much more. Collecting such documents became increasingly easy over the course of my study, as the Internet became ubiquitous, more historical and contemporary content was made available in digital form, and online search tools improved. Whether from my home office or the neighborhood coffee shop, I found myself able to instantly access a mountain of information that otherwise would have required the services of a full-time staff of research librarians.

Informal Interactions

Over my ten years of participant-observation and interviews, I participated in thousands of informal conversations with Success for All teachers, leaders, and staff members. Opportunities for such conversations were plentiful. These informal conversations functioned as opportunities to learn about the use of Success for All in schools, to learn about the work of SFAF, and to discuss my on-going analysis and interpretation of the work of SFAF. All training events were constructed intentionally to create social opportunities for participants and SFAF staff, including breakfast, snacks, lunch, and evening social gatherings. Further, training sessions themselves were designed to encourage social interaction and collaboration among participants. Finally, I had running phone and email conversations with school leaders and SFAF representatives throughout the course of my study, including leaders and representatives who left the program and the organization. I maintained records of particularly interesting informal conversations as notes and observations in my field notes. I used these notes to identify interpretations, perspectives, and concerns that I then pursued further through document analysis, as a participant-observer in training events, and through formal interviews.

Organizing the Data

In preparing our preliminary reports in 2000, my colleagues and I attempted to use qualitative analysis software to maintain and to analyze our data. While the software proved serviceable with small amounts of data, we stopped using it early during our formal data collection. The sheer volume of data, the rate at which we collected it, and its many different formats complicated the use of qualitative analysis software, as did differences in computing platforms (Windows and Macintosh), changes in operating systems over time, and changes in the qualitative analysis software over time. As such, I maintained all hardcopy and physical materials in chronologically sequenced files. I maintained all digital documents in differently named folders on my computer: for example, "Field Notes," "Interview Transcripts," "SFA Research," "External Research," "SFA Controversies," and so forth. In that I work on the Macintosh computing platform, I was able to index documents differently using aliases for files names, and, beginning in 2005, I was able to easily search the content of digitized documents using the "Spotlight" feature. As I analyzed these data, I did it very much the old fashioned way: pulling and printing documents; stacking and restacking; cutting and pasting; and marking pages and passages with different color Post-It notes and highlighters.

MAKING SENSE

My data collection strategy had the advantage of providing multiple close perspectives on very complex activity over a very long period of time. It wasn't just that I had a front row seat. I also had seats in the dug out, in the locker room, and in the press box. The disadvantage was that, between 2000 and 2010, I lived under a torrent of data that came at me so fast that, at times, it left my head spinning. Indeed, the preceding account brings artificial order to a set of experiences that, in the moment, often felt chaotic.

Thus, my seeing complexity in Success for All was not only a matter of watching, asking, and reading. Informally, it was also a matter of constantly trying to make sense of all that I was seeing, hearing, and reading. Formally, it was a matter of analyzing my data, processing my experiences, and validating my understandings, simultaneously and continuously. Extending my earliest work on SII, I did just that, collaboratively and individually, from 2000 through 2010.

Collaborative Analysis

Collaborative analysis was conducted with SII team members in the second case study component: the case study of the design and organization of the participating programs. David K. Cohen was the principal investigator. SII researcher Karen Gates was the lead analyst for the Accelerated Schools Project, Joshua Glazer was the lead analyst for America's Choice, and I was the lead analyst for Success for All. SII researchers Matthew Janger, James Taylor, and Christopher Weiss were early members of the team, though they moved on to new positions soon into our formal data collection. SII researcher Simona Goldin joined us in 2002 to complete the team.

In beginning our work together, we adopted a disposition to the organizations and programs under study that that mirrored my disposition as a systems analyst and teacher. On the one hand, my colleagues and I intentionally "went native."

We became closely involved with the organizations and programs that we were studying, and we sought to see, experience, and understand their goals, methods, successes, and failures as they did. On the other hand, we also sought to develop critical perspective on the organizations and programs, both by taking seriously the perspectives of external critics and by cultivating our own critical understandings. My framing of this disposition as a "strengths-as-weaknesses" dialectic captures the language that our team eventually used to describe this disposition.

This is not to say that sustaining a sympathetic-yet-critical disposition was either easy or natural. Quite the contrary. There was the straightforward problem of multi-mindedness: that is, concurrently developing and engaging multiple, possibly competing understandings of the three different programs and organizations. Further, we often found that it was easier to be critical of each others' work than sympathetic towards it (due, in part, to extensive graduate training in critical analysis and virtually no graduate training in sympathetic analysis). In fact, lead analysts (myself included) found ourselves having to advocate for our programs and organizations among our own (very critical) research team to ensure even-handed consideration, deep understanding, and rich comparisons.

With that as our disposition, we began our work in early 2000 as reported above: that is, with a provisional set of analytic categories and a summary report of all preliminary data. As we continued into our period of formal data collection, we initiated a process that would extend into 2010, and that would become our primary method of collaborative analysis. Specifically, we produced three individual memos (one per program) either weekly (most often) or bi-weekly (on occasion). In these memos, we continuously sorted newly collected and existing data into analytic categories. Our individual memos were then compiled into a collective memo for review by the group. Among ourselves, we described this as a process of "writing into" our analytic categories. From two to four times per month for nearly a decade, we met as a team to compare and contrast our program-specific analyses, review interpretations of data, press each other to push harder on the data, adjust our categories, and identify needs for additional data collection.

The initial intent was for our weekly memos to serve as the basis of a series of technical reports. The early-career academics among us imagined that the technical reports would serve as the basis for journal articles. However, by December of 2000, our attention turned toward using our weekly memos as the basis for a book comparing the design and organization of the Accelerated Schools Project, America's Choice, and Success for All. Our initial chapter structure drew directly from our early categories, with each chapter focused on a particular topic relevant to all three programs: for example, instructional designs; organizational designs; human resource development; managing environmental relationships; and so forth.

Thus, from the very beginning of our work together, our project team abandoned the goal of developing an array of stand-alone analyses that would lead to more targeted scholarly products in favor of a comprehensive, comparative, book-length treatment of America's Choice, the Accelerated Schools Project, and Success for All. In retrospect, when matched with the extensive resources afforded by SII, this decision was instrumental in creating both the time and the intellectual space to consider the full complexity of the phenomena under study.

As our data collection and analysis continued, our focus shifted in two directions. The first was to adapt our initial chapter structure to correspond to a set of emerging analytic themes that captured key challenges of large-scale, externally sponsored efforts to improve underperforming schools. The second (and one for which I advocated strongly) was to structure the chapters so that they provided a narrative account of activity across the three programs over time. A key outcome of our shift to an "analytically focused narrative" was the need to sequence our data and analyses chronologically. That, in turn, enabled us to compare across programs to identify overlaps and gaps in our data and analyses, which then became the focus of further data collection and analysis.

Throughout this process, our initial categories evolved into five cross-cutting themes that structure our forthcoming book: the design problem (which focuses on the challenge of designing for improvement in weak schools and complex environments); the challenge of moving externally developed models into practice; the challenge of improving implementation while working at scale; problems that arise from environmental turbulence (and the subsequent challenge of devising solutions to those problems); and the meta-problem of building coherent, instructional-focused networks of schools in the turbulent and resource-thin environments of U.S. public education.[4] Collaboratively, we also arrived at an interactive framework of schools, designs, environments, and sponsoring organizations as at the heart of these problems and challenges.

Individual Analysis

In the fall of 2002, after my first two years of participant-observation, I began a second, stand-alone analysis of Success for All that eventually led to this manuscript. The move was motivated by three things. The first was as described above: I had become convinced that Success for All was a story in-and-of itself. The second was the need recommence my doctoral studies and complete my dissertation. The third was that I had opened two lines of scholarship into the broader literature: one on the development and management of innovation; and another on "organizational replication" as a particular form of innovation. Both were motivated by ideas encountered in lectures by leading scholars sponsored by the Interdisciplinary Committee on Organizational Studies at The University of Michigan.

With the agreement and support of SII's principal investigators, this second line of analysis opened in 2003 as reported above: with me requesting and conducting interviews with SFAF staff members. As I conducted the interviews, I immediately began noticing interview subjects identifying and addressing a common set of issues, events, and problems within Success for All. No doubt due to the sequence of topics in my initial, 2003 interview protocol, I began noticing that many of the interviews had a narrative structure (i.e., personal beginning, organizational middle, and future prospects for self and organization at the end). To be sure, the interviews were not nearly so neat, and they jumped around a fair amount. Even so, the pattern was clear.

I continued by formally coding the interview transcripts. As described above, I produced an initial memo per interview at the time of each interview that captured key topics and themes. After completing all interviews for 2003, I read across the individual memos to produce an initial, summary memo. That memo included (among other things) a set of eight categories (and 44 subcategories) with which to begin coding interview transcripts: individual background and responsibilities; core principles of the program and the organization; evolution of the program; evolution of the organization; the social/informal organization of Success for All; knowledge acquisition/organizational learning; and environments. While derived inductively from the interviews, I recognized these categories more as an evolution of our initial categories from 2000 than as a new beginning.

Because we had abandoned qualitative data analysis software by this point, I adopted a self-devised method for coding the interview transcripts. For each interview, I created a new Microsoft Word document that included headings for each primary category, along with a "residual" category. With repeated readings of the transcript, I then literally cut-and-pasted the entire transcript so that all passages fell into one or more categories. Once "coded" in this way, I read within each category and re-sequenced the passages so that they read as a coherent, mini-narrative. I then wrote an introduction to each of these mini-narratives and what I thought of as "connective tissue" to stitch everything together. I was then able to read across interviews to compare accounts, identify where accounts overlapped or diverged, and begin to compile a general narrative.

Three things came of this exercise. The first was a general set of themes that cut across all of the interviews. These themes appeared to capture a great deal of the functional work of SFAF as an organization: designing, supporting, scaling up, organizing internal operations, and continuously improving. The second was recognition that different dimensions of the functional work appeared to have been particularly salient for SFAF at particular moments in its history, thus allowing me to sequence the themes chronologically. The third was my sense that I had the potential to represent what I was learning about Success for All in the form of a story. As mentioned above, I was drawn to this approach prior to encountering Success for All. My experience analyzing the 2003 interviews renewed my interest in it. This understanding and interest, in turn, led me to advocate to my research group that we adopt a similar approach (which, as described above, we did).

The five themes identified in my 2003 interviews became the focus of my follow-up interviews in 2004. My analysis of these interviews led me to expand and refine what I came to call my "functional framework": designing, elaborating, scaffolding, scaling up, continuously improving, and strategizing and adapting. My analysis of the 2004 interviews also yielded what I described at the time as a "contingency framework" that had schools, the program, and broader environments interacting in positive and negative ways to complicate the work of SFAF as the sponsoring organization. Each chapter of my dissertation (which I defended in July of 2005) focused on one of these functional themes, and each chapter examined how schools, the program, environments, and the organization interacted to complicate the work.[5] Subsequent data collection and analysis from 2005 through 2008 led me to refine the functional framework as it appears in this book: that is, designing, supporting, scaling up, continuously improving, and sustaining. Further, over this same period, changes within Success for All led me to refine the contingency framework as *clients* (i.e., schools, districts, and states), programs, environments, and the organization.

Establishing Validity

With those as my strategies for data collection and analysis, I arrived at several interpretations that gave me pause. For example, I arrived at an interpretation of SFAF that runs counter to widely held understandings of the organization as a perpetrator of bureaucratic, top-down programs. I arrived at an interpretation of Success for All that runs counter to its carefully cultivated image as a research-based program, by arguing that its evolution has been informed as much by experiential learning as by research. And I arrived at an interpretation of the work of large-scale, systemic educational reform that belies the rhetoric of rationality that surrounds it.

That my primary interpretations ran counter to widely held understandings placed a premium on establishing the validity of my analysis. But the press to establish validity went further. From the outset, I consciously drew on my training and experience as a systems analyst and a teacher in coming to understand, appreciate, and criticize SFAF and Success for All, especially their blending of simultaneous centralization and decentralization. With that, I recognized the need to ensure that my interpretations of Success for All were grounded in evidence, that others saw the possibility of interpreting this same evidence as I did, and that I represented the perspectives of those who advanced other interpretations.

Further, I recognized that my disposition toward my work would foster concerns of bias. In intentionally "going native," I developed close, personal relationships with Success for All executives, staff members, teachers, and leaders. Over the course of a decade, we came to know, understand, and appreciate each other, both professionally and personally. We shared elevators, cabs, and meals in all four corners of the United States. I cultivated these relationships both to understand and appreciate the work of these good people and to establish the trust that would allow me to air, discuss, and ultimately publish contrary understandings. Reflecting on the experience of "going native," my concern lies less in intentionally over-representing either the positive or the negative. Rather, my concern lies in the risk we run in all close relationships: that is, becoming so familiar as to look past the positive, and becoming so accepting as to look past the negative.

There were likely many more good things going on in SFAF than I report here, and many more problems, too.

Beyond my disposition as a researcher, I recognized that writing anything *at all* about Success for All (either positive or negative) risked concerns of bias. SFAF and its critics have been engaged in long and very public battles over the design of the program, the influence of the organization, the quality and independence of research, and the interpretation of findings. As is made clear in my account of Success for All, writing anything critical about the program or the organization risked a swift and direct response from SFAF's well-oiled public relations machine. At the same time, writing anything sympathetic risked charges from critics that I was doing SFAF's bidding. In intentionally taking a sympathetic stance toward Success for All, I was worried about the potential for my research to be marginalized and my integrity questioned. Indeed, the standards of evidence for a slash-and-burn, fear-and-loathing account of Success for All struck me as much, much lower than for a sympathetic account, and comparatively free of professional consequences.

With the preceding, I began to recognize a flip side to concerns about bias: that is, bias on the part of readers. Just as my personal background and experiences framed my understanding of Success for All, I began to fully appreciate that readers' backgrounds and experiences would frame their reading of my account. While readers beyond the field of education may have few preconceptions, many readers within the field of education will come to this account with highly developed interpretations of Success for All, and convinced that they already know the story. Some interpretations will be rooted in deep knowledge and experience: for example, the millions of students and tens of thousands of teachers and leaders who have co-enacted Success for All in schools. Absent careful, independent investigation, others will be rooted in cursory engagement and the flimsiest of caricatures, with Success for All pigeon-holed as bureaucratic, controlling, and bad. Still others will be somewhere in between. Indeed, there are many, many stories of SFAF and Success for All, both richly and variably informed. Mine is just one of them.

While all of the preceding may strike some as debilitating, I ultimately found it liberating. In my efforts to establish validity, I came to understand that all I could do was my best, and that the chips would fall where they may. As such, I structured my procedures for data collection and analysis to incorporate multiple means for establishing validity, with the goal of meeting personal standards for rigor and integrity. My means for establishing validity included: creating time for extended observation of the organization and phenomena under study; creating opportunities to investigate "negative cases" that did not square with emerging categories and themes; triangulating among different categories of evidence (i.e., field notes, interviews, and documents/artifacts); engaging in extended critical analyses with colleagues; triangulating among complementary analyses of Success for All, America's Choice, and the Accelerated Schools Project; and engaging in on-going member checking (formal and informal) with Success for All leaders and teachers and with SFAF staff members.

My efforts to establish validity went further. For example, my colleagues and I periodically intersected our work with work on the other two components of SII, with particular attention to comparing anecdotal reports from SFAF staff members about patterns of implementation and effects with evidence generated on SII. I invited Professor Jeffrey Mirel, a critic of comprehensive school reform, to join Professors David K. Cohen (chair), Annemarie Palincsar, and Michael D. Cohen on my dissertation committee, thus incorporating a thoughtful, caring, but passionate critic into the mix. In 2006, I began drawing from my work on Success for All to write and present seven conference papers (several in collaboration with colleagues), thus opening an avenue of criticism and feedback beyond our research team. As a professional courtesy, I solicited comments from SFAF executives on my dissertation, this manuscript, and my conference papers. To gain perspective on SFAF's interpretations of NCLB-effected environments, I interviewed an official from a state department of education and a researcher who was conducting an evaluation of state departments of education. To gain perspective on criticism of Success for All, I talked either via phone or email with three of the program's most vocal critics to inform them of my work and to affirm their views, each of whom was most gracious and most helpful: Herbert Walberg, Georgia Hedrick, and Stanley Pogrow. I engaged in extended forays into the literature to deepen my understanding of key phenomena under investigation. And I subjected my final manuscript to the evaluation and criticism of the editors and reviewers of the Oxford University Press.

Key to my efforts to establish validity was to establish the legitimacy of my disposition as researcher: that is, my commitment to examining the interdependent strengths and weaknesses of SFAF. For this, I drew confidence from my growing understanding of the Center for Positive Organizational Scholarship at The University of Michigan. While acknowledging the value of critical perspective, the Center holds that scholarship exploring the virtues, vitality, meaningfulness, and resilience of organizations is legitimate, and that richer understandings of organizations arise from careful examination of both positive and negative dynamics. While I sometimes worried that my research group and I were going it alone, it is heartening to know that there exists a worldwide community of scholars organized around this orientation to organizational analysis.

Finally, three additional efforts were particularly useful for testing the ideas developed in my analysis. The first was to begin incorporating these ideas into my teaching. My first attempt was early in my experience on SII, when I constructed internal training sessions for SII staff members who were responsible for conducting field work in Success for All schools. Later, in collaboration with Professor Melinda Mangin (a colleague at Michigan State University), I drew heavily on these ideas in designing a multi-course sequence at MSU in which masters students learn to analyze schools as complex systems operating in turbulent environments. The second was in an action research project in which Professor Gary Marx (a colleague at Eastern Michigan University) and I used my functional and contingency frameworks to structure feedback to a regional educational service agency as it worked with districts and schools on a systemic improvement effort.

The third was by actually doing the work. After joining the College of Education at Michigan State University, I assisted members of the Office of K–12 Outreach in designing and implementing the Michigan Principals Fellowship, a key component of Michigan's state system of support for chronically underperforming schools. I found the work to be most challenging, indeed.

While my data collection was extensive and my analysis careful, I am still concerned that my account does not captured the full complexity of effective, large-scale, sustainable education reform, either as a general matter or as experienced by SFAF. For example, even with extensive validation, the orderliness with which past events were represented to me (in contrast to the messiness of the current events that I observed directly) has me convinced that my account does not adequately capture disorder and complexity that likely existed during the emergence and scale up of Success for All between 1987/1988 and 1998/1999 (the beginning of my participant-observation). Further, in some cases, I subordinate what could clearly be a stand-alone domain of work to one or more of my five functional domains. The best example is my treatment of SFAF's financial operations, which I spread across the work of scaling up, continuously improving, and sustaining. Finally, as is made clear in research from the other components of SII, program implementation and effects are much more nuanced than suggested by this account. Thus, while my account provides perspective in broad strokes, there is clearly much, much more to be learned, and many other ways to learn it.

Reporting

The final component of my analysis was to leverage all of the preceding to render my account of SFAF as a narrative. In doing so, I heeded my sense of Bruner's verisimilitude. I used the work of SFAF to structure a sensible and authentic narrative. Within that narrative, I developed and probed ideas about what made the work so difficult, in specific environments, at specific points in time.

As I engaged my strategies for data collection, analysis, and validation, rendering my account as a narrative had gone beyond a matter of intellectual curiosity and analytic method. It had become a very real need. Affirming the early decision of our project team to forego technical reports in favor of a book, there was something about all that I had seen, heard, and read that required dealing with it in its entirety. With everything of interest seemingly contingent and dependent on everything else, writing a collection of independent, stand-alone analyses simply did not appear possible. That assessment became clearer as I began trying to extract parts of the story in order to develop them as conference papers and journal articles. For any given topic, the amount of necessary context and the number of relevant interdependencies challenged the conventional limits of 40 pages and 10,000 words for journal articles.

In talking to other researchers on SII, I was heartened to learn that this realization was not mine alone. In a conversation with Richard Correnti, a lead researcher on the quantitative component of SII, I learned that he, too, was struggling to tell anything less than the whole story of what he and his colleagues had learned about the complex dynamics driving changes in student achievement over time. In a later conversation with Seneca Rosenberg, an SII researcher who was leveraging her experience on SII to begin her own research, I learned that she was struggling to examine charter school networks as collections of stand-alone parts. Instead, she described herself as being drawn into a more holistic, systemic analysis—and, with that, into the challenge of explaining to people all that she was learning.

I came away from my experiences and these conversations recognizing that there is something organic and real about the advantages and challenges of analyzing education phenomena as complex systems. I also came away recognizing the challenges of reporting new knowledge in conference papers and journal articles, which require dealing with education and its improvement in targeted, focused pieces. With that, I came to the same conclusion as my project team: A book-length narrative was the only way to go.

Convergence

I continued my data collection and analysis through the first half of 2010. This included attending SFAF's Experienced Sites Conference in January of 2010 (in part so as not to miss out on any breaking news). It also included following SFAF's efforts in the summer of 2010 to secure a grant through the federal Investing in Innovation (I3) program.

Even so, I had decided before that to end my story of SFAF with the 2007/2008 school year. The timing seemed right. I felt that I had reached a point of convergence in my analysis, as did my colleagues in our collective analysis. While I always learn through my interactions with SFAF, I was finding that additional data collection and analysis were reinforcing my conceptual, analytical, and narrative work (rather than taking it in new directions). Also, as described in Chapter 5, the Success for All enterprise appeared to reach its own, momentary point of convergence and stability. Finally, with the change in presidential administrations and the pending reauthorization of No Child Left Behind, there appeared to be a moment of comparative calm before what was sure to be another storm in SFAF's turbulent environments.

As I wrapped up my data collection and analysis, I also began to transition out of my role as "embedded researcher" and into the role of "the guy who wrote that SFA book." In October of 2009, after completing a draft of this manuscript, I was invited to SFAF's headquarters to present and discuss my work with SFAF executives, developers, researchers, and staff. I did just that, in a meeting of the SFAF Operations Team and in an informal lunch with 40 SFAF staff members. In January of 2010, I was invited to present and discuss key findings from the Study of Instructional Improvement at the 2010 Experienced Sites Conference. And in June of 2010, I was invited to SFAF's Experienced Trainers Institute to present and discuss my work with members of SFAF's training organization.

As I engaged these opportunities, I realized that the tables had turned. I was doing all the talking, and other folks were scribbling furiously and asking questions. That is when I realized that I had transitioned from learner to teacher. The realization had begun creeping up on me in 2006, when I left SII as a full time researcher to accept a faculty position at Eastern Michigan University. I could feel it breathing down my neck in 2007, as I moved from there to Michigan State University. With my experiences through late 2009 and the first half of 2010, and with the opportunity in early 2011 to return to The University of Michigan as a faculty member, it became clear that the transition was complete.

REFLECTION

I hope that the preceding functions not only as a serviceable account of my research methods but, also, as a serviceable response to the questions posed at the outset. Looking back, I realize that I learned to "see complexity" in public education through extensive academic and professional learning in several different fields under the guidance of brilliant teachers, by using multiple strategies to generate a huge amount of data about a thoughtful and sprawling program, by enacting these strategies over a long and interesting period of time, by hanging out with groups of really smart people who helped me make sense of it all, and by trusting my gut feeling that I needed to deal with all of this in its entirety (and not in its parts). I hope that this account also functions as a serviceable answer as to why somebody might care about what I have to say.

Finally, I hope that the preceding account makes clear that my story of SFAF, even though independent, is anything but objective. It is one man's subjective account of exceedingly complex activity, studied and analyzed to the best of his ability given who he is as a person, his knowledge and capabilities, and the resources and opportunities available to him.

Notes

1. National Commission on Excellence in Education (1983).
2. Bruner (1986:11).
3. Peurach and Rowan (1999).
4. See Cohen, Gates, Glazer, Goldin, and Peurach (in press).
5. Peurach (2005).

BIBLIOGRAPHY

Adler, P. S. & Borys, B. (1996). Two types of bureaucracy: Enabling and coercive. *Administrative Science Quarterly, 41 (1)*, 61–89.

Aladjem, D. K. & Borman, K. M. (2006). *Summary of findings from the national longitudinal evaluation of comprehensive school reform.* Paper presented at the Annual Meeting of the American Educational Research Association, San Francisco, CA (April, 2006).

Aldrich, H. (1999). *Organizations evolving.* Thousand Oaks, CA: Sage.

Allen, J. D., Halbreich, R., Kozolvsky, J. D., Morgan, R. D., Payton, F. R., & Rolewski, M. T. (1999). *Quality leadership for SFA schools: Suggestions for school leaders.* Towson, MD: Success for All Foundation.

Allington, R. L. (ed.) (2002). *Big brother and the national reading curriculum: How ideology trumped evidence.* Portsmouth, NH: Heinemann.

Allington, R. L. & Johnston, P. (1989). Coordination, collaboration, and consistency: The design of compensatory and special education interventions. In R. E. Slavin, N. L. Karweit, & N. A. Madden (Eds.). *Effective programs for students at risk* (pp. 320–354). Boston: Allyn and Bacon.

Argyris, C. & Schön, D. (1974). *Theory in practice: Increasing professional effectiveness.* San Francisco: Jossey-Bass.

Argyris, C. & Schön, D. (1978). *Organizational learning: A theory of action perspective.* Reading, Mass: Addison Wesley.

Barr, R. & Dreeben, R. (1983). *How schools work.* Chicago, IL: University of Chicago Press.

Barr, R. & Sadow, M. W. (1989). Influence of basal programs on fourth-grade reading instruction. *Reading Research Quarterly, 24 (1)*, 44–71.

Berends, M., Bodilly, S. J., & Kirby, S. N. (2002). *Facing the challenges of whole school reform: New American Schools after a decade.* Santa Monica, CA: Rand Corporation.

Berman, P. & McLaughlin, M. W. (1975). *Federal programs supporting educational change* (Vol. 4): *The findings in review.* Santa Monica, CA: Rand.

Berman, P. & McLaughlin, M. W. (1978). *Federal programs supporting educational change (Vol. 8).* Santa Monica, CA: Rand Corporation.

Bidwell, C. (1965). The school as a formal organization. In J. G. March (Ed.), *Handbook of research on organizations*, pp. 972–1019. New York: Rand McNally.

Bodilly, S. J. (1996). *Lessons from New American Schools Development Corporation's demonstration phase: Prospects for bringing designs to multiple schools.* Santa Monica, CA: RAND.

Bodilly, S. J. (1998). *Lessons from New American Schools' scale-up phase: Prospects for bringing designs to multiple schools*. Santa Monica, CA: RAND.

Bodilly, S. J., Purnell, S., Ramsey, S., & Smith, C. (1995). *Designing New American Schools: Baseline observations on nine design teams*. Santa Monica, CA: RAND.

Borman, G. D. & D'Agostino, J. V. (1996). Title I and student achievement: A meta-analysis of federal evaluation results. *Educational Evaluation and Policy Analysis, 18 (4)*, 309–326.

Borman, G. D. & Hewes, G. (2002). Long-term effects and cost-effectiveness of Success for All. *Educational Evaluation and Policy Analysis, 24 (4)*, 243–266.

Borman, G. D., Hewes, G. M., Overman, L. T., & Brown, S. (2003). Comprehensive school reform and achievement: A meta-analysis. *Review of Educational Research, 73 (2)*, 125–230.

Borman, G., Slavin, R. E., Cheung, A., Chamberlain, A., Madden, N. A., & Chambers, B. (2005a). Success for All: First year results from the national randomized field trial. *Educational Evaluation and Policy Analysis, 27 (1)*, 1–22.

Borman, G., Slavin, R. E., Cheung, A., Chamberlain, A., Madden, N. A., & Chambers, B. (2005b). The national randomized field trial of Success for All: Second-year outcomes. *American Educational Research Journal, 42 (4)*, 673–696.

Borman, G., Slavin, R. E., Cheung, A., Chamberlain, A., Madden, N. A., & Chambers, B. (2007). Final reading outcomes of the national randomized field trial of Success for All. *American Educational Research Journal, 44 (3)*, 701–731.

Borman, G. D., Stringfield, S. C., & Slavin, R. E. (eds.). (2001). *Title I: Compensatory education and the crossroads (sociocultural, political, and historical studies in education)*. Mahwah, NJ: Lawrence Erlbaum Associates.

Bracey, G. W. (2000). Backtalk: A new award. *Phi Delta Kappan, 81 (5)*, 416.

Bracey, G. W. (2005). *No Child Left Behind: Where does the money go?* Tempe, AZ: Arizona State University, Educational Policy Research Unit.

Bradach, J. L. (2003). Going to scale: The challenge of replicating social programs. *Stanford Social Innovation Review, Spring 2003*, 19–25.

Bridges, E. M. (1982). Research on the school administrator: The state of the art 1967–1980. *Educational Administration Quarterly, 18*, 12–33.

Brophy, J. E. & Good, T. L. (1974). *Teacher-student relationships: Causes and consequences*. New York: Holt, Rinehart & Winston.

Brown, S. L. & Eisenhardt, K. M. (1998). *Competing on the edge: Strategy as structured chaos*. Boston, MA: Harvard Business School Press.

Bruner, J. (1986). *Actual minds, possible worlds*. Cambridge, MA: Harvard University Press.

Burnett, G. (1993). Chapter 1 schoolwide projects: Advantages and limitations. *ERIC/ CUE Digest*, Number 92. Retrieved June 30, 2005, from http://www.ericdigests. org/1994/chapter.htm.

Calderon, M. (1984). *Training bilingual teachers: An ethnographic study of coaching and its impact on the transfer of training*. Unpublished doctoral dissertation. San Diego, CA: San Diego State University.

Camburn, E., Rowan, B., & Taylor, J. T. (2003). Distributed leadership in schools: The case of elementary schools adopting comprehensive school reform models. *Educational Evaluation and Policy Analysis, 25 (4)*, 347–373.

Canady, R. L. (1988). A cure for fragmented schedules in elementary schools. *Educational Leadership, 46 (2)*, 65–67.

Canady, R. L. & Rettig, M. D. (2000). Block scheduling: What we have learned. In W. G. Wraga & P. S. Hlebowitsh (Eds.), *Research review for school leaders* (pp. 347–374). Mahwah, NJ: Lawrence Erlbaum Associates.

Carnegie Forum on Education and the Economy. (1986). *A nation prepared: Teachers for the 21st century.* Washington, DC: The Task Force on Teaching as a Profession.

Center for Data Driven Reform in Education. (2007a). *Gremlin Card.* Retrieved December 22, 2007, from http://www.cddre.org/Resources/GremlinCard.pdf.

Center for Data Driven Reform in Education. (2007b). *The Center for Data Driven Reform in Education.* Retrieved October 1, 2007, from http://www.cddre.org.

Center for Data Driven Reform in Education. (2007c). *The Data-Driven District (3D).* Retrieved October 1, 2007 from http://www.cddre.org/Mission.cfm.

Center for Data Driven Reform in Education. (2008a). *Achievement Planning.* Retrieved October 21, 2008 from http://www.cddre.org/achievement/achievement.html.

Center for Data Driven Reform in Education. (2008b). *Current CDDRE Research.* Retrieved August 1, 2008, from http://www.cddre.org/research/research.html.

Center on Education Policy. (2005). *Ensuring academic rigor or inducing rigor mortis: Issues to watch in reading first.* Washington, DC: Center on Education Policy.

Center on Education Policy. (2008). *Has student achievement increased since 2002? State test score trends through 2006–07.* Washington, DC: Center on Education Policy.

Center on Education Policy. (2009). *Improving low-performing schools: Lessons from five years of studying school restructuring under No Child Left Behind.* Washington, DC: Center on Education Policy.

Center for Research and Reform in Education. (2008a). *Center for Research and Reform.* Retrieved October 22, 2008 from http://education.jhu.edu/crre/.

Center for Research and Reform in Education. (2008b). *Projects and research.* Retrieved October 22, 2008 from http://education.jhu.edu/crre/projects/.

Chambers, B., Abrami, P. C., Tucker, B. J., Slavin, R. E., Madden, N. A., Cheung, A., et al. (2005). Computer assisted tutoring in Success for All: Reading outcomes for first graders. *Journal of Research on Educational Effectiveness, 1 (2),* 120–137.

Chambers, B., Cheung, A., Madden, N., Slavin, R. E., & Gifford, R. (2006). Achievement effects of embedded multimedia in a Success for All reading program. *Journal of Educational Psychology, 98 (1),* 232–237.

Cheung, A. & Slavin, R. E. (2005). Effective reading programs for English language learners and other language minority students. *Bilingual Research Journal, 29 (2),* 241–267.

Coalition for Evidence-Based Policy. (2008). *Initial results: Congressionally reviewed initiative to identify social programs backed by top-tier evidence.* Retrieved December 8, 2008 from http://ceg.files.cms-plus.com/Evidence/Announcement%20of%20results %2012.3.08.pdf.

Cohen, D. K. (1985). Origins. In A. G. Powell, E. Farrar, & D. K. Cohen, *The shopping mall high school: Winners and losers in the educational marketplace* (pp. 223–308). Boston: Houghton Mifflin Company.

Cohen, D. K. & Ball, D. L. (2007). Educational innovation and the problem of scale. In B. Schneider & S. K. McDonald (Eds.), *Scale-up in education: Ideas in principle* (pp. 19–36). Lanham, MD: Rowman and Littlefield Publishers, Inc.

Cohen, D. K. & Barnes, C. A. (1993). Conclusion: A new pedagogy for policy? In D. K. Cohen, M. W. McLaughlin, & J. E. Talbert (Eds.), *Teaching for understanding: Challenges for policy and practice* (pp. 240–275). San Francisco: Jossey-Bass.

Cohen, D. K. & Spillane, J. P. (1991). Policy and practice: The relations between governance and instruction. In S. H. Fuhrman (Ed.), *Designing coherent education policy: Improving the system* (pp. 35–95). San Francisco: Jossey-Bass.

Cohen, D.K., Gates, K., Glazer, J.L., Goldin, S., and Peurach, D.J. (In press). *Improvement by design.* Chicago, IL: University of Chicago Press.

Cohen, J. (1988). *Statistical power analysis for the behavioral sciences* (2nd ed.). Hillsdale, NJ: Erlbaum.

Cohen, W. M. & Levinthal, D. A. (1990). Absorptive capacity: A new perspective on learning and innovation. *Administrative Science Quarterly, 35,* 128–152.

Coleman, J. S., Campbell, E. Q., Hobson, C. J., McPartland, F., Mood, A. M., Weinfeld, F. D., et al. (1966). *Equality of educational opportunity.* Washington, DC: U.S. Government Printing Office.

Comprehensive Center—Region VI. (2005). *CSRD road map.* Retrieved June 30, 2005 from http://ccvi.wceruw.org/ccvi/csrdroadmap/ResrcReformModels.asp.

Comprehensive School Reform Quality Center. (2005). *CSRQ Center report on elementary school comprehensive school reform models.* Washington, DC: American Institutes for Research.

Comprehensive School Reform Quality Center. (2008). *About this site.* Retrieved July 7, 2008 from http://www.csrq.org/default.asp.

Conley, S. & Levinson, R. (1993). Teacher work redesign and job satisfaction. *Education Administration Quarterly, 29,* 453–478.

Correnti, R. (2007). An empirical investigation of professional development effects on literacy instruction using daily logs. *Educational Evaluation and Policy Analysis, 29 (4),* 262–295.

Correnti, R. & Rowan, B. (2007). Opening up the black box: Literacy instruction in schools participating in three comprehensive school reform programs. *American Educational Research Journal, 44,* 298–338.

Council of Great City Schools. (2003). Urban school superintendents: Characteristics, tenure, and salary. *Urban Indicator, 7 (1),* 108.

Cuban, L. (1992). *The managerial imperative and the practice of leadership in schools.* Albany, NY: State University of New York Press.

Cuban, L. (1993). *How teachers taught: Constancy and change in American classrooms, 1880–1990 (2nd ed.).* New York: Teachers College Press.

Cusick, P. A. (1983). *The egalitarian ideal and the American high school: Studies of three schools.* New York: Longman.

Darling-Hammond, L. & Snyder, J. (1992). Curriculum studies and traditions of inquiry: The scientific tradition. In P.W. Jackson (Ed.), *Handbook of research on curriculum* (pp. 41–77). New York: MacMillan.

Darling-Hammond, L. & Sykes, G. (1999). *Teaching as the learning profession: Handbook of policy and practice.* San Francisco: Jossey-Bass.

Datnow, A. (2000). Power and politics in the adoption of school reform models. *Educational Evaluation and Policy Analysis, Vol. 22, No. 4,* 357–374.

Datnow, A. & Castellano, M. (2000). Teachers' responses to Success for All: How beliefs, experiences, and adaptations shape implementation. *American Educational Research Journal, 37 (3),* 775–799.

Datnow, A. & Park, V. (2009). Towards the co-construction of educational policy: Large-scale reform in an era of complexity. In D. Plank, B. Schneider, & G. Sykes (Eds.), *Handbook of Education Policy Research* (pp. 348–361). New York: Routledge Publishers.

Datnow, A. & Stringfield, S. (2000). Working together for reliable school reform. *Journal of Education for Students Placed at Risk, 5(1)*, 183–204.

Desimone, L. (2002). How can comprehensive school reform models be implemented? *Review of Educational Research, 72 (3)*, 433–480.

Donmoyer, R., Imber, M. & Scheurich, J. J. (Eds.). (1995). *The knowledge base in educational administration: Multiple perspectives*. Albany, NY: State University of New York Press.

Dow, P. B. (1991). *Schoolhouse politics: Lessons from the Sputnik era*. Cambridge, MA: Harvard University Press.

Durkin, D. (1979). What classroom observations reveal about reading comprehension. *Reading Research Quarterly 14 (3)*, 481–533.

Edmonds, R. (1979). Effective schools for the urban poor. *Educational Leadership, 37 (1)*, 15–24.

Elmore, R. F. (1979–80). Backward mapping: Implementation research and policy decisions. *Political Science Quarterly, 94*, 601–616.

Elmore, R. F. (1990). Introduction: On changing the structure of public schools. In R. F. Elmore and Associations, *Restructuring schools: The next generation of educational reform* (pp. 1–28). San Francisco: Jossey-Bass.

Elmore, R. F., Peterson, P. L., & McCarthey, S. J. (1996). *Restructuring in the classroom*. San Francisco: Jossey-Bass.

Erickson, D. A. (1979). Research on educational administration: The state of the art. *Educational Researcher, 8*, 9–14.

Erlichson, B. A. & Goertz, M. E. (2002). Whole school reform and school-based budgeting: Three years of implementation in New Jersey. In C. Roellke & J. K. Rice (Eds.), *Fiscal ssues in urban schools*. Greenwich, CT: Information Age Publishing.

Evers, C. W. & Lakomski, G. (1991). *Knowing educational administration: Contemporary methodological controversies in educational research*. Oxford: Pergamon Press.

Fashola, O. S. & Slavin, R. E. (1998). Schoolwide reform models: What works? *Phi Delta Kappan, 79 (5)*, 370–379.

Feldman, M. S. & Pentland, B. T. (2003). Reconceptualizing organizational routines as a source of flexibility and change. *Administrative Science Quarterly, 48*, 94–118.

Firestone, W. A. & Corbett, H. D. (1988). Planned educational change. In N. J. Boyan (Ed.), *Handbook of research on educational administration* (pp. 321–340). New York: Longman.

Garan, E. M. (2002). *Resisting reading mandates: How to triumph with the truth*. Portsmouth, NH: Heinemann.

Garan, E. M. (2004). *In defense of our children: When politics, profit, and education collide*. Portsmouth, NH: Heinemann.

Gibbons, M., Limonges, C., Nowotny, H., Schwartzman, S., Scott, P., & Trow, M. (1994). *The new production of knowledge: The dynamics of science and research in contemporary societies*. Thousand Oaks, CA: Sage.

Glennan, T. K., Jr., Bodilly, S. J., Galegher, J. R., & Kerr, K. A. (Eds.) (2004). *Expanding the reach of educational reforms: Perspectives from leaders in the scale-up of educational interventions* (pp. 647–685). Santa Monica, CA: Rand.

Goertz, M. E. (2001). *The federal role in defining "adequate yearly progress:" The flexibility/accountability trade-off*. Philadelphia, PA: Consortium for Policy Research in Education, University of Pennsylvania.

Good, T. L. (1987). Two decades of research on teacher expectations: Findings and future directions. *Journal of Teacher Education, 38 (4)*, 32–47.

Greenfield, T. B. (1986). The decline and fall of science in educational administration. *Interchange, 17*, 57–80.

Griffiths, D. E. (1979). Intellectual turmoil in educational administration. *Educational Administration Quarterly, 15*, 43–65.

Guin, K. (2004). Chronic teacher turnover in urban elementary schools. *Education Policy Analysis Archives, 12(42)*. Retrieved August 1, 2009 from http://epaa.asu.edu/epaa/v12n42/.

Hale, S. V. H. (2000). *Comprehensive school reform: Research-based strategies to achieve high standards. A guidebook on school-wide improvement.* San Francisco, CA: WestEd.

Hart, A. W. (1990). Impacts of the school social unit on teacher authority during work redesign. *American Education Research Journal, 27*, 503–532.

Haxby, B., Lasaga-Flister, M., Madden, N. A., Slavin, R. E., & Dolan, L. J. (1995). *Family support manual for Success for All/Roots and Wings.* Baltimore, MD: Johns Hopkins University, Center for Research on the Education of Students Placed at Risk.

Haxby, B., Lasaga-Flister, M., Madden, N. A., & Slavin, R. E. (1999). *Success for All: Family Support Manual.* Towson, MD: Success for All Foundation.

Heartland Institute. (2009). *Welcome to the Heartland Institute.* Retrieved December 1, 2009 from http://www.heartland.org/about/.

Hedrick, G. (2000). *A veteran teacher looks at "Success for All"—SFA.* Retrieved June 15, 2009 from http://teachers.net/gazette/NOV00/hedrick.html.

Herdman, P. A. (2002). *Unraveling the basic bargain: A study of charter school accountability in Massachusetts and Texas.* Paper presented at the Annual Meeting of the American Educational Research Association, New Orleans, LA (April, 2002).

Herman, R. (1999). *An educator's guide to schoolwide reform.* Arlington, VA: Educational Research Service.

Herszenhorn, D. M. (2007, April 27). *Klein specifies restructuring of city schools.* Retrieved June 1, 2007 from http://www.nytimes.com/2007/04/17/nyregion/17schools.html.

Hess, F. M. (1999). *Spinning wheels: The politics of urban school reform.* Washington, D.C.: The Brookings Institution.

Hobbie, K. (2001). *Leave no child behind.* Retrieved August 1, 2009 from http://www.reed.edu/reed_magazine/Feb2001/index.html.

Holmes Group. (1986). *Tomorrow's teachers: A report of the Holmes Group.* East Lansing, MI: The Holmes Group, Inc.

Hord, S. M., Rutherford, W. L., Huling-Austin, L., & Hall, G. (1987). *Taking charge of change.* Alexandria, VA: Association for Curriculum and Development.

Hoy, W. K. (1982). Recent developments in theory and research in educational administration. *Educational Administration Quarterly, 18*, 1–11.

Huberman, M. (1993). The model of the independent artisan in teachers' professional relations. In J. W. Little & M. W. McLaughlin (Eds.), *Teachers' work: Individuals, colleagues, and contexts,* (pp. 11–50). New York, NY: Teachers College Press.

Institute for Education Sciences. (2009a). *Effectiveness of selected supplemental reading comprehension interventions: Impacts on a first cohort of fifth-grade students.* Washington, DC: Institute for Education Sciences.

Institute for Education Sciences. (2009b). *The evaluation of enhanced academic instruction in after-school programs.* Washington, DC: Institute for Education Sciences.

Institute for Effective Education. (2008a). *About the Institute.* Retrieved October 22, 2008 from http://www.york.ac.uk/iee/about.htm.

Institute for Effective Education. (2008b). *Welcome to the Institute for Effective Education.* Retrieved October 22, 2008 from http://www.york.ac.uk/iee/.

Jones, E. M., Gottfredson, G. D., & Gottfredson, D. C. (1997). Success for some: An evaluation of the Success for All program. *Evaluation Review, 21 (6),* 643–670.

Joyce, B. R. (1999). The great literacy problem and Success for All. *Phi Delta Kappan, 81 (2),* 129–131.

Joyce, B., Hersh, R., & McKibbin, M. (1983). *The structure of school improvement.* New York: Longman.

Joyce, B. & Showers, B. (1995). *Student achievement through staff development.* New York: Longman.

Katz, M. B. (1992). Chicago school reform as history. *Teachers College Record, 94,* 1–17.

Kearns, D. T. & Anderson, J. L. (1996). Sharing the vision: Creating New American Schools. In S. Stringfield, S. Ross, & L. Smith (Eds.), *Bold plans for school restructuring: The New American Schools designs* (pp. 1–23). Mahwah, New Jersey: Lawrence Erlbaum Associates.

Kearns, D. T. & Harvey, J. (2000). *A legacy of learning.* Washington, DC: Brookings Institution Press.

Kominski, R., Jamieson, A., & Martinez, G. (2001). *At risk conditions of U.S. school-aged children: Working paper series No. 52.* Washington, D.C.: U.S Bureau of the Census.

Kozol, J. (2005a). Confections of apartheid. *Phi Delta Kappan, 87 (4),* 265.

Kozol, J. (2005b, September). Still separate, still unequal: America's educational apartheid. *Harpers Magazine, 311 (1864),* 41–54.

Kozol, J. (2005c). *The shame of the nation: The restoration of apartheid schooling in America.* New York: Crown Publishers.

Kozol, J. (2006). Success for All: Trying to make an end run around inequality and segregation. *Phi Delta Kappan, 87 (8),* 624–626.

Larson, M. S. (1977). *The rise of professionalism: A sociological analysis.* Berkeley, CA: University of California Press.

Latour, B., 1986: Visualization and cognition: Thinking with eyes and hands. In H. Kuklick & Long, E. (Eds.), *Knowledge and society. Studies in the sociology of culture past and present, 6,* 1–40.

Lave, J. & Wenger, E. (1991). *Situated learning: Legitimate peripheral participation.* Cambridge: Cambridge University Press.

Lemann, N. (1998, November). *"Ready? READ!"* Retrieved on February 1, 2008, from http://www.theatlantic.com/issues/98nov/read.htm.

Lewin, R. (1999). *Complexity: Life at the edge of chaos.* Chicago, IL: University of Chicago Press.

Lindblom, C. E. (1959). The science of "muddling through." *Public Administration Review, 39,* 79–88.

Little, J. W. (1990). The persistence of privacy: Autonomy and initiative in teachers' professional relations. *Teachers College Record, 91,* 509–536.

Livingston, M., Cummings, N., & Madden, N. (1996). *Success for All facilitator's manual.* Baltimore, MD: Johns Hopkins University, Center for Research on the Education of Students Placed at Risk.

Lortie, D. C. (1975). *Schoolteacher: A sociological study.* Chicago: The University of Chicago Press.

Madden, N. A. (1996). *Reading Roots: Teacher's manual.* (1998 Edition). Baltimore, MD: Johns Hopkins University, Center for Research on the Education of Students Placed at Risk.

Madden, N. A. (1999). *Reading Roots: Teacher's manual.* Towson, MD: Success for All Foundation.

Madden, N. A., Slavin, R. E., Farnish, A. M., Livingston, M. A., & Calderon, M. (1999). *Reading Wings: Teacher's manual.* Towson, MD: Success for All Foundation.

Madden, N. A., Wasik, B. A., & French, M. (2000). *Success for All: Tutoring manual.* Towson, MD: Success for All Foundation.

Manzo, K. K. (2004, February 4). Reading programs bear similarities across states. *Education Week, 23 (21),* p. 1, 13.

Manzo, K. K. (2005a, June 22). Complaint filed against reading initiative: Success for All officials request investigation of federal program. *Education Week, 24 (41),* p. 3.

Manzo, K. K. (2005b, September 7). States pressured to refashion Reading First grant designs. *Education Week, 25 (2),* pp. 1, 24–25.

Manzo, K. K. (2007, April 25). "Reading First" information sent to Justice Department. *Education Week, 26 (34),* p. 26.

Manzo, K. K. & Washington, E. W. (2002, May 1). States unclear about ESEA rules about reading. *Education Week, 21 (33),* p. 1, 26.

March, J. G. (1996). Exploration and exploitation in organizational learning. In M. D. Cohen & L. S. Sproull (Eds.), *Organizational learning* (pp. 101–123). Thousand Oaks, CA: Sage Publications. (Reprinted from Organization Science, 2 (1), February, 1991).

Mathews, J. (2002, July 21). Success for some. The Washington Post, p. W30.

McCorduck, P. (2007). *The edge of chaos.* Sante Fe, NM: Sunstone Press.

McLaughlin, M. W. (1976). Implementation as mutual adaptation: Change in classroom organization. *Teachers College Record, 77,* 339–351.

McLaughlin, M. W. (1990). The Rand Change Agent Study revised: Macro perspectives and micro realities. *Educational Research, 19 (9),* 11–16.

McLaughlin, M. W. (1991). The Rand Change Agent Study: Ten years later. In A.R. Odden (Ed). *Education Policy Implementation* (pp. 143–155). Albany, NY: SUNY Press.

McClure, P. (2005). *School improvement under No Child Left Behind.* Washington, DC: Center for American Progress.

Meier, D. & Wood, G. (Eds.). (2004). *Many children left behind: How the No Child Left Behind Act is damaging our children and our schools.* Boston, MA: Beacon Press.

Meyer, J. W. & Rowan, B. (1983). The structure of educational organizations. In J. W. Meyer & W. R. Scott (Eds.), *Organizational environments: Ritual and rationality* (pp. 71–98). Beverly Hills, CA: Sage Publications. (Reprinted from Environments and Organizations, pp. 78–109, by Marshall W. Meyer (Ed.), 1978, Jossey-Bass, Inc.)

Meyer, J. W., Scott, R. W., & Deal, T. E. (1983). Institutional and technical sources of organizational structure: Explaining the structure of educational organizations. In J. W. Meyer & W. R. Scott (Eds.), *Organizational environments: Ritual and rational-ity* (pp. 45–70). Beverly Hills, CA: Sage Publications. (Reprinted from Environments and Organizations, pp. 151–178, by H.D. Stein (Ed.), 1981, Philadelphia: Temple University Press.)

Millot, M. D (2006, December 20). "Reading First-Gate": A predictable failure of public education's market transition. *Education Week, 26 (16),* 30.

Mirel, J. (2001). *The evolution of New American Schools: From revolution to mainstream.* Washington, DC: Thomas B. Fordham Foundation.

Mirel, J. (2002). Unrequited promise: Tracing the evolution of New American Schools, from feisty upstart to bulwark of the education establishment. *Education Next, 2 (2),* 64–72.

Miskel, C. & Song, M. (2004). Passing Reading First: Prominence and processes in an elite policy network. *Educational Evaluation and Policy Analysis, 26 (2),* 89–109.

Moskowitz, J., Stullich, S., & Deng, B. (1993). *Targeting, formula, and resource allocation issues: Focusing federal funds where the needs are greatest.* Washington, DC: U.S. Department of Education.

Murphy, J. (1988). Methodological, measurement, and conceptual problems in the study of instructional leadership. *Educational Evaluation and Policy Analysis, 10,* 117–139.

Murphy, J. & Datnow, A. (2003). The development of comprehensive school reform. In J. Murphy & A. Datnow (Eds.), *Leadership lessons from comprehensive school reforms* (pp. 3–18). Thousand Oaks, CA: Corwin Press, Inc.

National Commission on Excellence in Education. (1983). *A nation at risk: the imperative for educational reform.* Washington, DC: U.S. Department of Education.

National Conference of State Legislatures. (2005). *Task force on No Child Left Behind: Final report.* Washington, DC: National Council of State Legislatures.

National Education Association. (2005). *Stand up for children: Pontiac vs. Spellings.* Retrieved on June 30, 2005, from http://www.nea.org/lawsuit/index.html.

National Reading Panel. (2000). *Teaching children to read: An evidence-based assessment of the scientific research literature on reading and its implications for reading instruction.* Rockville, MD: NICHD Information Resource Center.

Nelson, C. (1994). *Organizing for effective reading instruction: ERIC Digest 369034.* Bloomington, IN: ERIC Clearinghouse on Reading, English, and Communication.

Nelson, R. R. & Winter, S. G. (1982). *An evolutionary theory of economic change.* Cambridge, MA: Harvard University Press.

New American Schools. (2005a). *About us: Our history.* Retrieved June 30, 2005 from http://www.naschools.com/contentViewer.asp?highlightID=6&catID=105.

New American Schools. (2005b). *NAS to merge with AIR, creating powerful K–12 consulting practice.* Retrieved June 30, 2005 from http://www.naschools.org/news/news viewer.asp?highlightID=20&docID=826.

New Jersey Department of Education. (1997). *A study of supplemental programs and recommendations for the Abbott districts.* Retrieved on June 30, 2005, from http://www. state.nj.us/njded/abbotts/archives/abbottstudy.htm.

North West Regional Education Laboratory. (2001). *About the CSRD Program: What is comprehensive school reform.* Retrieved June 01, 2005 from http://www.nwrel.org/ csrdp/about.html.

Nunnery, J. (1998). Reform ideology and the locus of development problem in educational restructuring: Enduring lessons from studies of educational innovation. *Education and Urban Society, 30 (3),* 277–295.

Nunnery, J., Ross, S., Smith, L., Slavin, R., Hunter, P., & Stubbs, J. (1996). *An assessment of Success for All program component configuration effects on the reading achievement of at-risk first grade students.* Paper presented at the annual meeting of the American Educational Research Association, New York, NY, 1996.

Nunnery, J., Slavin, R. E., Madden, N. A., Ross, S., Smith, L., Hunter, P., et al. (1997). *Effects of full and partial implementations of Success for All on student reading achievement in English and Spanish*. Paper presented at the annual meeting of the American Educational Research Association, Chicago, IL.

O'Day, J. A. & Smith, M. S (1993). Systemic reform and educational opportunity. In S. H. Fuhrman (Ed.), *Designing coherent education policy: Improving the system* (pp. 250–312). San Francisco: Jossey-Bass.

Olson, L. (1998, February 4). *Will success spoil Success for All?* Retrieved on February 1, 2008, from http://www.edweek.com/.

Paley, A. R. (2007, April 21). *Key initiative of "No Child" under federal investigation: Officials profited from Reading First program*. Retrieved on October 1, 2009, from http://www.washingtonpost.com/wp-dyn/content/article/2007/04/20/AR2007042002284_pf.html.

Palincsar, A. S. (1986). The role of dialogue in scaffolded instruction. *Educational Psychologist, 21(1 and 2)*, 71–98.

Palincsar, A. S. (1998). Keeping the metaphor of scaffolding fresh. A response to C. Addison Stone's, The metaphor of scaffolding: Its utility for the field of learning disabilities. *Journal of Learning Disabilities, 31 (4)*, 370–374.

Park, V. & Datnow, A. (2008). Collaborative assistance in a highly prescribed school reform model: The case of Success for All. *Peabody Journal of Education, 83*, 400–422.

Pearson, P. D. (2004). *The reading wars*. Educational Policy, 18(1), 216–252.

Peurach, D. J. (2005). *Designing and managing comprehensive school reform: The case of Success for All*. Unpublished doctoral dissertation. Ann Arbor, MI: The University of Michigan.

Peurach, D. J. & Rowan, B. (1999). *Organizational perspectives on instructional improvement*. Paper presented at the Annual Meeting of the American Educational Research Association. Montreal, Quebec, Canada: April 1999.

Pfeffer, J. & Salancik, G. (1978). *The external control of organizations: A resource dependence perspective*. New York: Harper and Row.

Phenix, D., Siegel, D., Zaltsman, A., & Fruchter, N. (2004). *Virtual district, real improvement: A retrospective evaluation of the Chancellor's District, 1996–2003*. New York: New York University.

Pogrow, S. (1998). What is an exemplary program, and why should anyone care? A reaction to Slavin and Klein. *Educational Researcher, 27 (7)*, 22–29.

Pogrow, S. (1999). Rejoinder: Consistent large gains and high levels of achievement are the best measures of program quality: Pogrow responds to Slavin. *Educational Researcher, 28 (8)*, 24–31.

Pogrow, S. (2000a). The unsubstantiated "success" of Success for All. *Phi Delta Kappan, 81(8)*, 596–600.

Pogrow, S. (2000b). Success for All does not produce success for students. *Phi Delta Kappan, 82 (1)*, 67–80.

Pogrow, S. (2002). Success for All is a failure. *Phi Delta Kappan, 83 (6)*, 463–468.

Powell, A. G., Farrar, E., & Cohen, D. K. (1985). *The shopping mall high school: Winners and losers in the educational marketplace*. Boston, MA: Houghton Mifflin Company.

Pressman, J. & Wildavsky, A. (1984). *Implementation*. Berkeley, CA: University of California Press.

Puma, M. J. (1999). *The "Prospects" study of educational growth and opportunity: Implications for policy and practice*. Paper presented at the Annual Meeting of the American Educational Research Association, Montreal, Quebec, Canada. April 19–23, 1999.

Puma, M. (2000). *Exploring new directions: Title I in the year 2000*. Alexandria, VA: National School Boards Association.

Puma, M., Raphael, J., Olsen, K., & Hannaway, J. (2000). *Putting standards to the test: A designing for evaluating the systemic reform of education*. Washington, DC: Urban Institute.

Purkey, S. & Smith, M. S. (1983). Effective schools: A review. *Elementary School Journal, 83*, 427–452.

Purkey, S. & Smith, M. S. (1985). School reform: The district policy implications of the effective schools literature. *Elementary School Journal, 85*, 353–389.

Ravitch, D. (1983). *The troubled crusade: American education 1945–1980*. New York: Basic Books.

Ravitch, D. (2005). *Recycling reforms*. Retrieved on June 30, 2005, from http://www.educationnext.org/20041/34.html.

Riddle, W. C. (1989). *Education for disadvantaged children: Major themes in the 1988 reauthorization of Chapter 1*. Washington, D.C.: Library of Congress, Congressional Research Service.

Rogers, E. M. (1962). *Diffusion of innovations*. New York: Free Press of Glencoe.

Rogers, E. M. (1995). *Diffusion of innovations*. Fourth edition. New York: The Free Press.

Ross, S. M., Smith, L. J., Slavin, R. E., & Madden, N.A. (1997). Improving the academic success of disadvantaged children: An examination of Success for All. *Psychology in the Schools, 34(2)*, 171–180.

Ross, S. M. (2000). When a debate becomes a feud. *Phi Delta Kappan, 82 (4)*, 337–340.

Rowan, B. (1990). Commitment and control: Alternative strategies for the organizational design of schools. In C. Cazden (Ed.), *Review of research in education* (pp. 353–389), Volume 16. Washington, DC: American Educational Research Association.

Rowan, B. (2002). The ecology of school improvement: Notes on the school improvement industry in the United States. *Journal of Educational Change, 3*, 283–314.

Rowan, B., Camburn, E., & Barnes, C. (2004). Benefiting from comprehensive school reform: A review of research on CSR implementation. In C. Cross (Ed.), *Putting the pieces together: Lessons from comprehensive school reform research* (pp. 1–52). Washington, D.C.: National Clearinghouse for Comprehensive School Reform.

Rowan, B. & Correnti, R. (2009). Interventions to improve instruction: How implementation strategies affect instructional change. In W. K. Hoy & M. DiPaola (Eds.), *Studies in school improvement: A volume in research and theory in educational administration* (pp. 45–74). Charlotte, NC: Information Age Publishing, Inc.

Rowan, B., Correnti, R. J., Miller, R. J., & Camburn, E. M. (2009a). *School improvement by design: Lessons from a study of comprehensive school reform programs*. Philadelphia, PA: Consortium for Policy Research in Education.

Rowan, B., Correnti, R. J., Miller, R. J., & Camburn, E. M. (2009b). School improvement by design: Lessons from a study of Comprehensive School Reform programs. In G. Sykes, B. Schneider, & D. Plank (Eds.) *AERA Handbook on education policy research* (pp. 637–651). New York: Routledge.

Rowan, B., Guthrie, L. F., Lee, G. V., & Guthrie, G.P. (1986). *The design and implementation of Chapter 1 instructional services: A study of 24 schools*. San Francisco, CA: Far West Laboratory for Educational Research and Development.

Rowan, B. & Miller, R. J. (2007). Organizational strategies for promoting instructional change: Implementation dynamics in schools working with comprehensive school reform providers. *American Educational Research Journal, 44 (2)*, 252–297.

Schemo, D. J. (2007, April 21). *Justice Dept. is asked to investigate reading plan*. Retrieved on October 1, 2009, from http://www.nytimes.com/2007/04/21/us/21reading.html?_r=1.

Schoenfeld, A. H. (2006). What doesn't work: The challenge and failure of the What Works Clearinghouse to conduct meaningful reviews of studies of mathematics curricula. *Educational Researcher, 35 (2)*, 13–21

Sebring, P. B., & Bryk, A. S. (2000). School leadership and the bottom line in Chicago. *Phi Delta Kappan, 81 (6)*, 440–443.

Sergiovanni, T. J. (1992). Reflection on administrative theory and practice in schools. *Educational Administration Quarterly, 28*, 304–313.

Shedd, J. B. & Bacharach, S. B. (1991). *Tangled hierarchies: Teachers as professionals and the management of schools*. San Francisco, CA: Jossey-Bass.

Sherman, L. (1999). *Putting it all together: Schools reinvent themselves so every child can succeed*. Retrieved June 30, 2005, from Northwestern Regional Education Laboratory Web site: http://www.nwrel.org/nwedu/fall99/article2.html.

Shulman, L. S. (1987). Knowledge and teaching: Foundations of the new reform. *Harvard Education Review, 57*, 1–22.

Simmons, D. C. & Kame'enui, E. J. (2003). *A consumer's guide to evaluating a core reading program grades K–3: A critical elements analysis*. Eugene, OR: University of Oregon, National Center to Improve the Tools of Educators/Institute for the Development of Educational Achievement.

Simon, H. A. (1962). The architecture of complexity. *Proceedings of the American Philosophical Society, 106*, 467–482.

Simon, H. A. (1996). *The sciences of the artificial*. Third edition. Cambridge, MA: The MIT Press.

Slavin, R. E. (1980). Cooperative learning. *Review of Educational Research, 50 (3)*, 315–342.

Slavin, R. E. (1983). *Cooperative learning*. New York: Longman.

Slavin, R. E. (1986). Best-evidence synthesis: An alternative to meta-analytic and traditional reviews. *Educational Researcher, 15 (9)*, 5–11.

Slavin, R. E. (1987). Ability grouping and student achievement in elementary schools: A best-evidence synthesis. *Review of Educational Research, 57*, 347–350.

Slavin, R. E. (1991). Synthesis of research on cooperative learning. *Educational Leadership, 48 (February)*, 71–82.

Slavin, R. E. (1994). School and classroom organization in beginning reading: Class size, aides, and instructional grouping. In R. E. Slavin, N. L. Karweit, B. A. Wasik, & N. A. Madden (Eds.), *Preventing early school failure: Research on effective strategies* (pp. 122–142). Boston: Allyn and Bacon.

Slavin, R. E. (1996). *Education for all*. Lisse, The Netherlands: Swets and Zeitlinger.

Slavin, R. E. (1998, April 29). *Slavin responds to essay's "ad hominem" critique*. Retrieved February 1, 2008, from http://www.edweek.com/.

Slavin, R. E. (1999). Yes, control groups are essential in program evaluation: A response to Pogrow. *Educational Researcher, 28 (3)*, 36–38.

Slavin, R. E. (2000a). Research overwhelmingly supports Success for All. *Phi Delta Kappan, 81 (9)*, 720.

Slavin, R. E. (2000b). Success for All works. *Phi Delta Kappan, 82 (4)*, 337–340.

Slavin, R. E. (2001). How Title I can become the engine of reform in America's schools. In G. D. Borman, S. C. Stringfield, & R. E. Slavin (Eds.), *Title I: Compensatory education at the crossroads*. Mahwah, NJ: Erlbaum.

Slavin, R. E. (2002a). Evidence-based education policies: Transforming educational practice and research (2002 Dewitt Wallace-Reader's Digest Distinguished Lecture). *Educational Researcher, 31(7)*, 15–21.

Slavin, R. E. (2002b). Mounting evidence supports the achievement effects of Success for All. *Phi Delta Kappan, 83 (6)*, 469–480.

Slavin, R. E. (2003). Change schools, change districts? How the two approaches can work together. *Education Week, 22 (25)*, (March 5), 44–64.

Slavin, R. E. (2005). *Evidence-based reform: Advancing the education of at risk students*. Washington, D.C.: Center for American Progress.

Slavin, R. E. (2006). Shame indeed. *Phi Delta Kappan, 87 (8)*, 621–623.

Slavin, R. E. (2008). Perspectives on evidence-based research in education: What works? Issues in synthesizing educational program evaluations. *Educational Researcher, 39 (1)*, 5–14.

Slavin, R. E. & Fashola, O. S. (1998). *Show me the evidence! Proven and promising programs for America's schools*. Thousand Oaks, CA: Corwin Press, Inc.

Slavin, R. E., Karweit, N. L., & Madden, N. A. (1989). *Effective programs for students at risk*. Boston, MA: Allyn and Bacon.

Slavin, R. E., Leavey, M., & Madden, N. A. (1984). Combining cooperative learning and individualized instruction: Effects on student mathematics achievement, attitudes, and behaviors. *Elementary School Journal (84)*, 409–422.

Slavin, R. E. & Madden, N. A. (1996a). *Built to last: Long term maintenance of Success for All*. Paper presented at the Annual Meeting of the American Educational Research Association, New York, NY (April, 1996).

Slavin, R. E. & Madden, N. A. (1996b). *Disseminating Success for All: Lessons for policy and practice*. Baltimore, MD: Johns Hopkins University, Center for Research on Education for Students Placed at Risk.

Slavin, R. E. & Madden, N. A. (1999a). *Disseminating Success for All: Lessons for policy and practice*. Baltimore, MD: Johns Hopkins University, Center for Research on Education for Students Placed at Risk.

Slavin, R. E. & Madden, N. A. (1999b). *Disseminating Success for All: Lessons for policy and practice*. (Revised, September 1999.) Baltimore, MD: Johns Hopkins University, Center for Research on Education for Students Placed at Risk.

Slavin, R. E. & Madden, N. A. (2000). Research on achievement outcomes of Success for All: A summary response to critics. *Phi Delta Kappan, 82 (1)*, 38–40, 59–66.

Slavin, R. E. & Madden, N. A. (2001a). Disseminating Success for All: Lessons for policy and practice. In R. E. Slavin & N. A. Madden (Eds.), *Success for All: Research and reform in elementary education*. New York: L. Erlbaum Publishers.

Slavin, R. E. & Madden, N. A. (2001b). *One million children: Success for All*. Thousand Oaks, CA: Corwin Press, Inc.

Slavin, R. E. & Madden, N. A. (2001c). *Success for All: Research and reform in elementary education*. New York: L. Erlbaum Publishers.

Slavin, R. E. & Madden, N. A. (2007). Scaling up Success for All: The first sixteen years. In B. Schneider & S. McDonald (Eds.), *Scale-up in education volume 2: Issues in practice* (pp. 201–228). Lanham, MD: Rowman and Littlefield.

Slavin, R. E., Madden, N. A., Dolan, L. J., & Wasik, B. A. (1996). *Every child, every school: Success for All.* Thousand Oaks, CA: Corwin Press, Inc.

Slavin, R. E., Madden, N. A., Dolan, L., Wasik, B. A., Ross, S. M., & Smith, L. J. (1994). "Whenever and wherever we choose": The replication of Success for All. *Phi Delta Kappan, 75 (8),* 639–647.

Slavin, R. E., Madden, N. A., Dolan, L. J., Wasik, B. A., Ross, S., Smith, L., et al. (1996). Success for All: A summary of research. *Journal of Education for Students Placed at Risk, 1,* 41–76.

Slavin, R. E., Madden, N. A., Karweit, N. L, Dolan, L., & Wasik, B. A. (1992). *Success for All: A relentless approach to prevention and early intervention in elementary schools.* Arlington, VA: Educational Research Service.

Slavin, R. E., Madden, N. A., Karweit, N. L., Livermon, B. J., & Dolan, L. (1990). Success for All: First year outcomes of a comprehensive plan for reforming urban education. *American Educational Research Journal, 27 (2),* 255–278.

Slavin, R. E., Madden, N. A., Shaw, A. H., Mainzer, K. L., & Donnelly, M. C. (1993). Success for All: Three case studies in restructuring of urban elementary schools. In J. Murphy & P. Hallinger (Eds.), *Restructuring schooling: Learning from ongoing efforts,* pp. 84–113. Newbury Park, CA: Corwin Press, Inc.

Smith, L. J., Maxwell, S., Lowther, D., Hacker, D., Bol, L., & Nunnery, J. (1997). Activities in schools and programs experiencing the most, and least, early implementation success. *School Effectiveness and School Improvement, 8(1),* 125–150.

Smith, M. S. & O'Day, J. (1991). Systemic school reform. In S. H. Fuhrman & B. Malen, (Eds.), *The politics of curriculum and testing: The 1990 Yearbook of the Politics of Education Association* (pp. 233–267). New York: The Falmer Press.

Smylie, M. A. & Smart, J. C. (1990) Teacher support for career enhancement initiatives: Program characteristics and effects on work. *Educational Evaluation and Policy Analysis, 12,* 139–155.

Spillane, J. P. (2004). *Standards deviation: How schools misunderstand education policy.* Cambridge, MA: Harvard University Press.

Stern, S. (2008). *Too good to last: The true story of Reading First.* Washington, DC: Thomas B. Fordham Institute.

Stevens, R., Madden, N. A., Slavin, R. E., & Farnish, A. (1987). Cooperative Integrated Reading and Composition: Two field experiments. *Reading Research Quarterly, 22 (4),* 433–454.

Stevens, R. J. & Slavin, R. E. (1995). The Cooperative Elementary School: Effects on students' achievement, attitudes, and social relations. *American Educational Research Journal, 32 (2),* 321–351.

Stringfield, S. C. (1998, August 5). *Science, cynicism and Diogenes' double-edged lamp.* Retrieved February 1, 2008, from http://www.edweek.com/.

Stringfield, S. C. (2000). A response and a hope for a better day. *Phi Delta Kappan, 82 (4),* 337–340.

Stringfield, S., Ross, S., & Smith, L. (1996). *Bold plans for school restructuring: The New American Schools designs.* Mahwah, New Jersey: Lawrence Erlbaum Associates.

Stullich, S., Eisner, E., & McCrary, J. (2007). *National Assessment of Title I Final Report.* Washington, DC: U.S. Department of Education.

Success for All Foundation. (2002a). *Success for All: Leadership guide.* Towson, MD: Success for All Foundation.

Success for All Foundation. (2002b). *Success for All—Reading First: Cover letter*. Retrieved on August 28, 2002, from http://www.successforall.net.

Success for All Foundation. (2002c). *Success for All—Reading First: Fulfilling the requirements of the Reading First legislation*. Retrieved on August 28, 2002, from http://www.successforall.net.

Success for All Foundation. (2008a). *About SFAF—history*. Retrieved on May 10, 2008, from http://www.successforall.net/about/about_history.htm.

Success for All Foundation. (2008b). *Active Benchmarks - 2008-2009 School Year*. Retrieved on October 21, 2008, from http://www.successforall.net/ayp/benchmarks.htm.

Success for All Foundation. (2008c). *Success for All schools in New York City's chancellor's district gain on the CTBS*. Retrieved June 1, 2008, from http://www.successforall.net/_images/pdfs/410045000_NYC_Chancell_ROPE.pdf.

Success for All Foundation. (2008d). *Success for All schools in New York City gain on ELA*. Retrieved June 1, 2008, from http://www.successforall.net/_images/pdfs/410034001_ROPE_NYCity.pdf.

Szulanski, G., Winter, S. G., Cappetta, R., & Van den Bulte, C. (2002) *Opening the black box of knowledge transfer: The role of replication accuracy*. Philadelphia, PA: University of Pennsylvania, Wharton School of Business.

Traub, J. (1999). *Better by design? A consumer's guide to schoolwide reform*. Washington, D.C.: Thomas Fordham Foundation.

Traub, J. (2003, August 3). *New York's new approach*. Retrieved June 1, 2008, from http://www.nytimes.com.

Tuckman, B.W. (1965). Developmental sequence in small groups. *Psychological Bulletin, 63*, 384–399.

Tushnet, W. C., Flaherty (Jr.), J., &* Smith, A. (2004). *Longitudinal assessment of comprehensive school reform program implementation and outcomes: First-year report*. Los Alamitos, CA: WestEd.

Tyack, D. & Cuban, L. (1995). *Tinkering toward Utopia: A century of public school reform*. Cambridge, MA: Harvard University Press.

Tyack, D. & Tobin, W. (1994). The "grammar" of schooling: Why has it been so hard to change? *American Educational Research Journal, 31*, 453–479.

U.S. Department of Education. (1994a). *Improving America's Schools Act of 1994: Section 1112 Local education agency plans*. Retrieved on May 12, 2008, from http://www.ed.gov/legislation/ESEA/sec1112.html.

U.S. Department of Education. (1994b). *Improving America's Schools Act: Section 1114: Schoolwide programs*. Retrieved March 1, 2008 from http://www.ed.gov/legislation/ESEA/sec1114.html.

U.S. Department of Education. (1997). *Tried and true: Tested ideas for teaching and learning from the Regional Educational Laboratories, September, 1997*. Retrieved August 20, 2006, from http://www.ed.gov/pubs/triedandtrue/success.html.

U.S. Department of Education. (1999a). *Reading Excellence Act, State competitive grant program: Non-regulatory guidance for state applicants*. Washington, D.C.: U.S. Department of Education.

U.S. Department of Education. (1999b). *Statement by Richard W. Riley, Secretary, before the United States House of Representatives Committee on the Budget, on Fixing Our Schools From the Bottom Up: State, Local, and Private Reform Initiatives*. Retrieved on June 30, 2005, from http://www.ed.gov/Speeches/09-1999/990923.html.

U.S. Department of Education. (2002). *Guidance for the Reading First program.* Washington, DC: U.S. Department of Education.

U.S. Department of Education. (2005). *No Child Left Behind: Part F—Comprehensive School Reform.* Retrieved on June 30, 2005, from http://www.ed.gov/policy/elsec/leg/esea02/pg13.html.

U.S. Department of Education. (2008a). *Funds for State Formula-Allocated and Selected Student Aid Programs, by Program.* Retrieved October 22, 2008 from http://www.ed.gov/programs/compreform/awards.html.

U.S. Department of Education. (2008b). *Reading first implementation evaluation final report.* Washington, DC: U.S. Department of Education.

U.S. Department of Education, Office of Inspector General. (2006). *The reading first program's grant application process: Final inspection report.* Washington, DC: U.S. Department of Education.

U.S. Government Accountability Office. (2007). *Reading First: States report improvements in reading instruction, but additional procedures would clarify education's role in ensuring proper implementation by states.* Washington, DC: United States Government Accountability Office.

Valentine, J. C. & Cooper, H. (2003). *Effect size substantive interpretation guidelines: Issues in the interpretation of effect sizes.* Washington, DC: What Works Clearinghouse.

Van de Ven, A. H., Angle, H. L, & Poole, M. S. (Eds.) (2000). *Research on the management of innovation: The Minnesota studies.* Oxford: Oxford University Press.

Van de Ven, A. H., Polley, D. E., Garud, R., & Venkataraman, S. (1999). *The innovation journey.* Oxford: Oxford University Press.

Venezky, R. L. (1994). *An evaluation of Success for All: Final report to the France and Merrick Foundations.* Newark, DE: University of Delaware.

Viadaro, D. (2007, October 17). "Scientific" label in law stirs debate: Proposals could reduce focus on randomized experiments. *Education Week, 27 (8),* p. 1, 23.

Walberg, H. J. & Greenberg, R. C. (1998, April 8). *The Diogenes factor: Why its hard to get an unbiased view of programs like "Success for All."* Retrieved February 1, 2008, from http://www.edweek.com/.

Walberg, H. J. & Greenberg, R. C. (1999). The Diogenes Factor: Why its hard to get an unbiased view of programs like "Success for All." *Phi Delta Kappan, 81 (2),* 127–128.

Walberg, H. J. (2000). Backtalk: The author responds. *Phi Delta Kappan, 81 (5),* 416.

Waldrop, M. M. (1992). *Complexity: The emerging science at the edge of order and chaos.* New York: Simon and Schuster.

Wasik, B. A. & Bond, M. A. (1999). *Early learning: Teacher's manual for prekindergarten and kindergarten.* Towson, MD: Success for All Foundation.

Wasik, B. A., Bond, M. A., & Waclawiw, I. (1995). *Early learning: Teacher's manual for prekindergarten and kindergarten.* Baltimore, MD: Johns Hopkins University, Center for Research on the Education of Students Placed at Risk.

Wasik, B. A. & Madden, N. A. (1992). *Success for All: Tutoring manual.* (Updated July 1995). Baltimore, MD: Johns Hopkins University, Center for Research on the Education of Students Placed at Risk.

Wasik, B. A. & Slavin, R. E. (1993). Preventing early reading failure with one-to-one tutoring: A review of five programs. *Reading Research Quarterly, 28,* 178–200.

Weick, K. E. (1976). Educational organizations as loosely couple systems. *Administration Science Quarterly, 21,* 1–19.

Wenger, E. (1999). *Communities of practice: Learning, meaning, and identity*. Cambridge: Cambridge University Press.

Wenger, E. (2008). *Communities of practice: A brief introduction*. Retrieved October 10, 2008, from http://www.ewenger.com/theory/.

What Works Clearinghouse. (2007). *WWC intervention report: Beginning Reading, Success for All*. Washington, D.C.: U.S. Department of Education, Institute for Education Sciences.

Wilde, S. (Ed.). (1996). *Notes from a kidwatcher: Selected writings from Yetta Goodman*. Portsmouth, NH: Heinemann.

Williams, A., Blank, R. K., Toye, C., & Petermann, A. (2007). *State education indicators with a focus on Title I 2002/2003*. Washington, D.C.: Council of Chief State School Officers.

Winter, S. G. & Szulanski, G. (2001). Replication as strategy. *Organization Science, 12 (6)*, 730–743.

Wong, K. K. & Meyer, S. J. (1998). *Title I schoolwide programs: A synthesis of findings from recent evaluation*. Washington, DC: U.S. Department of Education, Office of Educational Research and Improvement.

Zehr, M. A. (2009a, May 13). Supplementary reading programs found ineffective. *Education Week, 28 (31)*, p. 11.

Zehr, M. A. (2009b, September 30). Supplementary reading programs found ineffective. *Education Week, 29 (06)*. Retrieved November 1, 2009, from http://www.edweek.org/ew/articles/2009/09/30/06ies.h29.html.

Zollo, M. & Winter, S. G. (2002). Deliberate learning and the evolution of dynamic capabilities. *Organization Science, 13 (3)*, pp. 339–351.

INDEX

Page numbers followed by "f", "t", or "n" indicate figures, tables, and notes, respectively.